DISCARD

Senses
948.53

DEMCO

WORLD WAR II

AN ILLUSTRATED HISTORY

Sir Basil Liddell Hart, Litt.D.
Editor In Chief

Barrie Pitt
Editor

Created in collaboration with the
Imperial War Museum, London, England

PURNELL REFERENCE BOOKS
Milwaukee • Toronto • Melbourne • London

Reference Edition © 1977, Purnell Reference Books, a division of Macdonald-Raintree, Inc.

Library of Congress Number: (77-11939)

1 2 3 4 5 6 7 8 9 0 81 80 79 78 77

Printed in Great Britain and bound in the United States of America.

Library of Congress Cataloging in Publication Data

Main entry under title:

World War II: an illustrated history.

   Bibliography: v. 16
   Includes index.
   1.   World War, 1939-1945—Addresses, essays,
lectures. I. Purnell Reference Books (Firm)
D743.W67 940.53 77-11939
ISBN 0-8393-6003-7

© 1973, B.P.C. Publishing Limited

© 1966, 1967, 1968, 1973, Purnell and Sons Limited

Table of Contents

Barrie Pitt, editor of the *History of the Second World War*, was born in 1918, the son of a naval officer. Educated at Portsmouth, he joined the army in 1939, serving in France and the Middle East. After demobilisation, he continued his military associations by joining the 21st Special Air Service Regiment (Artists Rifles), specialising as an instructor in close-quarter fighting. In 1953 he left London and took an appointment with the Atomic Weapons Research Establishment at Aldermaston. He began writing on military matters in 1954; in 1958 his first book, on the Zeebrugge Raid, was published, followed by a novel of behind-the-lines activities in North Africa in 1942. In 1960, his third book *Coronel and Falklands* appeared, and two years later the much-acclaimed *1918 — The Last Act.*

In June 1963 he was invited to become Chief Historical Consultant to the BBC film series *The Great War*, and resigned from the Atomic Energy Authority to do so. He is a contributor on naval war to the *Encyclopædia Britannica*, has reviewed books on military subjects for newspapers in Britain and the U.S.A., and is currently editor of the paper-back series *Illustrated History of World War II* and *The Illustrated History of the Violent Century.*

The late **Sir Basil Liddell Hart**, Editor-in-Chief. Born in 1895, Sir Basil was wounded and gassed on the western front during World War I. At the age of 24, he wrote the first post-war manual on *Infantry Training* and subsequently edited the weapon manual *Small Arms Training.*
In 1924 he was appointed Military Correspondent of *The Daily Telegraph*. Ten years later he moved to *The Times* as its adviser on defence as a whole. Meanwhile he had also been Military Editor of *Encyclopædia Britannica*. In 1937 he became personal adviser to the War Minister, Mr Hore-Belisha. He resigned in 1938 to press the needs of Britain's army publicly, but once war began he felt it necessary to remain silent in case his writings betrayed the military weaknesses of the country.
After the war he spent many months interviewing captured German generals and analysing their campaigns with them. Sir Basil Liddell Hart wrote some thirty books and his writings have been translated into more than thirty languages. He was awarded the Chesney Gold Medal of the Royal United Service Institution in 1964 (along with Major-General J. F. C. Fuller), and Hon. D.Lit. of Oxford University the same year. He was also an honorary fellow of Corpus Christi College, Cambridge. In 1966 he was knighted.

A few of the many distinguished writers

Sir Basil Liddell Hart
Editor-in-Chief

Barrie Pitt
Editor

A. J. P. Taylor
Fellow of Magdalen College, Oxford. Historian, journalist and broadcaster and a distinguished contributor on political and diplomatic subjects

Constantine FitzGibbon
Best-selling author

Sir Francis de Guingand
Chief of Staff to Montgomery

Major-General Eric Dorman O'Gowan
Chief of Staff to Auchinleck

Alistair Horne
Hawthornden prizewinner; best-selling author

Christopher Hibbert
Heinemann Award winner; best-selling author

John Connell
Well-known journalist and historical writer

General Walter Warlimont
On the staff of Oberkommando der Wehrmacht

Generalleutnant Alfred Gause
Chief of Staff to Rommel

General Walther Nehring
Ex-tank expert, Chief of Staff to Guderian, Panzer division commander in desert and Russia

Alan Clark
Author of Barbarossa

Olivia Manning
Best-selling author

John Erickson
Head of Dept of Govt, Manchester University, and expert on Russian campaigns

Sir Francis Tuker
Commander of the famous 4th Indian Division

Sir Geoffrey Evans
Commanded brigades in desert and divisions in Burma. Since written many books on war

Major Tokuji Morimoto
Japanese officer

Joseph Baritz
Expert on Russian partisan warfare

Hervé Laroche
French banker and social historian

Commander M. G. Saunders
Ex-head of Foreign Documents, Admiralty; author and translator

Denis Richards
Official Historian for Air Ministry, ex-head of Morley College

Peter Elstob
Author (Warriors of The Working Day)

Jerrard Tickell
Best-selling author (Odette, Appointment with Venus)

Lt-Commander Peter Kemp
Head of Admiralty Library, author

Pieter Lessing
South African writer, soldier, and political journalist

Alan Palmer
Author, head of History Department, Highgate College

Wing Commander Asher Lee
Journalist and writer on aviation matters

Freiherr von der Heydte
German airborne commander and historian

Dan Davin
Official historian of Crete campaign for New Zealand government

Arthur Slater
Ex-Under Secretary, Air Ministry

J. M. Mackintosh
Foreign Office expert on Red Army

John Foley
Author of The Boilerplate War, etc

Major T. W. Williams
Commander of British airborne Pathfinder unit, pioneer in free-falling technique

Ralph Barker
Journalist and author

Rt Hon Sir John Smythe
VC, MC, divisional commander in Burma

J. H. Huizinga
Foreign affairs expert

Roger Manvell and Heinrich Fraenkel
Best-selling authors. Books on Goebbels, Goering, etc

Melita Maschmann
Ex-Nazi youth leader (reformed) now journalist

Colonel Sawczynski
Head of Sikorski Historical Institute

Donald Watt
Lecturer in Political Science, London School of Economics

Colonel Antonov
Battalion commander, Red Army

Kapitän zur See Bidlingmaier
German Admiralty historian

Dudley Pope
Best-selling author

Sir Henry McCall
Ex-naval attaché at Buenos Aires

A. F. Upton
Department of History, St Andrews. Author of books on Finnish war

Major-General R. H. Barry
Chief of Intelligence to Lord Gort at Dunkirk

Major Macksey
Tank expert and author

Major-General J. L. Moulton
Writer on military history, ex-head of Combined Ops

Dr Jean Charles
Belgian historian at École Royale Militaire, Brussels

Oberst Witzig
Commander German airborne detachment at Eben-Emael

John Hillaby
Scientific writer, author of Journey to the Jade Sea

Colonel A. Goutard
French historian

A. Swinson
Author

Generalleutnant Walter Charles de Beaulieu
Chief of Staff, 4th Panzer Group

Generalmajor Alfred Philippi
Infantry commander

Allied Strategic Bomber Offensive, 1941/1945/**Dr Noble Frankland**

Was the strategic bombing of Germany really necessary? Did it help to shorten the war at all? What was its actual effect on the German economy, on German morale, on the effectiveness of the German fighting machine? Dr Noble Frankland, official historian to Bomber Command, puts the RAF case for the strategic bombing offensive, which reached its climax in the still controversial raid on Dresden

Brown Bros

BOMBING
THE RAF CASE

Smoke markers indicate targets for B-17 Flying Fortresses during a raid on Berlin—a major target, along with Dresden, of Operation 'Thunderclap'

Three underrated factors led to the failure of the early Allied raids . . .

Civilian and industrial resilience

Effective fighter and AA resistance

Dispersal of bombing effort

In the last year of the war the Allied bomber forces possessed and meted out to the Germans a huge destructive power. Between them the Lancasters, Halifaxes, and Mosquitoes of the British Bomber Command and the Fortresses and Liberators of the US 8th and 15th Air Forces knocked out Germany's oil supply by the almost total destruction of her synthetic oil industry, rendered her transport system chaotic by the dislocation of railway, road, and canal systems throughout the Reich, and left many of Germany's cities in utter ruins—especially the Saxon capital Dresden, which in February 1945 suffered a comprehensive disaster greater than anything witnessed in any other European city during the Second World War.

These achievements of strategic bombing had a decisive effect upon the outcome of the war. Obviously Germany could not continue an effective military resistance when there was no more fuel to keep her tanks moving and her aircraft flying in effective strengths. Nor could she look to any future recovery when her industries lay either in ruins or without their essential supplies through the collapse of her transport systems. The ruin of her cities probably helped to signalise at last to the masses of the German people that further resistance was impossible.

Even so this great contribution to Allied victory by strategic bombing came late in the day, and it made itself felt only in combination with the products of military and naval victory. Though the eventual achievement at least approached the estimates of bombing effectiveness which had been made before the war by its advocates, it took much longer to get the results than most of them had expected. For this disappointment there were three main reasons:

● Effective damage by bombing required a much more sustained and greater weight of attack than had been expected. This was because people in general and the Germans in particular proved to be enormously more resilient to the horrors and hardships of bombing than had seemed likely and because the organisation of repair, recovery, and substitution, again especially in Germany, was greatly more efficient than expected.

● Second, the efficiency of bombing was in proportion to the effectiveness of the opposition from anti-aircraft guns and more particularly of fighters to a much greater degree than had ever been envisaged before the war. So much was this so that in fact bombing, though heavy and sustained, had a minimal effect upon Germany's war effort until her air defences were overcome and command of the air won. It then had its maximum effect.

● Third, even when command of the air existed and the Allied bomber forces had reached mammoth proportions, the maximum concentration of effort upon the most decisive targets was prevented not only by weather considerations but by disagreements within the high command as to what were the best targets. Thus, in the final phase of the war, the efforts of the heavy bombers were divided between a variety of aims to an extent which delayed the fulfilment of any of them. In this last phase the combined Anglo-American bombing offensive had three main themes: oil, transport, and general attack on major cities.

Ever since there has been a continuous controversy as to the wisdom or otherwise of the various schools of thought and experience which produced these competing themes and even now, a generation later, we seem to be no nearer the realisation of what may be the verdict of history than in those critical days of 1944 to 1945 when the issues were hotly disputed by the great protagonists upon whom the responsibility for decision or for command fell: Churchill, Portal, Harris, Tedder, Roosevelt, Arnold, and Spaatz. In the public eye this controversy has assumed the appearance of being crystallised in the issue raised by the bombing of Dresden, and on this there is still a regular and voluminous outpouring of explanations, sentiments, judgments, and statistics in the popular press and other media of publicity.

This crystallisation and the mode of debate which has stimulated it are especially unfortunate. In the first place the bombing of Dresden is not an event which can be understood, as so often the attempt to understand it has been made, in isolation from the bomber offensive and the war situation as a whole. The motives for the attack were complex and in view of the results produced they deserve to be clearly and objectively understood before the stage of moral judgments and the like is reached. Moreover, it is as well to remember that sensational statistics, for example of the deaths caused in Dresden, are liable to leave a profound public impression long after they have been withdrawn by their originators; that those near the centre of government or high command in war are as liable as anyone else to have faulty memories or even, perhaps, to have missed the point at the time; and, last but not least, that the partial digestion of bits of the documentary evidence is liable to produce very misleading conclusions. As one particular example of this danger, the recent so-called discovery of a document gives the implication that Portal relentlessly pursued the destruction of Dresden even after being warned off it by Churchill. In fact, as will be shown in the course of this article, this charge against the war-time Chief of the Air Staff is not only quite unfounded but is absolutely contrary to incontrovertible evidence.

These alone, in addition to the Dresden raid's intrinsic interest, are perhaps sufficient reasons to analyse the course of the strategic air offensive.

'The bomber will always get through'

Before the war the British air staff, on the principle that the bomber will always get through, had evolved a doctrine of air power which has since become known as the Trenchard doctrine, suggesting that the only defence against bombing was counter-bombing and that the side which would win the war was that which could first develop and then sustain the heaviest air attack upon the sources of the opposing war strength. Trenchard's ideas as to what constituted the sources of enemy war strength were only loosely defined, but it is certain that he regarded the moral effect of bombing—that is, of course, the effect upon the people being bombed—as much more important than the material—that is, the systems such as marshalling yards and power grids, or the structures such as oil plants and factories. It is also certain that he did not regard fighter defence as a major consideration in a strategic bombing offensive. If the enemy air defence, or for that matter his air offence, became too strong, the balance, it was supposed, could be restored by attack upon his aircraft factories. Thus the heavy bomber was the heart of air power, and in all probability, Trenchard thought, of the war effort. Other elements of air power—such as defensive fighters, or naval and military supporting squadrons—were at worst a waste of effort and at best subordinate and marginal instruments.

When in the last three or four years of peace it became increasingly obvious that the enemy in the next war would be Germany, the Trenchard doctrine was however somewhat watered down. For one thing, by the time that the British rearmament programme began to get into its stride it became apparent that the Germans had built up an important lead in air strength which, especially because it looked more impressive than it really was, rather suggested that a slogging match between the bombers of Germany and Britain might well end rather quickly in a victory or knock-out blow in favour of Germany.

For another thing the British, when they came to the brink, found themselves unwilling to initiate unrestricted bombing—or, to use the jargon of the time, 'to take the gloves off'. Thus Bomber Command's war plans, known as the Western Air Plans, consisted mainly of highly selective attacks which were to be applied with extreme precision against key points in the German war economy such as power, oil production, or transport. Even these were only to be carried out in certain circumstances which it was hoped would not, and in the event did not, prevail at the outset of the war. Even so, the heavy bomber was still regarded as the main weapon with which both to prosecute the offensive and to reduce the scale of the enemy offensive.

This was strange, because the development of techniques in Fighter Command which was going on at the same time began already to indicate somewhat different probabilities. The introduction of high-performance interceptor fighters represented by the Hurricane and later the Spitfire, coupled with the introduction of radar, gave air defence the real prospect, at least in daylight, of getting effectively to grips with air offence. Indeed Sydney Camm who designed the Hurricane, R. J. Mitchell who designed the Spitfire, Sir Robert Watson Watt who evolved the principle of radar, Sir Henry Tizard who seized upon its military application, and Sir Hugh Dowding who commanded the force which received these nourishing reinforcements, released the potential which made possible the first wholly decisive air battle in history: the victory in the Battle of Britain. The victory was one of the British air defence over the German air offence.

But even before this crucial battle began, the British Bomber Command had discovered that its plans for precision bombing of German targets in daylight were impracticable. Sufficient proportions of the Wellingtons and Hampdens simply could not survive the onslaught of the German defending fighters, which also, though less effectively than the British, had the early warning of radar. And so before the war was six months old, Bomber Command had turned for all save exceptional purposes to night bombing.

In the course of 1940 and 1941, rather slowly but nevertheless clearly enough in the end, it became obvious that at night in the face of the enemy defences the Bomber Command crews could not find such precision targets as oil plants or even marshalling yards. If these were to remain as

The defenders take their toll. (Top) A B-24 Liberator receives a direct hit on its way to bomb the Kiel and Hamburg U-boat pens. Of 1,000 bombers in this raid, 9 were lost. (Bottom) A B-17 Flying Fortress scatters smoke and debris as it disintegrates in the sky after being hit by German AA fire. The nose and one engine have been completely torn off

'We can smash the German machine by the bomber blitz'

(Air Marshal Lord Trenchard, 1942)

'Our aircraft occasionally killed women and children'

(Air Chief Marshal Sir Arthur Harris: Bomber Offensive)

'In spite of all that happened at Hamburg, bombing proved a comparatively humane method'

(Air Chief Marshal Sir Arthur Harris: Bomber Offensive)

the aiming points, the bulk of Bomber Command's tonnages would continue to fall harmlessly in fields. Since by the end of 1941 Britain's armies had been defeated or driven on to the defensive wherever they had appeared; since her navy was engulfed in a desperate struggle for survival in the Battle of the Atlantic; since the Russians had been driven back almost to Moscow; and since the Americans had hardly recovered from the shock of Pearl Harbor, it was utterly inconceivable that the one and only Allied force which could so much as cast a shadow over Germany should not exert every possible effort to do so.

Thus Bomber Command turned not surprisingly—indeed in the circumstances of the time inevitably—to the attack of targets which at any rate to some extent it could find and hit. These targets were whole German towns. The policy was at the time described, and has since become famous, as that of 'area bombing'.

Though it was the response of Britain to an utterly desperate war situation in which Germany and Japan were everywhere victorious and Russia, America, and Britain everywhere vanquished, it was not simply an emotional outburst of frustrated rage leading to wanton terror bombing. General area attack upon German towns was a carefully conceived strategic plan to undermine the basis of the German war effort by the dislocation of her industries, sources of power, and communications through the general destruction of the towns associated with them. The hope was that the aim would be realised by a combination of the material damage caused in the towns themselves and the moral effect upon the workers who lived in them.

However well- or ill-founded were these hopes, and many of them proved to be based on not much more than wishful thinking, the fact remained that if Bomber Command was to achieve any effects at all, this was the only policy open to it. In war, as Moltke observed, one must do what one can and not what one ought. Here then were the foundations of one of the great elements in the final bombing offensive against Germany: the general area attack upon towns in which by aiming at the centres of the target areas it was intended to cause such destruction and dislocation that one industrial area after another would seize up.

Thus daylight bombing had to be abandoned because the Wellingtons and Hampdens (and later the Lancasters, Halifaxes, and Stirlings) could not survive in the face of the German fighters. The cover of darkness had to be sought. But this meant that small targets such as those offered by particular factories could not be found or aimed at, at least by the squadrons of the main force. So came the attack on the larger areas offered by whole towns.

While these developments took place and while in the course of 1942 Bomber Command began under the leadership of its new Commander-in-Chief Sir Arthur Harris to win its first major successes over Lübeck and Cologne, the Americans were preparing to join in the bombing offensive. But they were not, as the RAF originally hoped, prepared simply to reinforce the Bomber Command squadrons any more than a generation earlier they had been willing simply to reinforce Haig's divisions in France. As Pershing had then resolved to lead an independent American army into the alliance so now Arnold, the Commanding General of the American

Army Air Forces, determined to send an independently commanded American force into the combined bomber offensive.

The Americans in their Fortresses and Liberators were not going to follow the British into the night area bombing offensive, for they were determined to mount a daylight attack which would enable them to launch precision attacks against key points in the German war economy. The British, who had, of course, had exactly the same idea before and at the outset of the war, explained that such a plan was impracticable and that it would be better to convert the American aircraft and crews to night work.

The Americans were unmoved. Their bombers could reach much greater altitude than the British and they carried heavier guns. By the use of highly disciplined formation flying tactics they would be able to provide such concentrated fire-power that their formations would be able to fight their way to and fro between base and target—and, so far as their ranges permitted, they would have the benefit of escorting fighters, Spitfires from RAF Fighter Command and in time their own machines, for the 8th Air Force was to include both bombers and fighters under the command of General Ira Eaker.

Heavier and heavier US losses

On August 17, 1942, the Americans opened their offensive with an attack on the marshalling yards at Rouen. It was carried out by 12 aircraft. All returned safely, and for the rest of the year the Americans continued the working up of their force by attacks on targets in France, picking usually on submarine bases. This was a beginning—but, as Churchill hinted to Roosevelt at the time, not all that impressive a beginning, especially by comparison with the widespread and increasingly heavy attacks being carried out in many parts of Germany, including three 'thousand' raids by the night bombers of Bomber Command.

Nor did this comparison seem to improve in 1943 when the American bombers, from the beginning of the year, began operations against German targets. While Bomber Command cut a swathe of devastation through the Ruhr valley, Hamburg (the scene of a singular calamity for the Germans), and towards Berlin, the 8th Air Force tried to begin its selective attack upon key industries. The heavy losses which it soon began to suffer from the German day fighter force led it to concentrate its effort more and more upon aircraft factories in the hope that this would reduce the effectiveness of the German air defences. The trouble was that aircraft factories were particularly difficult targets in inaccessible and therefore dangerous places such as, for example, Regensburg and Wiener Neustadt.

The American losses became heavier and heavier and neither the scale nor the effectiveness of the German air defences declined. On the contrary, they steadily increased. Moreover, the German night fighter force, developing upon the basis of primitive beginnings, was now becoming a formidable menace to the night bombers of Bomber Command. The very means which the latter used to reduce the disadvantage of having to navigate and bomb in the dark—such things as radar transmissions, flares, and route and target markers—disclosed the position of the force to the German night fighters, now skilfully directed and scientifically equipped.

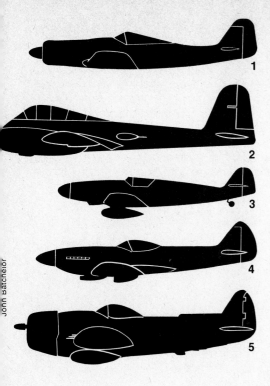

John Batchelor

Escorts and defenders

Two of the fighter aircraft that escorted the bombers – and three that flew against them

(1) The FW-109D ground attack fighter was also used to great effect for bomber interception
(2) The ME-410, a high-altitude fighter
(3) The ME-109G was used to 'bomb' Allied formations with a 500-lb bomb slung under the fuselage
(4) The Spitfire, the RAF's only escort, was hampered by very short range
(5) The Thunderbolt, 8th Air Force's high-altitude, long-range escort fighter, was the first airscrew fighter to fly faster than 500 mph

Thus not only the obstacle of the darkness but also its cover was being removed from the night bombers, while the American day bombers, despite their formation tactics, their gunnery, and their high altitude, were, once they had crossed the Rhine, beyond the range of fighter support and all on their own. As the British had feared they were almost sitting ducks for the high-performance German interceptors – the Me-109 and the FW-190 – as well as such heavier machines as the Me-110 and the Ju-88.

If Bomber Command could not quickly induce a German collapse under the impact of its area offensive, or if the Americans could not strangle the German fighter force in production, then the combined bomber offensive was heading straight for a crisis of the first magnitude.

Berlin: climax of the offensive

Some specialised crews in Bomber Command who had gained exceptional experience, who had enjoyed statistically unlikely good luck, and who were nourished by extraordinary resources of courage and a specially developed Barnes Wallis bomb, had evolved a technique of night precision attack which had enabled them to breach the Möhne and Eder Dams in May 1943. But although this technique later produced a method of night precision marking which revolutionised the possibilities of night bombing, nothing of this kind was possible for the main force of Bomber Command in 1943 or for much of 1944. The general area offensive remained the only recourse, and in November 1943 Bomber Command opened its greatest and most ambitious assault, the Battle of Berlin, which raged throughout the winter and until March 1944. It was to be the climax of the offensive. It was intended to complete the wreck of Germany from end to end.

A month earlier, in October 1943, the Americans had determined to attempt a rapier blow against Schweinfurt, the centre of German ball-bearing production, whose destruction they believed would cripple the Luftwaffe, and lay the foundation of their selective attack on German industry.

These operations, those of Bomber Command in the Battle of Berlin and that of the Americans against Schweinfurt, were therefore of critical importance. If the Battle of Berlin had ended in the collapse or virtual collapse of Germany the policy of area bombing would have been wholly vindicated and the invasion of Europe would have become a formality required only to collect the surrender. If the American operation against Schweinfurt had caused a seizure of the German aircraft industry and had resulted in the collapse of the German fighter force, the American bombers would then have had the way open to the destruction of such vital industries as oil production.

On October 14, 1943, some 291 Flying Fortresses set course in formation for Schweinfurt. As they neared Aachen their fighter escorts, running out of range, turned about and went home. They were quickly replaced by wave after wave of German fighters. Single-engined aircraft came in firing 20-mm cannon and machine-guns, twin-engined fighters fired rockets, and meanwhile the single-engined aircraft landed, refuelled, rearmed, took off, and attacked again.

The Americans pressed on against hopeless odds with the utmost gallantry and even managed to inflict considerable damage upon the ball-bearing factories in Schweinfurt.

Sixty of their bombers were shot down, 17 more were heavily damaged, another 121 sustained some damage. Nor was this an isolated disaster. It was the climax of a frightful week in which, in four attempts to break through the German fighter defences, the Americans lost 148 bombers and crews shot down.

Operations on such a scale and of such a type could not be continued, for if they had been they would rapidly have led to the strangulation in infancy of the American strategic bombing forces. Whether successful or not, they had to be called off. General Arnold, who had his ear close to public opinion in his country, let it be thought that the attack on Schweinfurt had been so successful that it *need* not be repeated. The harsh truth was that it *could* not be repeated.

Nor had it been very successful. No great harm was done to any vital element in the German war effort. Repairs were quickly made, stocks were drawn upon, and where neither expedient answered the German requirement, substitutes were used. The American plan to strike selectively at German industry by daylight heavy bombing precision attacks had apparently been decisively defeated by the German fighter force. The Battle of Britain seemed to have been refought on a greater scale with the same outcome: the victory of the defence over the offence.

'Strong medicine'

Appearances in war, when so much is on the other side of the hill, are often, as in this case they were, deceptive. From March 1943 great developments in the application of area bombing had taken place. New strengths had come to Bomber Command. Lancasters, the best of the heavy bombers, and Mosquitoes, the best of the light ones, had come more and more into service. The scope of radar had also been enlarged and techniques greatly improved. The Battles of the Ruhr and of Hamburg had demonstrated a new degree of air warfare. For the first time Essen, the home of Krupps, and, on account of industrial haze and especially heavy defences, an exceptionally difficult target, was severely damaged. In Hamburg nearly 50,000 people were killed in a series of attacks to which the Americans contributed but in which the British were predominant.

Surely this medicine would prove too strong. Surely the destruction of Berlin, and the other towns which would go with it, would be the *coup de grâce* for Germany. Even the German Economics Minister Speer thought so at the time. Six more attacks on the Hamburg scale would, he feared, finish the war. Later he realised his fear was exaggerated, but he did fear it at the time.

Success in the Battle of Hamburg had turned not only upon the great weight of the attack delivered but upon the unusually high degree of accuracy achieved and the very short space of time into which the operations were compressed. Apart from some harassing and the light American daylight attacks, Bomber Command completed the Battle in four major operations, each mounted by over 700 bombers, on the nights of July 24, 27, 29 and August 2, 1943. Some 3,095 sorties were flown and nearly 9,000 tons of bombs dropped. In all but the last attack, when the weather was bad, highly concentrated patterns of incendiary bombs, of which about 4,500 tons were dropped, were achieved, with the result that the fires in Hamburg got out of control and built up to such an **2192** ▷

New Allied Weapons in the Air War

British doctrine had maintained that the heavy bomber would always be the most important factor in air power— 'The bomber will always get through'. But the unexpected effectiveness of fighter resistance and AA fire dispelled this illusion, and early attempts by the RAF at daylight raids incurred wholly unacceptable casualties. It became obvious that bombers without fighter protection could operate only at night, and also that the RAF's heavy bomber, the Lancaster, was inadequately armed, particularly its underside. The US 8th Air Force, with its better armed Flying Fortresses and Liberators, in its turn adopted a policy of unescorted bombing. Though American bombers flew in 'impregnable' formations, they too, like the RAF, suffered heavily and soon realised the vital necessity of an escort fighter. Because of its superior range, the American Mustang, illustrated below, was adopted to fill the rôle.

Lancaster B-3: *Length:* 69 feet 6 inches. *Wingspan:* 102 feet. *Top speed:* 275 mph. *Armament:* eight or ten ·303 machine-guns. *Bomb load:* 18,000 lb. *Crew:* seven. *Range:* 2,530 miles with 7,000 lb bomb-load

P-51C Mustang: *Speed:* 439 mph. *Armament:* four ·50 Browning machine-guns. *Bomb load:* two 1,000-lb bombs. *Range:* 2,700 miles (max)

John Batchelor

Gen H. H. Arnold, Chief of the US Army Air Force: he urged a sole commander for the joint bombing commands

Air Chief Marshal Sir C. F. A. Portal, Chief of the Air Staff: he favoured selective targets but was ultimately unable to change the area bombing school of thought

Wing Commander Guy Gibson VC: a pilot with Bomber Command from the first days through to the '1,000-bomber' raids, he led the famous 'Dam Buster' raid

Lieutenant-Colonel Lent had a total score of 110 Allied aircraft, only 8 of them by daylight

Major Prince Sayn-Wittgenstein, credited with a score of 83 Allied aircraft, was shot down on January 21, 1944

Colonel Werner Streib was credited with 66 kills over Germany, a remarkable total for a night-fighter pilot

Boeing B-17G Flying Fortress: *Length:* 74 feet. *Wingspan:* 103 feet. *Top Speed:* 287 mph. *Cruising speed:* 182 mph. *Armament:* thirteen ·5-inch Browning machine-guns. *Bomb load:* 8,000 lb in various combinations. *Crew:* ten. *Range:* 2,100 miles with 5,000 lb bomb-load

The bomber crews – and where they sat
(1) The Lancaster's crew of seven consisted of (from left to right), bomb aimer (who also operated the forward gun turret), flight engineer, pilot, wireless operator, navigator, mid-upper gunner, and rear gunner. (2) The Flying Fortress, more heavily armed, carried a crew of ten: (left to right) bomb aimer, navigator (with two 'window' guns to operate), pilot and co-pilot, flight engineer (also responsible for the top turret guns), wireless operator, belly gunner, two waist gunners, and tail gunner

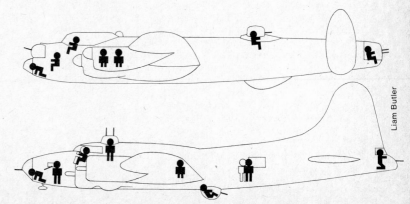

extent that firestorms were set up. The result was an exceptionally severe scale of devastation.

Berlin was, however, an altogether more formidable target than Hamburg. It was much farther from England, which meant that the petrol/bombload ratio had to be less favourable, and also that there was a greater problem of navigation and risk of destruction en route. Unlike Hamburg, Berlin gave a very confusing radar response since it was a huge built-up area without the clarifying factor of the contrast given by sea and land. It was also densely packed with anti-aircraft guns and searchlights. Finally, Bomber Command's device for confusing the German radar which guided night fighters and guns, the so-called 'Window', was now familiar to the Germans and therefore less confusing than when it was first used on the opening night of the Battle of Hamburg.

There was never the possibility that the attack could be exclusively concentrated against Berlin. The weather often made operations in one area impossible but left them possible in another; moreover, operations concentrated in one area for too long would enable the German defences to concentrate there too. The concentration of 3,000 sorties against Hamburg in summer time within a week, and with the special advantage conferred by the Window surprise, was one thing; a corresponding concentration against Berlin in the winter was quite another. In fact, the Battle of Berlin can only be understood if it is taken to include not only the 16 major attacks on Berlin itself, but also the 19 major attacks on other German towns which were carried out within the same period between the middle of November 1943 and the end of March 1944.

The main attacks on Berlin involved 9,111 bomber sorties. The other main attacks involved 11,113 sorties. Thus, the Battle of Berlin amounted to 20,224 sorties of which 19,914 were flown by four-engined bombers including 14,652 by Lancasters.

Great damage was wrought in Berlin and in the other towns attacked, but nowhere did it approach the extent of the catastrophe which had been inflicted on Hamburg and at no time did it threaten a fatal undermining of the German capacity to continue the war. Indeed, as events were to show, the Germans continued to fight on an increasing scale for more than a year after the end of the Battle of Berlin, and they then succumbed only to much more grievous blows than they suffered in that battle.

RAF losses become intolerable

Bomber Command, on the other hand, had suffered a severe reverse. Of the 20,224 sorties flown in the Battle of Berlin, 1,047 aircraft failed to return. Another 1,682 returned with degrees of damage varying from minor to complete wreckage. The gravity of these losses and the strain which they imposed upon Bomber Command is made apparent by the realisation that the average daily availability of aircraft with crews in the Bomber Command squadrons during November and December 1943 and January, February, and March 1944 was only 890. Thus in an engagement lasting four and a half months Bomber Command lost substantially more aircraft and crews than it had available for action at any one given moment in the battle. Moreover the longer the battle lasted the worse the casualties tended to become. Indeed, in the final major action on

An interlocking box
Unlike the RAF, which never evolved a special formation for its massive night attacks, the US 8th AF soon adopted a strict formation (left) which gave its daylight bombers maximum firepower against the German fighters. Three sections of six bombers, flying in an interlocking 'box', would form up in a horizontal 'Vee' formation with each section slightly above the other. The wings then formed up into larger units flying above and beside each other. The key aircraft in each unit was the leader (red) on whom all the aircraft formed up. The navigator of this aircraft led the whole formation and gave the signal for all aircraft to drop their bombs. After escort fighters had been introduced, these rarely flew in formation, but 'swept' ahead to engage the German defences rather than waiting to be attacked

Some of the Allies' bombs
Although a high-explosive-filled steel case was the accepted bombing weapon, the Allies developed many variations for special purposes. Below are the main types of bomb the Allies used

USA: (1) 100-lb Mk 4: TNT-filled steel case with impact fuse. (2) 500-lb Mk 12: TNT-filled with nose and tail fuses. (3) 4,000-lb AN-M56: TNT- or Amotol-filled, with nose and tail fuses. (4) 1,000-lb armour-piercing bomb: solid steel nose. (5) 2,000-lb AN-M66: TNT- and Amotol-filled, with impact fuse. (6) 500-lb M9 Cluster: 128 4-lb incendiary sticks, thermate-filled **RAF:** (7) 22,000-lb 'Grand Slam': Torpex-filled deep-penetration bomb. Delay fuse. (8) 12,000-lb 'Tallboy': Torpex-filled deep-penetration bomb. Delay fuse. (9) 4,000-lb heavy capacity: Amotol- and TNT-filled. Impact fuse. (10) 1,000-lb medium capacity: Amotol-filled. Delay or impact fuse. (11) 600-lb anti-sub bomb: Torpex-filled, with depth fuse. (12) 2,000-lb armour piercing: Shellite-filled, with solid nose. (13) 500-lb general purpose: TNT-filled. Delay or impact fuse. (14) 100-lb anti-sub bomb. TNT-filled. Delay tail fuse

the night of March 30, 1944, some 795 bombers were dispatched to Nuremberg. Ninety-four of them failed to return and another 71 returned damaged, including 12 totally destroyed at or near their bases.

Such losses could not of course have been sustained for much longer. Bomber Command would soon have consisted almost exclusively of new and inexperienced crews. Those who argue that this great campaign, the Battle of the Ruhr, the Battle of Hamburg, and the Battle of Berlin, would have proved decisive if there had been less diversion from it and if it had been continued in the spring of 1944, reckon without the fact that at the end of March 1944 Bomber Command, like the Americans in October 1943, had reached the point at which the casualty rate could no longer be sustained. Thus, as Schweinfurt had seemed to mark the failure of the American daylight precision bombing offensive, so the Battle of Berlin, culminating in the Nuremberg operation, seemed to do the same for the British night area bombing offensive.

A plan laid before these sombre events had disclosed themselves, however, now led Bomber Command to shift the centre of its attack from Berlin and the great German towns, to the railway system of northern France. This was part of the direct preparation for the invasion of Europe by the Anglo-American armies, which was to follow in the summer. Though the casualties in these attacks on French installations presently began to result in severe losses as the Germans redeployed their fighter defences, they did give Bomber Command a breathing space. They also produced most impressive results, which had very important military effects when General Eisenhower's invading armies, working on exterior lines of communication, engaged the Germans working on destroyed interior lines of communication. This, in turn, had another important result. It re-emphasised the possibilities which had long been considered of transport bombing as a main air strategy.

These possibilities were especially impressed upon the mind of the Deputy Supreme Commander, Sir Arthur Tedder. It was he who had adopted the plan for railway bombing in France and who presently foresaw that an extended application of the same principle to Germany herself might be the quickest and most effective way of assisting the advance of the Allied armies while at the same time bringing about the destruction of the German war economy.

The 'Oil Plan'
Meanwhile, however, the possibilities of another air strategy were also being heavily underlined. This was the attack upon German synthetic oil production. Throughout the war and before it, Britain and the United States knew that oil was among the weakest links in the German war machine. Its limited availability made Germany critically dependent upon a relatively small number of rather delicate synthetic oil plants and the Rumanian supplies. Clearly if their production could be drastically reduced and stocks diminished the effect would be reflected in a seizure of mechanised armed forces and much of war industry as well. To General Carl Spaatz, who on New Year's Day 1944 assumed the overall command of the 8th Air Force in England and the 15th in Italy (henceforth known jointly as the United States Strategic Air Forces in Europe), oil was the target *par excellence*. He foresaw

that the main target must be one which the Luftwaffe would be compelled to defend against all odds and one whose destruction would immediately and directly lead to the downfall of the Luftwaffe. For General Spaatz, the destruction of the German air force in being was a preoccupation.

To Sir Arthur Harris, the now famous Commander-in-Chief of Bomber Command, most arguments about so-called key targets were unconvincing. Nor was his scepticism without reason. Near the coat tails of the Air Staff and all the other staffs were large bodies of apparent experts. Much of the advice they gave was inappropriate or too clever by half. Harris believed that what would tell in the end was the destruction of the great towns of Germany themselves.

These beliefs, that of Tedder that the way ahead lay in transport bombing as the common factor between the military requirements of the armies and the strategic potentialities of the air forces, that of Spaatz in the attack on oil as the means of bringing down the Luftwaffe and Germany in turn, and that of Harris that general area attack would capitalise on the past efforts of Bomber Command and crown its future, were highly influential. Tedder, though not Churchill's favourite air commander, had the prestige of success won as the air commander in the Middle East and now enjoyed the full confidence of the Supreme Commander, General Eisenhower. Spaatz, commanding the greatest volume of air power yet seen in history and backed to the last ditch by Arnold from Washington, was in a position to make his opinions count. Harris, redoubtable, resolute, and convinced, had already demonstrated his status as one of the greatest leaders of men in the Second World War. Bomber Command without Harris was virtually inconceivable.

Moreover, as the last year of the war began, these different and even conflicting views assumed a real strategic importance. This was because in the American pause after Schweinfurt and the British one after Nuremberg, new factors arose or were injected into the situation which immensely, almost unrecognisably, increased the effectiveness of strategic bombing. Thus the options were increased and the importance of choosing the right ones enhanced.

A new Allied fighter
Among many, there were two principal factors bringing about this change. The first arose from the introduction of a highly effective long-range fighter, the P-51 Mustang, an American airframe now fitted with a Rolls-Royce Merlin engine. Between December 1943 and March 1944 this aircraft was worked up in the 8th Air Force until by the end of that period it could engage anything German as far afield from its British bases as Berlin. Now there was almost nowhere in Germany where, at least in daylight, any German pilot could enjoy any real security. Wherever he was, whether training or operating, he was liable to encounter increasing numbers of more and more aggressive Mustang pilots.

The result was that in a short time the daylight air over Germany was American dominated. Not only did this have a generally disruptive effect upon the Luftwaffe but it had a particularly favourable one upon the daylight bombers which, up to Schweinfurt, had taken such a hammering. Their ambitions became greater; their casualties became lighter; their attacks became more

accurate. These favourable tendencies set in in February 1944 and developed steadily thereafter, and in March 1944, operating on an ambitious scale, the percentage loss rate of the Americans fell to a third of what it had been in October 1943.

The second great factor was the advance of the Allied armies from the Normandy beach-head across France and eventually towards the Rhine. In August 1944 the armies over-ran the front line of the German fighter defence and their radar early warning posts, so that Bomber Command, already enjoying the symptoms of air superiority in daylight, now had the way at night opened as well. In the course of August 1944 the German air defences more or less folded up and an effective command of the air passed to the Americans and the British. The weather was still an obstacle, however, and anti-aircraft guns remained in action. Occasionally the remnant of the German fighter force concentrated to gain a temporary and local superiority. But the conditions of bombing were now unrecognisable by comparison with what they had been throughout the war up to then. In September 1944 Bomber Command flew more than three times as many sorties against major German targets as it had done in June 1944, but it lost only about two-thirds as many aircraft.

And so it seemed in September that the strategic air forces were poised for a final knock-out blow against Germany. They had already made substantial progress with the destruction of her oil production and her transport system, and the general area offensive against her towns had been resumed on a major scale. The military situation too looked good, for the Anglo-American armies were at the Rhine and the Russians also were on the way. There was hope that the war would be over by Christmas.

One reason for the disappointment of this hope was the failure of the Arnhem operation, which might have got the military advance going again. Another was the continuing failure of the strategic air forces to concentrate their immense potential effectively enough to produce immediately decisive effects. The competing claims of oil, transport, and general industrial dislocation, though theoretically given their order of priorities in the bombing directives, could not, in practice, be adequately adjusted.

Knowing how well the oil offensive was going and seeing from Intelligence appreciations (which in this case were remarkably accurate) how critical the German oil position was becoming, the Chief of the Air Staff, Sir Charles Portal, weighed in on the side of the oil advocates. He pressed Harris strongly to increase his effort against oil targets, even if it did mean a reduction in the area offensive against towns. Though Bomber Command, which carried much heavier bombs than the Americans, did play a major role in the oil offensive, it was, so far as Harris was concerned, rather a reluctant one. The eventual almost complete oil famine in Germany might have come earlier if Portal had been more insistent. But if he had been, he would probably have had to find a replacement for Harris. This, not surprisingly in the circumstances, he was unwilling to do. The resulting spread of bombing between oil, cities, and transport (as well as some other target systems) produced in the end perhaps a more certain and a more comprehensive collapse in Germany than any other method could have done. But it may all the same have delayed the moment **2196** ▷

The bombing was costly in life to both sides. *Below:* A Liberator bursts into flames after being hit by flak. Over Schweinfurt the Americans lost 60 aircraft in one raid alone. And the RAF lost 95 aircraft (of 795) over Nuremberg in one night. *Bottom:* Bomb damage in Hannover. In one raid on October 19, 1943, 2½ square miles of this city were destroyed

US Air Force

US Air Force

Below: The bodies are counted after one of the RAF's raids on Hamburg, in which 42,000 people were killed. According to the estimates compiled by Germany's Federal Statistical Office, the total German civilian losses due to bombing between 1939 and 1945 were 593,000. The total British civilian losses due to bombing during the same period were 65,000

at which collapse occurred by comparison with what might have happened if there had been a greater concentration against oil, especially in the last four months of 1944. This, however, is a speculative conclusion of which the probable validity is easier to assess now than it was at the time.

The war drags on

Thus the Anglo-American offensive of all arms against Germany lost its momentum in the autumn of 1944 and the war, after all, was to drag on into 1945. Indeed, for the Western camp of the Grand Alliance, 1945 opened in a distinctly depressing atmosphere. Discussion in the councils of strategic bombing left all—Portal, Tedder, Spaatz, and Harris—with a feeling of frustration. Nor was it only the air force high command which suffered this frustration, for Eisenhower's plan for the final advance into Germany had received a rude check from the German counteroffensive in the Ardennes.

These delays may now seem inconsequential. The Allies had a vast preponderance of military power, the Russians were about to resume their offensive, the damage done in the Ardennes was soon repaired, and the bombers now had Germany at their mercy.

But the prospect did not appear quite in that light in January 1945. The Germans had shown an alarming ingenuity in the development of new weapons. Schnorkel breathing threatened to give their U-boats a new lease of life. In the development of high-speed flight they led the world. Jet-propelled aircraft might yet unmake the Allied command of the air. The V-weapons (and the V-2 was no less than a partly guided missile) might portend even more alarming possibilities. There could be no certainty that Germany would not produce an atomic bomb.

Moreover, the support given by the German people to Hitler was still very real. Hitler survived all attempts at assassination or deposition; his armed forces fought on with courage and determination despite the odds; the civil population endured with a stoicism which is one of the wonders of history. Even when Hitler had been disposed of, there still remained the problem of Japan, so it was hardly strange that the Allies were urgently seeking a means of accelerating their victory over Germany.

In January, with the Anglo-American armies temporarily halted, there seemed to be two main possibilities. One was that the Red Army would advance rapidly into the heart of Germany; the other was that the heavy bombers might strike a mammoth pulverising blow at a German city, or group of cities, which would amount to the last straw. The Chiefs-of-Staff of Britain and America had had such an idea (given the code-name of 'Thunderclap') in mind for some time, but they had not found any specific plan sufficiently convincing to be worth attempting, for an air strike of this character, it seemed, would in itself be insufficient to cause the collapse which was sought. But, as occurred to them in January, such a blow might, if aimed at Berlin and timed to coincide with the westward flow of refugees fleeing before the Russian advance, have at least a markedly helpful effect upon the Russian advance.

On January 25, 1945, the Deputy Chief of the Air Staff, Sir Norman Bottomley, discussed these ideas on the telephone with Sir Arthur Harris, and the next day he reported

Harris's suggestion to Portal: that the main attack on Berlin should be supplemented by operations of a like nature, against Chemnitz, Leipzig, and Dresden. These cities, with Berlin, would be trying to house refugees fleeing from the Russians and were, also like Berlin, focal points in the German system of communications behind their eastern front.

Churchill demands action

On the same day as this telephone conversation, January 25, 1945, Churchill spoke to the Secretary of State for Air, Sir Archibald Sinclair, about the same possibilities. In particular, as he explained on the following day in a minute to Sinclair, he wanted to know whether Berlin and other large cities in east Germany should not now be considered especially attractive targets. In a somewhat peremptory manner he indicated that what was now required was not consideration, but action.

Portal, however, was somewhat doubtful of the wisdom of the whole idea. He did not think that Thunderclap, even on the heaviest scale, would prove decisive. He feared that the bombers might suffer heavy losses over Berlin. He firmly believed that the oil offensive should continue to have absolute priority. He also insisted that attacks on U-boat and jet aircraft factories should be kept up, but subject to all those considerations, and if the Americans would join in, he was prepared to agree that one big attack on Berlin supported by severe blitzes on Dresden, Leipzig, and Chemnitz and perhaps some other places would cause confusion in the evacuation from the east, and hamper the Germans in moving their troops from the west.

On January 27, Sinclair sent a minute to Churchill telling him that the Air Staff had now arranged to make attacks on Berlin, Dresden, Chemnitz, and Leipzig or other cities where severe bombing would destroy communications vital to the evacuation from the east and would also hamper the movement of troops from the west. He made it absolutely clear that this would be done only subject to the over-riding claims of the oil offensive and other approved target systems.

Such was the plan, its origin, and its motive; and thus, a little reluctantly, because he feared that it might detract from the oil offensive, Portal assented to it.

The plan, then, arose from the application of the Thunderclap idea to the particular situation created by the Russian advance. The actual targets selected came from the telephone conversation between Bottomley and Harris and the urgency with which the idea was pressed forward proceeded directly from the very insistent prodding administered by Churchill.

Perhaps these facts will serve to make clear the development of events up to this stage which has been so widely misunderstood in so many places. But now there is a new misunderstanding which has to be cleared up. This is the extraordinary suggestion that on January 28 Churchill tried to call off the Dresden attack but that Portal nevertheless persisted with it. In fact on January 28 Churchill only told Portal in a minute that he felt doubtful about the wisdom of so much *transport* bombing when oil was meant to be the first priority. Portal assured him that oil was still the first priority, though he put in a reminder that there would shortly be heavy attacks on certain eastern towns including Dresden.

This of course merely confirmed what had just been arranged and agreed.

General Spaatz was now consulted about the plan. Though the severe sudden damage required was thought to be especially appropriate to heavy night attacks by Bomber Command, American daylight operations were also required and, in the event, forthcoming. The plans were also touched on at the Yalta Conference, which followed immediately upon these events, and though the Russians did not specifically call for the bombing of Chemnitz or Dresden, they did ask for the paralysis of Berlin and Leipzig as centres of communication behind the German front against which they were about to speed up their advance.

The plan was now nearing execution, but it could not be initiated until the moon had waned and until the weather was right. On the night of February 13, 1945, Bomber Command set course in two waves over 800 strong for Dresden. In daylight on February 14 the American 8th Air Force followed, more than 400 strong. The Americans went again, about 200 strong, on February 15 and finally 400 strong on March 2. Meanwhile, on the night of February 14, Bomber Command made a major night attack on Chemnitz and the Americans carried out other related attacks including one on February 26 on Berlin by over 1,000 bombers.

These were the operations designed to speed up the Allied victory by causing confusion behind the German line, urged upon the Air Staff by the Prime Minister and, in their generality, asked for by the Russians. If they had not been carried out people would no doubt now be wondering why the strategic air forces had not exerted their power against these targets at this critical moment in the war. They fitted the general conception of the area bombing offensive now more than four years old, they fitted the immediate military situation, and they were executed without undue prejudice to the main priority, the oil campaign.

Most of these attacks, like so many others carried out by Bomber Command, have long

The crucial equation: bombs dropped against German production

The ultimate justification for the Allied bomber offensive was that it struck directly at the German war machine and could thus cripple her forces at the front. The graphs below, taken from figures published in the British Official History, show the mounting total of bombs dropped, and the output of three key German industries

◁ Part of the Krupp Works (Essen) in ruins

Ullstein

BOMBS DROPPED

It was not until the war ended that the Allies were able to take stock of the effect of the vast weight of bombs which they had hurled at Germany, and realise that in almost all types of production German output had risen almost as swiftly and steadily as the weight of bombs. The massive rise of bombs dropped during 1944 reflects the achievement of a continuous day-and-night offensive co-ordinating the attacks of RAF Bomber Command and the USAAF

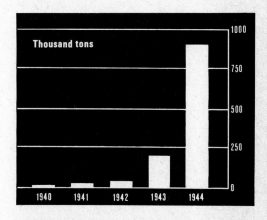

AIRCRAFT PRODUCTION

One way in which the attacking forces were to gain air supremacy over their targets was by smashing the air frame and aero engine factories of the defenders. This the Allies tried, but German countermeasures proved so successful—dispersing the large factories into small units scattered all over the country which were difficult to locate and attack—that their aircraft production rose steadily, and it was not until the Allies were able to introduce long-range escort fighters for their daylight raids that they were able to achieve a reasonable level of superiority

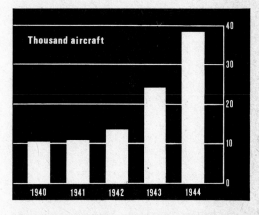

TANK PRODUCTION

During the years before D-Day while the Russians had complained that they were bearing the whole brunt of the war, the British and American strategic bombing offensive had been the great symbol of what the Western Allies were doing to strike directly at Germany. But in tanks, as in aircraft, the German production totals continued to rise—although this is not to say that they would not have risen considerably faster had the bombing not taken place

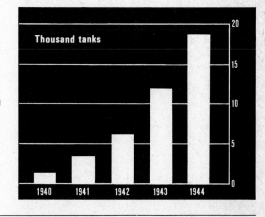

OIL PRODUCTION

The assault on German oil production was one of the fields in which the Allied bomber offensive was shown to be conspicuously successful. The Germans had long realised the threat which hung over this most vital and vulnerable part of their economy, but, except for two raids on Ploesti, it was not until October 1943 that US bombers were unleashed in concentrated attacks on the plants in the Ploesti and South German areas. At first the damage to production was slight, but during the summer of 1944 German oil output collapsed and her forces were condemned to near immobility during their most vital battles

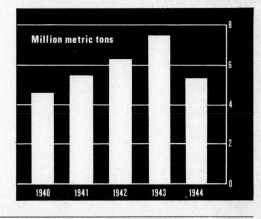

---

since been forgotten, but not so the Dresden one. The conditions proved to be virtually perfect and the defences nil. The success of the raid, unlike that of the following night against Chemnitz, was overwhelming. Huge but uncertain numbers of Germans were killed. In all probability the death roll was even greater than that caused in Hamburg in July to August 1943. By far the greater part of the damage was done by Bomber Command in the night attack.

Some newspaper men at the time thought it represented a change of policy and referred to it as terror bombing. This caused embarrassment in America, where bombing was thought to be a different sort of thing to what it was, and even in Britain, where at least some had deluded themselves into thinking of bombing as surgery instead of what it was: an element in nearly total war.

Perhaps it may suffice to say that Dresden was the logical climax of the strategic air offensive against Germany, which as a whole played a major part in the defeat of Nazi hegemony; that it was dramatically more successful than could reasonably have been anticipated; and that, while it seemed to be urgently necessary at the time of its execution in the middle of February, it was possible to wonder as soon afterwards as the end of March how the Germans, then visibly and rapidly crumbling, could have merited such an ultimate punishment.

NOBLE FRANKLAND was born in 1922 and educated at Sedbergh and Trinity College, Oxford, where he was a Scholar. During the war he served as a navigator in Bomber Command and was awarded the DFC. After a period as a Narrator in the Air Historical Branch of the Air Ministry and after taking a doctorate at Oxford, he was in 1951 appointed, jointly with the late Sir Charles Webster, as official historian of the *Strategic Air Offensive Against Germany*. The History was published in four volumes in 1961. Dr Frankland is the author of several other works. From 1956-1960 he was Deputy Director of Studies at the Royal Institute of International Affairs. Since then he has been Director of the Imperial War Museum.

The Key Raids against Germany

[Statistics compiled by the IWM.]

1940, May 15/16: RAF Raid on the Ruhr
Night precision raid on oil plants and marshalling yards. Of 99 planes involved, 1 lost. Amount of damage unknown but probably negligible. This raid opened strategic air offensive against Germany. (RAF had previously confined itself to raids on coastal targets and military communications, and to dropping leaflets.)

1940, December 16/17: RAF Raid on Mannheim
Night area raid on city centre. Of 134 planes involved, 3 lost. Only scattered damage inflicted: many bombs fell outside target area. First RAF 'area' raid. Lacking means to carry out effective precision attacks, Bomber Command bombed main industrial cities. Object was to disrupt German war production and break civilian morale.

1942, March 28/29: RAF Raid on Lübeck
Night area raid on town centre. Of 234 planes involved, 12 lost. Some 1,500 houses destroyed, much damage to factories. But production nearly normal one week later. First large-scale incendiary raid.

1942, April 17: RAF Raid on Augsburg
Daylight precision raid on MAN diesel engine factory. Of 12 Lancasters involved, 7 destroyed, 5 damaged (no fighter cover). Main assembly shop and other buildings damaged but production hardly affected. Raid showed that it was impractical for heavy bombers to make precision attacks in daylight, and reinforced RAF's faith in the night offensive.

1942, May 30/31: RAF Raid on Cologne
Night area raid on city centre. Of 1,046 planes involved, 40 destroyed, 116 damaged. Nearly half of city devastated, 474 people killed, over 40,000 homeless. But Cologne made a surprisingly rapid recovery. First of the 'Thousand Bomber' raids.

1942, August 17: 8th AF Raid on Rouen
Daylight precision raid on Sotteville marshalling yards. Of 12 B-17s involved, no losses. Some damage to rolling stock and rails but only temporary. US 8th AF's first attack. US firmly committed to daylight precision raids.

1943, March 5/6: RAF Raid on Essen
Night area raid on Krupp works. Of 442 planes involved, 14 destroyed, 38 damaged. Heavy damage to Krupps, 160 acres of Essen devastated. But British estimates exaggerated effect of raid on production. First use of 'Oboe' radar device helped to overcome industrial haze in the Ruhr area.

1943, May 16/17: RAF Dams Raid
Night precision raid on Möhne, Eder, and Sorpe dams. Of 19 Lancasters involved, 8 destroyed, 6 damaged. Möhne and Eder dams breached; Sorpe dam only damaged. Some 1,000 people drowned and severe flooding, but raid had no appreciable effect on German war economy. Landmark raid in development of precision bombing techniques.

This map shows the main Allied bombing targets in Europe between 1942 and 1945. Unless otherwise specified, the cities listed below were general industrial targets.

Key Allied Airbases
A. Sunninghill Park (HQ US 9th Air Force)
B. High Wycombe (HQ RAF Bomber Command/HQ US 8th Air Force)
C. Bushy Park (HQ US Strategic Air Force)

1. Bordeaux (U-boats)
2. La Pallice (U-boats)
3. Lorient (U-boats)
4. St Nazaire (U-boats)
5. Nantes (aircraft)
6. Brest (U-boats)
7. Le Mans (aircraft)
8. Paris
9. Rouen
10. Martinvast (V-bombs)
11. Sottevast (V-bombs)
12. Siracourt (V-bombs)
13. Lottinghem (V-bombs)
14. Mimovecques (V-bombs)
15. Watten (V-bombs)
16. Wizernes (V-bombs)
17. Lille
18. Brussels (aircraft)
19. Rotterdam
20. Amsterdam (aircraft)
21. La Rochelle
22. Cherbourg
23. Le Havre
24. Boulogne
25. Dunkirk
26. Metz
27. Emden (U-boats)
28. Wilhelmshaven (U-boats)
29. Vegesack (U-boats)
30. Bremen (aircraft)
31. Hamburg
32. Flensburg (U-boats)
33. Kiel (U-boats)
34. Lübeck
35. Hannover
36. Brunswick
37. Magdeburg
38. Oschersleben (aircraft)
39. Dessau (aircraft)
40. Essen
41. Dortmund
42. Duisburg
43. Düsseldorf
44. Cologne
45. Bonn
46. Möhne Dam
47. Wuppertal
48. Eder Dam
49. Sorpe Dam
50. Kassel (aircraft)
51. Leipzig (aircraft)
52. Dresden
53. Liegnitz
54. Berlin
55. Rostock
56. Peenemünde (V-bombs)
57. Stettin
58. Danzig (U-boats)
59. Erfurt
60. Gotha (aircraft)
61. Schweinfurt (ball-bearings)
62. Fürth
63. Nuremberg
64. Regensburg (aircraft)
65. Augsburg (aircraft)
66. Munich
67. Ulm
68. Stuttgart
69. Ludwigshafen
70. Saarbrücken
71. Bochum
72. Karlsruhe
73. Friedrichshafen
74. Chemnitz
75. Prague
76. Wiener Neustadt (aircraft)
77. Frankfurt
78. Hanau
79. Aschaffenburg
80. Koblenz
81. Oberlahnstein
82. Giessen
83. Siegen
84. Schwerte
85. Soest
86. Hamm
87. Löhne
88. Osnabrück
89. Rheine
90. Bielefeld
91. Altenbecken Neuenbecken
92. Seelze
93. Lehrte
94. Hameln
95. Paderborn
96. Bebra
97. Stendal
98. Halle
99. Gera
100. Breslau
101. Oppeln
102. Heydebreck
103. Bohumin
104. Minden
105. Mulhouse
106. Freiburg
107. Offenburg
108. Rastatt
109. Karlsruhe
110. Heilbronn
111. Treuchtlingen
112. Pasing
113. Munich
114. Rosenheim
115. Salzburg
116. Strasshof
117. Würzburg
118. Mannheim
119. Darmstadt
120. Mainz
121. Bingen
122. Vienna
123. Münster
124. Wesseling
125. Reisholz
126. Dülmen
127. Gelsenkirchen
128. Salzbergen
129. Nienburg
130. Farge
131. Heide
132. Hitzacker
133. Dollbergen
134. Derben
135. Pölitz
136. Salzgitter
137. Lützkendorf
138. Leuna
139. Ruhland
140. Böhlen
141. Rositz
142. Mölbis
143. Zeitz
144. Brüx
145. Deschowitz
146. Blechhammer
147. Auschwitz
148. Neuburg
149. Freiham
150. Linz
151. Moosbierbaum
152. Korneuburg
153. Floridsdorf
154. Schwechat
155. Lobau
156. Budapest

Legend:
- Allied airbase
- Industrial target
- Rail target
- Oil target
- Operation Thunderclap

Allied fighter ranges

0   50   100   150 miles

Aug/Dec 1942
Dec 1942/Jul 1943

1943, July 24/25: RAF Raid on Hamburg
Night area raid on city centre. Of 791 planes involved, 12 destroyed, 31 damaged. Over 2,200 tons of bombs dropped. Widespread damage to residential areas. Fires still burning 24 hours after raid. Major success for Bomber Command. German radar confused by 'Window'—strips of tinfoil used for first time. This raid followed by mass attacks on nights of July 27, 29, August 2. Hamburg left in ruins. Over 42,000 people thought to have been killed.

1943, October 14: 8th AF Raid on Schweinfurt
Daylight precision raid on ball-bearing works. Of 291 planes involved, 60 destroyed, 138 damaged. Most damaging of the 16 Schweinfurt raids but caused only temporary setback in production. Germans reorganised ball-bearing industry before next attack 4 months later. Bombers escorted only part of way to target. Crippling losses caused by German fighters exploded theory of self-defending bomber formation, forced US to curtail daylight bombing offensive.

1943, November 18/19: RAF Raid on Berlin
Night area raid on city centre. Of 444 planes involved, 9 lost. Some 1,500 tons of bombs dropped. Damage unknown but probably considerable. First of 16 mass raids on Berlin, involving over 9,000 planes in all. These raids less effective and more costly than ones on Hamburg and the Ruhr, owing to distances, strength of defences, weather.

1944, March 8: 8th AF Raid on Berlin
Daylight precision raid on Erkner ball-bearing works. Of 590 planes involved, 37 lost. Heavy damage to works (75 direct hits). Production at standstill for some time. Third US raid on Berlin. Bombers escorted by large force of P-51s. Beginning of US daylight air command.

1944, March 30/31: RAF Raid on Nuremberg
Night area raid on city centre. Of 795 planes involved, 95 destroyed, 71 damaged. Some 2,500 tons of bombs dropped but raid too dispersed to cause serious damage. Heaviest defeat suffered by Bomber Command in war. Nuremberg was to RAF night raids what

Schweinfurt was to US day raids. Both showed that without command of the air long-range bombing could not be kept up indefinitely. After Nuremberg RAF broke off mass raids on distant targets.

1944, September 23/24: RAF Canal Raid
Night precision raid on Dortmund-Ems Canal, inland waterway linking Ruhr with other industrial areas. Of 141 planes involved, 14 lost. 11 'Tallboy' bombs (12,000 lb each) dropped. Canal breached, 6-mile section drained.

1945, February 13/14: RAF Raid on Dresden
Night area raid on city centre. Of 805 planes involved, 8 lost. Immense damage to old town and inner suburbs: 1,600 acres devastated. Incendiaries kindled worst firestorm of war. Estimates of killed range from 35,000 to 135,000 (latter figure almost certainly too high). Most destructive—and most controversial— European raid of war. Dresden, whose strategic importance is questionable, was crowded with refugees and virtually undefended. Bombed again next morning by 400 planes of US 8th AF.

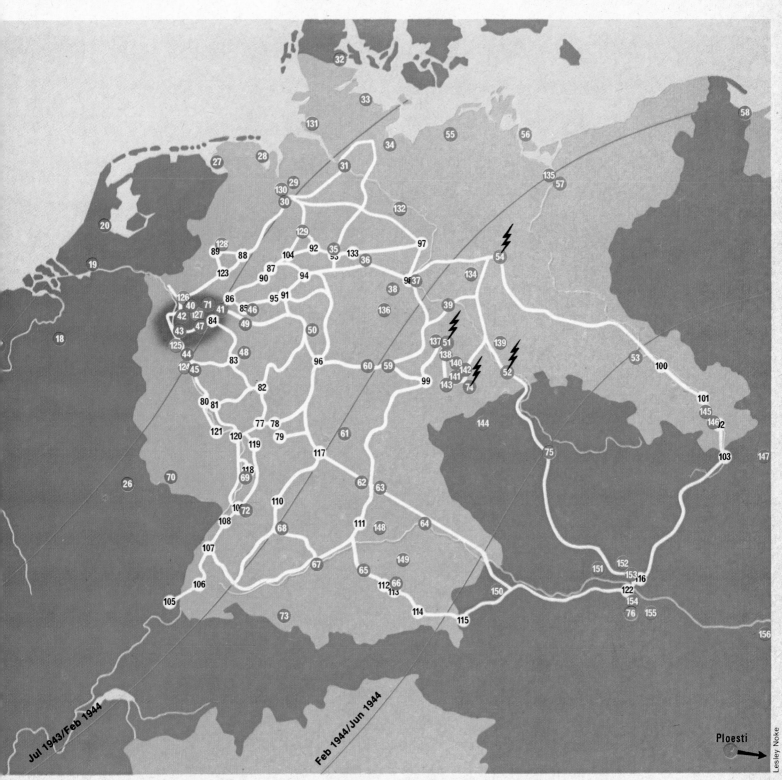

2199

The Allied Strategic
Bomber Offensive,
1941/1945
Gregor Janssen

THE EFFECT OF THE BOMBING

By the beginning of 1944, the cities of Germany had been under heavy attack by British Bomber Command for more than 18 months yet German war production was higher than ever before, and civilian morale showed no signs of cracking. But less than a year later the German economy was shattered and her forces were grinding to a halt through lack of fuel. Here a German economic historian considers the whole Allied bomber offensive, and decides that the turning point came when the Americans were able to mount the massive pin-point raids which wrecked the fuel and supply systems of the Reich

Keystone

△ The wrong target: German morale survived even Dresden
▽ The right target: A B-24 takes its toll of oil production

Associated Press

Germany's industrial centre of gravity lay in the west. Coal, coke, and crude steel production was concentrated in the Rhine and Ruhr basins, the chemical and chemical engineering industries in the Rhineland and to a lesser extent in the east (see map on p. 2199). Steel construction work was distributed over the whole Reich though again with the Ruhr area as its focus, and similarly with vehicle construction. The electro-technical, precision engineering, and optical manufacturing centres were widely scattered, and so were the petroleum production sites.

When Hitler was preparing German industry for war, the danger of these regional agglomerations was clearly recognised. With most industry tied to the Ruhr or to Upper Silesia, and shipbuilding to the coast, there was little hope of escaping attack. And so a relocation programme was initiated in 1936, run on the following lines. The industrial areas near the frontiers—the Ruhr, Saxony, and Silesia—were to be thinned out in favour of the relatively safe central region. The area between Hannover, Magdeburg, and Halle was considered immune from military operations, which were of course expected to threaten on land rather than from the air. It was in accordance with this idea that German industrialists created the Herman Göring *Reichswerke* around Hannover and Brunswick out of nothing.

But the limitations of the economy meant that the schemes for construction and relocation could only be implemented to a minor extent, and in the following period were in fact restricted to the steel industry and to the expansion of the petroleum output, which was the weakest link in the chain of economic preparations for war.

However, the lightning campaigns of the first war years brought additional capacity into German industry and at the same time encouraged the decentralisation of production sites. The successes won in those lightning campaigns eliminated, in the minds of Hitler and his close associates, all possibility of military defeat or of any threat from the air to Germany's arms industry. The course of the First World War and the kind of strategic thinking evolved from it gave no grounds for such anxieties. Moreover the prowess of the Luftwaffe, which had justified itself up to 1941, promised security against hostile activity in the air. The initial air operations against shipping outside Wilhelmshaven, in the English Channel, and around the Shetlands did nothing to shake air staffs on either the German or the British side from the view that aircraft were to be used in support of the army's land operations. The British air attacks of summer 1940 were, it is true, aimed at the enemy's war economy, but they were completely inadequate to disrupt manufacture.

It was not till he failed in his attempt to blockade Germany that Churchill hit on the idea of attacking it with bombers based on Britain. After the first raids Göring, as Commander-in-Chief of the Luftwaffe and at the same time manager of German industry, announced a policy of reprisals. Absorbed in the awkward problem of pinpointing targets from great heights, Britain and Germany found themselves involved in an air war whose intensity and limits were unforeseeable. When Hitler broke off the Battle of Britain and gave precedence to preparations for the land campaign against

Russia, the initiative in the air passed to the British.

The year 1941 proved to have been the calm before the fatal storm. Britain readied herself for a long air war and steadily expanded her bomber fleet. As soon as Churchill was able to win the American President over to his armament plans, the US started building her own bomber fleet.

On the German side, Göring's personality put a brake on any forward thinking. His bombastic prophesies about the future course of the war, his vast underestimation of his opponent's arms production, and his ignorance of technology allowed no scope for sober calculations. The British air strategy seemed at first, moreover, to bear out Göring's views. The RAF launched one night sortie after another without effectively damaging German arms manufacture. On August 12, 1941, the Ruhr suffered its first daylight attack, but after its heavy losses the RAF soon reverted to night-flying. Like the Luftwaffe it was not yet capable of undertaking a prolonged daytime offensive. As long as it stuck to the hours of darkness, losses were kept within bearable limits. Between May and December 1941 the RAF entered German airspace 105 times. Yet the damage suffered by German industry was almost negligible. The British greatly overrated the effect, whereas Hitler's real anxieties during the winter of 1941/42 lay in the Eastern theatre.

Churchill's notion of forcing Germany to her knees through the RAF was based on the assumption that the enemy would be attacked not by a co-operating, but by an independently operating, air force. This approach, formulated shortly after the First World War by the Italian Douhet (whence the term *douhetism*), won increasing support among Britain's leading airmen. It was under their influence that the War Cabinet decided, on February 14, 1942, in favour of 'area bombing'—not narrowly defined targets but whole areas were now to be destroyed from the air. The method did not appear to be a quick one, but did seem to promise the best results. This was the great hour of Sir Arthur Harris, whom Churchill put in command of the British bomber fleet. In Germany, in the same month of February 1942, Albert Speer became head of the Arms Ministry.

Hitler's protégé takes charge

In the spring of 1940 Hitler had appointed the constructor of the autobahns and the Siegfried Line, Dr Fritz Todt, Reichsminister for Arms and Munitions. The impressive title could hardly conceal the scanty authority of this prosaic technician. It was only the army's weapons which came under his purview; the navy and Luftwaffe controlled their own procurements. Todt's meticulously calculated production targets were meant to take care of the armies in the East. When the losses of equipment and ammunition during the winter of 1941/42 became known in Berlin, Todt urged Hitler to put an end to the whole grim operation. After an interview on these lines in the Führer's headquarters, Todt flew off. His aircraft crashed within sight of the building.

A few hours later Hitler's young architect protégé Albert Speer arrived at his headquarters. At 36, Speer already had to his credit Hitler's new party buildings, the Nazi Congress stadium at Nuremberg, and the new Reich Chancellery in Berlin. Hitler had entrusted him with the development of

the capital and showered every favour on him. He was no 'old warrior', and had only joined the party in 1932 under the attraction of its building programme. It was February 8 when Todt had his fatal crash; on February 9 Hitler appointed Speer in his place. The decision caused great surprise: several of Todt's collaborators would have been obvious choices and the young architect knew nothing about armaments. Nevertheless Hitler's choice was in this case a fortunate one. In Speer's person the leading group acquired a man who did not altogether conform to their pattern, but who exceeded all expectations and resisted the anti-war elements in Germany as long as this was practicable and indeed a little longer. Hitler was right when he said that without Speer the war would have ended two years earlier.

With the appointment of Arthur Harris as head of Bomber Command a new chapter began for the British. Churchill thought he had found in the new Air Marshal the man to implement Douhet's theories. Harris had been able to try out his air warfare concepts on a miniature scale against tribesmen in Mesopotamia, Transjordan, and India. Now he hoped to apply them with greater effect in the European theatre.

The chief instrument for bringing the Germans to their knees was to be the four-engined bomber carrying a load of 9 tons, with a range of 3,000 miles and a ceiling of more than 30,000 feet, equipped with radio instruments for navigation and bomb-dropping. Harris demanded 4,000 such machines, plus another 1,000 fighter-bombers, so as to keep 1,000 aircraft in the air over German territory at all times. In view of Britain's shortage of raw materials, however, Harris never had at his disposal in the following years more than 1,350 bombers altogether.

In his first six months Harris's achievements were almost negligible: the Luftwaffe was in command of too much air space. Even the spectacular attacks on Rostock and Lübeck and the first 1,000-bomber raid on Cologne were more useful as sources of Intelligence data for planning air strategy than for their military impact. A similar verdict must be passed on the subsequent series of attacks on German cities. Bombing the Ruhr, where arms production centres were likely to be hit by area bombing because of the high concentration of industrial sites, was made very difficult by the permanent haze which hung over the region. This was another technical consideration which determined the British air strategy we must now describe.

In his book *Bomber Offensive,* Sir Arthur Harris had this to say about the birth of 'area' bombing after the Casablanca Conference in January 1943:

The subject of morale had been dropped, and I was now required to proceed with the general 'disorganisation' of German industry, giving priority to certain aspects of it such as U-boat building, aircraft production, oil production, transportation and so forth, which gave me a very wide range of choice and allowed me to attack pretty well any German industrial city of 100,000 inhabitants and above.

The assumption that the bombing of German towns could be equated with the destruction of German industry was the most persistent fallacy in this air strategy. Submarine construction had been concentrated on the coast and was not dispersed over the whole country till 1943. Aircraft manufacture and, still more markedly, fuel production were scattered throughout the Reich

and were not represented in the major cities at all. The attacks launched later against these sectors clearly refute Harris's supposition. The only system of targets represented in every town was the transportation network, but this could only be put permanently out of action by precision bombing.

With area bombing, direct hits on armament factories were merely a by-product of a different intention, that of instilling war-weariness into Germany's civilian population. Churchill and his Air Marshal decided to go in for 'morale bombing' and recommended the policy openly at the Casablanca Conference. The middle of 1942 saw the start of that 'death dance of German towns' which began with the 1,000-bomber raid on Cologne, reached its first climax with blazing Hamburg as its symbol, and culminated in the destruction of a defenceless and economically irrelevant Dresden at a time when the outcome of the war was no longer in doubt.

For a long time, Churchill was convinced that this strategy was the weapon to beat Germany with. Yet the British air assaults on the Ruhr, the Rhine towns, the towns east of the Ruhr, and Berlin itself, did nothing to advance the military prosecution of the war and left the flow of arms production almost unimpaired—on the contrary, they strengthened the public's will to resist and brought bloody grist to the mills of Goebbels' propaganda machine. After the war was over, Churchill and Harris had to admit that the unending giant air raids had in no way accelerated the collapse of the Reich. True, Harris maintained that he would have attained his object if he had had 1,000 bombers continually in the air over Germany; but even that remains a question-mark. We have examined the record of 'morale bombing' because this technique in the event merely postponed the decisive weakening of German industry. It was British air strategy, in fact, that turned the cities of Germany into bastions of her industrial strength.

The arrival on the scene of the American air arm dramatically increased the threat to the arms industry. The US Army Air Force took on the dangerous task of precision bombing against arms and communication targets. Speer and Milch, Inspector-General of the Luftwaffe, recognised the danger now looming for their production plans and saw the bitter truth that German air strength was incapable of meeting it. In numerous conversations with Hitler, Speer described the rising toll of industrial damage. On February 12, 1943, in the planning centre of the Material Allocations Board, he painted a grim picture of worse to come: 'You must reject the childish notion that the air threat will remain as mild as it is today. Things are going to be quite different,' he said. And he was right.

On July 4, 1942, the 8th USAAF started its operations in Western Europe by raiding airfields and railway stations in Holland and France. On December 21, 1942, they attacked the Krupp factory in Essen, unsuccessfully at first. The threat became clearly discernible when the American bomber fleet took steps to paralyse German industry as a whole by destroying key sectors. One of the most important was the manufacture of ball-bearings, more than half of which was concentrated in Schweinfurt. Göring had opposed the relocation of industries, believing that the Luftwaffe had only temporarily lost control of the air.

On August 17, 1943, the production sites were heavily damaged in a daylight raid which reduced current output to 35%. The same day, Speer flew with a collection of photographs of the destruction to Hitler's headquarters and gave a report of this appalling attack. As so often before, he demanded better protection for sensitive links in the arms production chain, including Schweinfurt. The arrival of a second swarm of bombers on October 14, intent on hamstringing German ball-bearing manufacture completely, found the air defences ready. One of the biggest air battles of the war was fought out in the sky above Schweinfurt, and American losses were so high that the city was immune to attack for the next two months. The industrialist Kessler, who had been brought in by Speer, managed during this breathing-spell to restore output to its previous level. He achieved this by switching production to other sites. But this solution would have been ruled out if many factories had been raided simultaneously. And the way things were going in the German skies, that was precisely what could be expected.

1,500 drowned by the 'Dambusters'

The barrage dams were of special importance to the industries of the Ruhr. Those which blocked the valleys of the Möhne and Sorpe provided industrial water for 70% of the Ruhr factories and supplied nearly 5,000,000 people with drinking water. The Eder valley barrage regulated the level of the Weser and controlled flooding on the Eder and Fulda rivers. They all provided power for numerous generators. These facts led the British Air Ministry to think that it could hobble the Ruhr industries at a single blow. Bomber Command calculated that an attack launched in the high-water season would bring the Ruhr factories to a complete stop in July and August 1943. Destruction of the retaining walls of the Eder valley dam, moreover, would halt river traffic on the Weser for months on end and would strike a heavy blow at the aircraft armament industry around Kassel. If only a successful raid could be launched the effects, it was felt, must be catastrophic.

The raid which Harris had been preparing since March 1943 was carried out on the night of May 17/18. The few 37-mm anti-aircraft guns positioned on the dams had no time even to take aim at the British aircraft approaching low over the water. Two dams were hit and collapsed, but the third was not spotted. This partial success no doubt gave joy in London, but the hopes rested upon it were not fulfilled. The main effect was not economic but psychological, for 1,500 people were drowned in the flooding and the RAF had demonstrated that it could reach any target in the Reich with its bombs. The German armament experts supposed that incendiary raids would be launched against the Ruhr towns during the following night. The failure to launch them saved the population of that region from catastrophe, for there would have been no water with which to put out the fires. This alone makes it clear that the primary motives for that daring venture were economic ones.

As soon as the news of the attack arrived, Speer flew to the dams and started reconstructing them with the aid of his Todt Organisation. By September 23, the walls were closed up again and better protected, this time, by anti-aircraft units. The event gave Speer sufficient grounds to press Hitler

once more for anti-aircraft cover for the entire Ruhr industry, and this time Hitler consented. The Armaments Minister himself was also moved to pay more attention to the seriously threatened Ruhr valley. He set up a 'Ruhr Staff' in Krupp's residence, the Villa Hügel: this consisted of a number of industrial managers whose job was to prevent output declining in the event of air raids on armament works.

The story of effective air raids in 1943 cannot be completed without mention of that on the peninsula of Peenemünde. The attacks on Schweinfurt, the Ruhr and its nearby dams, and the mysterious Peenemünde were not of course the only ones; but they were the conspicuous highlights of the year and harbingers of the coming air offensive against Germany's arms supply.

Ever since 1932 General Dornberger and the young Wernher von Braun had been working on projectiles capable of carrying bombs over great distances. During 1942 and 1943 the finishing touches were put to 'Aggregat 4' and 'Fieseler 103', which had been developed under the army's and Luftwaffe's aegis on Peenemünde and became known as the V-1 and V-2. Speer and Milch, who had taken the initiative over Germany's most costly arms items, had been pressing ahead energetically since 1943 though without – like Goebbels – expecting miracles. The more the test-site expanded, the greater the danger of its being discovered by the British secret service and attacked by the RAF. As early as May 14, 1943, the temperamental Field-Marshal Milch was prophesying that the enemy would soon notice where the 'infernal machines' were being created.

On August 17 the USAAF had paid a visit to Schweinfurt. It was on the night immediately following that Air Marshal Harris fulfilled General Milch's fears by starting up Operation 'Hydra'. While the German air defences were awaiting a raid on Berlin, the RAF, after a successful feint flight, turned off to Peenemünde and dropped its bombs on the army's experimental station. The V-1, which was the Luftwaffe's child, remained intact, but Braun's V-2 suffered a severe setback. Clouds of smoke still hung over the peninsula when Speer's aircraft arrived and a sleepless and dust-caked Dornberger was able to report to him. Speer flew back to Hitler via the ruins of Schweinfurt to tell him of the damage. The RAF had won more than a psychological success this time. The completion date for the V-2 had been postponed and the people of London remained immune for several months longer to the effects of that devastating weapon.

'The growing strength of the enemy's air force obliges us to speed up our plans for relocating production facilities of important armaments.' At the time when Speer sent this message on December 19, 1942, to the arms factories, the threat from the air was very small and relocation was more a matter of prudent foresight than an urgent necessity. But the very possibility of the RAF making unwelcome visits brought about expensive transfers of entire sectors of production. 'Unique manufactures' were subjected to 'immediate transfer orders' and had to leave any specially vulnerable sites without waiting for the first raids. Then there was a second category of 'emergency transfer orders' which came into effect as soon as the first hits were registered. But this migrating frenzy did not affect the whole armament industry. The big production centres on the Rhine and Ruhr and on the

Saar, in Upper Silesia and the Austrian Salzgitter, were in any case tied down by geography and could not be split apart. These could only be protected by strong air defences, which Speer proceeded to demand of the Führer in countless conversations.

The stream of evacuated German armament factories ran first into the occupied territories of the West. France, Belgium, and Holland were roped into the German arms industry, as were later Italy, the Balkans, and the countries of northern Europe. Earlier, there had been transfers within the Reich frontiers. As a result of these shifts it was hoped that the most essential manufacturing processes would remain immune to air attack, and this remained true as long as Allied aircraft was reluctant to fly across the German border. But the more command of the air passed to the Allies, the more pointless it became to shift production around within Germany or indeed to the occupied territories, since these too were not immune to attack. By the winter of 1943/44 there was only one way to protect manufacture effectively: to carry it out underneath thick layers of concrete, or to put it right underground. This solution was in turn limited by the capacity of German civil engineering, which was largely taken up with repairing the mounting total of air raid damage.

Signs of an ominous tendency

With the development of round-the-clock bombing, the danger for the arms factories grew bigger every day. Speer, who had to produce the weapons without having any control over their utilisation, had been pressing since 1942 for massive protection of the key arms factories. In the spring of that year he had numerous interviews with Hitler, urging the acceleration of the anti-aircraft gun and ammunition programmes and a switch to heavier calibres. In September Hitler congratulated his minister on this crash programme, but by the end of the month Speer was having to ask for the transfer of several anti-aircraft units to Friedrichshafen so as to better shield the extremely exposed aircraft industry there.

There were already signs of an ominous tendency: Speer only got protection for his factories after the first damage had been suffered. This trend, made inevitable by the shortage of defensive artillery, can be traced right through the records of 1943. Speer had to demand anti-aircraft protection successively for Friedrichshafen, Schweinfurt, Kassel, and then for the 'Reich territory' of the Hermann Göring Works. The demands alternated with orders from Hitler for the expansion of anti-aircraft weapon and ammunition output. On May 30, 1943, he even came up with the idea of using rockets to break up whole formations of aircraft. Speer passed the problem to his technical expert Dornberger, but nothing came of it. Early in 1944, when the Allied air raids began to reveal a pattern, Speer pressed more vigorously than ever for active air protection and Hitler, impressed by the continuous influx of air raid damage reports, made a lavish distribution of special powers to people involved in armaments.

It was hoped that a combination of anti-aircraft activity with searchlights, smoke-screens, mock factories, and jamming devices would deter the enemy from his systematic attacks. But the growing number of bottlenecks in every sphere made the planning targets unattainable from the start. Speer was moved to the sarcastic comment that German industry no longer had enough 'fog acid' (phosphoric acid) to put up a fogscreen round the plants responsible for making it.

In mid-August 1944 the arms experts attempted another crash programme for anti-aircraft production, and even Speer's conversation of early January 1945 contained figures which were entirely unrealistic. But the armaments sector had since mid-1944 been putting all its hopes in the new Messerschmitt 262 jet-fighter, and paid little attention to anything else.

1944: the fatal turning-point

Up to the end of 1943 Allied air attacks had spoilt the appearance of a lot of German towns, but the output of war material under Speer's guidance was. greater than ever before. It was early 1944 that saw the turning-point here, when attacks on the Luftwaffe's arms base commenced. In mid-1944 military production received another jolt when the German fuel installations went up in flames. And the fatal blow came when the transportation network, under the continuous downpour of bombs, fell apart and the German war machine was deprived of the freedom of movement essential to it.

Since August 1943 Allied aircraft had been able to fly up from airfields in Italy and to reach without difficulty both the Rumanian airfields of Ploesti—Germany's biggest petroleum source—and the southern area of the Reich itself. The Luftwaffe was given the insoluble task of defending vast regions of airspace in all parts of the country. A further difficulty was that the American bomber squadrons, ever since 1943, had been accompanied right up to their targets by Allied long-range fighters. Not only did this spare the Allies the kind of losses they had suffered over Schweinfurt: it led to a dramatic increase in losses of defence fighters. And the more the German air defences were enfeebled, the more frequent and precise the attacks on German arms installations became.

The high hopes placed in the new Messerschmitt fighter become clear from Milch's remark that 'without it, no more arms manufacture will be possible'. The Luftwaffe officer's judgement was correct; but his hopes could not be fulfilled because of the rivalry between army and Luftwaffe interests. Production capacities were just not sufficient to meet all the top priority arms manufacture programmes. The Luftwaffe's plan foresaw a monthly output of 2,000 fighters, 750 Junkers 88 bombers, and 200 Heinkel 177s. But such figures would have been beyond the ability of all the aircraft factories combined, even if they had not been declared the special target of American bombing. On February 20, 1944, Operation 'Big Week' began. For six days on end the German aircraft factories endured a constant rain of bombs from the USAAF. The destruction reached such proportions that if it had continued the Luftwaffe would have been completely eliminated from the war. On that same day, February 20, Milch and his staff visited all the major aircraft works. During this visit there was born the idea of a Fighter Staff. Part of Germany's aircraft production was to be transferred to the control of Speer, who had been considerably more successful than the Luftwaffe organisers. Milch was enthusiastic: *No other solution is possible. I shall have to tell Reichsmarschall Göring and Hitler today: 'The arms production programme as we have imagined it is no longer anywhere*

near a practical proposition. By the time when you, Führer, trust that we shall have 2,000 planes, we shall be lucky to have 600, and this would make a decisive difference to the whole course of the war. . . .'

The whole aircraft industry was hamstrung. On February 28 Milch informed Speer that output in March 1944 would only be 30% to 40% of that for the preceding month. The Fighter Staff which Speer had thought up and put under the command of his ruthless colleague Saur set about forcing up fighter production again by any means available. By July 31, 1944 – the day when Speer took over the entire responsibility for

'The death dance of the German towns'

Dresden, symbol of the horror of 'area bombing', counts its dead (below) and, for lack of any alternative, burns them by the thousand (left)

Erich Andres

aircraft production – fighter output had been more than doubled. But not even that was sufficient now.

German fuel production is smashed

Fuel, the very lifeblood of modern military operations, had so far remained incomprehensibly immune from Anglo-American air attack even though the Americans, at least, had at an early stage given some thought to this matter. The raid on the Ploesti oilfields in 1942 had left little trace, but these and the German hydrogenation works (for converting coal into liquid fuel) exercised a fascination over the American bomber fleet. The German Armaments Ministry was aware of the constant threat looming over the installations, but few people were in a position to envisage the consequences of an attack on such sensitive targets. The special protection which Hitler granted to the oilfields soon seemed to be superfluous, for no fresh raids took place and it was more urgent to strengthen the anti-aircraft defences round the cities in Germany itself. Then, on August 1, 1943, a fleet of 177 American bombers – of which 54 failed to return – attacked the Ploesti fields. It proved possible, however, to make up for the damage by reactivating idle plant. In the following period there were no more of these large-scale raids, nor any on the few German hydrogenation plants because of their great distance from the enemy bases.

In October 1943, however, American bombers were let loose both on Ploesti and on the South German area. The raids on Leuna (1940), the Gelsenberg-Benzin works (1941), Scholven and Ludwigshafen (1943), and Wesseling (1944) were by way of experiments rather than exercises in systematic destruction. According to the Armaments Ministry's Planning Office, the total loss of petroleum up to the end of 1943 had not exceeded 150,000 tons – a trivial fraction of the total production.

This state of affairs, so favourable for the German side, was due in part to the lack of unanimity in the American Bomber Command. It took the staffs a long time to agree on target priorities. Among many other proposals, General Spaatz put forward a plan in March 1944 for a two-week continuous bombardment of the German fuel sector as the weakest element in the armaments industry. Since there were others who thought it more urgent to disrupt communication lines, Spaatz did not find acceptance for his ideas. Eisenhower, with the current land operations in mind, also gave priority to the communication targets; but on April 19 he gave way to Spaatz' insistence and allowed an experimental two-day attack on the German hydrogenation plants. When the American aircraft accordingly dropped their bombs on May 12 over the east German plants in Leuna, Böhlen, Zeitz, and Lützendorf, some of these installations were so severely damaged that they made no contribution to output for several weeks. The Ruhr refineries came under the RAF's jurisdiction and were spared major attacks for a little while longer.

Speer doubts a German victory

Recently recovered from a severe illness, Speer went to see the still-smoking Leuna factory on May 16 and next day gave the necessary procurements and repairs the highest priority classification. But repairs were hardly started when, on May 28 and 29, a second wave of bombers visited this

sensitive installation. The maintenance or loss of German fuel output now acquired decisive importance for the issue of the war. Despite the doubts he felt about the possibility of a German victory, Speer applied all his might to the tiller. He was completely aware of the magnitude of the new danger. 'The preservation of the hydrogenation plants is the most important task at present on the domestic scene. The outcome of the war virtually depends upon its fulfilment,' he wrote.

On May 23 Speer went with his closest colleagues in the fuel sector to see Hitler in his headquarters and give him an unvarnished picture of the situation. The Führer ordered intensification of anti-aircraft and smokescreen measures along with many other individual steps, the total effect of which still seemed inadequate to his Armaments Minister. After the second series of raids began, Hitler accepted a further suggestion of Speer's and agreed to appoint a plenipotentiary with full powers of decision. On June 30 the appointment went on Speer's advice to the steel specialist Edmund Geilenberg. This man and his staff now had to compete with their enemy on most unequal terms. Early in June 1944 target priorities were set for the American 8th and 15th Air Forces – petroleum, ball-bearing factories, and thirdly tank manufacture; the jet-fighter and V-weapon installations came lower on the list. On the German side, the protection of petroleum production was also the No. 1 priority, so that the struggle over this item was seen as decisive by all protagonists.

While repairs continued, Speer gave orders that enemy air reconnaissance should be prevented at all costs in order to keep the reactivation of the plants secret for as long as possible. But Germany's air defences were no longer able to accomplish even this. As soon as June 10 bombs were falling on Ploesti again; on June 12 the RAF raided the west German hydrogenation plants; on June 20 the first factories in eastern Germany were completely put out of action. The same day, Speer visited Hitler's headquarters and reported the catastrophic consequences, and on June 30 he handed over his first Hydrogenation Memorandum, giving statistical data which clearly showed the rapid drop in German fuel output since May 28. Assuming a constant tempo of repair work, he prophesied disaster by September.

Despite all manner of defence measures the 8th Air Force struck again in July, this time with heavy losses. Speer's forecast looked like coming true, now that fresh raids were following hard on the resumption of production. Early in July Speer gave Hitler another report on the fuel situation and on July 30 handed him his second memorandum, envisaging the utter paralysis of the Luftwaffe. On August 30 he ended his third memorandum with the words: 'If the Allies continue to gain successes in the air, we shall soon lack the materials necessary for prosecuting modern warfare.' As he had expected, fuel output sank by September to 8% of its April level and supplies were soon completely exhausted, whereas the production of German fighter aircraft now reached its zenith.

The attacks from the air continued without respite. The hope of bad weather bringing a temporary pause was not fulfilled. With over 300,000 workers under him, Geilenberg went on with the unequal struggle even when further carpets of bombs descended in

November until Pölitz and Leuna were the only plants still turning anything out. In December a few installations resumed work, only to go up in flames in January 1945. Speer's memorandum of January 19, 1945, was an admission of defeat in the armaments battle. But by this time his energies were being devoted to ends other than the production of war material.

The Allied bombers had attained their objective — although the efforts of Speer and Geilenberg had forced the bomber commands to undertake new and often costly sorties. Lack of fuel had condemned the German air defences, the armies on the front, and the whole war economy to immobility. The German fuel industry was bound to lose this fight, but it did not admit defeat until the enemy tanks drove into the very factory yards. On Speer's instructions they kept at it, not so much with a view to continuing a pointless military resistance as to avoid a complete breakdown of traffic in the devastated ruins of Germany.

Roads and rails: the decisive blow

Greatly though the German war machine was enfeebled by the failure of the fuel industry, it cannot be claimed that this was the decisive blow. That term applies rather to the assaults on the transportation net.

At the start of the war Germany enjoyed a transportation system that was in every respect balanced and appeared to be little susceptible to damage. But the transport crisis of spring 1942 showed clearly how dependent German armament production was upon this network.

The junctions in the vicinity of major industrial centres soon became an attractive target for Allied aircraft. It was nevertheless possible for some time to repair any damage speedily, until the autumn of 1943 when it was recognised that a new situation had arisen: the enemy was set upon systematic destruction of Germany's transportation. The transport problem acquired special importance because of its close connection with coal, so vital for the sustenance of industry. Damage to railway tracks meant non-delivery of essential coal supplies; destruction of transport routes hit not only industry as a whole but military operations too. On December 16, 1943, Speer visited Hitler to give him an anxious account of the traffic situation.

Up to the spring of 1944 the transport sector had managed, as Speer's confidant Kehrl put it, to muddle through somehow. Then, however, transportation was put at the top of the Allied targeting lists, for one thing as part of the preparations for invasion in the West, and for another to hold up German arms supplies. On May 18, 1944, Speer received an utterly depressing verdict from the Transport Minister. It was not so much the air attacks on travelling trains as the carpet-bombing of rail junctions which had produced the most appalling results. At the worst hit place, Hamm, 9,000 workers were continually engaged in repairs. As with the hydrogenation works, so here a race began between bombers on the one hand and anti-aircraft gunners and repair gangs on the other. When the Transport Minister suggested that workers should be shifted from repair jobs to anti-aircraft production, Speer's resigned reaction was to say: 'We have no choice any more.' The only hope lay in utilising the brief intervals between completion of a repair and the next air raid.

When on June 30 Speer met the transport

The German answer to the bombers — flak

Just as the Germans had been the first to realise and exploit the offensive power of aircraft, so they were among the first to provide their forces with a wide range of anti-aircraft equipment, ranging from the multiple 20-mm cannon to the legendary 88 and even larger weapons. All the guns illustrated below in their mobile versions could also be used to provide static defence for strategic targets, and combined with radar and searchlights to form a series of defensive belts

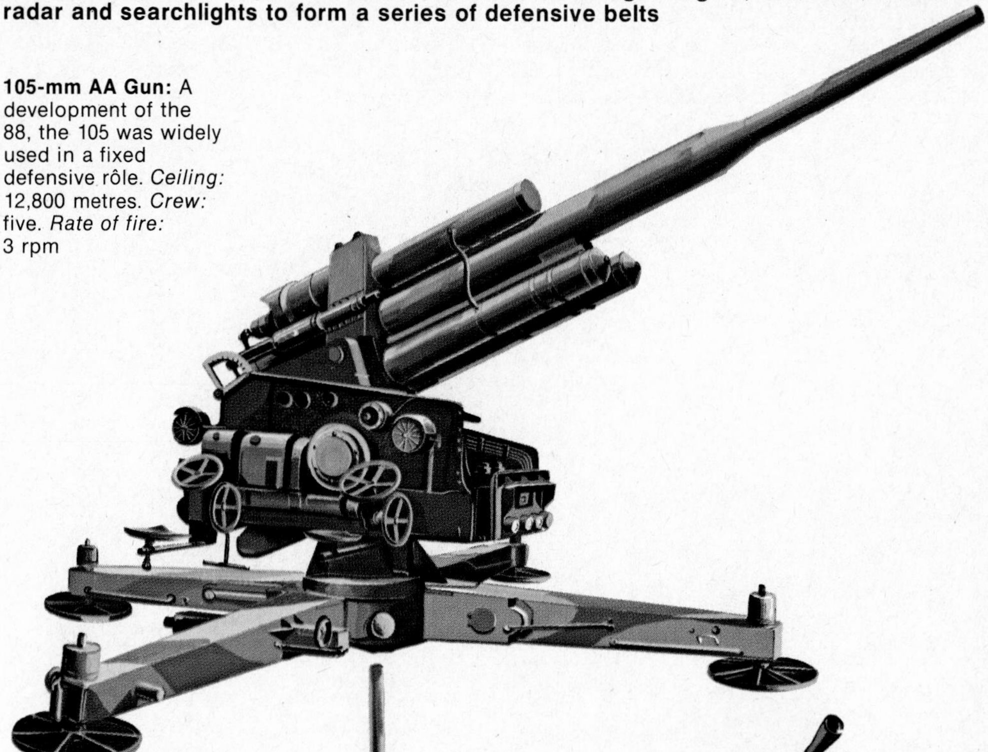

105-mm AA Gun: A development of the 88, the 105 was widely used in a fixed defensive rôle. *Ceiling:* 12,800 metres. *Crew:* five. *Rate of fire:* 3 rpm

20-mm Flakvierling 38: This version of the quadruple 20-mm was mounted on a small trailer and could be towed behind a light vehicle

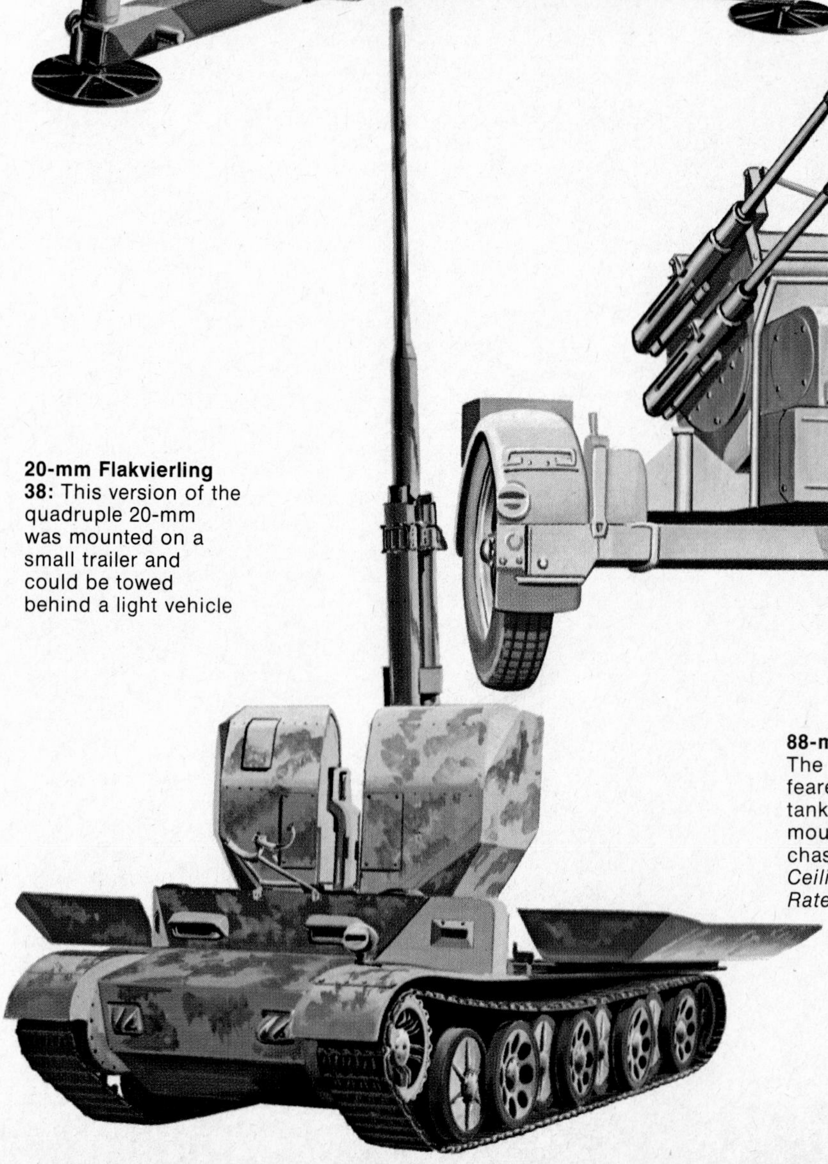

88-mm Grille 10: The most tested and feared German anti-tank and AA gun, mounted on a Pzkw-IV chassis. *Crew:* six. *Ceiling:* 10,800 metres. *Rate of fire:* 3 rpm

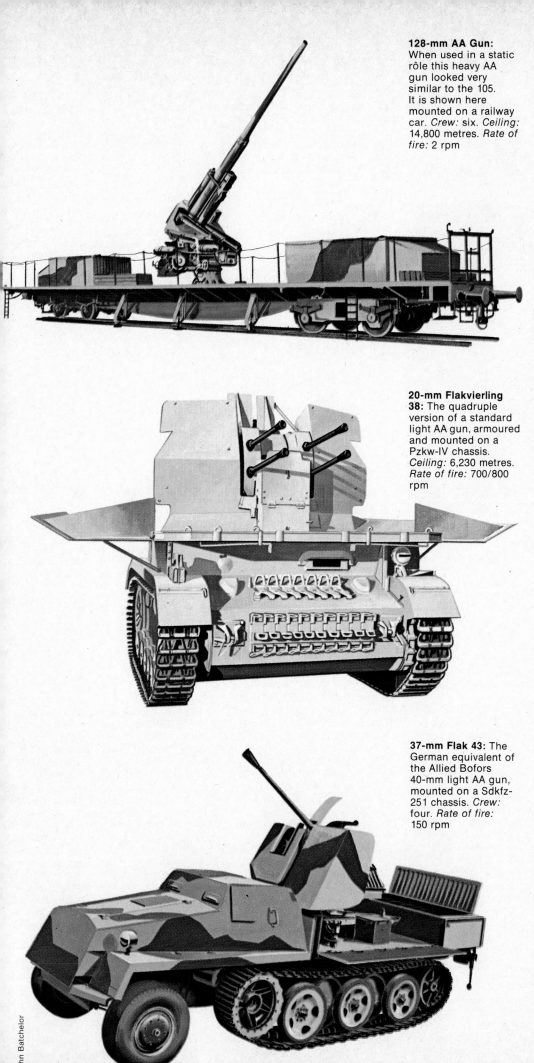

128-mm AA Gun: When used in a static rôle this heavy AA gun looked very similar to the 105. It is shown here mounted on a railway car. *Crew:* six. *Ceiling:* 14,800 metres. *Rate of fire:* 2 rpm

20-mm Flakvierling 38: The quadruple version of a standard light AA gun, armoured and mounted on a Pzkw-IV chassis. *Ceiling:* 6,230 metres. *Rate of fire:* 700/800 rpm

37-mm Flak 43: The German equivalent of the Allied Bofors 40-mm light AA gun, mounted on a Sdkfz-251 chassis. *Crew:* four. *Rate of fire:* 150 rpm

experts in the Ministry, there was no longer any question of repelling an invasion. Indeed the network was already so impaired that even a long gap between raids was now insufficient for transport inside Germany to be got going again. Trains were running mostly under cover of night, scantily equipped with anti-aircraft artillery, between one break in the track and the next. The short-haul traffic managers were able to deliver a great many goods despite almost insuperable obstacles, but as the year 1944 wore on, Germany's economic terrain came to resemble a transportation wilderness.

While Speer and Transport Minister Ganzenmüller were still discussing ways of clearing the congestion, the triangle Hamm/Osnabrück/Münster, so vital to the arms industry, was completely paralysed. Speer tried to keep at least the most essential arms materials flowing, but when frost and snow came in the second half of January 1945 and refugee transports began arriving from the East, inter-regional planning became impossible. On January 23 Speer drew the only reasonable conclusion in the circumstances: he declared food and clothing to be higher priority items than arms supplies. When on February 18 Hitler entrusted Speer with the formation of a Transport Staff, expecting his successful minister to solve this problem too, the effect was tragi-comic. But by using his appointment to facilitate the feeding of the population, as far as this was possible, Speer gave it some retrospective point. A few days after he had taken over the transport sector, the US air force embarked on Operation 'Clarion' and gave it the *coup de grâce*. Complete military collapse was expected hourly. Speer postponed it day by day, bringing 2,000,000 workers to the damaged sites. But it was in vain. Germany's armament economy fell finally to pieces as Allied troops entered the Reich.

Collapse due to transport, not towns

While Operation Big Week had weakened Germany's air defence capability by smashing aircraft factories, the attacks on arms production facilities throughout the Reich had not had their desired effect. Speer, with his flexible leadership system and an endless succession of improvisations, had managed to continue providing Hitler with the weapons and equipment he wanted. It was only the attacks on coal-hydrogenation plants and the bombing of the transportation network which injured Germany's operational capability on the war fronts, and the internal mobility of her armaments industry, grievously enough to lose her the war. It was not the bombing of towns but the destruction of her transport system that broke the economic resistance of the Reich. The pressure on her frontiers, and then the occupation of her soil, finally throttled the war economy so that military operations and arms production collapsed of necessity at the same moment.

GREGOR JANSSEN was born in Bottrop (Westphalia) in 1938, and grew up in Cologne during the war. Afterwards he was at school in Cologne, and for some time in York. Since 1959 he has studied history and philosophy at the Universities of Cologne, Bonn, and Tübingen. His studies concentrated particularly on the German economy during the Second World War; and his thesis was on German armaments under the Speer ministry between 1942 and 1945.

John Batchelor

UNDER THE

Germany, August 1944
For the Allied bomber chiefs, the bombing of Germany soon became an interesting problem which could be argued about, calculated, and indulged in, as if it were largely theoretical. But for the people of Germany the massive offensive meant at best a radical change in their way of existence and at worst a savage and horrifying death

In August 1944 my parents, who were then living in Darmstadt, were bombed out for the first time. Their house had been burnt to the ground, but they had been able to rescue their possessions from the ruins and had been taken in by relatives. They intended moving to a small town in the Odenwald on September 11, and I had come to Darmstadt from Berlin two days earlier to help with the move. The van driver, who was to take us and our possessions to Michelstadt, sent a message in the morning of the 11th to say that he was tired out and would come to move us the following day.

Neither he nor my parents lived to see that day. Overnight, Darmstadt became a smoking heap of ruins, almost 80% destroyed. About 15,000 people were killed.

The sirens started to wail 20 minutes before midnight. I was already in bed but had not yet fallen asleep. I had been used to such nightly disturbances in Berlin. Automatically I got dressed, reached for the small suitcase standing ready, and groped my way through the darkness to the door. My mother's shouts made me hasten my step. I was not familiar with the plan of the house in which my relations had given us refuge, but I only needed to follow the hurrying shadows which were crowding on to the unlit stairs. Somebody pushed me into a corner of the cellar, where space had been allocated to my relations. I sat shivering between my parents on a rough wooden bench. The room was poorly lit and filled with the silent anguish of people doing their best to control their own fear in order to reassure the children and old people. There were two or three prams with babies crying in them, a few small children on their mothers' laps, and I also noticed two or three soldiers in uniform. All told, we were about 30 people. Apart from my parents and a cousin, I knew no one.

Our hope that the enemy bombing unit would fly straight past soon changed to dreadful certainty: this time, it was our turn! The hum of the approaching engines became a roaring hurricane and the crashes of the first explosions could already be heard. At that moment, the light went out. Folding our arms over our heads in an instinctive gesture of self-defence, we cowered in the darkness and listened to the explosions. The bombers came in waves. The infernal roar of destruction drew near, moved away, approached again and then withdrew, only to return yet again. For a few seconds, a frantic hammering of the heart shut out all other sensations. Then came a somewhat longer pause. The explosions had receded to the edge of the town and the humming of the engines

resounded like a distant bass chorus.

Here and there a torch was turned on and its reflector cut a dazzling pathway through the thick, white haze which filled the air. The explosions in the neighbourhood had rocked the house to its foundations. The bricks in the walls had grated against each other in their beds of mortar and a dry, white dust poured out in clouds from the countless thin cracks in the wall. This made breathing a torment, but out of the suffocating haze came moaning and shouting.

Suddenly I found my cousin standing in front of us, her hair hanging dishevelled over her face, which was streaming with blood. She was the owner of the house. She had tried in vain to rescue some people from the neighbouring house and bring them to our cellar, but the way was blocked by rubble. She told us that it was impossible to get back up to the bedrooms as the stairs had been blocked by the falling walls, and had also caught fire. So now the only way left to us out of the cellar was through a small window covered by an iron flap just beneath the ceiling and reached by a ladder. Passing through this window you could crawl out on to the street; but for the moment we stayed where we were.

I don't know how many seconds of relative calm passed before the next wave of attack. Perhaps we were granted one or two minutes, even, to struggle for breath. In this brief interval I talked to my mother for the last time. The war had torn her nerves to shreds, and now she acted like a desperate child. She cried out loud and implored one of the nearby soldiers to help us. But he was as powerless as the rest of us. Then her cries for help turned to God and she started fumbling for an exit in the walls of our prison, as if she were out of her mind. I took her in my arms and pressed her tightly to me. At that moment, as I felt the helpless trembling of her body, a feeling of great calm surged over me and I heard myself say: 'Why are you crying out to God? From now on, we can only help ourselves!' 'But how, child?' 'By submitting to what He has ordained for us!'

For a moment all was still between us, and then I heard my mother say softly, but with deep emotion: 'Yes.'

Just then, a fresh wave of attack roared overhead. As it moved on, I laid my mother in my father's arms. I had noticed that one of the soldiers had climbed up the broken steps and pushed open the iron trap of the escape window, only to drop it immediately afterwards. A flame had lashed at him from outside. As he came back down the steps, he said: 'We're all done for.'

BOMBING

Melita
Maschmann

Ullstein

Erich Andres

What happened next was no longer dictated by reason. Strangely enough, I was, in my mind, completely convinced that we had to die here, and, deep down in my heart, I was quite prepared to die. This preparedness, which I experienced at all moments of great danger in the war, gave me inward calm. I was a convinced National Socialist and the war held meaning and purpose for me, so that I was ready to accept all sacrifices which it might impose. Yet, although I was ready to die—then and there—I nevertheless became, so far as I know, the only person to escape from the cellar, or, as I prefer to say, to be saved from it.

I opened the small window and found myself looking into a sea of fire. The street was strewn with burning wreckage from the roof of the house opposite and—as I now suspect—pools of burning phosphorus. I hardly stopped to think: with a jacket soaked in water over my head and shoulders, I ran straight into the fire and out on to the large square beyond. There it was easier to breathe and I could dip my smouldering shoes in a water tank. I then ran back to the window, which could only be opened from inside, and banged on it with my feet, and shouted; but after a few seconds, I was forced back to the square—otherwise I should have suffocated and burned on the spot.

I risked this same desperate deed just once more, getting no reaction from below, and then the human in me collapsed and the animal took over—the urge to save one's own skin and let the others die like cattle in their horrible prison! For the next two or three minutes, I ran to save my life, desperately summoning every scrap of energy. There was not a house anywhere in the street which had not turned into a blazing fire-brand. Above the sea of flames, a glowing cyclone raged over the town; and whenever it caught the bodies of people in flight, it shrivelled them in a second to the size of a child, and the next day they lay all over the streets, hardly burnt, but like mummified children.

I kept to the edge of this burning hurricane, but at one time had to clutch at a tree with both arms to avoid being swept into a burning house by the draught. Finally I reached a small park—here, at least, one could breathe, and I fell to the ground.

By now, the bombers had turned back, but for hours afterwards explosions from delayed-action bombs re-echoed through the night.

When I had regained my strength, I asked a man wearing a swastika on his armband to lend me his gas mask. I wanted to go back and do what I could to save whoever was still left, but he refused to hand over the mask, and I shouted at him: 'How can you just stand there with your swastika? There are women and children dying in there in their thousands. Come on, come with me, come and help!' But he still refused, and I tore his party armband off his arm. I felt ashamed that someone who wore this badge could be such a coward.

A little later, I came upon a group of soldiers standing together and grumbling about their officers: 'That gang sit safely in their bunkers, giving orders, and leave us here to roast.' I urged these men to help, too, beseeching them to come back with me as far as the square with the water tank. About a hundred people, mostly women and children, had crowded into the square by now, and we had to get them moving somehow before they choked to death in the heat.

Some of the soldiers followed me, but there was only one who didn't turn back before we reached the water tank. Of course, I had been that way before and knew that it could be done, and this knowledge gave me an advantage over those who turned back.

By the tank, the people who had fled from the fire were in a state of collapse. Many were lying unconscious—or were they dead?—and some were floating in the water. The air was so unbearably hot and contained so little oxygen that it stifled the will to live. I drove the people out of their lethargy and begged them to risk that last part of the road to safety, which I, myself, had already taken twice. Little by little, some stood up, and here and there a group was formed.

Gradually the fury of the fire abated. I made that journey many a time in the course of the night, past the heap of burning rubble below which my parents were buried. I was helped by a Hitler Youth leader about 14 or 15 years old; he had a bicycle with burnt tyres, but it ran all right on the wheel rims. We hung the unconscious over the crossbar and brought them in this way to the small park, where we unloaded them, and then went back for more. We sat people with burnt feet on the saddle and carried children on our backs. When we found somebody on the way who had collapsed from exhaustion, we helped him to pull himself together and continue his flight.

We worked with silent ferocity until morning, not stopping to reflect for a moment. If we had waited to consider, we would have been paralysed by despair. But we belonged to the generation which had learnt early not to ask questions, but to get on with the job.
[*Melita Maschmann's biography is in Vol 1, p. 56.*]

2209

'That bombing German towns could be equated with the destruction of German industry was the most persistent fallacy in the Allied air strategy.'

THE YALTA CONFERENCE

By the end of 1944 the Allies were reluctantly facing up to the possible problems of winning the war. For the last time, Britain tried to act as an independent Great Power as Churchill persuaded Stalin and Roosevelt to meet him at Yalta and discuss the shape of the future world. A. J. P. Taylor describes the 'moment of greatest optimism in the Second World War', the decisions which were made, and the miscalculations and suspicions which were soon to lead to the Cold War

The Anglo-American operations in north-west France from D-Day (June 6, 1944) onwards marked the beginning of a new period in relations between the three Great Powers. It was clear from this moment that Germany would be totally defeated, and within a fairly short time. Indeed, after the German collapse in Normandy, British and American generals expected that the war might well be over by the autumn of 1944. The earlier prospect that the Russians might liberate, or conquer, most of Europe, while the Western Powers would be left with only Italy and perhaps Greece, was now dispelled. On the contrary, it seemed that the western armies might arrive at the heart of Germany before the Russians. There was urgent need to reach agreement about the future of Germany. By the end of July the zones of military operation were drawn—lines which, though no one realised this, determined the later partition of Germany. The terms for Germany's surrender were also settled. Beyond this all was still in flux.

The approaching end of war in Europe raised other problems. The war in the Far East would soon take first place, and the Americans were eager to secure Soviet, less eager to secure British, assistance. Roosevelt, with his mind set on a stable world order, wished also to secure Soviet co-operation in the United Nations and was ready to pay a high price for this, at any rate in words and gestures. The British concerns were of a more practical kind. They wanted to ensure free conditions in a liberated Europe and believed that the terms should be laid down while the war was still in progress. They feared an immediate withdrawal of American forces from Europe as soon as the war was won and dreaded that they would be left alone to face a victorious Russia. They knew from previous experience that their own forces would run down when the fighting stopped. This time, as well, they were at the end of their resources. British economy had gone to the limit and had now passed it. The approaching end of the war raised a still more desperate question. American Lend-Lease would be automatically terminated, and the British did not see how they could survive without it.

It is not surprising therefore that Churchill took the initiative in approaching his two partners. For the last time, Great Britain strove to act as an independent Great Power, and Churchill appeared as the man who held the Grand Alliance together. From September 11 to 19, 1944, Churchill and Roosevelt met in conference at Quebec. It was their first meeting since Tehran and Cairo, and Churchill aimed to restore the exclusive Anglo-American association which Tehran had weakened. He immediately offered full British participation in the war against Japan. Roosevelt, never unwilling to make an honest buck, at once accepted, to the annoyance of his naval advisers, who preferred to conduct the Far Eastern war on their own. This was a great alleviation of the British position. Though 'Stage I', the war against Germany, would be over, 'Stage II', the war against Japan, and with it Lend-Lease, would continue. Hence the British were now eager to end Stage I as soon as possible and to prolong Stage II at least until they could play a decisive part in Burma.

Churchill aimed higher: to justify Anglo-American association in Europe as well as in the Far East. He breathed hints of the approaching Bolshevik danger, against which only Great Britain, sustained by Lend-Lease, would be an effective bulwark. Roosevelt did not respond. It is probably that he did not believe in the Bolshevik danger or at any rate imagined that he could deal with it in his well-tried way of softening Stalin up. Besides, he never faced difficulties until he reached them. The future of Germany arose however in an unexpected way. Henry Morgenthau, the secretary of the American treasury, was summoned by Roosevelt to Quebec. Presumably he was expected to discuss Lend-Lease. Instead he produced a plan for 'pastoralising' Germany, that is, for virtually destroying her industrial power. Churchill at first rejected the proposal violently, declaring that it would chain Great Britain to a dead body. Morgenthau held out the bait of $3,500,000,000 for Great Britain under Lend-Lease during Stage II and a further credit of $3,000,000,000 for non-military purposes. Churchill, perhaps encouraged by his private adviser Cherwell, agreed. Roosevelt, who needed Morgenthau's support at the coming presidential election, agreed also.

Churchill back on his own

The Morgenthau plan did not last long. The British war cabinet rejected it unanimously. So, more decisively, did all Roosevelt's advisers in Washington. He himself repented and pleaded that he had signed without thinking what he was doing. A few days later, he put a stop to all planning over the future of Germany until the war was over. Thus ultimately Churchill had drawn a blank with Roosevelt so far as Europe was concerned. The dual negative of no plans for Germany and no fear of Bolshevism meant also that there was no need of an Anglo-American partnership in Europe. Churchill was back on his own. Failing agreement with Roosevelt, his only resource, whether he liked it or not, was agreement with Stalin.

The sequel of the Quebec meeting therefore was Churchill's journey to Moscow, where he conferred with Stalin from October 9 to 17. This, too, was a memorable meeting: the last time that Churchill saw Moscow and the last time also that

Smiling for the camera, but clad as if against the Cold War to come — the 'Big Three' at Yalta

Great Britain and Soviet Russia met on more or less equal terms, virtually without American participation. The real significance of the meeting is a mystery. On the surface, both men were still confident and confiding; underneath they were suspicious, or so it seemed later. Perhaps the suspicions were in the nature of afterthoughts. Certainly, at the time, they claimed to be in warmer agreement than ever. Churchill produced his old idea by which spheres of military operation were gradually turned into spheres of political influence. Stalin responded. Churchill wrote the percentages on a scrap of paper: Rumania— 90% Russian; Greece—90% British; Hungary and Yugoslavia—50-50. Stalin initialled the deal. This was the most practical treaty ever made between Great Britain and Soviet Russia. The deal did not cover Poland, but here too the differences seemed less acute. Stalin had by this time sized up the exiled Polish government. He realised that, whatever concessions he made, they would not yield an inch. Therefore, by appearing conciliatory, he could increasingly win Churchill's sympathy.

The Moscow meeting opened another topic. An American observer was present, and Stalin gave him the precise assurance that Soviet Russia would enter the Far Eastern war three months after the defeat of Germany. Roosevelt was naturally pleased and in return gave his unofficial blessing to the Anglo-Soviet partition of the Balkans. Churchill returned home triumphant. He told the House of Commons: 'Relations with Soviet Russia were never more close, intimate and cordial than they are at the present time.' Probably Stalin would have said the same. Both men were aware of the differences which divided them. But both believed that by the partition-agreement they had avoided clashes in the Balkans and had set the pattern for similar deals elsewhere. The value of the agreement was demonstrated in December, when the British were able to crush the Greek Communists without a word or sign of protest from Stalin. He was honouring his bond and expected the same attitude from the British in his sphere.

There was of course a mutual equivocation. Both partners assumed that a freely-elected government would be anti-Communist. But they drew opposite conclusions. The British suppressed Communist governments as axiomatically not freely elected; the Russians worked against freely-elected governments as inevitably anti-Communist.

Much grander than Tehran
However all seemed set fair for agreement at the end of 1944. It was the Americans, not the Russians, who complained about British policy in Greece and to a lesser extent in Italy—complaints which drew from Churchill to Roosevelt

'the most violent outburst of rage in all of their historic correspondence'. Russian stock rose still higher in the west, when the Soviet armies advanced the date of their winter offensive in order to relieve the British and Americans after the German surprise attack in the Ardennes. The Western powers appeared once more as suitors to Soviet Russia, and the impression grew even stronger when Churchill and Roosevelt agreed to meet Stalin on Russian soil.

The conference at Yalta, from February 4 to 11, 1945, was a much grander affair than Tehran. The earlier meeting was really a matter of conversation between the three great men, with a few military advisers. At Yalta, there were full-scale military and political delegations, and the three leaders had less time for private discussion. Roosevelt was a little irritated at having been dragged so far and was eager to be off again. Hindsight later suggested that he was already a dying man, with his powers of judgement failing. Nobody however remarked on this at the time, and Roosevelt achieved most of what he had set out to do.

Roosevelt had an overriding aim at Yalta. He wished to make absolutely sure that Soviet Russia would enter the Far Eastern war. His principal motive was the unanimous opinion of his military advisers that, without Soviet intervention, the Far Eastern war would drag on for 18 months at great expense in money and lives. Roosevelt made the further calculation that action in the Far East would draw Soviet strength out of Europe. Stalin met Roosevelt's wishes fully and, since Soviet Russia was clearly a Far Eastern power, this was not surprising. Stalin further pleased Roosevelt by declaring his readiness to work with Chiang Kai-shek, and not with the Chinese Communists.

To crown all, Stalin agreed to join the United Nations Organisation virtually on Roosevelt's terms. This series of agreements was neither hypocritical nor misleading. Roosevelt's ideas and Stalin's were at this time close together. Both wanted to prolong and to strengthen their partnership. Contrary to what was said later by Roosevelt's enemies in the United States, Roosevelt had much the best of the bargain. He did not yield anything except what Soviet Russia possessed already or could easily acquire without asking anyone's permission. In exchange, he got the solid reward of Soviet intervention and the less solid one of Soviet participation in UNO.

Churchill was less successful. The prospect of Soviet intervention eclipsed Great Britain's role in the Far East. As well, Churchill wished to settle the affairs of Europe in advance, and Roosevelt refused to assist him. Hence there was much talk about Poland and about the reparations to be taken from Germany, without any firm decisions at the end. Churchill seems to have believed that

Great Britain would be too weak after the war to oppose Soviet Russia on any question and therefore strove to tie Stalin down while the war was still on. Roosevelt had every confidence that United States strength, to say nothing of his own skill, would go on increasing and was delighted to see questions indefinitely postponed. Stalin also assumed that he would get his own way, at any rate over Poland and reparations, and his gestures of agreement were made primarily to keep Roosevelt in a good temper.

Nevertheless Yalta was much more than a matter of mutual deception, whatever might be said later. It represented an attitude of firm agreement between Stalin and Roosevelt, based on compromises genuinely offered and accepted. Soviet distrust was less at Yalta than at any time since the Bolshevik revolution, and Roosevelt was on the way to winning his great stroke: he had opened the door to One World instead of two. Churchill and Great Britain generally had been pushed to one side, but this is exactly what was happening in practice. The days of Great Britain as a Great Power were nearly over. Soviet Russia and the United States had found the bases for understanding and co-operation. Yalta was the moment of greatest optimism in the Second World War.

Symbols of a deeper discontent
The optimism began to crumble almost as soon as the conference broke up. Roosevelt and Churchill were both criticised when they returned to their own countries—Roosevelt for allowing Soviet Russia to have three seats in the United Nations Assembly, Churchill for failing to insist on free elections in Poland. The criticism of Churchill came from disgruntled Conservatives and, since he was planning to lead the Conservative Party after the war, it alarmed him more than criticism from the Left would have done.

The actual points of criticism were only symbols of a deeper discontent. British and American hostility towards Soviet Russia had been abandoned, or at any rate submerged, during the war. In Great Britain particularly, declarations of friendship with Soviet Russia were an essential contribution to good labour-relations in the factories. As the war drew to an end, those who had always been anti-Soviet no longer kept quiet in the national interest. Moreover the conservatively-minded only realised the full consequences of the defeat of Germany when it was actually happening: by destroying Nazi Germany the Allies had inevitably made Communist Russia the only Great Power on the continent of Europe. It was not surprising that those who had spent sleepless nights over the Bolshevik peril ever since 1917 were now more apprehensive than ever before.

[A. J. P. Taylor's biography is in Vol 4, p. 1523.]

ANTWERP: THE VITAL PORT

Belgium and Holland, September/October 1944

Major-General J. L. Moulton

For the Allies, Antwerp was a vital prize—but Montgomery was convinced that the Ruhr could be attacked without the clearing of this key port to provide a short cut for supplies. His view prevailed: the 'Market Garden' paratroop attack went in—but the shortage of supplies (because Antwerp had not been made a prior objective) contributed to the British failure at Arnhem. Too late, attention turned to solving the supply crisis, and once again it fell to Canadian troops to bear the brunt in the battles for Antwerp, the Scheldt estuary, and the stronghold of Walcheren

Above: Ashore on Walcheren— and an early prisoner

In the early days of September 1944, the Reich seemed to the German generals to lie open to the Anglo-American armies advancing against it from their victories in France. That these armies failed to continue their advance, cross the Rhine, enter Germany, and bring the war to an end before the winter came, seemed a miracle comparable to that of the Marne, which in 1914 halted the German armies short of Paris.

Yet there was in reality nothing miraculous in the slowing down of the Allied advance. An army, said Napoleon, marches on its belly, and now it was supply that set limits to the Allied advance and gave the Germans time to recover and organise resistance. It had happened before in the Second World War, to both sides in Russia and in North Africa. As a victorious army advances, its lines of communication become strained, until the time comes when sheer lack of petrol and ammunition brings it to a halt. Added to that, there are the losses in battle of men and armour and—harder to pinpoint but still very real—psychological reaction both in the front line and in the command echelons.

Churchill recognised early what was happening, and minuted the British Chiefs-of-Staff on September 8:
One can already foresee the probability of a lull in the magnificent advances we have made. General Patton's army is heavily engaged on the line Metz-Nancy. Field Marshal Montgomery has explained his misgivings as to General Eisenhower's future plan. It is difficult to see how the Twenty-First Army Group can advance in force to the German frontier until it has cleared up the stubborn resistance at the Channel ports and dealt with the Germans at Walcheren and to the north of Antwerp.

The British and Canadian armies were by the beginning of September feeling the strain on their manpower of the Normandy casualties, although fresh American divisions were arriving at Cherbourg in a steady stream. But logistics were a different matter, for in the early weeks of September a supply famine developed.

Hitler's insistence that the German VII Army should hold its ground in Normandy had led to its destruction in August. Montgomery and Patton had then brilliantly seized the opportunity thus given them to drive ahead for the German frontier. Largely because the Germans did not withdraw from Normandy, the Allied advance had thus been slower than expected for the first seven weeks and stores had piled up in the beach-head. Then it had leapt ahead of schedule. Eisenhower's armies reached the Seine 11 days before they expected to, freed Paris 55 days ahead of programme, and by mid-September the American 1st Army was approaching Aachen, which on pre-invasion estimates it had not been expected to reach until May 1945. Garrisoning the Britanny and Channel ports in the face of this advance, Hitler gambled another 130,000 men on the Allied supply famine, adding desperately to Germany's own manpower famine.

Soon the beaches, Mulberry harbour, and Cherbourg were 400 to 500 miles behind the Allied front line. The American 'Red Ball Express'—heavy lorries and tank transporters converted to carry stores, with drivers briefed to rush them through—started to run on August 25. Airlifts brought stores direct from Britain, delivering 1,000 tons a day in the second week of September. Closer to the front than Normandy were the Channel ports. The Canadians entered Dieppe without resistance on September 1 and Ostend on the 10th, but the Germans still held Le Havre, Boulogne, Calais, and Dunkirk. Moreover, except for Le Havre—which would later discharge 14,000 tons a day—these were primarily passenger ports.

Antwerp—ideal for supply
Antwerp was in a different class. It could take ships up to 19,000 tons burden and 30 foot draught, and berth nearly 1,000 ships of varying sizes at a time. There were 10 square miles of docks, 20 miles of water frontage, 600 cranes, plus marshalling yards, granaries, cold storage plants, coal hoists, and oil tankage. Before the war it handled up to 60,000 tons a day, and SHAEF planners counted on it for 40,000 a day. With Antwerp a mere 25 miles from Brussels, hauls to the fighting front were correspondingly short. But, between Antwerp and the sea stretched 80 miles of the lower Scheldt river and its seaward approaches, commanded by German guns, blocked by German minefields.

On September 3, as General Dempsey's British 2nd Army crossed the Belgian frontier, Montgomery issued new instructions, ordering Dempsey to advance with utmost speed to the Rhine in the hope of a surprise crossing. The Guards Armoured Division reached Brussels that night. On its left the 11th Armoured Division, momentarily held up near Lille, entered Antwerp next day. There was some fighting in the dock area, but, with the aid of the Belgian Resistance, these were captured almost intact in the next few days. The 12th Corps, coming up, took over Antwerp, and 30th Corps swung away east, heading for the Dutch frontier beyond Brussels

and ultimately for the Rhine, with 12th Corps guarding its left flank.

Eisenhower had also issued instructions on the 3rd, giving Montgomery the multiple tasks 'to secure Antwerp, breach the sector of the Siegfried Line covering the Ruhr and then seize the Ruhr'. On September 10 he authorised Montgomery to carry out the Arnhem attack. The airborne divisions dropped on the 18th, and from then until the 25th, when the remnants of the 1st Airborne Division were ordered to withdraw, all eyes and all hopes were fixed on the battle there.

The German XV Army had escaped the worst of the Normandy fighting. Responsible for the defence of the Pas de Calais, it had remained waiting for the second landings which never came. Towards the end of July, Hitler, who had guessed right over Normandy but then changed his mind, at last allowed divisions to be taken from the XV Army for Normandy. By the end of August only six of its original 19 divisions were left intact.

General von Zangen, newly appointed to its command and ordered to hold the line of the Somme, found Allied armour streaming around his southern flank where the VII Army should have been. Making up with remnants of seven other divisions nearly 100,000 men, the XV Army began to withdraw eastwards. Then, on September 6, Zangen was told that Brussels and Antwerp were in British hands, that he should garrison Le Havre, Boulogne, Calais, and Dunkirk, and bring the rest of his men out across the mouth of the Scheldt to Walcheren, and thence back to the mainland via South Beveland (see map).

86,000 men got away
Merchant ships, Rhine barges, and rafts were rounded up for the crossing, and marching troops were directed to Breskens and Terneuzen for embarkation. Most of the crossings were made by night, with some by day. Allied air attack took its toll, but by September 23, when the crossing was complete, 86,000 men with 616 guns, 6,200 trucks, and 6,000 horses had got away. On the mainland German 719th Division, arriving too late to hold Antwerp, was ordered to cover the exit from South Beveland, and General Student's I Parachute Army brought in on Zangen's left. Later, under Lieutenant-General Chill, remnants of three infantry divisions, together with the crack VI Parachute Regiment and part of the Göring Training Regiment, were formed into a reserve.

To hold the mouth of the Scheldt, Zangen left the 64th Infantry Division (Major-General Eberding), west of the river, and the 70th (Lieutenant-General Daser), in Walcheren and South Beveland. The 64th had been hastily formed in Germany from men on leave from the Russian and Italian fronts and from Norway. Its men were therefore fresh and experienced, if new to their present units. The 70th was also newly formed, in its case from men invalided from Russia and elsewhere with gastric conditions needing special diet. At Breskens, Cadzand, and Zeebrugge, and on the dunes of Walcheren, there were powerful coastal defence batteries manned by fresh, fit men.

Walcheren had not been on Hitler's original list of 'fortresses', whose garrisons were individually sworn to hold them at all costs. On September 4, however, he named Walcheren and Boulogne, and the men there and in the 64th Division were duly sworn. 'In this hour,' said Zangen, echoing Hitler in a special order issued on October 7 as the pressure came on, 'the fortifications along the Scheldt occupy a role which is decisive for the future of our people.'

On September 3, General Crerar's Canadian 1st Army was crossing the Somme, having been held back to ease the supply situation for the British 2nd Army. All that Montgomery's directive issued that day required of Crerar was to 'clear the coastal belt and advance to the area of Bruges and Calais'. The British 1st Corps (Lieutenant-General Crocker), took Le Havre on September 12; the Canadian 3rd Infantry Division took in succession Boulogne on the 22nd, the Gris Nez batteries on the 29th, and Calais on October 1. Advancing eastwards, the Canadian 4th Armoured Division (Major-General Foster) forced the crossings of the Ghent Canal on September 8 and entered Bruges that day. Shortly afterwards, its patrols made contact with German positions on the double line of the Leopold Canal and the Canal de la Derivation de la Lys.

On September 14, issuing his Arnhem directive, Montgomery gave Crerar the task of opening Antwerp as first priority, but still with paragraphs directing him to open Boulogne and Calais. Lieutenant-General Simonds, commanding the Canadian 2nd Corps, had already on the 12th directed the Polish 1st Armoured Division to clear the area south and west of Antwerp as far as Terneuzen on the Scheldt, and the Canadian 4th Armoured to clear what became known as the Breskens pocket, the area at the mouth of the Scheldt between Terneuzen and Zeebrugge.

On the night of the 13th, four companies of the Algonquin Regiment crossed the double canal line at Moerkerke by assault boat, meeting German fire. After initial success they were heavily counterattacked and forced to withdraw the following morning, losing 35 killed, 53 wounded, and 60 prisoners. Survivors had to swim the canal to escape. No further attempt was made at Moerkerke, but on the 15th the Canadians followed up German withdrawals further east to the Leopold Canal beyond its point of separation from the Canal de la Derivation. On the 22nd the Algonquins lost an entire platoon, trying to get a foothold across the canal at Isabella Polder at its eastern end.

Further south, the Polish 12th Dragoons, advancing from Ghent across polder country very unsuited to armour, reached Hulst on September 17, but there they were fiercely counterattacked by German infantry and tanks and forced to give up a bridgehead. Attacking the next day, the Polish 3rd Infantry Brigade bridged the branch canal at Kijkuit, and reached Terneuzen late on the 20th. By the 22nd the Poles had cleared the south bank of the Scheldt back to Antwerp, sinking or capturing boats used by the Germans to cross the river. The operations cost them 75 killed, 191 wounded, 63 missing, and they took 1,173 prisoners. Clearly the Canadian and Polish armour had run into something very different from the disorganised and scattered resistance that 30th Corps had overcome on its way to Antwerp and Brussels a fortnight earlier.

Much of the low-lying polder country—big open fields separated by raised dykes—was below sea level and either inundated or liable to be. From the coast at Zeebrugge, floods, 5 miles wide, stretched 7 miles south to the Bruges-Sluis Canal; then came a smaller flooded area on the Canadian side of the double canal line most of the way to Moerkerke. Beyond that for 5 miles the floods stopped, but the flat coverless country was crossed by the formidable obstacle of the double canal. After Eede, where the canals part company, came 11 miles of flood along the Leopold Canal, a single dry polder, the Isabella, and the Braakman, an inlet 1 mile wide and 5 miles long, leading to the Scheldt. No country, this, for armour.

Baulked by canals

Simonds realised that, but until the Canadian 3rd became available from Boulogne and Calais, he had no infantry division available for the Breskens pocket. His other, the Canadian 2nd Infantry Division (Major-General Foulkes), had moved up to Antwerp, starting to take over from the 53rd (Welsh) Division on September 18. It found Merxem, a suburb of Antwerp north of the Albert Canal, still in German hands, with civilians crossing the canal on their daily business. There were patrol clashes, and a German counterattack, which the Canadians drove back on the 20th. Next night, at second attempt, the Canadian 5th Infantry Brigade established a bridge-head across the Albert Canal some miles east of its junction with the Turnhout Canal.

On the 24th, and again on the 26th, the Canadians attempted without success to force the Turnhout Canal. Further east, however, the 49th (West Riding) Division, which had come up from Le Havre, gained a bridgehead, which it gradually extended against stiff opposition. On the 28th the Canadians crossed the canal behind it, and began to work back along the north bank to their own sector. On that day, Crocker, who had taken charge of operations in the Antwerp area, ordered the Polish 1st Armoured Division to break out north-east for the next canal line 20 miles on, the Wilhelmina Canal. Against heavy resistance, the Poles took Merxplas on the 30th, but thereafter progress was slower.

So here, too, German resistance had hardened. It was becoming clear that a long and difficult battle lay ahead of the Canadian, British, and Polish divisions of the Canadian 1st Army, ordered to clear the approaches to Antwerp.

Montgomery issued another directive to his two armies on September 27. He still held to the double objective—Antwerp and the Ruhr. Antwerp got first mention for the Canadian 1st Army, but, as well as to open the Scheldt, it was to advance north-eastwards for 's Hertogenbosch and Tilburg to protect the flank of the British 2nd Army's thrust for the Ruhr.

Crerar was temporarily invalided to England on the 27th; Simonds moved up to command the army, and Foulkes to command Canadian 2nd Corps. Simonds gave Crocker at British 1st Corps the task of supporting British 2nd Army, and added to it that of developing operations towards Breda and Roosendaal, covering the flank and rear of the Canadian advance towards the Beveland isthmus. Foulkes got the task of clearing the Scheldt, taking over the Canadian 2nd Infantry Division (now Brigadier Keefler) for the isthmus and South Beveland, and the 3rd (Major-General Spry) for the Breskens pocket, as it came up from Boulogne and Calais, freeing Canadian 4th Armoured for the 1st Corps. On October 3, the Polish armour, leading 1st Corps' advance, took Barle-Nassau, but was later checked by vigorous counterattacks near Alpen.

Canadian 2nd Infantry Division began its new advance on October 2. Making at first good progress, it took Lochtenberg that day, Camp de Brasschaet on the 3rd, Putte on the Dutch-Belgian border on the 5th, and on the 6th was 3 miles from Woensdrecht. Woensdrecht, almost surrounded by flooded polder, and Hoogerheide, half a mile to its east on rising heathland, were the turning point around the floods for the isthmus. A village road through Woensdrecht connects with the station of that name on the isthmus line, while the main road branches off at the hamlet of Korteven,

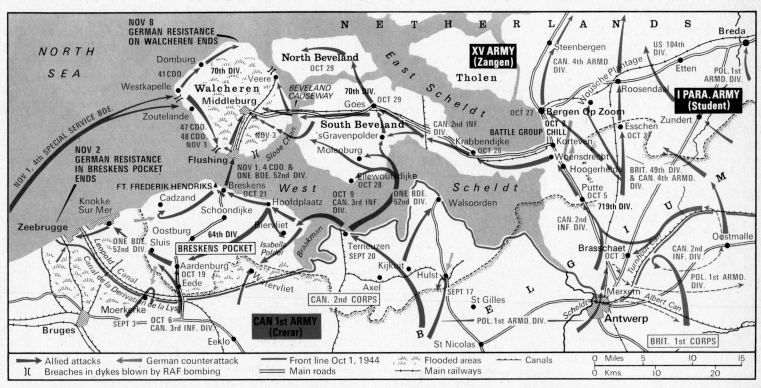

| Allied attacks | German counterattack | Front line Oct 1, 1944 | Flooded areas | Canals |
| Breaches in dykes blown by RAF bombing | | Main roads | Main railways | |

Although the Allies had captured Antwerp on September 4, they could not use the great port until the Germans had been cleared from both sides of the Scheldt estuary. But the Channel ports were holding out in the rear of 21st Army Group, tying down much-needed infantry—and Montgomery insisted that the Arnhem venture take priority over the clearing of the Scheldt. The result was a costly series of setbacks for the Allied forces attacking along the Scheldt estuary. It took the combined arguments of Admiral Ramsay and Sir Alan Brooke to persuade Montgomery that the job must be done promptly. Not until October 9 was Canadian 1st Army ordered to clear the approaches—and fighting lasted a month

British 'Wasp'
The Wasp, a flame-throwing Bren-gun carrier, assisted the infantry attacks across the canals of the Scheldt region. *Crew:* two. *Range:* 117 miles. *Speed:* 20 mph. *Range of flamethrower:* 50/60 yards

German Sd Kfz-251
Another German attempt to marry firepower and mobility, this machine mounted the hitting-power of a Nebelwerfer rocket-mortar on a half-track hull. *Crew:* three or four. *Range:* 187 miles. *Speed:* 31 mph. *Armament:* six Wurfrahmen rockets, two 7·92-mm machine-guns

US 'Weasel'
The M-29C light carrier proved of great use during the campaign in the flat, soft polder country. It was an amphibian machine, with a remarkably light ground pressure —2 lbs per square foot, which was lighter than the pressure of a man's foot

John Batchelor

a mile north of Hoogerheide. On the 7th the Calgary Highlanders, after a stiff fight, got into Hoogerheide, but the Black Watch of Canada, attacking Korteven on the 8th, was forced back to its start line in Hoogerheide. Air reconnaissance reported a large German force with armour and guns in the woods south of Bergen-op-Zoom, and prisoners were identified as paratroops—Battle Group Chill coming south to hold the isthmus. That night and through the next day, the Canadians in Hoogerheide and in the heathland to its east had to beat off German attacks.

Check to the Canadians
On the 9th a detachment from the Canadian 4th Armoured Division came up to protect the Canadian 2nd Infantry Division's long, exposed right flank, and in a new attack on the 11th the Royal Regiment of Canada and the Canadian Black Watch, crossing flooded polder short of Woensdrecht, reached the isthmus railway, all but cutting off the Germans in the islands. Further bloody fighting followed. On the 13th the Black Watch got into Woensdrecht, but later was ordered to withdraw, having lost 145 officers and men, 56 of them killed. The Germans held on.

On the 16th the Royal Hamilton Light Infantry fought its way into Woensdrecht with intensive artillery support, and the next day the Essex Rifles beat off renewed enemy counterattacks, losing 161, 21 of them killed, in the two days. 'It is close hard fighting,' the Essex commanding officer reported, 'the enemy is not giving up here the way he did in the past.' That day Rundstedt wrote in his diary: 'In the area of the Scheldt estuary a permanent recapture of the land connection with Walcheren can no longer be expected. C-in-C West, therefore, consents to the flooding of the area.' But for the moment Canadian 2nd Infantry Division was checked.

Calais fell on October 1, freeing the Canadian 3rd Infantry Division for the Breskens pocket. At 0530 hours on the 6th, the Canadian 7th Infantry Brigade, having moved up 90 miles from Calais, attacked across the Leopold Canal near Eede. Under cover of flame thrown by 27 'Wasps' (flamethrowing Bren-gun carriers), the Canadian Scottish and the Regina Rifles crossed in assault boats and secured two small bridgeheads. After the initial surprise and the shock of the flame, the Germans reacted violently, pouring in mortar and machine-gun fire and counterattacking with heavy losses to both sides, despite massive Canadian artillery and air support. That night the third battalion, the Royal Winnipeg Rifles, crossed by kapok assault bridge. On October 9, after severe fighting, the two bridgeheads were joined up and, on the night of the 13th, Royal Canadian Engineers completed a heavy bridge, enabling tanks to cross the following morning. By then the Canadian brigade had lost 533 officers and men, 111 of them killed.

Two days after the 7th Brigade's assault on the left, the Canadian 9th Infantry Brigade attacked across the mouth of the Braakman. The British 79th Armoured Division had provided specialised armour for the Normandy landings. Recently re-equipped, its two Royal Engineer assault regiments now provided 100 Buffaloes (American tracked amphibians), and 40 Terrapins (British wheeled amphibians) for the attack. After a 24-hour delay caused by difficulty in reaching the Scheldt past a damaged lock, the Buffaloes, carrying the North Nova Scotia Highlanders and the Highland Light Infantry of Canada, set off from Terneuzen by bright moonlight at 0200 hours on October 9 for 'beaches' on dykes 5 miles away across the Braakman.

Surprise was complete. German shelling did not start until after dawn, and by then the beach-head was firm. At 0930 hours the reserve battalion, the Stormont, Dundas, and Glengary Highlanders, came ashore under smoke cover. Eberding scraped up reserves to meet the threat, but the Canadians took Hoofdplaatz, 2 miles along the Scheldt, on October 10 and, swinging around towards Isabella Polder, took Biervliet on the 11th.

A renewed attempt on the Isabella by the Algonquins failed on the 10th, and now Spry sent his third brigade, the 8th Infantry, to land in the beach-head. On the 14th patrols crossing the floods at Watervliet linked up with the Isabella, and on the 16th the Germans were found to have gone from Eede. On the night of the 18th, the 157th Infantry Brigade from the 52nd (Lowland) Division took over from the Canadians there and, advancing on the 19th, met the 7th Canadian Reconnaissance Regiment at Aardenburg.

On October 1 Admiral Sir Bertrand Ramsay, Eisenhower's naval commander, wishing to concentrate landing-craft in readiness for an attack on Walcheren, was told by 21st Army Group Headquarters that other operations had priority. Four days later at Versailles, Ramsay attended Eisenhower's conference of army group, naval, and air commanders. 'Monty made the startling announcement that we could take the Ruhr without Antwerp,' wrote Ramsay in his diary. 'This afforded me the cue I needed to lambast him for not having made the capture of Antwerp the immediate objective at

highest priority, and I let fly with all my guns at the faulty strategy we had allowed . . . had we now got Antwerp and not the (Arnhem) corridor, we should be in a far better position for launching the knockout blow.' Sir Alan Brooke, back from the Second Quebec Conference, was present and told Ramsay afterwards that he agreed with him. Ramsay later believed that Brooke now persuaded Montgomery to give real urgency to opening the Scheldt. A few days later a severe gale damaged the Mulberry harbour and interrupted unloading, rubbing in Ramsay's argument.

Now at last the job got the priority it needed. On October 9 Montgomery, in a new directive, instructed the Canadian 1st Army to concentrate all available resources on opening Antwerp, and gave that operation 'complete priority over all other offensive operations in 21st Army Group without any qualification whatsoever'. The US 104th Infantry Division, moving up from Cherbourg, and the 52nd (Lowland) Division (Major-General Hakewell-Smith), fresh from the United Kingdom having missed Arnhem, were placed under the Canadians, and the British 2nd Army ordered to take over the north-eastward advance on 's Hertogenbosch and Tilburg, freeing the Canadians to concentrate on opening Antwerp. As a postscript to the controversy, Montgomery took Ramsay to task for planning the amphibious operation direct with the Canadians.

With this new priority, Simonds's plan could take final shape. His armour, the Canadian 4th and the Polish 1st Armoured Divisions, was concentrated east of Antwerp where it could operate effectively under Crocker together with the 49th (West Riding) and the US 104th Infantry Divisions, to attack north-westward for Roosendaal, Breda, and the Maas, hacking out the underpinning of the German defence on the Scheldt. To deal directly with this latter, Foulkes would have the Canadian 2nd and 3rd Infantry Divisions, already engaged respectively at the isthmus and in the Breskens pocket; the 4th Special Service Brigade—Commandos—for amphibious assault on Walcheren; and in reserve the 52nd (Lowland) Division. The attacks would be simultaneous except that Walcheren would have to wait until supporting artillery could be sited near Breskens to fire across the Scheldt.

On October 17, the Canadian 4th Armoured Division completed its concentration north-east of Antwerp and came under command of 1st Corps. Then on the 20th, Foster launched his attack towards Esschen and Bergen-op-Zoom. Esschen fell on the 22nd. Resistance stiffened as the XV Army and the I Parachute Army struggled to keep touch with the isthmus, but the Canadian armour took Wousche Plantage on the 26th, and entered Bergen-op-Zoom the next day. Further east the 49th Division was by then approaching Roosendaal; the 104th, Zundert; and the Polish 1st Armoured, on Crocker's extreme right, Breda, which it entered next day. On the 2nd Army front, 12th Corps entered 's Hertogenbosch on the 24th and Tilburg on the 28th. In front of the two corps, the Germans pulled out across the Maas to avoid capture.

Around Woensdrecht, the Canadian 2nd Infantry Division met fierce resistance on October 23 as the Canadian 5th and 6th Infantry Brigades closed in on Korteven and the isthmus. Next day, however, the Germans on the mainland, threatened by the Canadian armour, began to withdraw northwards, and the 2nd Division started its advance westwards along the isthmus. Two flooded areas blocked the isthmus; and beyond them, the South Beveland Canal, a wide, deep ship canal, blocked the eastern tip of South Beveland.

A difficult assault crossing
Early on the 24th, the Royal Regiment of Canada, attacking with massed artillery support, crossed the first floods, but, in the restricted area available, armour from the 4th Division, which it was hoped would then be able to rush the canal crossing with the Essex Scottish, was stopped by anti-tank guns. Once more infantry would have to fight its way across flooded polder land. Attacking that night and again on the 25th, the Canadian 4th Infantry Brigade reached Krabbendijke on the 26th very tired. There the 6th Brigade passed through, prepared for a difficult assault crossing.

But a better way was available. In the early hours of October 27, the 4/5th Royal Scots and the 6th Cameronians, both of the 156th Infantry Brigade, 52nd (Lowland) Division, embarked in Buffaloes at Terneuzen—137 of them manned by the 5th Assault Regiment Royal Engineers and the 11th Royal Tanks, both from the 79th Armoured Division. Guided by a landing-craft and by Bofors firing tracer, they made the 9-mile trip successfully, and at 0450 hours landed at two 'beaches' on the dykes of the South Beveland coast. On the right, the Fusiliers suffered some casualties from shellfire, but the Cameronians, a short distance to their left, landed almost completely unopposed.

Meeting only desultory resistance, the two battalions linked up at 0635 hours. Eleven DD Shermans of the Staffordshire Yeomanry, which reached the beach after swimming from Terneuzen, had great difficulty in climbing out, and in the end only four were able to get into action. Brigade reserve, the 7th Cameronians, landed behind the 6th Cameronians at 1100 hours. There was a counter-attack during the day, but by then the beach-head was firmly held. The Buffaloes continued running during the 27th and 28th, supplying and reinforcing the 156th Brigade, and on the 28th brought across the 157th. In all the Buffaloes carried 700 loads across the Scheldt, bringing light vehicles as well as men and stores but, in view of the difficult beach exits, not mountain artillery as at first intended.

Mopping-up on Beveland

On the 28th the 7th Cameronians took Ellewoutsdijke, 4 miles from the beaches, and later that night the 5th Highland Light Infantry, Molenburg. The Canadian 6th Infantry Brigade crossed the ship canal on the night of the 27th and later met the 156th Brigade at 's Gravenpolder. On the 29th the 5th Brigade took Goes, and Canadians and Lowlanders reached the causeway leading from South Beveland to Walcheren. On the same day detachments of the Canadian and Lowland divisional reconnaissance regiments cleared North Beveland.

The causeway, 1,200 yards long, dead straight and coverless, flanked by marshes impenetrable either to land vehicles or boats, had been cratered in its middle; German infantry positions on the far side covered it, and German artillery was registered on it. The Canadian Black Watch made the attempt that afternoon, to be driven back when within 25 yards of the far end. That night the Calgary Highlanders made another attempt without success. Then, on the morning of November 1, the Calgaries with heavy artillery support got a company across, only to be driven back 300 yards.

Meanwhile in the Breskens pocket, the Braakman attack had loosened the German hold on the Leopold Canal, and Eberding withdrew to an inner line from Breskens through Schoondijke to Sluis. Renewing their attack, the Canadians took Breskens on October 21; they were repulsed at Fort Frederik Hendriks on the 22nd, but on the 25th the fort surrendered. On the 27th, the Canadian Scottish were strongly counterattacked when trying to by-pass Cadzand, but Knokke-sur-Mer fell on November 1, and the same day Eberding was captured. The next day the Canadians entered Zeebrugge. German resistance ended. The Breskens pocket had cost the Canadian 3rd Infantry Division 2,077 casualties, 314 of them killed and 231 missing, almost all of whom were dead. They had captured 12,707 prisoners.

Walcheren, dangling like a hard stone at the end of the necklace of the German Scheldt defences, had exercised the minds of Crerar, Simonds, and Ramsay since mid-Sptember. On the 21st of that month, Simonds, challenging the opinion of planners that an amphibious attack was ruled out, had demanded that preparations for one should be put in hand, and had suggested that the island should be flooded by bombing its sea dykes.

Approximately rectangular in shape, 12 miles by 9 in dimension, Walcheren lies mostly below sea level, but along three of its sides there is a rim of dunes up to 100 feet high connecting with an area above sea level in the eastern corner, where the causeway from South Beveland joins the island. On the dunes of the north-west and south-west coasts, the Germans had mounted powerful batteries in concrete, covering respectively the sea approaches and the mouth of the Scheldt. In all there were eight batteries capable of firing to seaward or on the Scheldt, mounting some 26 guns of 75-mm calibre or over. In addition the coast was defended against infantry attack by barbed wire, mines, and machine-guns, many of the latter in concrete emplacements.

Simonds's proposals were discussed at a conference on September 23. By then Eisenhower, on the advice of his air and airborne army commanders, had decided that airborne assault on Walcheren was unlikely to succeed, but agreed that full bomber support should be available for the attack on it. About this time the 4th Special Service Brigade (Brigadier Leicester) was earmarked for the assault, and Captain Pugsley RN, who had commanded Force J in the Normandy assault, was sent for by Ramsay to take charge of the naval side and assemble landing and support craft for it.

In the early afternoon of October 3, 247 Lancasters and Mosquitos of RAF Bomber Command attacked the dyke at Westkapelle. The attack was completely successful: 120 yards of dyke were demolished; the sea rushed in to flood the polder land and the village, and continued to rise for 48 hours. An attack on the dyke either side of Flushing on October 7 was less successful, but on the 11th the dykes were breached there and near Veere on the north-east coast. Thereafter bombing turned to the batteries. In all, Bomber Command dropped 8-9,000 tons on Walcheren; in the last

▷ Through the ruins of Breskens, British troops move down to the embarkation-beach for the assault on Walcheren island

Centre: British and Canadian troops wait to embark in Buffaloes before crossing from Beveland to Walcheren

▽ RAF bombs burst on the Walcheren dyke to flood the island. In all, Bomber Command dropped more than 8,000 tons of bombs on Walcheren

Associated Press

Imperial War Museum

Imperial War Museum

△ Ashore on Walcheren: troops advance along the Flushing waterfront while Allied guns shell the German defences

▷ Scene on a be head in Walche landing-craft, dozer, and Buffa

◁ Buffalo amphibians carry Commandos across the Scheldt to Walcheren. Despite a difficult landing, these veterans of D-Day secured their beach-head and began to work through the town

▽ Troops abandon a landing-craft after a direct hit from one of the German batteries. Out of Eastern Flank Support Group's 28 craft, nine were sunk and 11 put out of action

◁ Final stage, November 8, 1944: British infantry wade ashore to complete the occupation of Walcheren. The action had cost the 4th Special Service Brigade some 500 casualties

days of October 2nd Tactical Air Force flew 650 sorties against it. The batteries, however, remained almost undamaged.

The decision to break the dykes had not been taken lightly. Inevitably it must cost the lives of Dutch civilians by bombs and drowning. Less important but still very serious was the loss of property and the probable after-effects to the rich polder land, won from the sea by generations of Zeelanders, now contaminated by salt water. For the attackers the Dutch government had reluctantly agreed to the flooding, and later the stout-hearted Zeelanders were to say that water was at least preferable to Germans. The bombing and floods cost them lives, but it immobilised the German defence and isolated the deadly batteries along the dunes.

Like the Canadians and the landing and support craft crews, the Commandos had taken part in the Normandy landings. On the afternoon of October 31, the brigade, except for 4 Commando, embarked for the new assault at Ostend, sailing early next morning for Westkapelle. The 4 Commando, the single army Commando in the brigade, its strength increased by three troops of Fighting French, embarked in assault landing-craft at Breskens early on November 1. Crossing the Scheldt, its leading troops landed at the Orange Mole on the Flushing seafront at 0620 hours in darkness as an intensive artillery bombardment from guns in the Breskens area lifted. Despite a difficult beaching, obstacles, barbed wire, and fire from German pillboxes, the Commando secured a beach-head and began to work through the town.

In a second landing at Flushing at 0800 hours, the landing-craft brought the 4th Kings Own Scottish Borderers and the 452nd Mountain Battery, followed later by the rest of the 155th Infantry Brigade from the 52nd Division. By evening the Commandos and the Borderers, fighting their way through the streets, had captured the seafront and central area of the town.

Although a very large concentration of artillery had been assembled in the Breskens area to support the attack as it came within range, only heavy and super-heavy artillery, unsuitable for the close support of infantry, had the range to fire on the Westkapelle gap from the Breskens pocket. The *Warspite* and the monitors *Erebus* and *Roberts* would add the fire of their 15-inch guns, but for close support the assault must rely on light support craft accompanying the landing-craft on either flank. The morning of November 1 dawned rough and overcast, but rather than risk prolonged postponement of the attack, Pugsley and Leicester decided it should go in. They did not know it then, but Bomber Command aircraft, intended for a final heavy raid on the batteries as the assault came in, were grounded by fog in England. Typhoons and Spitfires of 2nd Tactical Air Force, however, gave the landings and the battle on shore close and effective support.

At first the German batteries were silent. Then they opened fire with deadly effect, not on the landing-craft, but on the support craft which engaged them hotly. Commander Sellar's Eastern Flank Support Group on the right, closing the range to protect the landing-craft, suffered severely. Out of its 28 craft, nine were sunk, and 11 put out of action with severe damage; 20 officers and 172 men were killed or drowned, 15 and 111 severely wounded.

The 41 and 48 (Royal Marine) Commandos landed within minutes of each other left and right respectively of the now vast gap in the dyke, through which a tidal current streamed. Making their best speed on foot outwards along the narrow strips of dunes, and overrunning German defences as they met them, 41 reached the outskirts of Domburg that evening, and 48 took a battery 2 miles from the gap. Twelve Shermans, of the 1st Lothian and Border Horse, had great difficulty in landing north of the gap, and only four were able to support 41 Commando; on the other side no attempt was

Temporary home for German POWs — in the lion cage of the Antwerp zoo

made to land armour, but 48 Commando came within range of medium and field artillery support as it advanced. Buffaloes proved invaluable in crossing the gap and bringing up ammunition, but the whole area was soon under heavy shellfire, and on the 2nd, when a gale blew up, the beach was closed.

That day 47 Commando went through 48 beyond Zouteland, reaching the gap west of Flushing on the evening of the 3rd and making contact with 4 Commando. On the 4th a company of the 7/9th Royal Scots from the 155th Brigade reached Middleburg in Buffaloes swimming through the floods. Taken by surprise, Lieutenant-General Daser surrendered, and 2,000 of his garrison there followed his example.

Meanwhile at the causeway Le Régiment de Maisonneuve and the 1st Glasgow Highlanders established a bridgehead early on the 2nd but were driven back that night. The night before, Royal Engineers had discovered a just possible way across Slooe Channel, 1½ miles south of the causeway. After they had established a track through mines and mud the 6th Cameronians got across early on the 3rd. They were counterattacked, but held on, and the next night they were joined by the 5th HLI. At dawn on the 5th the Lowlanders advanced westwards to meet the Royal Scots from Middleburg, and the 7th Cameronians reached Veere. By then the Commandos had reached the northern corner of the island, where the last Germans surrendered to them on the 8th. The 4th Special Service Brigade had lost 103 killed, 325 wounded, and 68 missing, almost certainly dead.

Reviewing the mistakes
Minesweeping began on November 4. Ten flotillas were used, some going through to Antwerp to start work at that end, but it was not until November 26, when 267 mines had been swept, that the first coasters could be sent through. Two days later the first heavy cargo ships reached Antwerp, the leading one, appropriately, the Canadian-built *Fort Cataraqui*. On December 1 some 10,000 tons were unloaded at Antwerp, and by the end of the second week of that month, 19,000 tons a day.

From October 1 to November 8, the Canadian 1st Army took 41,043 prisoners, and lost 703 officers and 12,170 other ranks killed, wounded, and missing. Of these, half—355 officers and 6,012 other ranks—were Canadians. To these losses must be added those at sea and in the air. On January 2, 1945, Admiral Ramsay, naval commander for the Dunkirk evacuation and for the Normandy invasion, chief advocate for opening the Scheldt, was killed in an air accident.

Reviewing the Antwerp campaign, Montgomery wrote:
. . . I must admit a bad mistake on my part—I underestimated the difficulties of opening up the approaches to Antwerp so that we could get free use of the port. I reckoned that the Canadian Army could do this while we were going for the Ruhr. I was wrong.

Eisenhower, too, while clearly understanding the need for Antwerp, was tempted by the glittering prize of the Ruhr and, with whatever doubts, gave Montgomery his head. The failure to concentrate on a single objective was reflected at the time of the Arnhem battle, in the two armoured divisions misemployed in the Scheldt polders, and in numerous infantry divisions, mostly American, grounded for lack of transport all the way back to Cherbourg. So Arnhem was not taken, and the Scheldt opening was delayed. With supply restricted, concentration against Arnhem was not possible. The conclusion, seen early by Ramsay and by many others later, seems inevitable: Antwerp should have been opened before the Arnhem attempt was made.

[*Major-General Moulton's biography is in Vol 1, p. 74.*]

Admiral Sir Bertram Ramsay, born in 1883, went to sea at the age of 16 as a midshipman. He served two years on the epoch-making battleship *Dreadnought,* qualified as a signals officer, and later attended the newly-established Naval War College.

In the First World War he served in the Grand Fleet and the Dover Patrol; between the wars he lectured for a time at the Imperial Defence College; in 1935, promoted to Rear-Admiral, he became Chief-of-Staff to the C-in-C Home Fleet, Admiral Sir Roger Backhouse. After clashes over their respective areas of responsibility, Ramsay felt obliged to resign, and in 1938 he was put on the retired list.

In 1939 he was recalled to take over the Dover command, and on the collapse of France in 1940 he was charged with 'Dynamo', the evacuation of the BEF from Dunkirk, a brilliantly improvised rescue operation. In 1942 he left the Dover command to study the problems of invading France. When this was postponed, he helped with the planning of the 'Torch' landings in North Africa and in the invasion of Sicily, once again displaying his outstanding gifts as an organiser. As commander of the Allied Naval Expeditionary Force for 'Overlord', he played a leading part in the planning of the D-Day landings, the most momentous amphibious operation in history. His last operation was the attack on Walcheren to open the great port of Antwerp for the Allies; on January 2, 1945, he was killed in an air crash on the way to attend a conference in Brussels

Keystone

BATTLE OF THE BULGE: THE ONSLAUGHT

**Ardennes, Belgium
December 16/19, 1944**

Peter Elstob

By early December 1944, Hitler had achieved a near-impossible: out of the armies which had fought, lost, and disintegrated in Normandy, France, Belgium, and the approaches to the German frontier, he had built up a new army group on the Western Front. What was more, this new force was intended not merely to hold the front, but to hurl itself on the weakest American sector, sweep westward to the Meuse as in 1940, and reach the Channel in one of the most daring armoured counteroffensives in history. The onslaught was the heaviest Panzer attack ever seen on the Western Front, and its success depended on the strictest adherence to a taut timetable of vital objectives. This is the story of how the disorganised and often panic-stricken American defenders met the full fury of what soon became known as the 'Battle of the Bulge'.

Right: German soldiers advance on the first day of the Ardennes offensive

As early as August 19, 1944, just after the successful Allied landings on the Mediterranean coast of France and on the actual day that almost the last of the German armour in the West was destroyed in the Falaise pocket, Hitler issued the following order: 'Prepare to take the offensive in November . . . some 25 divisions must be moved to the Western Front in the next one to two months.'

But how? Where, after the gigantic losses of men and material, could Germany find 25 divisions? The Führer's generals told him it would be a miracle if the Wehrmacht could replace half its losses; to create a whole new army group was impossible. Hitler replied that he would once again show them how to achieve the impossible.

For the first time Germany was put on a total war footing. Dr Goebbels was given dictatorial powers to increase war production and direct men into the army. The call-up age was lowered to 16, and no one escaped the scraping of the manpower barrel: non-essential workers, small shopkeepers, civil servants, university students, officer candidates in training, men formerly listed as unfit, prisoners from the jails—all were sucked into the great maw. Despite the heavy bombing, German war production actually increased to all-time records. After six to eight weeks' concentrated training, these new soldiers, *Volksgrenadiers* (People's Infantry), were equipped and ready to go into the line; and by the beginning of November Hitler had, to the amazement of his generals, replaced his lost mobile reserve and sent 18 new divisions to the West.

The problem of where to mount his great offensive occupied a lot of Hitler's thinking, but one area had long attracted him—the heavily wooded hills where Luxembourg, Belgium, and Germany meet, known in Germany as the Eifel and in Belgium and Luxembourg as the Ardennes. It was an historic German invasion route, the scene of his great success in 1940. And—miraculously—it was the weakest-held section of the entire 450 miles of the Western Front.

That fact was decisive: once again it would be the Ardennes.

This time Hitler planned everything himself and although, for the sake of morale, the old but still much respected Field-Marshal Gerd von Rundstedt was persuaded to come out of retirement and assume nominal command, the Führer actually directed the battle from a new headquarters in the West.

Three armies—two armoured and one infantry—were joined to make Army Group B, commanded by Field-Marshal Model, an aggressive attacker and master of improvisation, who had prevented total defeat on the Eastern Front three times. The VI SS Panzer Army, which would spearhead the attack, was given to one of Hitler's oldest comrades, Josef 'Sepp' Dietrich, ex-sergeant-major in the regular German army, the Führer's personal bodyguard in the early street-brawling days of the Nazi Party, and former commander of the famous I SS Panzer Division, 'Leibstandarte Adolf Hitler' (Hitler's Bodyguard).

Moving alongside VI SS Panzer Army and adding weight to the left hook would be V Panzer Army commanded by another of Hitler's 'fighting generals' from the Eastern Front, Hasso von Manteuffel. The important task of throwing up a wall to cover the southern flank of the attack was given to the German VII Army commanded by Erich Brandenberger, a general of the old school, unimaginative but dogged.

Hitler also decided to use the shattered German Parachute Corps once more to seize important crossroads behind the American lines and hold them open for his beloved SS Panzer divisions, and Colonel von der Heydte, a veteran of Crete, was ordered to get a force together. Also the Führer had one of his famous unorthodox ideas and sent for Otto Skorzeny, the man who had 'rescued' Mussolini. Skorzeny was ordered to train special units of German commandos dressed in Allied uniforms who would travel in captured vehicles ahead of the main force to seize bridges over the Meuse, the first big obstacle, and, as well, cause chaos behind the American lines by giving false orders, upsetting communications, and spreading rumours of great German successes.

An 85-mile sector of the front from Monschau in the north to Echternach in the south was chosen for the breakthrough. After a tremendous opening barrage, infantry in overwhelming strength would breach the American line in a dozen places through which the Panzers would pour in a classic Blitzkrieg, racing for the Meuse crossings before the Allies could regain their balance. Once across the Meuse the second phase of the offensive, a double-pronged drive northwest to Antwerp, would begin. Army Group B's attack would be supported by one from General Student's XV Army in Holland, and when Antwerp and the Scheldt estuary had been taken the Allied forces in Europe would be cut in two and their four armies in the north—US 9th, US 1st, British 2nd, and Canadian 1st—could be destroyed. Then, Hitler thought, the Western Allies would be ready to make a separate peace, and Germany could switch all her forces to the East.

The German commanders in the field protested that the plan was far too ambitious. Old Field-Marshal von Rundstedt was scathing. 'Antwerp? If we reach the Meuse we should go down on our knees and thank God!'

But Hitler refused even to consider any of their alternative plans, insisting on his own and reminding them that their sole duty was to obey his orders. The field commanders' opposition and the tremendous logistic problems involved made the original date impossible and Hitler was forced to agree to several postponements. In the end he lost his patience, saying that generals are never ready to attack, and set a last unalterable hour, 0530 hours on Saturday December 16, 1944.

The final German strength was less than had been promised but more than the generals had expected, and their mood changed from deep pessimism to mild optimism. Without alerting Allied Intelligence, they had been able to move 20 divisions, including seven armoured, into the attack front which the Americans were holding with only six divisions, of which one was armoured.

The overall superiority in manpower was no more than five to two, which is about the minimum required for a successful attack. But the attacker chooses the ground as well as the time, and the main weight of the offensive—eight *Volksgrenadier* divisions and five Panzer divisions—was concentrated on 45 miles of the Ardennes held by two American infantry divisions, a squadron of reconnaissance cavalry, with the only reserve a single combat command of an untried armoured division.

In the north, this blitz front took in the extreme right wing of 1st Army's 5th Corps, held thinly by the US 99th Infantry Division, six weeks in the line and yet to experience battle; and an inexplicably unguarded 2-mile gap between 5th Corps and General Middleton's 8th Corps front, the northernmost two-thirds of which was included in the mammoth breakthrough.

Next to the inter-corps gap, thinly stretched across a classic easy entry from Germany into Belgium known as the Losheim Gap (see map), were some 900 men of the 18th Cavalry Squadron who had not yet tied in with a newly-arrived division on their right. This was the 106th Infantry who, after a gruelling journey across France and Belgium, had taken over positions three days before on the forward or eastern slope of a high ridge known as the Schnee Eifel. Completely inexperienced and suffering from frostbite and 'trench foot' they were to prove easy meat for the attacking Germans.

The southern half of the blitz front, which was to be hit by V Panzer Army with three *Volksgrenadier* divisions, one parachute infantry division, and two Panzer divisions, was held by the 28th Infantry Division, holding US 8th Corps' centre. This veteran division had been badly mauled in the recent heavy fighting around Aachen, where it had lost 6,184 men, and had been sent to the quietest part of the Ardennes for rest and refitting.

Were five objectives possible?

The rest of Army Group B was to be committed on either side of the main thrust to destroy the American line and to supply flank protection for the advance. On 8th Corps' right General Patton's US 3rd Army was in the last stages of preparation for an all-out offensive through the Saar; on their left 5th Corps had begun, three days before the German attack, an attack north towards the Roer dams. Part of this attack entailed an unusual manoeuvre: the 2nd Infantry Division, greatly experienced and recently rested, had pushed an attack column through the middle of 99th Infantry Division and captured an important crossroads 4 miles inside Germany. The unexpected presence of this division and its supporting artillery was to help to upset VI SS Panzer Army's plans.

Army Group B would have to achieve five initial objectives, and achieve them quickly if there were to be any chance at all of reaching Antwerp. The first two objectives were the setting up of 'hard shoulders' at both ends of the assault front to secure the flanks and make sure that the attack could not be pinched out. Thirdly, Sepp Dietrich's crack SS Panzer divisions must quickly overrun the lightly held American line and race for the Meuse, securing the bridges within 24 or at the most 48 hours. Fourth, General von Manteuffel's right-hand armoured punch must move alongside the SS Panzer divisions and, even though their route was longer, keep up with them, and also capture the important road and rail centre of St Vith along the way. Fifth, Manteuffel's left-wing attack must first capture Bastogne, the equally vital communications centre in the south, and go on to seize bridges over a third section of the Meuse.

The long night of December 15, 1944, was one of the darkest and coldest of that dark, cold winter. By midnight everything was ready on the German side—some 200,000 men with more tanks, guns, and ammunition than for many months past, waited to start

The 'blitz front' of the Ardennes

The German plan *Wacht am Rhein* ('Watch on the Rhine') gambled on a surprise breakthrough against US 8th Corps, strung out weakly along the Ardennes front. Some 80,000 unprepared Americans were to be struck by 200,000 keyed-up Germans

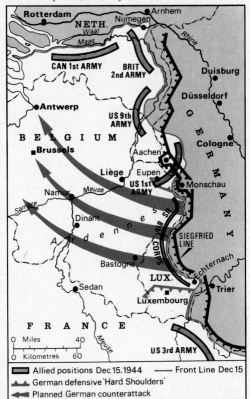

Allied positions Dec 15,1944 — Front Line Dec 15
German defensive 'Hard Shoulders'
Planned German counterattack

the biggest German offensive on the Western Front since 1940. Far to the rear Colonel von der Heydte's 1,250 paratroops, many about to jump for the first time, waited for trucks to carry them to the airfields. Skorzeny's men, in Allied uniforms and driving Allied vehicles, were lined up behind the leading tanks of the I SS Panzer Division, joking among themselves about it being too late to learn any more English and privately wondering if they would be shot if captured. The assault troops, many going into battle for the first time, tried to get some rest before the opening barrage. They had been thrilled by a multitude of stirring 'Orders of the Day'—from their own commanders, from the famous Field-Marshals von Rundstedt and Model and from the Führer himself. Many of them believed that they were about to take part in a great battle which would somehow miraculously win the war for Germany after all.

In the path of this mighty force were about 80,000 Americans, most of whom were sleeping peacefully, completely unaware of the storm that was about to break over them—for German security had been superb, Allied Intelligence sadly deficient. Some of these soldiers had not yet heard a shot fired in earnest; some had heard too many, and had been sent here so that their shattered nerves could recover. Most were thinking about their chance for leave at the many rest centres in the Ardennes or the promised Christmas festivities, a Christmas that many would never see.

Promptly at 0530 hours, the concentrated German artillery opened fire and almost all American positions were pounded heavily for periods from 20 minutes to an hour and a half. The startled Americans behind the front line tumbled out of their sleeping bags into shelters. At the forward outposts, where

the wire communications were quickly knocked out, the soldiers peered into the pre-dawn murkiness and asked each other what the hell had happened to this quietest of all fronts.

When the barrage stopped, hundreds of searchlights flicked on, reflecting off the low cloud to create 'artificial moonlight'. Moments later, before the dazed Americans could recover, German shock troops surged forward to make gaps for their tanks or to seize their own first-day objectives.

Tactically the most important of these was the securing of the flanks by setting up 'hard shoulders' at either end of the attack front. While not as dramatic as the Panzer thrusts these defence lines were absolutely vital, for without them the strong Allied forces north and south of the Ardennes could pinch out the offensive.

The northern 'hard shoulder' was to run from the town of Monschau along a ridge road to Eupen (see map). Sepp Dietrich decided first to attack on either side of Monschau, and after his other three infantry divisions had breached the American front lines and launched the SS Panzer divisions on their dash westwards, they would wheel right and continue the defence wall as far as Liège (see map on p. 2238).

A first, fatal setback

The attack north of Monschau was halted at a roadblock before dawn by the 102nd Cavalry Squadron who, in the light of star shells, inflicted 20% casualties on the *Volksgrenadiers,* and stopped the assault dead. South of Monschau the *Volksgrenadiers* hit a battalion of the 99th Infantry Division in good defensive positions on high ground. As soon as the barrage stopped, German assault troops, closely packed, advanced steadily on to the American dug in positions. The result was not battle, but slaughter, yet the young Germans kept coming—in at least three verified instances their bodies fell into the American foxhole line. They could not possibly succeed for they were too few (the unexpected US 5th Corps attack towards the Roer dams, which had started three days before, tied down most of the German troops assigned to the attack around Monschau) and without armoured support. The assault was broken off and an attempt later in the day to get it rolling again was repelled.

At the end of the first day the plan to set up the 'hard shoulder' in the north had failed completely—and this was a failure that was to become increasingly serious for the Germans.

Some 85 miles to the south, General Brandenberger's tactics called for one of his four *Volksgrenadier* divisions to cross the Sauer river before dawn east of Echternach (the Sauer runs west to east here) and another to cross west of the town. After joining up south of Echternach they would then seize high ground behind the American artillery, so forcing the guns to pull back. Once they had done so, pontoon bridges could be put in over the Sauer and the heavy guns and equipment needed to set up the southern 'hard shoulder' could be brought across. At the same time, a third *Volksgrenadier* division would cross the river further up and, after overrunning an unexperienced American armoured infantry battalion, wheel left to continue the southern 'hard shoulder'.

The Echternach sector of the American front was held by 4th Infantry Division's 12th Infantry Regiment, still about 500 to

600 men under strength. The *Volksgrenadiers* attacking them would number about 12,000—a four to one advantage—but many were newly-raised 17-year-olds, and they had few vehicles, no tanks, and only a handful of self-propelled guns—which helped to even out the odds.

The Sauer runs fast in December, and the German assault troops in rubber boats found the crossing difficult; some had to try several locations before getting across, thus upsetting the timetable; but the opening barrage knocked out communications and deluged the forward posts with shells. Many were overrun before they had time to give the alarm and at first—as elsewhere along the Ardennes front—there was complete confusion. Villages were taken, lost, and re-taken with captors and prisoners changing rôles. In some places small bodies of American troops held out against the odds: 21 men turned a thick stone farmhouse into a fort and beat off all attacks for four days. Elsewhere, 60 Americans with only one machine-gun made a tourist hotel into a strongpoint, and held up the German advance long enough for relieving infantry to besiege the besiegers. But in many places the small American forces were simply overwhelmed.

The 60th Armoured Infantry Battalion, which had been given a small section of front a few days before for 'battle indoctrination', had about an hour's warning because the *Volksgrenadier* division sent against them was delayed by fog. Although greatly outnumbering the defenders, the Germans had no self-propelled guns, while the American armoured infantry—whose job is to protect its division's tanks—were fully equipped and wrought terrible damage on the German horse-drawn artillery and unarmoured transport. Although the American main line of resistance was penetrated several times the arrival of their reserves saved the situation and by nightfall the armoured infantry were still in position, blocking the *Volksgrenadiers'* attempt to join the Echternach attackers in forming a southern wall.

On this front, too, the Germans had failed to reach their main objectives. The American forward outposts had been overrun and the Germans were in force west of the Sauer, but they had failed to dislodge 4th Infantry Division's artillery, whose gunners were able to knock out the temporary bridges and prevent self-propelled guns or heavy mortars from being brought into play. Although the position of the American troops at the extreme southern flank of the Ardennes front was precarious, and would become more so before reinforcements arrived, the German advance had slipped behind schedule. Like the failure in the north, it was to have far-reaching effects on the battle.

Heady successes, serious setbacks

Along the line of the main attack the first 24 hours brought the Germans two main successes, one partial success, one serious failure, and three temporary setbacks which the plan could not afford.

The major success, like the major failure, took place on VI SS Panzer Army's front: a battlegroup spearheading I SS Panzer Division got through the gap between US 5th Corps and US 8th Corps and broke out into the unguarded rear areas. On the other hand XII SS Panzer Division and two divisions of *Volksgrenadiers,* who were to open gaps for the tanks, were held up all day.

The other major success was achieved by Manteuffel's force north of the Schnee **2230** ▷

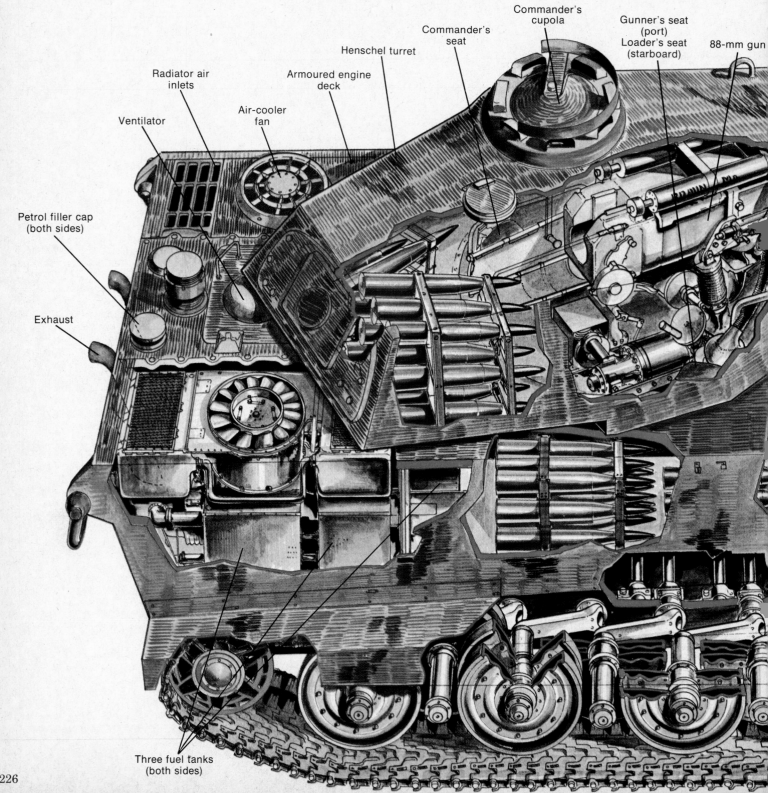

Commander's cupola

Commander's seat

Gunner's seat (port)
Loader's seat (starboard)

Henschel turret

88-mm gun

Armoured engine deck

Radiator air inlets

Air-cooler fan

Ventilator

Petrol filler cap (both sides)

Exhaust

Three fuel tanks (both sides)

John Batchelor

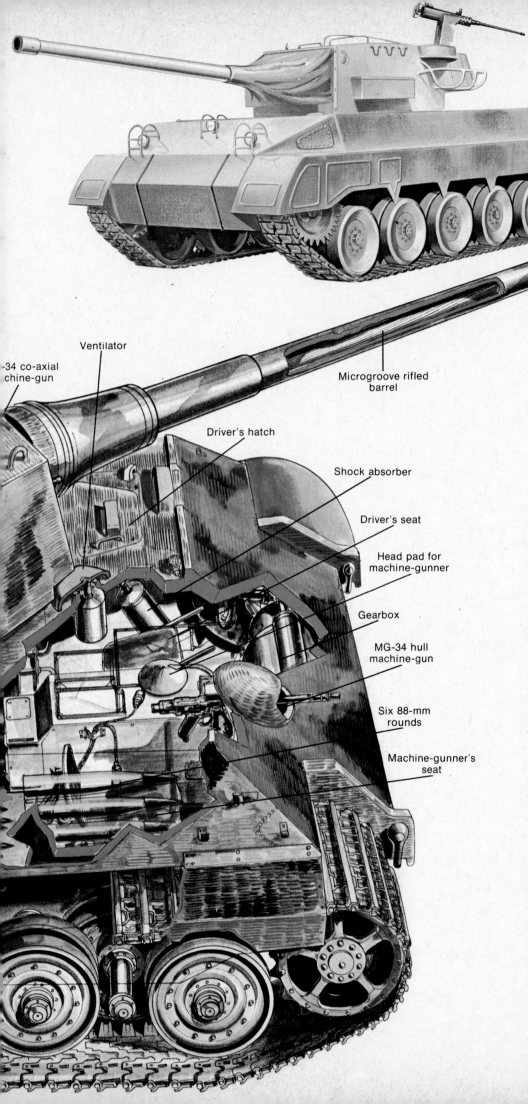

Ventilator

-34 co-axial
chine-gun

Microgroove rifled
barrel

Driver's hatch

Shock absorber

Driver's seat

Head pad for
machine-gunner

Gearbox

MG-34 hull
machine-gun

Six 88-mm
rounds

Machine-gunner's
seat

A new breed of tiger

'**King Tiger**' *(left)*. The Pzkw Mk VI Tiger II ('Königstiger') entered service in mid-1944 – and was one of the best protected, hardest-hitting tanks of the war. It was manufactured under the most difficult circumstances: Allied bombing of factories and the sources of essential materials produced a series of delays which limited the total production figure to 485 machines. Tiger II appeared with two different types of turret, Henschel (shown here), and Porsche. Both were used in a machine which was a vast improvement over Tiger I – with a longer gun, well-sloped armour, and a larger engine giving better all-round performance. Even so, Tiger II was underpowered and difficult to manoeuvre, particularly when crossing bridges. *Weight:* 68 tons. *Crew:* five. *Armour:* 185-mm (max), 40-mm (min). *Armament:* one 88-mm gun, two 7·9-mm MGs

'**Hunting Tiger**' *(top left)*. The Jagdpanzer VI ('Jagdtiger') was next in line of succession to the 'Elephant' heavy tank destroyer (see Vol 4, p. 1386). It was the heaviest armoured vehicle in use with the German army – but its manoeuvrability was hampered by excessive weight, and was in no way compensated by its immensely thick armour – or by its 128-mm gun, with its low rate of fire. *Weight:* 70 tons. *Crew:* six. *Armour:* 250-mm (max), 30-mm (min). *Armament:* one 128-mm gun, one 7·9-mm MG

'**Hellcat**' *(top right)*. The American M-18 ('Hellcat') was a lighter, high-powered version of the M-10 3-inch-gun motor carriage (see Vol 4, p. 1611). With a top speed of 55 mph, this fast, elusive tank-destroyer was used to hit and run rather than to stand and fight it out; and so it was the antithesis of the German Jagdpanzer. *Weight:* 20 tons. *Crew:* five. *Armour:* 25-mm (max). *Armament:* one 76-mm gun, two ·50-inch MGs

Rundstedt, C-in-C Western Front: nominal commander of the Ardennes *Wacht am Rhein* offensive

Model, the 'Führer's fireman': C-in-C of Army Group B, comprising the three assault armies

Manteuffel: C-in-C of V Panzer Army, the 'left hook' of the Panzer assault through the Ardennes

Dietrich, top general of the Waffen-SS: C-in-C of VI SS Panzer Army, spearhead of the assault

▷ As they had been promised: infantry advancing past blazing US vehicles

Centre: A patrol dashes across a road littered with US guns

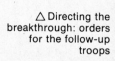

△ Directing the breakthrough: orders for the follow-up troops

▷ Scene of the Malmédy massacre, where SS troops shot 86 US POWs

▷By December 18, the German spearheads had driven 25 miles in only 36 hours

◁ The offensive rolls on, past more abandoned US vehicles

▽ *Left:* A captured SS trooper; many were cut off in over-enthusiastic advances

A la population de BASTOGNE

△ US soldiers await the crunch in Bastogne

◁ How it was in the early days: advance instead of retreat

Eifel, which swept through the strung-out positions of the 18th Cavalry Squadron in the Losheim Gap and reached the main road to St Vith less than 10 miles from that vital communications centre. But again, his centre thrust, intended to go round the south of the Schnee Eifel and join up with his right-wing attack, thus entrapping two regiments of newly-arrived infantry along the top of the hill, was held up all day only a mile or so from their start line.

General Manteuffel's main effort to reach the Meuse came from his left wing, where the élite XLVII Panzer Corps of one Panzer and two infantry divisions (plus a division of parachute infantry from Brandenberger's VII Army) planned to cross the Our, cut the main north/south highway, and seize bridges over the next river to the west (the Clerf) in the first 24 hours. This would enable them to take Bastogne the next day and also to get their Panzers on good roads to the Meuse.

His centre thrust also fumbled when a Panzer division and its supporting infantry division were unable to cross the Our in their sector at all and the armour had to be sent south to get over by another bridge. But the II Panzer Division, destined to advance further than any other troops in the Battle of the Bulge, got across the Our and moved up the wooded slopes to seize the main highway (known as 'Skyline Drive' to the heavily-shelled drivers of the lorries who used it to carry supplies to the American 9th Army in the north) thus achieving a partial success. Somehow the outnumbered and exhausted 28th Infantry Division was able to prevent them from crossing the Clerf for the whole of the second day, a gallant stand which bought the precious hours needed to reinforce Bastogne.

Although, at the time, neither side was able to see it, the pattern that emerged at the end of the first two days' fighting determined the outcome of the battle, and these events are worth examining a little more closely.

In VI SS Panzer Army confidence ran high, for it had not only the best and shortest route to the Meuse but had been given the most tanks, guns, and men. Two main armoured punches were planned: XII SS Panzer Division ('Hitler Jugend') was to lead the right-hand one and its great rival, I SS Panzer Division ('Leibstandarte Adolf Hitler') the left. Each waited behind a *Volks-grenadier* division which was to make the initial breakthrough; these four divisions were opposed by four *battalions*—less than half a division—of the green 99th US Infantry Division. But, because of the Roer dams attack going in just to the north, there was an exceptional concentration of American artillery on this front.

The German barrage here was the heaviest of all. A few days before, a US Intelligence report had said that the German front opposite one of 99th Infantry's battalions seemed to be very lightly held, adding that there were only two horse-drawn guns there. After an hour's non-stop shelling the battalion executive officer reported: 'They sure worked those horses to death.'

As soon as the shelling stopped, assault troops hit every American forward position in strength and most of the riflemen were killed or captured. But when the *Volks-grenadiers* tried to exploit this success they were hammered by heavy howitzer and artillery fire and went to ground. Some of the 'Hitler Jugend' Division, impatient at the delay, tried to advance their tanks alone,

but were stopped by large-calibre, high-explosive shells.

By dusk, about 1630 hours, the American survivors had formed strongpoints around their battalion command posts in the woods and, though reduced to half strength, somehow preserved a front. After only six weeks in the line these young soldiers had held up two élite SS Panzer divisions for an all-important 24 hours, the time needed to bring in other troops to hold the high ground behind the Elsenborn Ridge against which the 'Hitler Jugend' division was practically to destroy itself in the next few days before giving up and being moved to another part of the front.

But the leading battle group of the 'Leibstandarte Adolf Hitler' was commanded by one of Germany's toughest, most ruthless, and most daring SS Panzer leaders, Colonel Joachim Peiper, who demanded and got almost suicidal devotion from his men.

Disgusted at the failure of the *Volks-grenadiers* to open a breach for his battle group, he went forward and personally led his Panzers through the snarled-up rear areas, ordering them to run down anything that did not get out of their way. Breaking out into no-man's-land after dark, his spearhead lost five Panzers to old German mines. Carrying on all through the night, they seized the town of Honsfeld, far behind the American lines, at dawn on Sunday, December 17, capturing many vehicles and anti-tank guns and shooting down 19 unarmed American soldiers, the first of a number of atrocities perpetrated by these veterans from the bitter no-quarter fighting in Russia.

Peiper's vital breakthrough

In need of fuel, Peiper's men swung 2 miles off route into the 'Hitler Jugend' Division's zone and seized a large petrol dump at Büllingen, forcing 50 American soldiers to fill their tanks and then shooting them down in cold blood too, before swinging back on to their own route and pushing west as fast as possible.

Just after noon Peiper's men pierced an American column moving down from the north as reinforcements. This was part of the US 7th Armoured Division, on its way to St Vith. Only half an hour earlier Peiper's column would have run head on into their Armoured Combat Command and a great tank battle would have developed, but this had passed through and blind chance brought a field artillery observation battery of 125 men to the Malmédy crossroads at that precise moment. They could do nothing against the tanks and guns of a Panzer division and all were quickly captured. A couple of hours later, while standing in a field waiting to be marched back, these prisoners were machine-gunned by passing SS. Some were unconscious or feigned death but 86 died and the news of this massacre, reaching the Americans in front line positions that night by 'latrine telegraph', was responsible for a stiffening of the will to resist and an unwillingness to surrender.

Having apparently achieved a clean break-through, Peiper hoped to reach his objective —the bridge over the Meuse at Huy—by late that night or early the next morning. A few miles ahead of him lay Stavelot, and from there a good road ran almost due west 40 miles to the Meuse.

What happened next is something of a mystery still. His spearhead, racing on, was stopped when the leading half-tracks were knocked out; but this was no more than had

been expected; and German countermoves knocked out two American tanks and captured more prisoners. But the encounter bred caution in the leaders, and the battle group's advance guard did not get to the high ground across the river from Stavelot until dusk. There they saw hundreds of American vehicles and jumped to the conclusion that they had reached a heavily defended position.

In fact the only combat troops in Stavelot were a single battalion of engineers who were constructing a roadblock: there were no tanks or anti-tank guns at all. The vehicles were trucks engaged in moving fuel out of a huge dump a few miles away. The leading German tanks ran on to a newly-laid American minefield and the commanders who, after all, had been on the move for 36 hours and advanced 25 miles, must have decided that they had pushed their luck far enough for they greatly exaggerated the strength of the defences. Uncharacteristically, Peiper did not come up to see for himself but consented to a halt—probably realising that he must now wind up his tail anyway.

Whatever the explanation the stopping of Battle Group Peiper at Stavelot on the second night of the offensive was the turning point in VI SS Panzer Army's offensive, for although in the next week this strong force would remain the main threat on the northern front, lack of support and particularly lack of fuel prevented its breaking out to the west. American reinforcements from the 82nd Airborne Division, the 30th Infantry Division, the 3rd Armoured Division, and other units bore down heavily on Battle Group Peiper, which became isolated from the rest of I SS Panzer Division.

The unexpected stiff resistance of the US 99th Infantry Division in front of I SS Panzer Corps and the delay caused by the extensive minefields on that front brought about colossal traffic jams behind the German attack front as horse-drawn artillery, supply trains, bridging equipment, reserves, and huge siege guns all pressed forward trying to keep to their time-tables.

Skorzeny—master of confusion

Otto Skorzeny personally led his group through this tangle, bypassing clogged roads by cutting across fields (and losing his most experienced commander on an old German mine) and so was able to dispatch three of his disguised commando teams towards the Meuse crossings. One actually got to the bridge at Huy and 'guarded' it all day, doling out terrifying rumours to passing American units. Other teams blew up ammunition dumps and destroyed communications but the main result of the presence of German soldiers in American uniforms far behind the front was to set in motion the most elaborate measures to check on everyone's identity. All jeeps or staff cars were stopped and passengers asked the names of comic strip characters, the league positions of baseball teams, or details of the private lives of film stars. Often the more senior American officers did not know the correct answer and many spent a few hours in custody. All this, combined with the stories of German paratroops dropping everywhere, tied up troops who were desperately needed in the fighting.

In fact, like Skorzeny's operation, the parachute drop was something of a farce, for lack of fuel for the transport trucks stopped the paratroops on the first night and postponed their drop for 24 hours, when the element of surprise was lost and it was almost certain that American reinforcements would be moving through the drop zone.

Strong crosswinds scattered the aircraft and the paratroops came down at widely separated spots. Many of these young, courageous volunteers, jumping in the black, freezing night for the first time, came down in remote parts of the Ardennes, far from houses or roads. Some broke arms or legs on landing and although some were found by American search parties or local people others lay in the snow and slowly died. Bodies were still being found the following spring.

Only ten or 15 bombers found the drop zone and Colonel von der Heydte discovered that he had only about 350 men, little food, no blankets, no weapons larger than small mortars and machine-pistols, and no radios working. Just after first light the paratroops heard the noise of heavy trucks climbing towards them from the north and moments later trucks crammed with American infantry rolled through their position. This was the 1st Infantry Division, the most experienced in the American army, veterans of three beach assaults—Africa, Sicily, and Normandy. Now they were on their way to reinforce the 99th Infantry Division and the 2nd Infantry Division, now being pulled back from the Roer dams attack to screen 99th Infantry's withdrawal to the Elsenborn Ridge. 'The Big Red One' Division would arrive just in time to shore up the southern flank and help block VI SS Panzer Army's attack in which Hitler had such high hopes.

In the next few days Colonel von der Heydte had to watch two more American divisions, the 7th Armoured and the 30th Infantry, move into the attack zone without his being able to do anything about it. What Omar Bradley has described as America's 'secret weapon', mobility, was being brought into play.

After four days, out of rations and suffering severely from the intense cold, Colonel von der Heydte ordered his men to break up into small parties and find their own way back. He sent back his American prisoners and, with them, his own wounded with a request to the American commander to look after them. Two days later, exhausted and ravenous, he surrendered himself. It was the end of the once-great German Parachute Corps, whose exploits had won the admiration of soldiers everywhere.

On VI SS Panzer Army's left General von Manteuffel planned a double-pronged drive around the Schnee Eifel, which would first trap the green 106th Infantry Division's troops there and would then go on to take St Vith, whose road and rail communications were absolutely essential to the second phase of the German offensive.

Attached to the 106th Division and guarding its left flank were 900 men of the 18th Cavalry Squadron in village strongpoints across the Losheim Gap. At dawn they were hit by both Manteuffel's right-wing attack of reinforced *Volksgrenadiers* and Sepp Dietrich's left, a division of parachute infantry whose main axis ran from Germany to Manderfeld, the reconnaissance cavalry's headquarters.

The 18th Cavalry Squadron was part of the 14th Cavalry Group, whose commander, Colonel Mark Devine, went forward from Manderfeld to try to discover what was happening on his front. In some places the first German assaults had been beaten off,

but other small groups had been overwhelmed before they could do much more than radio for artillery support. Realising that this was a major attack and that his outposts were hopelessly outnumbered, Devine ordered those who were able to do so to disengage and fall back. He got through to his superiors at 106th Division HQ in St Vith and proposed a new flank defence line across the western end of the Losheim Gap to be followed by a counterattack as soon as his reserve squadron arrived. This was agreed to, for no one at divisional headquarters realised that both proposals were quite unreal in the light of the strength of the German attack.

Rumours, confusion—and panic

When Devine got back to his headquarters in Manderfeld about 1100 hours, he found it a shambles, with his staff frantically packing and trying to destroy their records. Floods of refugees had been pouring in with stories of terrible disasters and German successes. Their terror was unnerving. Panic swept through 14th Cavalry Group HQ and the staff piled into their vehicles with what personal possessions they could grab; and, in an attempt to destroy anything which might aid the Germans, they simply set fire to the whole town, destroying it completely. It was the beginning of a series of disorganised retreats which became a long nightmare, only ending some 60 hours and four commanding officers later, 25 miles to the rear, when the 14th Cavalry Group's survivors were attached to the 7th Armoured Division as part of the defence of St Vith.

When the cavalry broke off action and pulled back, Manteuffel's right wing raced through the Losheim Gap until it was halted by artillery near the village of Auw in front of St Vith. Here the commander of the 106th Infantry Division, General Alan Jones, only recently arrived on the Continent, was involved in his first battle. His main worry was the fate of his two regiments stuck out on the eastern side of the Schnee Eifel ridge. Wrongly believing that the 14th Cavalry was guarding his left flank, he sent one of his reserve battalions to stiffen his right flank and the other to engage Manteuffel's right wing, a mixed force of infantry and assault guns attacking the field artillery at Auw. These guns were then able to withdraw and take part in the all-important defence of St Vith itself, which took place over the next few days.

The southern prong of Manteuffel's attack around the Schnee Eifel had come under killing fire from 106th Division infantry on the southern slope of the hill, and after fierce hand-to-hand fighting in the streets of Bleialf, key to the road network there, the Germans had been halted less than 2 miles from their start line. Displeased, General Manteuffel ordered them to renew their attack at dawn, take Bleialf 'at all costs', and advance to join the northern prong, closing the trap on the two regiments of American infantry on the Schnee Eifel.

The 106th Division had lost little actual ground on the first day of the offensive and its inexperienced staff probably failed to realise the precariousness of their position. All through the night the Germans continued to move infantry and guns into the breaches they had made, in preparation for the next day's onslaught.

In answer to the 106th Division's request for reinforcements, 8th Corps gave it an armoured combat command, no longer needed for the Roer Dams attack, and during the evening of the 16th, promised that the 7th Armoured Division from the north was on its way and that its leading combat command would arrive at 0700 hours the next morning. This estimate was hopelessly out, for it had not taken into account either the winter road conditions or the traffic jams being caused by the disorganised headlong retreat of many rear troops. In fact the main body of tanks of the 7th Armoured did not arrive at St Vith until late on Sunday afternoon, too late to save the two regiments on the Schnee Eifel. It took the tanks five hours to cover the last 12 miles against a tide of panic-stricken staff and rear area troops.

By nightfall on December 17, some 8-9,000 American troops were surrounded in the Schnee Eifel. Two days later, without having incurred more than a few casualties or inflicted any serious damage on the encircling Germans who did not outnumber them but who did have tanks and self-propelled guns, they all surrendered. It was, as the official American history says, the most serious reverse suffered by American arms in the European theatre.

Jubilantly the Germans moved in for the kill at St Vith.

The central blow

The V Panzer Army's main effort, an attack by two Panzer corps in the centre, although destined to be the most successful of all, did not get off to the flying start planned. On the German right 58th Panzer Corps of a division of *Volksgrenadiers* followed by the 116th Panzer Division, planned to roll through a single regiment of the 28th Infantry Division (the 112th), holding trenches east of the Our river, and go flat out for the Meuse through the vacuum between Bastogne and St Vith, which it was expected the attacks on both those places would create.

South of this thrust XLVII Panzer Corps' XXVI *Volksgrenadier* Division would seize bridges over the Our for the armour of the élite II Panzer Division, and both infantry and tanks would smash through the centre of US 28th Infantry Division's front, held by their 110th Regiment, get across the Clerf river 6 or 7 miles further west, and go on to capture Bastogne. As an added precaution, one of General Brandenberger's divisions of parachute infantry would move alongside this attack, cutting the 110th Infantry Regiment off from the 109th further south.

It was a good plan and should have succeeded quickly, for the Germans numbered about 50,000 while the American defenders consisted of 14 companies of riflemen (about 3,250 combat troops) supported by artillery and howitzer positions, and one battalion of tanks. But, of course, only a part of the total German strength could be brought to bear at the beginning of the attack.

On 58th Panzer Corps' front the American defenders, being east of the Our, maintained intact bridges behind them capable of taking tanks and self-propelled guns. If these could be taken by surprise, the Panzers could get off to the flying start they needed to reach the Meuse.

To make sure of surprise General von Manteuffel ordered that this section of the front would not receive the pre-dawn opening barrage but, instead, white-clad *Volksgrenadiers* would quietly penetrate the rear areas of the American front line before dawn and, when the attack began, move swiftly to seize the two bridges.

Had the *Volksgrenadiers* on this front been more experienced or the defending infantry less so this plan might have succeeded, but the German division were a scratch lot of ex-garrison troops from Norway and Denmark, most of whom had never seen action. The first part of the plan worked—shock companies of *Volksgrenadiers* penetrated the American forward line during the night and, as soon as the barrage began—an hour later here than on the rest of the front—moved through the gaps in the long, deep, barbed-wire defences which the Americans had left open for moving up supplies at night.

The Germans achieved complete surprise. In one case they burst into a clearing just as a platoon was lined up for breakfast. The sudden fire of machine-pistols and exploding grenades killed a number of Americans and the rest broke. The white-clad shock troops moved swiftly towards the bridges—and here their inexperience was their undoing. Flushed with success they advanced openly on to defended pillboxes and manned trenches. The veterans of the US 112th Infantry Regiment, who had lost 2,000 out of 3,000 in the bitter Hurtgen Forest fighting the month before, picked the invaders off with rifle fire, sprayed them with machine-guns and, when they took refuge in gullies, plastered them with mortar fire. German casualties were very heavy here and elsewhere on this part of the front and by nightfall all the bridges were still in American hands.

The *Volksgrenadiers* had been badly mauled and the Panzer division had lost six tanks. Manteuffel's centre thrust was badly behind schedule and, in an attempt to catch up, the 116th Panzer Division was ordered to send a battalion of light tanks (Mk IVs) 5 or 6 miles south and cross the Our over a bridge which had been established by the XLVII Panzer Corps. The Mk IVs were then to turn north, come back along the American side of the Our, and take the bridges on 58th Panzer Corps' front from the rear.

The Panzer schwerpunkt

General Hasso von Manteuffel's main hope of reaching the Meuse lay with his XLVII Panzer Corps, the Wehrmacht's 'Number One Reserve' on the Western Front. For the Ardennes offensive this consisted of a first-class infantry division from the Eastern Front ('The Old XXVI', renamed the XXVI *Volksgrenadiers*) and the famous II Panzer Division, which had fought the Allies with spirit and courage all the way from Normandy to Germany. In reserve another crack division, Panzer Lehr, was to be thrown in to add weight to the *schwerpunkt*.

The XXVI *Volksgrenadiers* were given a particularly difficult rôle: they had to force the Our river, advance 7 or 8 miles and force the Clerf river, hold both these open for the armour to cross, and then follow the Panzers on foot 15 more miles to Bastogne, which it was then their task to take.

In order not to alert the Americans, *Volksgrenadier* shock troops were not allowed to cross the Our before the opening barrage but XXVI *Volksgrenadier's* commanding officer, Major-General Kokott, pointed out that he had been in the habit of putting men over the river at night and holding a line of outposts on the American side until dawn and not to do so would arouse sus-

Imperial War Museum

At the tip of the 'Bulge': SS Colonel Peiper with a scout team of his group. It was Peiper's battle group which committed the Malmédy massacre of US POWs in the early days of the breakthrough

picion. He was given permission to continue this practice on the night before the attack and, taking advantage of the concession, slipped two of his three regiments over the Our and moved them silently up through the woods to the north/south highway, 'Skyline Drive', on which the American 110th Infantry Regiment had based its main line of resistance. This highway was one of XLVII Panzer's first objectives.

General von Manteuffel's main armoured punch, II Panzer Division, was to cross the Our at Dasburg, move rapidly up 4 miles through wooded country to the small town of Marnach on Skyline Drive, seize this, and then move another 3 miles and capture the town of Clervaux, principal crossing place of the Clerf and headquarters of the 28th Division's 110th Infantry Regiment. From here good roads ran to Bastogne and beyond.

The German schedule called for all the Clerf river crossings to be held by nightfall of the first day—less than 12 hours after the opening barrage. It would be a tight schedule and unit commanders were impatient to get their men moving.

The 28th Infantry Division's 110th Regiment, holding this 10 miles of the Ardennes front, had based its defences on a series of fortified villages held in company strength and backed up by artillery positions. It was realised that the Germans could not be prevented from crossing the Our, and the ground between Skyline Drive and the Our was virtually no-man's-land used by both sides for patrolling. In the event of an attack, which as elsewhere in the Ardennes was regarded as almost an academic problem, it was intended first to hold Skyline Drive, the principal tactical feature, and next to deny the Germans the Clerf river bridges.

Fierce US resistance
On this front as elsewhere the opening barrage knocked out wire communications but the first contact was made, not at the front line, but at Holzthum west of Skyline Drive, 5 miles from the Our and only 4 miles from an important Clerf bridge. The attackers, of course, were some of the XXVI *Volksgrenadiers* who had quietly moved up during the night. They were beaten off by the Americans who had been alerted by the opening barrage and word was flashed at 0615 hours to regimental headquarters at Clervaux enabling 110th Infantry's other strongpoints to prepare to resist attack.

Failing to clear Holzthum by direct assault the XXVI *Volksgrenadiers* tried to work round north but came under fire from an artillery battalion which caused them to go to ground. Annoyed, the German commander ordered an attack against the guns which were without infantry support but this too failed. Again and again the *Volksgrenadiers* attacked the villages of Holzthum and Consthum, which barred their way to the Clerf crossing, but were unable to get past. It was an unexpectedly stubborn defence and it cost these German troops, who had hoped to be the first to cross the Clerf, all the time advantage they had gained by their night crossing of the Our. Desperately they attacked the American artillery position but the gunners put their shells on one-second fuses and fired over open sights—in some cases parts of the shells blew back on the gun positions. Although the battery commander and 15 of his gun crews became casualties, the position was held.

Other positions on this part of the American front also put up unexpectedly fierce resistance. At Wahlhausen, a cluster of houses on top of a hill with an all-round view, an American observation post of a single platoon beat off attack after attack until their ammunition ran out. After dark the Germans shelled them with anti-aircraft guns and came on in force. The last message from Wahlhausen was a request for American artillery fire on top of them; only one man survived. The rest of the company to which this platoon belonged were in the village of Weiler near the German start line, and they too beat off successive waves of brave but largely inexperienced young *Volksgrenadiers* all day, and were not eliminated until nightfall. The troops who finally captured these two positions should by then have been across the Clerf.

General Kokott had ordered his assault troops to bypass the defended village of Hosingen on Skyline Drive but a company of riflemen and another of combat engineers sallied out and engaged the German columns on either side and drew them into a pitched battle for the village. This threw the German timetable out here, too, and the outnumbered Americans held out for two and a half days when, cut off and out of ammunition, the survivors surrendered.

The tough defence of the 110th Infantry Regiment's right flank stopped the XXVI *Volksgrenadiers* from getting across the Clerf until the third day and undoubtedly enabled Bastogne to be reinforced—and so later to resist all the German efforts to capture it.

The left half of the 110th Infantry Regiment's sector, based on Clervaux, also put up an unexpectedly fierce fight. At Marnach, midway between the Dasburg crossing and the key town of Clervaux, a company of American infantry held off the German assault all the first day, only going down when the tanks of II Panzer Division crashed into the little town. At Clervaux itself a particularly spirited defence held up the combined German armour and infantry for two days, the regimental commander himself remaining in his headquarters until the attackers had broken into the downstairs rooms. With survivors of his staff and some walking wounded he got out of an upstairs back door which led up the hill behind, but he was later captured.

The 28th Infantry Division's centre regiment, the 110th, lost about 2,750 men in two and a half days holding the Clerf crossings—but in doing so enabled Bastogne to be reinforced and later held, which in turn stopped General von Manteuffel from reaching the Meuse.

This then was the situation, after nearly 100 hours of continuous fighting in the Ardennes. On the northern flank the Elsenborn Ridge was securely held by four American infantry divisions and concentrated artillery—but it had been a near thing. The 99th Infantry Division was forced back by overwhelming infantry and tank attacks; the 2nd, breaking off its own offensive, had had to fight a desperate withdrawing action through the crumbling front. The 9th Division had moved in from Eupen to back up the Monschau position where no ground had been yielded despite wave after wave of attackers; and the veteran 1st Division had arrived just in time to hold the right of the ridge line against renewed SS Panzer attacks. Thus, with most of VI SS Panzer Army held almost at the start line and their

one success, Peiper's Battle Group (spearheading the 'Leibstandarte Adolf Hitler' Division) in a pocket, the main hope of a quick, unbroken advance to the Meuse in the north had failed. And with St Vith and Bastogne under attack but still in American hands, the original timetable had to be torn up.

'Our forces must now prepare to defend the territory we have already taken,' Field-Marshal von Rundstedt said as early as December 18. Although Hitler overruled him and ordered the Panzers to smash through regardless of casualties, even he was forced to face reality. On the 19th he cancelled the supporting attack from the German XV Army in the north.

The first crisis passes
But on the American side it was only after four days that some sort of order emerged from the confusion caused by the mass of small actions, the breakdown of communications, and the near panic in some of the rear areas. Now major decisions could be taken. Although at first General Bradley had thought the Germans were mounting a spoiling attack to stop General Patton's projected Saar offensive, he had immediately moved an armoured division into the attacked front from either side, the 7th from the north which saved St Vith, and the 10th from the south which got one combat command into Bastogne and another to the hard-pressed defenders around Echternach.

Also 9th Army's General Simpson voluntarily sent his 5th Armoured Division and his 30th Infantry to his old friend General Hodges' aid, and SHAEF's sole reserve, two airborne divisions, were also thrown into the battle. They had been resting and refitting at Rheims after nearly two months' fighting in Holland and were not supposed to be operational for another month: but after a wild 100-mile ride through the night the 101st came into Bastogne on December 19 and the 82nd arrived near the point of 'Liebstandarte' Division by the evening of the 18th.

Although the offensive was taking place entirely on the American front, Field-Marshal Montgomery moved part of his only reserve, 30th Corps, to backstop positions west of the Meuse.

When the full seriousness of the situation was realised at SHAEF on December 19, the offensive through the Saar was called off and General Patton was ordered to counter-attack the German left flank as soon as possible with two of 3rd Army's corps.

This, it was realised, would take time, and orders were given for Allied forces to fall back if necessary—but not further than the Meuse. General Eisenhower told General Bradley to 'choose the line he could hold most cheaply' and he asked Field-Marshal Montgomery to examine the possibility of giving up ground in Holland to shorten the line and amass a reserve.

While General Patton worked furiously to turn his whole front through 90°, and while Bastogne and St Vith waited for all-out assaults, General von Manteuffel drove his armour straight through the vacuum between these towns. This threatened to split the front in two, making it increasingly difficult for General Bradley to exercise control over both halves.

It was a situation which faced General Eisenhower with one of his most difficult command decisions.

[*Peter Elstob's biography is in Vol 5, p. 1848.*]

BATTLE OF THE BULGE: THE CRISIS

Imperial War Museum

Ardennes, Belgium, December 16/21, 1944
Charles B. MacDonald

While the hastily-deployed American defenders of St Vith and Bastogne fought desperately to stem the German tide in the Ardennes, another battle was being fought out in Allied headquarters. This involved the thorny subject of Montgomery's rôle in the Battle of the Bulge. It was clear to Eisenhower that Montgomery was in the best position to deal with the northern side of the Bulge until Patton was ready for his attack from the south—but Montgomery's approach aroused much surprise and resentment among the American generals. And while the Allied counterattacks hung in the balance, the Germans finally took St Vith, one of the vital obstacles in their path. Jubilantly, they moved in for the kill at Bastogne . . .
Above: US troops under shellfire near Houffalize

The bitter and costly battles for the Elsenborn Ridge, for the Schnee Eifel, for St Vith, for the Skyline Drive and Clerf, for the Sauer river crossings and Echternach—these did not decide the outcome of Hitler's winter counteroffensive. Yet taken together, these opening engagements drew much of the sting out of the total tactical and strategic surprise the Germans had scored, denying the German commanders the quick momentum they required if they were to achieve the strategic goal of Antwerp.

The grim fighting before the Elsenborn Ridge had jammed the northern shoulder of the German penetration, stalling the main effort of SS General Josef 'Sepp' Dietrich's VI Panzer Army. The battles on the Schnee Eifel and at St Vith had put the *verboten* sign on the vital roads that thread through St Vith, sharply restricting westward movement of the north wing of General Hasso von Manteuffel's V Panzer Army in the centre of the German line-up. These two stands together restricted Sepp Dietrich's Panzer columns to a corridor between St Vith and the Elsenborn Ridge only 4 miles wide.

The fight for the Skyline Drive and crossings over the little Clerf river at the town of Clerf had seriously slowed the V Panzer Army's main effort, scheduled to plunge swiftly through the centre of the Ardennes, taking the crucial road centre of Bastogne in the process, and seizing crossings of the Meuse river to protect the left flank of the VI Panzer Army. The determined American stand at crossings of the Sauer river and at Echternach at the southern base had similarly delayed General Erich Brandenberger's VII Army, which had to establish a solid shoulder extending far to the west if Manteuffel and Dietrich were not to be subjected to quick counterattack by a commander whom all the German generals respected—Lieutenant-General George S. Patton, Jr, commanding the US 3rd Army.

The stand at these forward positions also afforded time for the commander of the American 8th Corps, Major-General Troy S. Middleton—whose over-extended troops had borne the brunt of the German thrust—to dispose his reserves, however meagre, and contribute to the German delay. Of the two combat commands of the 9th Armoured Division that constituted the sole formal reserve, Middleton had sent one to St Vith. The other he had disposed on the roads behind the Clerf river leading into Bastogne. Also available were a few engineer combat battalions that Middleton turned from timber cutting and road building to reinforce various threatened sectors.

There were other reserves, though not formally designated as such, that would also have an impact, a kind of battlefield residue made up of headquarters companies, supply and service troops, and stragglers filtering back from broken or surrounded units. By turning to fight at critical road junctions, manning tanks pulled from repair shops, firing machine-guns for vital minutes while engineers demolished a bridge, these troops in hundreds of impromptu engagements had an effect in the sharply compartmented Ardennes terrain far out of proportion to their numbers.

That was what had happened, for example, at the town of Stavelot, in the deeply incised valley of the little Amblève river 15 miles south-west of the Elsenborn Ridge, where the one German force that had scored an unequivocal breakthrough in the early hours had become involved in a time- **2238** ▷

Within 48 hours, the Germans had trapped nearly 9,000 Americans in the heights of the Schnee Eifel.
Another 48 hours and they had all surrendered. They were not outnumbered; their casualties had been slight.
It was the most serious US defeat suffered in the European theatre.
And the Germans were quick to comment. 'Bearers of American culture' sneers the German caption to this picture of Negro POWs

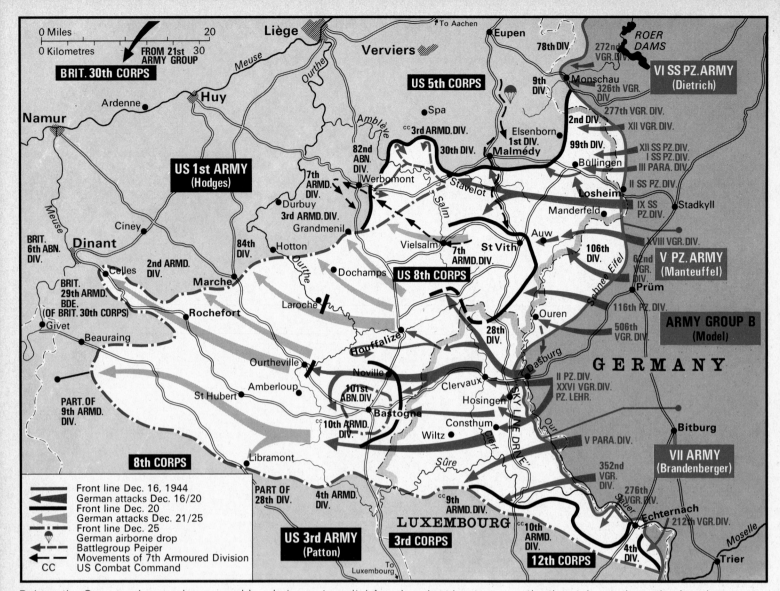

Map legend:
- Front line Dec. 16, 1944
- German attacks Dec. 16/20
- Front line Dec. 20
- German attacks Dec. 21/25
- Front line Dec. 25
- German airborne drop
- Battlegroup Peiper
- Movements of 7th Armoured Division
- CC — US Combat Command

Delays, the German planners knew, would be fatal for the Ardennes offensive—but the German flood was forced to stream between two vital American breakwaters: St Vith and Bastogne, holding out valiantly in the path of the advancing enemy. And the time taken to lever the Americans out of the St Vith horseshoe and besiege Bastogne crimped German operations

consuming fight. This was a task force commanded by *SS-Obersturmbannführer* Joachim Peiper of the I SS Panzer Division, which had plunged swiftly westward, murdering American prisoners in the process.

This delay alone would hardly prove fatal to Peiper, but little bands of die-hard defenders were waiting at other spots as well. An American major ordered Belgian troops manning a big fuel depot to pour petrol into a road cut, set it aflame, and deny Peiper access to the depot. A lone towed anti-tank gun at the next town delayed Peiper's tanks long enough for engineers to demolish two critical bridges. A brief break in heavy snow-clouds that had shielded the Germans since the start of the counteroffensive afforded American fighter-bombers a fleeting but sharp blow at the rampaging Panzers.

Yet without additional resources, these delays were temporary successes at best. If the overwhelming tide—some 200,000 men and more than a thousand tanks—that had surged into the Ardennes was to be fully and finally reversed, something other than that available to Middleton at the start—83,000 men and perhaps 300 tanks—had to be used.

Full realisation of what was happening in the Ardennes had been slow to come at head-quarters of Lieutenant-General Courtney S. Hodges' US 1st Army, located in the Hotel Britannique in the once fashionable watering place of Spa, whence the Kaiser had directed his armies in the First World War. Because the opening artillery bombardments had knocked out most telephone lines to forward units, reports from some sectors had been slow to emerge. Emanating mainly from the northernmost divisions, the first messages seemed to indicate only a local spoiling attack designed to thwart an American offensive against the Roer river dams near Monschau.

Local attack or not, the Supreme Allied Commander, General Dwight D. Eisenhower, and the commander of the 12th Army Group, Lieutenant-General Omar N. Bradley, who controlled the US 1st, 3rd, and 9th Armies, recognised immediately that Middleton would have to have help to meet it. That was what had started the 7th Armoured Division moving south from the 9th Army to bolster St Vith and the 10th Armoured Division from the 3rd Army to reinforce the southern shoulder near Echternach and Bastogne. General Hodges himself hastily pulled troops from unthreatened portions of the 1st Army's line farther north and sent them marching to help hold the Elsenborn Ridge, while Lieutenant-General William H. Simpson, commanding the 9th Army, sent two divisions hurrying south-

ward to extend the northern shoulder to the west along the Amblève river.

As awesome reports continued to reach Hodges' 1st Army HQ on December 17, Hodges asked General Eisenhower for the Supreme Commander's reserve, which consisted of only two US airborne divisions that were recuperating from a bitter fight in Operation 'Market Garden' in the Netherlands. On Bradley's recommendation, Eisenhower agreed reluctantly to part with these two units—the 82nd and 101st Airborne Divisions—and gave the order that sent them on a wild, 100-mile night ride through sleeting rain. As finally determined, the 82nd was to form a cordon far to the west near the town of Werbomont to contain Peiper's tanks, while the 101st rushed to reinforce Bastogne.

By midnight of December 17, the second day, some 60,000 men and 11,000 vehicles were on their way to reinforce Hodges' 1st Army in the Ardennes. In the next eight days, three times those numbers would be on the move. The name of the game now was mobility, and that the Americans knew how to play.

Almost instinctively, everybody from Middleton up to the Supreme Commander had begun to act in keeping with doctrine long taught in American staff schools. The way to contain and eventually erase a salient created by a major offensive – as proved in the First World War – was first to hold the shoulders of the penetration. Firm shoulders would deny the enemy the room he required if major forces were to be committed. Counterattack from the flanks then might eliminate the restricted penetration. As modified only by a determination to deny the Germans the critical road net at Bastogne, that was how the American command went about facing its task.

Yet all the early moves were makeshift, designed to meet the immediate emergency. The broad, long-range decisions remained to be taken. These General Eisenhower faced as he gathered on December 19 in a damp old caserne in Verdun with key members of his staff. With him were Bradley, Patton, and Lieutenant-General Jacob L. Devers, the latter commanding the 6th Army Group, which controlled an American army and a French army forming the southern end of the Allied line.

He wanted to see, Eisenhower said at the first, only cheerful faces.

A new infantry division, he revealed, already had arrived in France and would be moved forward quickly. Three new divisions were to accelerate their shipping schedules from way-stations in Britain, and he would ask that divisions alerted for early movement from the United States ship their infantry regiments in advance direct to French ports. He also would ask authority for artillery units to use the radar-controlled 'proximity' fuse (a scientific advance formerly deemed so secret that it had been employed only by anti-aircraft units protecting ships at sea), which caused shells to burst with deadly effect while still in the air above the target.

The American offensives that had been underway north and south of the Ardennes, Eisenhower directed, were to be halted. Both Bradley and the commander of the 21st Army Group, Field-Marshal Bernard L. Montgomery, were to look to the possibility of limited withdrawals to gain reserves, but in no event were withdrawals to be made beyond the west bank of the Meuse river. Simpson was to extend his 9th Army southward to release divisions of the 1st Army around Aachen, while Devers' 6th Army Group was to extend northward to free the bulk of Patton's 3rd Army for counterattack.

Although the more obvious and desirable method of counterattack was to strike simultaneously from north and south close along the base of the German penetration, so preoccupied was Hodges with trying to contain the penetration that only Patton would be able to move swiftly. That being the case, Patton was to attack not along the base of the penetration but toward Bastogne. From there he was to continue north-eastward to another road centre at Houffalize, there to meet Hodges' troops coming down from the north. While not eliminating the penetration, that at least would contain it.

As for the cheerful faces that Eisenhower requested, Patton gave him ebullience. He could start his counterattack, Patton insisted – despite looks of incredulity on the faces of his colleagues – in just over 72 hours, early on December 22.

The meeting at Verdun had not long adjourned when Eisenhower's Chief of Intelligence, a British officer, Major-General Kenneth W. D. Strong, remarked that soon the German thrust would so split the 12th Army Group that all forces north of the pene-

tration should be transferred to Field-Marshal Montgomery's command. It was an explosive suggestion, for Eisenhower had so far resisted placing large bodies of American troops under foreign command and had specifically rejected an oft-recurring proposal that Montgomery be made overall ground commander on the Western Front.

The proposal nevertheless made sense – as even a shocked and hurt Bradley would have to admit – for direct telephone communications already had been cut, long-range radio was no substitute for the telephone, and the German salient made travel between Bradley's headquarters in Luxembourg City and those of Hodges and Simpson in the north circuitous at best. Since the counteroffensive opened, Bradley had met Hodges face to face only once; and confusion there was, not only from streams of stragglers and civilian refugees but in the command structure as well. Neither Hodges nor the corps commander, Middleton, could possibly maintain contact with all units on the broken, fluctuating front. To pull Bradley's headquarters out of Luxembourg City to a position west of the Meuse whence Bradley might control the entire front would be to flirt with panic among the civilian population and possibly to damage the morale of the troops as well.

Yet what was more important to Eisenhower – and this sweetened the pill for Bradley – was that giving Montgomery command north of the penetration would assure use of British reserves, which included an entire corps with four divisions and several armoured brigades. It was a step that would pay off as planned, for Montgomery promptly ordered his 30th Corps to move to reserve positions between Liège and Brussels and announced that the British would assume responsibility for the Meuse bridges from Liège to the big bend in the river at Namur.

Had Montgomery been an American, or even had he been a less self-assured, imperious personality, the shift in command would have been easier for American commanders to take. As it was, Montgomery on the 20th strode into the 1st Army's HQ (in the words of one of his own staff) 'like Christ come to cleanse the temple'. He ignored the 1st Army's detailed operations map to consult a small one of his own, on which he had plotted information provided by British liaison officers. He also declined General Hodges' invitation to lunch, turning instead to eat alone from a lunch box and Thermos – which, to be fair, was his normal practice.

Montgomery nevertheless approved the dispositions and measures Hodges had already taken. The incoming 30th Division, Hodges reported, had cut Peiper's supply line by retaking Stavelot; other troops of the 30th were battling Peiper at the tip of his penetration to cover assembly of the 82nd Airborne Division; a portion of the 3rd Armoured Division was on the way; and St Vith was holding, although the American position there had been compressed into a horseshoe-shaped salient maintaining only tenuous contact with other American forces to the rear.

While approving Hodges' moves, Montgomery nevertheless urged withdrawal from two positions that the Americans considered to be key: the Elsenborn Ridge and St Vith. It was a typical Montgomery manoeuvre, a step to 'tidy the battlefield' by removing what by any standards was a dangerous salient at St Vith and to soften what was an admittedly sharp northern corner of the German penetration at the Elsenborn Ridge.

Yet when Hodges and his staff reacted with shocked disbelief, Montgomery desisted.

Having gone along with the American determination, Montgomery went even farther, sanctioning a move already planned by Hodges to send the 82nd Airborne Division skirting the south flank of Peiper's penetration to push westward to the Salm river, which represented the rear of the St Vith horseshoe. Other than Peiper's task force, which American reinforcements were now effectively bottling up, tanks of the VI Panzer Army had yet to get over the Salm, so few were the roads available in the narrow corridor between the St Vith salient and the Elsenborn Ridge. To hold the Germans even temporarily at the Salm was to afford an avenue of escape for the troops in St Vith while at the same time providing cover for assembling a force for counterattack.

Montgomery wanted for counterattack, he told Hodges, the corps commander whom he deemed the 1st Army's most aggressive – Major-General J. Lawton Collins, who long ago had earned the nickname, 'Lightning Joe'. Pulled from the line near Aachen, Collins' 7th Corps was to be filled out with infantry and armoured divisions and readied for counterattack to hit the Germans once they had extended themselves in their quest for bridges over the Meuse.

Closing in on Bastogne
As Montgomery was moving to shore up the extended northern shoulder, combat commands of the US 9th and 10th Armoured Divisions were fighting a bitter delaying action in front of Bastogne, enabling the 101st Airborne Division to beat the Germans into the town. Yet from Bastogne all the way north to where the 82nd Airborne Division was assembling near Werbomont, no American line existed, leaving a gap more than 20 miles wide that included the town of Houffalize.

Having passed to the south of St Vith, two of General von Mantueffel's crack Panzer divisions – the II and the 116th – were hurtling almost without check into this gap. By nightfall of December 19 one column of 116th Panzer had reached Houffalize while reconnaissance troops had pushed 10 miles farther to the south-west toward a west branch of the Ourthe river. This joins the east-west main branch at a point west of Houffalize, where the Ourthe makes a turn to the north-west for an eventual swing to the north.

Fortunately for the American cause, the troops forming for the defence of Bastogne had pushed their northern perimeter out as far as the town of Noville, almost half the distance to Houffalize, which left only one road leading west between Noville and Houffalize, that already taken by the 116th Panzer Division. The position at Noville blocked passage of the II Panzer Division.

Fortunately, too, General Middleton had rushed some of his conglomerate reserve – an engineer battalion, an independent tank destroyer battalion, even a Canadian forestry company – to destroy bridges and hold the west branch of the Ourthe. Before tanks of 116th Panzer could cross, the way was barred with outposts and demolished bridges.

Fortunately again, the II and 116th Panzer Divisions belonged to separate corps. Since the 116th had been scheduled to swing north-west after getting across the west branch of the Ourthe, the corps commander deemed he had no choice in the absence of a bridge but to recall his troops to Houffalize and resume his advance along the north bank of the main branch. In the countermarch he would lose 24 critical hours.

The II Panzer Division, meanwhile, battered against the defenders of Noville, finally pushing the Americans aside during the afternoon of December 20. This division belonged to the XLVII Panzer Corps, commanded by General Heinrich Freiherr von Lüttwitz, whose responsibility included Bastogne. Although Lüttwitz was preoccupied with taking the town, he had other troops to do it with, including the Panzer Lehr Division. While these troops probed the Bastogne perimeter, encircling the town in the process, Lüttwitz sent the II Panzer Division pushing on to the west.

That night (the 20th) the division's reconnaissance battalion got across the Ourthe at Ourtheville on a bridge that 116th Panzer had neglected to storm in the belief the Americans would destroy it, as they had all others. Yet the American demolitions unaccountably had failed, and the II Panzer Division got across the Ourthe dryshod.

The Meuse now lay only 23 miles to the west. But for a reason that seemed inexplicable at the time to the little bands of American defenders who still stood in the way, the II Panzer Division came to a halt.

In the north, in the meantime, the decision to send the 82nd Airborne Division skirting the south flank of Peiper's trapped tanks to push up to the Salm river behind the St Vith horseshoe proved to be exceptionally provident. Advancing without opposition, the airborne troops dropped off units along the way to face southward in the direction of Houffalize, thus affording some block should the 116th Panzer Division and accompanying infantry units swing northward. By the morning of the 21st, the rest of the paratroops were in position along the Salm, facing the west, where during the day the Germans were finally to wrest the town of St Vith from the 7th Armoured Division and the mixed units that had held it for over five days.

As nightfall came on December 21, the battle from the American viewpoint still was going badly:
● St Vith and its roads was now open to the Germans, with American withdrawal from the portion of the horseshoe still in their hands inevitable. Peiper was still dangerous, even though trapped;
● The situation on the southern shoulder of the German penetration was still fluid;
● The delaying forces in front of Bastogne were all but destroyed, leaving the lightly armed 101st Airborne Division, encircled in Bastogne, to muster such support as could be salvaged to defend against an entire German corps;
● One German Panzer division was across the Ourthe river 23 miles from the Meuse, another was at Houffalize presumably preparing to resume the trek westward;
● Ever since the start of the German attack on the 16th, fog and low overcast had denied all but the most daring (and usually unproductive) sorties by American fighter-bombers.

Yet, as is so often the case in battle, the other side saw the situation in another light.

As early as the third day, December 18, the German army group commander, Field-Marshal Walter Model, had come to the conclusion that the counteroffensive had fallen short. This may have been merely an initial reaction of surprise and frustration that the opening blows had failed to penetrate the

The price of violating the rules of war...

'Scarface' Skorzeny, Hitler's master commando. His men, dressed in American uniforms, spread chaos and confusion behind the US lines—but those who were caught paid the inevitable price before the firing squads

Südd Verlag

Imperial War Museum

Imperial War Museum

Imperial War Museum

American line as quickly as planned. Yet even Hitler had expressed at least tacit concern by cancelling a projected supporting attack by the XV Army against thinned American lines near Aachen. But that was before the II Panzer Division achieved its spectacular gain across the Ourthe river. So thrilled was the Führer with this development that he afforded Field-Marshal von Rundstedt two divisions from the general reserve to be employed as Rundstedt himself decided.

There were continuing problems on the German side nevertheless. The Americans at the northern corner on the Elsenborn Ridge still held, a rock against which the VI Panzer Army could but batter in vain, restricting Dietrich's armour to two of the four main roads intended for the advance westward, and one of those under heavy American artillery fire. That was why the remainder of the I SS Panzer Division was so slow to follow Peiper's lead, and why Peiper had been trapped. He eventually lost 39 tanks and the rest of his transport and equipment, with only 800 out of an original force of 2,000 men at last infiltrating back to safety.

Nor could Dietrich's other three SS Panzer divisions be brought to bear through this narrow passage: all efforts to do so produced traffic spill-over into the zone of the V Panzer Army around St Vith. At one point Field-Marshal Model personally helped direct traffic near St Vith and came upon General von Manteuffel doing the same thing. So critical was the jam that Field-Marshal von Rundstedt on the 21st ordered two of Dietrich's SS Panzer divisions transferred southward to Manteuffel, whose V Panzer Army henceforth would compose the German main effort. A shift southward of the boundary between the two armies, giving St Vith to Dietrich, was part of the plan.

For all the success of II and 116th Panzer Divisions in bypassing St Vith to the south and streaming westward between St Vith and Bastogne, the failure to capture these two road centres early in the fighting had sharply restricted Manteuffel's dash for the Meuse. And even after General von Lüttwitz's spearheads had drawn up to Bastogne on the 19th, he had been slow to launch a comprehensive attack because thawing roads leading up from the eastern river valleys slowed the arrival of supporting artillery.

Shortages of fuel crimped German operations everywhere, the most drastic shortage hitting II Panzer Division, preventing that front-running force from moving at all on the 21st. The shortages developed partly because the Germans had failed to capture any large American stocks, but also because awesome traffic jams plagued the steep, serpentine, icy roads behind the lines in the Eifel. One of Dietrich's Panzer divisions used up its fuel battering against the Elsenborn Ridge. When on the 21st Rundstedt ordered two of Dietrich's divisions to be transferred to Manteuffel, there would not—for 36 hours—be enough fuel to allow one of the divisions to move.

German commanders also had to keep looking over their left shoulders, for how long would it be before Patton would throw his 3rd Army against the German southern flank? How long, too, before the fog and overcast parted to enable the deadly American fighter-bombers to join the battle?

[*Charles B. MacDonald's biography is in Vol 5, p. 2016.*]

BATTLE OF THE BULGE: THE ALLIED COUNTERBLOW

Ardennes, Belgium, December 22, 1944/January 28, 1945

Charles B. MacDonald

On December 22, the Allies still seemed on the edge of disaster—the Germans were still advancing towards the Meuse, still confidently demanding the surrender of Bastogne. But in reality, despite the disagreements which were rending the Allied command, the worst was over: incredibly stubborn American resistance had sapped the strength of the German drive and soon the US forces would begin their counterattack—unfortunately settling for the 'small solution' of squeezing the Germans out of the Bulge instead of amputating it cleanly. *Below:* American infantrymen advance towards beleaguered Bastogne

No one could have discerned it with any certainty at the time, but the day of December 22, 1944, saw the beginning of the climax of the battle in the Ardennes.

On that day, in a blinding snowstorm, General Patton made good his promise to counterattack. While rushing an infantry division into the line north-east of Luxembourg city to bolster a weakening American position at the southern base of the bulge, he threw another infantry division and the veteran 4th Armoured Division into a drive to break through to encircled Bastogne. The 3rd Army had withdrawn in the face of the enemy and executed a 90° shift in direction of attack with a speed unparalleled in military history.

On that day, too, the Germans surrounding Bastogne tightened their encirclement and delivered a surrender ultimatum, only to be left to ponder the meaning of the reply that came back in American slang: 'Nuts!'

Also on the 22nd, the Germans launched what they hoped would be the last leg on the drive to the Meuse—the II Panzer Division already across the west branch of the river and the 116th Panzer Division driving from Houffalize along the north bank of the main branch with plans to cross the river where it swings north near

Out of the east emerged what weathermen call a 'Russian high', bringing in the wake of the day's heavy snowfall sharply dropping temperatures that froze the ground, allowing tanks—both American and German—to manoeuvre freely, but also bringing weather that allowed aircraft to operate again.

Given the overwhelming Allied superiority in aircraft, the advantage of clear skies rested fully with the Allied side. As December 23 dawned, fighter-bombers and mediums would be out in force, wreaking havoc on German columns that heretofore had enjoyed virtual immunity to punishment from the air. Out in force, too, would be big C-47 transport aircraft, looking like pregnant geese against the sky and dropping multi-hued parachutes bearing critical supplies to the troops in beleaguered Bastogne.

For all the assistance from the air, by mid-day of December 23 a hasty line thrown up by the 84th Division beyond the Ourthe around Marche was in serious trouble. So was the American line between the Salm and the Ourthe, where the II SS Panzer Division attacked alongside the 116th Panzer Division. So devastating were the German strikes against the combat command of the 3rd Armoured Division that contingents of another infantry division ear-

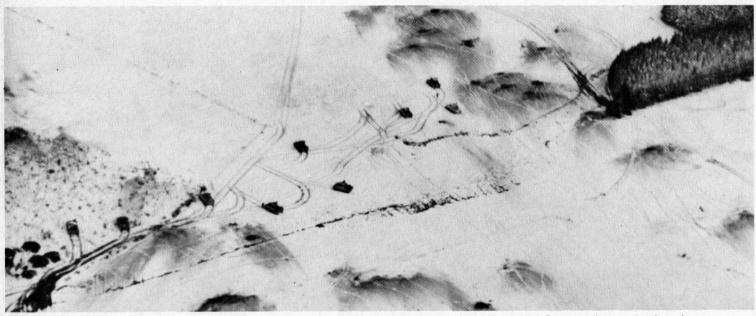

US Army

American armour deploys during a counterblow against the 'Bulge'. Within ten days of the initial German thrust, the American forces were again on the offensive, but their efforts were much hampered by weather conditions like this

Hotton. General von Manteuffel was hoping to reinforce these two divisions, the II Panzer with the Panzer Lehr once the latter could shake loose from Bastogne, the 116th Panzer with the II SS Panzer Division, shifted from Dietrich's army.

Yet the Germans had lost too much time getting through Noville, waiting for fuel beyond the Ourthe, and countermarching to Houffalize to enjoy the same free wheeling they had experienced in earlier days: for the divisions scheduled to 'flesh out' Joe Collins' 7th Corps for counterattack were now arriving. First, a combat command of the 3rd Armoured Division, which Hodges committed astride the Houffalize-Liège highway to extend westward all the way to the Ourthe the southward-facing positions assumed by the 82nd Airborne Division between the Salm and the Ourthe. Second, the 84th Infantry Division, which in assembling behind the Ourthe near the town of Marche would lie full in the projected path of the II Panzer Division, north-westward from Ourtheville toward the Meuse. And before the battle south of the Meuse was over, the other two divisions joining Collins' corps also would enter the fight.

Another move began on the 22nd—American withdrawal from the St Vith horseshoe. Having lost 8,000 out of some 22,000 men, not counting the regiments of the 106th Division that had been trapped on the Schnee Eifel, the defenders of St Vith came back under orders from Montgomery. They were orders laced with the kind of accolade that had long ago endeared the Field-Marshal to the British Tommy: the heroic defenders of St Vith were authorised to withdraw 'with all honour . . . They put up a wonderful show'.

The last of them would make it before daylight on December 23, not to return to some warm, safe haven but to re-enter the line; for by this time the positions of the 82nd Airborne and 3rd Armoured Divisions between the Salm and the Ourthe were under heavy attack.

One final event on the 22nd would have an authoritative impact on the continuing battle. As darkness fell, chill winds began to blow.

marked to join Collins' counterattacking reserve were pulled into this fray, leaving only one division of armour from the counterattacking force still uncommitted. Once the remnants of the St Vith defenders were safely within American lines, Montgomery aided this fight by ordering the 82nd Airborne Division to withdraw from what had become a sharp corner at Vielsalm, along the Salm river west of St Vith.

Crisis there was between the Salm and the Ourthe; but to American commanders the most serious crisis was developing in what represented the tip of the bulge, beyond the Ourthe where the II Panzer Division bounced off the flank of the 84th Division and continued toward the Meuse. Here, by mid-day of the 23rd, the last of the units that Montgomery had hoped to assemble as a reserve, the 2nd Armoured Division, was arriving.

This development was destined to bring to a head a kind of covert contest of wills that since the day Montgomery had assumed command had been running between Montgomery and the commander of the US 1st Army, Courtney Hodges. As demonstrated by Montgomery's early wish to withdraw from St Vith and the Elsenborn Ridge, the British commander believed in a policy of rolling with the punches. The Americans, for their part, shocked at what a presumably defeated German army had done to them, were reluctant sometimes to the point of fault to give up any ground unless forced, particularly ground that American soldiers had bought with blood.

Montgomery's theory was that by holding the most economical line possible in the north and amassing a reserve in the process, he might force the Germans to overextend themselves, whereupon he would strike with Collins' 7th Corps. Montgomery was relatively unconcerned about the Germans reaching or even crossing the Meuse: by this time he had moved a British armoured brigade to cover the critical bridges on either side of the big bend at Namur. Furthermore, even should the Germans cross the Meuse, he had a reserve corps in position to annihilate them.

Possessed of no ready reserve, American commanders could hardly be so sanguine. As late as the 22nd, both Patton and Middleton were still concerned lest the Germans suddenly swing south-west in the direction of Sedan and the site of their triumph in 1940. Remembering 1914 and 1940, Paris had the jitters, and military police were enforcing a strict curfew in the French capital while guarding Eisenhower closely lest Otto Skorzeny's disguised raiders try to assassinate the Supreme Commander. Hodges and the staff of the 1st Army were still unconvinced that the Germans would not turn north to take Liège. Even the British were concerned enough to station guards and erect roadblocks on the outskirts of Brussels.

Having had close personal experience with the power of the German drive, Courtney Hodges remained most concerned of all. That he had been forced, contrary to Montgomery's plan, to keep committing incoming divisions as the Germans continued to work westward seemed to him under the circumstances the only way to run the fight. He saw the tip of Manteuffel's striking force embracing or soon to embrace four Panzer divisions—Panzer Lehr in the south, II Panzer and 116th Panzer in the centre, and II SS Panzer

The 'big' solution—severing the bulge completely—was rejected in favour of the 'small' solution: squeezing it out

1944 December 22: The Germans launch their last attempt to reach the Meuse. US forces withdraw from the St Vith area.
December 25: US 2nd Armoured Division attacks and turns back II Panzer Division 4 miles from the Meuse.
December 26: US 4th Armoured Division relieves Bastogne. Word reaches Hitler that Antwerp can no longer be reached.
December 30: A US attack north-east from Bastogne towards Houffalize is stalemated by a German attack on the corridor to Bastogne.

1945 January 3/4: The last German attack on Bastogne is defeated. The US counterattack begins.
January 8: Hitler authorises withdrawal to Houffalize.
January 16: US 1st and 3rd Armies link up at Houffalize.
January 20: General Patch's withdrawal from the north-eastern sector is complete.
January 22: The weather clears, allowing US pilots to take the air against German convoys.
January 28: The last vestige of the Bulge disappears.

in the north, while to the right of II SS Panzer, Sepp Dietrich was at last bringing his two remaining SS Panzer divisions to bear.

To Hodges, to withhold reserves while forces of such power were still on the move—even in view of radio intercepts indicating that the Germans were running short of fuel—was to flirt with disaster.

Without asking approval, the commander of the 2nd Armoured Division, Major-General Ernest Harmon, sent one of his combat commands southward on December 23 to investigate reports of German tanks passing south of Marche. Yet word came back of no contact except with British armoured patrols already working the area with no sign of the enemy.

Yet, in reality, the II Panzer Division had found free passage south of Marche and was toiling toward the Meuse at Dinant. (The only one of Skorzeny's disguised patrols to reach a Meuse bridge gained Dinant that night but was quickly captured by British guards.) By mid-afternoon of December 24—Christmas Eve—it was all too apparent to General Harmon that German tanks were present a few miles farther south in strength. He put in a call to Collins, his corps commander, for authority to turn the entire 2nd Armoured Division to the attack.

With Collins away from his headquarters, the 7th Corps' staff relayed the request to 1st Army HQ. Courtney Hodges was torn. Although still under Field-Marshal Montgomery's dictum to amass a reserve, and specifically to keep from getting the 2nd Armoured Division involved, Hodges' heart was with Collins and Harmon.

The word that came from Hodges was that Collins was 'authorised' to roll with the punch, to peel back to the north-west; but along with the failure specifically to order withdrawal, Hodges included no proviso denying attack. That was all the licence General Collins needed. That night he and Harmon mapped out an attack to begin early on Christmas Day, employing all of the 2nd Armoured Division.

Collins' decision represented the high-water mark of the German counteroffensive in the Ardennes. In conjunction with contingents

of British armour and American fighter-bombers enjoying another day in the sun, the 2nd Armoured Division on Christmas Day began to wipe out a II Panzer Division that at the height of its achievement had run out of gasoline at the town of Celles—only 4 miles from the Meuse and not quite 60 miles from the start line along the German frontier.

The Germans paid a price of more than 80 tanks. They left not only their spearhead but their ambition broken in the snow.

Bastogne relieved at last
There were two other events on Christmas Day equally disconcerting to the Germans. The first was in the north-west, where the US 3rd Armoured Division with help of infantry reinforcements brought to a halt an all-out attack by the II SS Panzer Division to break through between the Salm and the Ourthe, while on the west bank of the Ourthe other American troops dealt roughly with the 116th Panzer Division.

The second was at Bastogne.

Obsessed with the idea that the II Panzer Division was out on a limb, General von Manteuffel saw Bastogne as a boil that had to

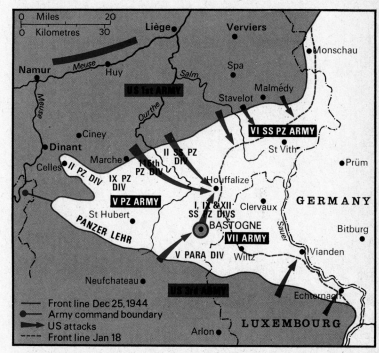

be lanced if the Panzer division were to be reinforced and if the entire German counteroffensive were not to be disrupted by Patton's counterattack. Rather than send the Panzer Lehr Division immediately to II Panzer's assistance, Manteuffel held on to it and ordered an all-out attack by Lüttwitz's XLVII Panzer Corps to be launched on Christmas Day to capture Bastogne. This time Lüttwitz was to hit a previously untested and presumably soft rear—or western—arc of the American perimeter.

Preceded by a heavy air bombardment of Bastogne the night before, the new attack posed such a threat that as the morning dawned many an American paratrooper shook hands with his buddies in a final gesture of salute. The farewells were premature. Before night came, the paratroops of the 101st with their *potpourri* of reinforcements had either held or quickly sealed off every penetration.

The next day, December 26, as dusk descended, an engineer battalion manning a portion of the southern fringe of the perimeter reported the approach of 'three light tanks, believed friendly'.

The 4th Armoured Division had arrived.

The siege was ended.

On this day after Christmas, the word reaching Hitler from Manteuffel, Model, and Rundstedt was that no chance whatever remained of reaching Antwerp. The only hope of salvaging any sort of victory from the Ardennes was to turn the V and VI Panzer Armies north to cross the Meuse west of Liège and come in behind Aachen. This presupposed the capture of Bastogne and a secondary attack from the north to link with the Panzer armies. Yet if these prerequisites were to be met, Hitler would have to abandon a new project he had been contemplating: a second counteroffensive in Alsace.

This was, in effect, a return to what Hitler earlier had labelled the 'Small Solution', a proposal his generals had championed when he first had broached the idea of a counteroffensive in the Ardennes. Deeming German resources too limited for taking Antwerp,

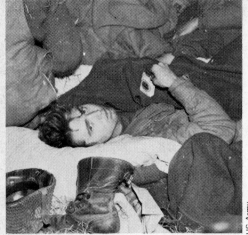
US wounded in makeshift conditions

Bastogne: 'bastion of the battered bastards of the 101st' ...

POWs dig mass graves, also makeshift

A vital communications centre, Bastogne was the key to the Ardennes—and the target of an all-out German attack

they had wanted instead a limited attack to take the American supply base of Liège and cut in behind the 1st and 9th US Armies around Aachen. Hitler long ago had scorned the 'Small Solution'. Again he rejected it.

'We have had unexpected setbacks,' the Führer acknowledged, but that was 'because my plan was not followed to the letter'.

So stretched had the Americans become in Alsace in order to release Patton for counterattack, Hitler believed, that the second counteroffensive he contemplated there would score such gains as to turn Patton away from the Ardennes. Given the code name *Nordwind* ('North Wind'), the counteroffensive was to begin on New Year's Day.

Nor would Hitler accept the contention that Antwerp lay beyond reach. While agreeing that, once Bastogne was captured, the two Panzer armies might turn northward to clear the east and south banks of the Meuse, he saw this as no switch to the 'Small Solu-

tion' but as a temporary diversion to trap the American units that had rushed to the north shoulder of the bulge. This would prepare the way for renewing the drive on Antwerp.

On the Allied side, Bradley on Christmas Day and Eisenhower a few days later urged Field-Marshal Montgomery to turn the 1st Army quickly to the offensive in order to take some of the pressure off Bastogne and Patton's efforts to carve a viable corridor into the town. Montgomery responded that he expected the Germans to hit the 1st Army one more blow; but if that failed to come he would attack on January 3.

Montgomery's reluctance to attack annoyed the American commanders. The British field-marshal, they knew, had an entire corps in reserve. Although neither Bradley, Hodges, nor Patton asked commitment of British troops, they believed that so long as Montgomery had this reserve he need fear no further German thrust.

Another German blow in the north never came, primarily because

2244

POWs: German casualties neared 100,000

. . . and the rock which broke the German offensive

The wrack of the receding German tide

Turret torn off by anti-tank fire, this shattered German tank symbolises the ferocity of the American defence of Bastogne

Patton's troops at Bastogne and on either side of the relief corridor that he opened on the 26th fought the V Panzer Army to a standstill. The battle reached a climax on December 30 when Patton, his forces around Bastogne swollen now to six divisions, tried to resume his attack north-east toward Houffalize. At almost precisely the same moment, General von Manteuffel launched another major attempt to cut the corridor into Bastogne and take the town.

Casualties on both sides mounted, and bitterly cold weather took an inevitable toll; but the American troops held firm, even after the Germans had driven a salient into the east side of the corridor. It was a struggle for survival such as Bastogne had not known even in the critical days of encirclement.

Threat to the 'Colmar Pocket'
As events strode to a climax at Bastogne, a crucible similarly demanding was beginning to develop for troops of the US 7th Army,

commanded by Lieutenant-General Alexander M. Patch, and some of their compatriots in General Jean de Lattre de Tassigny's French 1st Army, which together made up General Devers' 6th Army Group. Undermined by any standards of comparison with Bradley's 12th Army Group or Montgomery's 21st Army Group, Devers' forces had had to stretch already thin lines even thinner to absorb former positions of two of the 3rd Army's corps in order to release Patton for counterattack.

The new arrangement charged General Patch's 7th Army with 124 miles of front, the bulk of it along the German frontier facing the Saar industrial region, 40 miles of it along the Rhine to include the city of Strasbourg. From that point southward General de Lattre's French took over, containing what Allied troops called the 'Colmar Pocket', an expansive German bridgehead on the Rhine's west bank around the town of Colmar, a hold-out position that Devers' undermanned forces had yet been unable to eliminate and one that had posed a constant threat in General Eisenhower's mind ever since the counteroffensive had begun in the Ardennes.

Because General Patch's positions formed a right angle where the Franco-German border meets the Rhine, those American divisions in this extreme north-east corner of France would be threatened by entrapment should the Germans launch converging thrusts against them or should the Germans strike swiftly to deny the few passes through the Vosges Mountains, which stood behind them. Recognising that little of strategic importance lay in this low plain alongside the Rhine, General Eisenhower had told Devers at the meeting in Verdun to yield ground rather than endanger the integrity of his forces.

To withdraw all the way to the Vosges would nevertheless involve giving up Strasbourg, a city which the French looked upon symbolically as the capital of Alsace and Lorraine, the provinces lost to the Germans from 1870 to 1918 and again from 1940 until late 1944. To the French, to abandon Strasbourg was to relinquish a part of the soul of France.

Yet to defend 124 miles of front, including Strasbourg, the 7th Army had only seven divisions, plus the infantry regiments of three new divisions, only recently arrived from the United States in response to Eisenhower's call for assistance at the start of the Ardennes counteroffensive. Also available as a last resort were two divisions that Eisenhower had managed to cull from the line to recreate a Supreme Headquarters reserve; but these might at any time have to be sent into the Ardennes.

That left the stratagem of withdrawal in the event of a major German attack perhaps the only recourse.

That the Germans planned to attack either on New Year's Day or soon thereafter became clear to the 6th Army Group during the last week of December. The attack actually was to begin an hour before the first stroke of the New Year.

The American soldier, victor of Bastogne…

When Hitler had first proposed a counteroffensive in Alsace, the idea had been a heavy strike all the way to the American supply base of Metz, but even Hitler had to accept that this was too ambitious for the available resources. As in the Ardennes, the Führer himself planned the blow actually delivered—Operation *Nordwind*.

Attacking west of the Vosges Mountains, two divisions under the aegis of Army Group G (Generaloberst Johannes Blaskowitz) were to make a penetration, whereupon a reserve of two armoured divisions was to strike swiftly southward to seal from the rear the vital Saverne Gap, which separates the High Vosges in the south from the less imposing Low Vosges in the north. At the same time a supporting effort by three infantry divisions was to push down the spine of the Low Vosges. A few days later, a lone division was to cross the Rhine north of Strasbourg, while two divisions were to attack northward from the Colmar Pocket, link with the Rhine bridgehead (encircling Strasbourg in the process), then swing westward to the Saverne Gap.

The net effect would be to trap all American units east of the Low Vosges, the equivalent of five divisions, and those French troops guarding the northern periphery of the Colmar Pocket.

Sharply conscious of this possibility, General Eisenhower moved swiftly once the German attack began, and ordered General Devers to pull back from his north-eastern salient all the way to the Vosges, leaving only delaying forces on the low-lying plain.

That meant abandoning Strasbourg, a condition that prompted the head of the provisional French government, Charles de Gaulle, to send an emissary to Eisenhower's headquarters to express his dismay. Rather than relinquish the city, the word was, de Gaulle already had ordered General de Lattre to extend his lines north and take over the defence.

Struck by this defiance, Eisenhower's Chief-of-Staff, Lieutenant-General Walter B. Smith, threatened to cut off American supplies and equipment, without which the French army would be powerless —to which de Gaulle's man responded that the French were prepared to withdraw their troops from Eisenhower's command.

Although it sounded like an argument in a schoolyard, it was a serious confrontation. De Gaulle even went so far as to cable the American President and the British Prime Minister for support; but intercession proved unnecessary. When apprised by General Smith of the fervour of de Gaulle's objections and when apprised, too, by the end of the second day (January 2) of the success of Patch's troops in constraining the German main effort toward the Saverne Gap, Eisenhower withdrew the order. While directing the French to take responsibility for defending Strasbourg, he told General Devers to withdraw from the north-eastern salient only as far as the little Moder river, some 20 miles behind the existing lines.

By January 20 this withdrawal was complete. The Germans, meanwhile, had succeeded in establishing a Rhine bridgehead north of Strasbourg, advancing to within 8 miles of the city, and inducing near panic in the civilian population before commitment of a portion of General Eisenhower's reserve brought them to a halt. The attack northward out of the Colmar Pocket got within 13 miles of Strasbourg, but the French stopped it at the last bridge short of the city.

While Devers' 6th Army Group retained its integrity, Strasbourg stayed French. Having committed so much to the Ardennes, the Germans had simply been unequal to a second blow: ten under-

Thick fog and low clouds, combined with high winds, deprived the American armour and infantry of much-needed air support. Here men of the 82nd Airborne Division move through typical Ardennes Forest terrain

US Army

Although both Model and Rundstedt gave their endorsement, Hitler refused. The counteroffensive under the original concept of taking Antwerp and trapping Allied armies, he at last admitted, no longer had any chance of success; but he had arrived at definite ideas of how the bulge in the Ardennes might be turned to German advantage.

In creating the salient, Hitler reasoned, he had forced General Eisenhower to employ almost all his resources. That Eisenhower used élite airborne divisions to do the brutal defensive work of infantry was proof enough of that. By holding the bulge, he might keep the Allies widely stretched while pulling out some German units for spoiling attacks elsewhere—like Operation *Nordwind*. That way he might prevent the Allies from concentrating their forces in the north for a renewed offensive to cross the Rhine and capture the Ruhr industrial region.

Yet even this strategy begged the capture of Bastogne, for Hitler required the town both to anchor the southern flank of the bulge and to deny its nexus of roads to the Americans.

To American troops, Manteuffel's final offensive at Bastogne, aimed at severing the corridor into the town, appeared less a concerted attack than reaction to counterattack to Patton's efforts to drive on to Houffalize. Lasting two days—January 3 and 4—the German offensive delayed the drive on Houffalize; but it was too feeble either to pose any genuine threat to Bastogne or to thwart the American offensive entirely. What was more, it operated on borrowed time, for it opened on the same day that Field-Marshal Montgomery at last released Hodges' 1st Army to attack from the north.

The pattern of the drive to eliminate the bulge had been set at the Allied conference in Verdun on December 19 with the decision to send the 3rd Army to Bastogne. Although Patton insisted, once Bastogne was relieved, on shifting to the classic though venturesome manoeuvre for eliminating a deep penetration—cutting it off

...and of the whole Ardennes campaign

at its base—he found no support from either Hodges or Bradley. They were concerned about the limited roadnet at the northern base and about the effect of winter weather in the more sharply compartmented terrain along the German frontier. Montgomery conformed, moving parts of two British divisions to the tip of the bulge to enable General Collins to shift his 7th Corps slightly northward and drive from the north-west for Houffalize. Once the 1st and 3rd Armies met at Houffalize, both were to sweep, after the manner of synchronized windshield wipers, on to the German frontier.

In other words, they were going to push in the bulge rather than cut it off. It was—Field-Marshal von Rundstedt would observe after the war—the 'Small Solution'.

The nadir of winter

The snow was deeper than ever in the Ardennes, the temperatures lower, the fog thicker, the winds more penetrating when, early on January 3, General Collins sent two armoured divisions backed by infantry south-east toward Houffalize across ground featured by stretches of high marshland, dense patches of firs, and deep-cut streambeds. Only three of Sepp Dietrich's badly damaged divisions barred the way, including fragments of the mauled II Panzer Division. But that was enough, in view of the weather and the terrain, to slow the Allied advance to a crawl.

So murky was the atmosphere that not a single tactical aircraft could support the attack all day, and sorties by little artillery observation aircraft were possible for no more than an hour. It was a pattern that would undergo little change for a fortnight. On only three days would fighter-bombers be able to take to the air at all. Much of the time the men advanced through snow flurries, followed on the fourth day by a heavy snowfall that piled drifts in places to a depth of several feet.

Tanks stalled on icy hillsides in long rows. Trucks towing anti-tank guns or artillery pieces skidded, jack-knifed, collided, and blocked vital roads for hours. Two trucks towing 105-mm howitzers plunged off a cliff. Deliberate roadblocks formed by felled trees with anti-tank mines on the approaches could be eliminated only by

strength divisions were not enough. The fighting in bitter cold and snow nevertheless cost the Americans 15,600 casualties; the Germans, 25,000.

As the 6th Army Group was meeting its test in Alsace, the Germans managed two last spasms in a dying effort in the Ardennes.

One came from the air, an extraordinary effort by the Luftwaffe. Early on New Year's Day, 700 German planes struck at Allied airfields in Belgium and the Netherlands. The blow took Allied airmen by surprise and cost 156 planes, most of them destroyed on the ground.

The second blow again was aimed at Bastogne, where General von Manteuffel had seen his offensive of December 30 collapse in the face of Patton's renewed attack. It was a blow of which Manteuffel himself disapproved. The time had long come, he believed, to abandon all attempts at maintaining the offensive in the Ardennes. Lest the troops in the tip of the bulge be trapped between Patton and what appeared to be a pending attack by the US 1st Army from the north, he appealed to Field-Marshal Model late on January 2 for permission to pull back to a line anchored on Houffalize.

These POWs, promised a quick victory in December, were humbled by defeat and capture in February

dismounted infantry making slow, sometimes costly flanking moves through deep snow. Bridges everywhere were demolished, the sites defended, so that, just as with the roadblocks, winter-weary infantry had to plod upstream or down to find an uncontested ford, then wade the icy stream to take the Germans in flank, finding in most cases that the foe at the last moment pulled back to fight again another day. The Germans occasionally counterattacked: five or six tanks, a company or a battalion of infantry at a time. Under these conditions, to advance 2 miles a day was a major achievement.

The 3rd Army had it as hard and more so, for the defences in the vicinity of Bastogne reflected the large concentration of German forces there for the various efforts to take the town. Bitterly cold, stung by biting winds and driven snow, nostrils frozen, Patton's troops saw little change in a pattern too long familiar. The Germans opposing them were old and dreaded foes—such units as the I, IX, and XII SS Panzer Divisions, the V Parachute, the Panzer Lehr. Accustomed too were the place names, the same towns and villages where little clots of tanks and infantry a fortnight before had thwarted the Germans in the race for Bastogne, although these were less towns and villages now than macabre monuments to the destructiveness of war.

Yet for all the rigour of the fighting, it became apparent on January 5 that the final crisis at Bastogne had passed. When Field-Marshal Model pulled out one of the SS Panzer divisions to go to the aid of the VI Panzer Army in the north, General von Manteuffel took it upon himself to pull another of the SS Panzer divisions from the line to form a reserve. Three days later, on January 8, Hitler himself authorised withdrawal from the tip of the bulge, not all the way back to Houffalize as Manteuffel had asked, but to a line anchored on a series of ridges 5 miles west of Houffalize.

This was the Führer's first grudging admission that the counteroffensive in the Ardennes had failed utterly. Dietrich's VI Panzer Army, he directed, was gradually to relinquish control of all but the SS Panzer divisions to Manteuffel's V Panzer Army, whereupon these four divisions were to assemble in the rear at St Vith. There they were ostensibly to guard against attacks near the base of the bulge: but in reality they were executing the first step in leaving

the Ardennes entirely. As Hitler's advisers in the East had long been warning, a powerful new Russian offensive was destined to begin any day. It would actually start on January 12, and Hitler on January 22 would order the VI Panzer Army to move with all speed to the Eastern Front.

Meanwhile, early on January 16, patrols of the US 1st and 3rd Armies met at Houffalize. Rent apart by the counteroffensive, the two armies had joined hands at the waist of the bulge, failing to trap many of the elusive foe but setting the stage for the return of Hodges' 1st Army to General Bradley's command. This General Eisenhower would order, effective the next day, at the same time retaining Simpson's 9th Army under Montgomery with an eye toward renewing an Allied offensive toward the Ruhr.

It would take another eight days to push in what was left of the bulge in a slow contest against weather and long-proven German ingenuity on the defence. Back to St. Vith, back to Clerf, back to Echternach, back to the Skyline Drive, back to many another spot where American infantrymen, surprised, frightened, but determined, had purchased a commodity called time.

On January 22 the clouds finally cleared dramatically. A brilliant sun came up, its rays dancing on a new snow cover. Pilots were early in the air, jubilant to find German vehicles stalled bumper to bumper waiting their turn to cross ice-encrusted bridges over the Our river into Germany. Astride the Skyline Drive, infantrymen cheered to see the carnage that both air and artillery wrought.

By January 28 the last vestige of the bulge in the Ardennes had disappeared.

The cost of the campaign
Of some 600,000 Americans who fought in the Ardennes—more than participated on both sides at Gettysburg—81,000 were killed, wounded, or captured, and the British incurred 1,400 casualties. The Germans probably lost 100,000 killed, wounded or captured.

Both sides lost heavily in weapons and equipment, probably as many as 800 tanks on each side, and the Germans 1,000 aircraft. Yet the Americans could replace their losses in little more than a fortnight, while the Germans could no longer make theirs good. The Germans nevertheless had managed to extricate almost all

THE GERMAN TANK-SMASHERS

During the Battle of the Bulge, the Americans lost a total of 733 tanks and tank destroyers. Many of these of course fell to German armour, but many also were destroyed by infantry and artillery anti-tank weapons. A good anti-tank weapon needed three essentials: a high muzzle velocity for good penetration, low silhouette for concealment, and accuracy. Here we show two of the most successful German anti-tank guns

PZB 41 (The 'Squeeze' gun): *Bore:* A continuous taper from 28-mm at the breech to 20-mm at the muzzle. *Weight:* 501 lb. *Muzzle velocity:* 4,600 feet per second. *Penetration:* 72-mm of armour at 400 yards, and 49-mm at 800. *Crew:* Two or three. The taper imposed a great strain, but each barrel had a life of 500 rounds

PAK 43: *Bore:* 88-mm. *Weight:* 11,225 lb. *Muzzle velocity:* From 1,968 feet per second to 3,282 depending on ammunition used. *Penetration:* 167-mm of armour at 1,000 yards. *Crew:* Five. This weapon could fire high-explosive as well as armour-piercing rounds. Its total length was 260·23 inches

John Batchelor

that they had taken into the Ardennes except that destroyed in the fighting—a ·combination of weather, the 'Small Solution' of reducing the bulge, and German ingenuity had seen to that.

Not only did the Germans fail to come close to achieving their strategic objective of Antwerp: they fell short even of the interim objective of the Meuse. Although they had failed to wring from General Eisenhower any 'Backs to the Wall' order like that proclaimed by Sir Douglas Haig in 1918, they had provided the American command many an anxious moment. Yet neither Patton, Bradley, Eisenhower, nor even Hodges—once the first brutal impact of what had happened to his command had passed—had displayed any indication but that matters would be settled their way in the end. That the Germans under Hitler's tutelage should act irrationally and come out of their defences into the open would in the long run do nothing to aid their plight.

In deluding himself that the Wehrmacht of 1944 had the power to repeat the performance of 1940, Hitler had accomplished nothing other than to assure swift victory for the new Russian offensive and possibly delay for a few weeks a final offensive by the Allies. Yet in delaying that offensive he probably speeded the final act, for he retained fewer resources with which to oppose it.

The victor in the Ardennes was the American soldier—he who had given his Allies some sharp concern almost two years before at the Kasserine Pass but who had come a long way since that first battle experience in North Africa. Purportedly pampered, lacking in motivation, he had met the test when it came, giving his commanders—for all their Intelligence failure—time to bring their mobility and reserve power into play. Although Allied power would have told in the end in any case, the American soldier in the Ardennes made the outcome a certainty by his valour and determination at the Elsenborn Ridge, St Vith, Echternach, Clerf, Stavelot, Bastogne, Celles, and countless untold places.

Footnote to the battle

One unfortunate footnote to the battle remained. Perhaps as a reflection of a campaign that had begun in the British press to revive the old issue of making Montgomery overall ground commander, the Field-Marshal in a press conference on January 7

indulged in an exaggeration that the record could hardly sustain.

'As soon as I saw what was happening,' he said, 'I took certain steps myself to ensure that if the Germans got to the Meuse they would certainly not get over that river.' He was 'thinking ahead'. When 'the situation began to deteriorate . . . national considerations were thrown overboard' and 'General Eisenhower placed me in command of the whole northern front'. He had, he claimed, 'employed the whole available power of the British Group of Armies', bringing it into play gradually and then finally 'with a bang'. The operation was 'one of the most interesting and tricky I have ever handled'.

While denigration of American commanders was probably far from Montgomery's mind, his remarks had much the same effect, particularly after the Germans broke in on a BBC wavelength to imitate a British broadcast and give a distorted version of Montgomery's remarks. So upset was General Bradley that he told Eisenhower that rather than serve under Montgomery he would ask to be relieved. Patton said that if Bradley went, so would he.

Bradley saw Montgomery's remarks as a reflection on his own ability as a commander, yet Eisenhower had called in Montgomery only because he hesitated to shift Bradley's headquarters from Luxembourg city to a point farther west and because he wanted to ensure the use of British reserves if needed. While those reserves had been conveniently at hand, few of them had been employed, certainly in no such force as Montgomery intimated in saying he had committed 'with a bang' the 'whole available power of the British Group of Armies'. At most, an armoured brigade and parts of two divisions had briefly entered the fight.

That Montgomery had withheld undermanned British units consciously to save them for the coming offensive against the Ruhr was, in the American view, fully justified. But to have withheld them and then boast otherwise was unjustified.

It remained for that splendid orator, Winston Churchill, to heal the wound. In an address before the House of Commons, he paid full tribute to the American soldier and made abundantly clear that the Ardennes was an American battle and one, he believed, that would be regarded as 'an ever famous American victory'. [*For Charles MacDonald's biography, see Vol 5, p. 2016.*]

BATTLE OF THE BULGE: THE LAST GASP

Belgium, December 1944

Peter Elstob

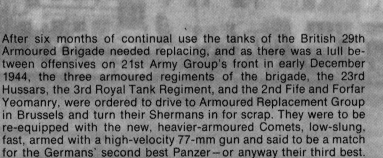

Few of the British troops preparing to celebrate Christmas 1944 in Brussels attached much importance to what seemed like a minor German counteroffensive which the Americans would extinguish quickly. But soon it was realised that the Germans were driving hard for Brussels, and that little stood in their way except one brigade— hastily re-equipped with the tanks it had turned in for scrap. Peter Elstob—whose unit was part of this 'death-or-glory' brigade—describes the skirmish which halted the last desperate German thrust. *Right:* Men of the 5th Bde Guards Armd. Div. watch for German paratroops in a battle-weary Sherman tank rescued from the scrap heap

After six months of continual use the tanks of the British 29th Armoured Brigade needed replacing, and as there was a lull between offensives on 21st Army Group's front in early December 1944, the three armoured regiments of the brigade, the 23rd Hussars, the 3rd Royal Tank Regiment, and the 2nd Fife and Forfar Yeomanry, were ordered to drive to Armoured Replacement Group in Brussels and turn their Shermans in for scrap. They were to be re-equipped with the new, heavier-armoured Comets, low-slung, fast, armed with a high-velocity 77-mm gun and said to be a match for the Germans' second best Panzer—or anyway their third best.

But the Comets had not yet arrived and the tankmen happily went into civilian billets around Ypres and started to make preparations for an unexpected merry Christmas. Leave was generous and two days after coming out of the line many of these men were watching the exciting performance by Errol Flynn as Robin Hood when a V-2, part of the opening of the Ardennes offensive, landed on the cinema. It killed twice as many British servicemen as were going to die in the Battle of the Bulge.

On that same day Field-Marshal Montgomery, having completed plans for his next offensive, the battle of the Rhineland, was playing a round of golf with Dai Rees at the Eindhoven Golf Club. He too was looking forward to Christmas, having got permission from his commanding officer to spend it in England. A message brought out to him on the fairway about the surprise German attack put paid to the golf game and the leave. Within minutes he was flying to his TAC HQ reflecting, among other things, that the only available reserve in 21st Army Group was 30th Corps' 29th Armoured Brigade—and they had no tanks.

No one in the three armoured regiments took much notice of what was happening some 150 miles away on the US 1st Army front. The only information came from two-day-old situation reports and the BBC news, and anyway the Intelligence experts had said so often that the Germans had very little armour left that it seemed that this could only be a local counteroffensive with which the Americans would quickly deal. The important matter of the moment was to get hold of sufficient food and liquor for the coming festivities.

This air of detachment was shattered in the early hours of Wednesday, December 20, by telephone calls to duty officers ordering them to see that their regiments moved immediately to the International Exhibition grounds in Brussels where they were to sort out their old tanks, put back their wireless sets, get the engines running, draw fuel, rations, and ammunition, and move as fast as possible to battle positions along the Meuse. Their task was to 'deny the enemy the river crossings' from Namur southwards for

US Army

about 30 miles, to Givet in France.

The 29th Armoured Brigade's motor battalion, the 8th Rifle Brigade, which had only just pulled out of the mud and cold of the front line in Holland, was sent on ahead and ordered to hold the bridges with its armoured cars and half-tracks until the tanks came up to it. No one knew how far the German armour had advanced and it must be prepared to run into a hostile column coming the other way. As this was in the American zone no one had any maps, so school atlases were in great demand.

A motley collection of defenders

The motor battalion moved through an alarmed and despondent Brussels—by this time the full menace of the great German attack had made itself felt—and, passing through hastily thrown up road blocks manned by a strange collection of rear area troops, arrived at the Meuse about noon the following day. The bridges were being stoutly held by 'R' Force, a scratch collection of sappers and elderly tank men in worn-out Shermans and veteran armoured cars. There was as yet no sign of the advancing German XLVII Panzer Corps.

At that moment its three Panzer divisions were driving hard for this section of the Meuse, the only part of the 90-mile-long German attack line that was still moving westward, and although great American strength was bearing down towards both flanks of this penetration, nothing yet lay between the point and the Meuse. Leading this attack was a battle group of the Wehrmacht's crack II Panzer Division, and as the British reached their battle positions the Panzers forced a crossing of the next river east, the Ourthe, giving them a practically unopposed run to the Meuse bridge at Dinant.

In Dinant the officer commanding G Company of the Rifle Brigade, Major Noel Bell, MC, co-ordinated the existing defences. A large detachment of the US Air Service Corps—officially non-combatants—and a company of American Military Police put themselves at his disposal, and there was a single platoon of American infantry under an enormous sergeant who was grimly determined 'to do a Horatio' on Dinant bridge. There was also a small force of British sappers who had mined the bridge and were standing by their plungers ready to blow it as soon as the Germans appeared in force on the other side.

Finally, the leader of the local resistance, Captain Jacques de Villenfagne, turned up and in those chaotic and suspicious times nearly got himself taken into custody by asking for supplies of hand grenades and offering to lead night patrols of officers—the more senior the better—forward to find the enemy. His *bona fides* were quickly established and for the next four critical days he moved about the woods and fields he knew so well, keeping tabs on the movement and disposition of the German tanks and guns, calling down artillery concentrations and afterwards happily counting dead Germans.

Just as the shortest day of the year was ending the leading squadron of the 3rd Royal Tank Regiment arrived in Dinant. Over-all command passed into the hands of Colonel A. W. Brown, DSO, MC: now the bridge was only to be blown on his personal order. Shortly afterwards the rest of the tanks arrived here—as elsewhere—and by 2000 hours Brigadier R. Harvey, DSO, was able to report to General Horrocks that 29th Armoured Brigade were 'complete on the river line'; the 2nd Fife and Forfar at Namur, the 3rd Royal Tanks at Dinant, and the 23rd Hussars at Givet—about 36 hours after receiving orders 100 miles away. General Horrocks was pleased—although his own reaction to the news of a German army advancing towards Brussels had been to suggest that they were allowed to come on so that he could fight the Battle of Waterloo over again.

Most of Dinant, a small town of narrow streets, is squeezed along the narrow strip of comparatively flat land on the east bank of the Meuse, between the river and steep bluffs. The main approach along which the Germans would come enters Dinant from the south and runs alongside the river—at one point passing through an opening cut out of solid rock. Here a check point was set up and a little further on a necklace of Hawkins mines was placed ready to be pulled quickly across the road should any vehicle refuse to stop. About midnight on December 23 a jeep with US markings crashed through the check point and was blown to bits by the mines, and as the dead occupants wore American great-coats it was feared that one of war's tragic mistakes had been made; but underneath were found SS uniforms—the men were part of Skorzeny's 'Operation Greif'

A 'death or glory' operation

Captured German orders for this offensive had stressed the importance of night fighting, so after the first night, when the defence had been concentrated around the bridge, a squadron moved across the river and one tank was put out to cover each approach road. If the Germans attacked in strength, the bridge would be blown and tanks on the wrong side of the river were to hold up the enemy as long as possible and then to place themselves in such a position as to form a road block when they were knocked out. None was to come back.

This was wryly called a 'death or glory' operation but as is so often the case when the worst is expected, nothing happened during the whole of that first night of waiting. Orders were un-changed for the night of December 23/24 but lack of sleep began to tell—so that when the point of the leading German armoured column, probing forward to test resistance, did advance up a road towards a hull-down Sherman, its exhausted crew was fast asleep. They were awakened by the noise of straining engines and clanking tracks, and in the confusion the startled sergeant tank commander shouted the order to fire. The equally confused gunner hastily aimed at the lead vehicle, but neglected to bring down the range on his sight, so his high-explosive shell hit a truck further down the German column—which was evidently full of ammunition: the resulting explosion set fire to another truck full of fuel—and successfully stopped the advance.

The Sherman's crew, now a little better organised, then methodic-ally worked down the line, destroying a Mark IV, a half-track, and a scout car before a German self-propelled gun, determinedly pushing past the blazing wreckage, opened fire and forced the Sherman back.

Radio crackled busily on both sides. 'Heavy armoured resist-ance', the Germans reported; 'We tore him apart!' was the modest British claim, and it was all a great boost for morale, in addition putting the rest of the tank crews on their toes. Quarter of an hour later, another Mark IV was destroyed on a different approach, followed by the destruction of two Panthers moving along yet another back road. The Germans were now fired at whenever they moved, and British artillery west of the Meuse, firing their mediums at maximum range, did such great damage that the II Panzer Division stopped where they were. They had advanced further than anyone else in Army Group B—some 60 miles in eight days and to within sight of the Meuse (just as they had got within sight of Dunkirk in 1940 *and* of the towers of the Kremlin in 1941)—but once again they were to be disappointed.

Almost another Waterloo

Had II Panzer not been held for two critical days at the very outset of the offensive by the US 28th Infantry Division, and then further delayed by the illogical refusal of the defenders of Bastogne to surrender, they would have reached Dinant earlier and would most certainly have formed a bridgehead through which the rest of XLVII Panzer Corps armour would have poured—and General Horrocks might well have had his Battle of Waterloo. As it was, the delays used up their ration of fuel and they found none to capture; the steam thus went out of their advance, and when they were met by the fire of a few British tanks and guns they most uncharacteristically hesitated for a fatal day: fatal because during that day there moved swiftly down from the north the US 2nd Armoured Division of 14,000 men, 3,000 vehicles, and 390 tanks—about a third as many tanks as the Germans were able to commit in all three armies that launched their offensive.

This mighty force swept from north to south between the thin line of British and the weary Germans, and very soon afterwards cab ranks of Lightnings came over and strafed everything that moved—including C Squadron, Third Royal Tank Regiment, who luckily incurred only one casualty.

The British from the Rifle Brigade and the Tanks had a grand-stand view of this attack. After the aircraft had reduced almost everything to rubble at least 50 American tanks moved slowly forward as though on parade, their machine-guns blazing con-tinuously against absolutely no opposition. 'There's no doubt,' said one of the British tank commanders wistfully, 'that if you've got the ammunition, that's the way to use it.'

The battered II Panzer Division was ordered to escape and, abandoning its vehicles—many were found undamaged but without a drop of petrol in their tanks—made its way back on foot. But not all, for in the area where the point of the German advance was broken it lost 1,100 prisoners and left behind 900 dead. After the battle was over and the fighting had moved on, the indefatigable Captain de Villenfagne 'went carefully over the battle-field. It was a great cemetery of destroyed vehicles and abandoned equipment half-buried in the snow. I counted 840 vehicles including 40 tanks'. It was a humiliating end to an advance that was to change the whole war on the Western Front.

[Peter Elstob's biography is in Vol 5, p. 1848.]

Glum US soldiers fall prisoner to the sudden German onset in December. US casualties in the Ardennes reached 76,890

Cheerful Americans recapture lost ground. By January the tide had turned, and by March the Germans had lost 81,834 men

'All I had to do was to cross the river, capture Brussels, and then go on to take the port of Antwerp. The snow was waist deep and there wasn't room to deploy four tanks abreast, let alone six armoured divisions. It didn't get light till eight and was dark again at four, and my tanks can't fight at night. And all this at Christmas time.'

Gen Sepp Dietrich, VI Panzer Army

'We pulled up along the road with 60 Panthers. Then came the endless convoy driving in two columns, side by side, hub on hub, filled to the brim with American soldiers. And then a concentrated fire from 60 guns and 120 machine-guns. It was a glorious bloodbath, vengeance for our destroyed homeland. The snow must turn red with American blood.'

Lt Rockhammer, a Wehrmacht officer

'If this proposal should be rejected, one German artillery corps and six heavy anti-aircraft battalions are ready to annihilate the US troops in and near Bastogne. All the civilian losses caused by this artillery fire would not correspond with the well-known American humanity.'

Gen von Lüttwitz, XLVII Panzer Corps

'Nuts.'

Brig-Gen McAuliffe

'The Ardennes battle drives home the lesson that a large-scale offensive by massed armour has no hope of success against an enemy who enjoys supreme command of the air. Our precious reserves had been expended, and nothing was available to ward off the impending catastrophe in the East.'

Gen von Mellenthin

It is almost inevitable that, when great soldiers of strong persuasions have to combine in the pursuit of a common objective, they will clash at one point or another—and when national interests supervene, the chances of disruption are redoubled. There can be no doubt that every ingredient of Allied distemper stood ready for injection in the autumn of 1944 and so it is a measure of the strength of the alliance that the internal rupture did not become public until after the Ardennes and only erupted when each general looked to his memoirs after the war.

Field-Marshal Montgomery never readily accepted General Eisenhower's interpretations as co-ordinator of army groups, preferring instead, and somewhat naively, that command should be central, military, and divorced from national politics. Coming late and in haste to the helm, Eisenhower's grip on Montgomery and General Bradley only slowly took hold: command at times seemed actuated more by committee than personality. But by mid-October, with Antwerp still blockaded and the drive deep into Germany quite sterile, plans to establish a new strategy had to be made.

At a meeting in Brussels on October 18 Eisenhower presented his ideas. In essence, he envisaged 12th and 21st Army Groups destroying the enemy west of the Rhine and thereafter developing mobile operations east of the river—with the emphasis on early elimination of the Ruhr, and the centre of gravity of the advance directed through the North German Plain. Turning to his own major commitment within this plan, Montgomery gave Canadian 1st Army the task of planning an offensive south-east from the Nijmegen area between the Rhine and the Maas. Called 'Valediction' at first, it assumed its final name, 'Veritable', at about the same time as Eisenhower's modified post-Ardennes strategy went into effect. With the US 1st and 3rd Armies deeply embroiled in driving the Germans out of the Ardennes salient and intent on projecting that same axis straight into Germany, 12th Army Group automatically shifted its centre of gravity south from the Ruhr, thrusting the capture of the Ruhr and operations across the North German Plain upon 21st Army Group and upon US 9th Army, which remained under Montgomery's command. To all intents and purposes this consigned the decisive battle to 21st Army Group since, although Hitler laid it down that every inch of Germany had to be defended, some parts had to be defended more than others and those acres protecting the Ruhr industrial complex took first priority: any Allied offensive launched here was bound to draw forth every fibre of desperate German resistance.

As finally evolved, Montgomery's execution of the west bank operations was attritional, and could hardly be otherwise. Canadian 1st Army could only introduce Veritable on a narrow front straight against prepared positions that guarded the Ruhr, just where the Allies had come closest: US 9th Army had then to launch Operation 'Grenade' by crossing the Roer river between Hilfarth and Hambach before converging north-east towards Veritable. Everywhere the enemy stood strong, but opposite 9th Army the flood-waters let free through enemy-held Roer dams barred the way and made eastwards movement impossible until the dams could be shut or the contents behind drained off. So, the original idea that US 9th Army should attack two days after

MONTGOMERY'S DRIVE TO THE RHINE

Rhineland, January/March 1945
Major K. J. Macksey

The Allied battle plan to seize the west bank of the Rhine underwent considerable modification, since most of the US forces were still embroiled in driving the Germans out of the Ardennes salient. It fell to Montgomery's 21st Army Group to overcome fanatical German resistance in the last great 'killing match' in the West

Imperial War Museum

Canadian 1st was less than a pious hope and, in fact, both Montgomery and Eisenhower realised and accepted the possibility that the northern attack might have to be sustained for a fortnight before US 9th Army could come to grips in the south. Thus, 21st Army Group would fight with one hand tied behind its back with Canadian 1st Army (comprising, to start with, two Canadian and five British divisions) taking the full brunt of a head-on assault.

The ground chosen for Veritable left no room for manoeuvre, its frontage certain to contract still further as operations progressed when the level of flood-water in the two rivers bounding its flanks rose higher. From Nijmegen to Udem a spine of higher ground, no more than 4 or 5 miles in width, dominated by the great Reichswald forest and interlaced by the partly resuscitated outer fringes of the Siegfried Line, ran between Rhine floods to the north and Maas lowlands to the south (see map). Poor roads converged on narrow but vital route centres while forest rides concealed mud of a tank-proof viscosity—this was certainly not ground fit for the practice of high mobility. Of course, Veritable, as first conceived before the Ardennes, would have taken place on frozen ground in January 1945: but, by February 8, a thaw had set in and flooding covered much of the land.

Vital race for the dams
Before Grenade could start, two territorial features had to be wrested from the Germans—the Roermond triangle in British 2nd Army's and the seven Roer dams in US 1st Army's sector. The former flanked and overlooked Grenade's prospective startline and the latter controlled the level of water which submerged it.

General Ritchie's British 12th Corps tackled the Roermond triangle in conditions of frost alternating with heavy rain on January 15, using two infantry and one armoured divisions, assisted by specialised armour and the usual liberal mass of artillery. Two German divisions waited stolidly behind concrete, wire, and mines—strong enough to exact a stiff penalty but not sufficiently strong to hold out for long. The weight of fire which engulfed them on January 15 did only part of its job, for although the British advanced, it was but slowly and at heavy cost in armour. Mines lay buried everywhere and the heavy ground hampered the flails: the water ways had to be bridged and the AVREs floundered in mud: pillboxes needed the attention of tank gunfire and Crocodile flame, but the German self-propelled guns hid in wait and picked them off. Nevertheless, by January 25, after over a fortnight's unpleasant intensive fighting, the triangle could be declared safe for US 9th Army.

Then General Hodges's US 1st Army started out for the Roer dams again, struggling forward against desperate resistance amongst a maze of mined and booby-trapped forests, snow-filled ravines, and along broken roads. Seven dams holding back 111,000,000 cubic metres of water, backed by thawing snow, had withstood RAF bombing and were now held open by the Germans at just the right volume to overbear the banks of the Roer along US 9th Army's front, with commensurate effects on the level of the Maas downstream by Canadian 1st Army. When, at last, on February 10, Hodges's men took final possession of the last dam, the damage had been done. Veritable was two days old and Grenade would have to wait until the dams had emptied through jammed valves.

On December 1, 1944, there were 68 Allied divisions under General Eisenhower's command, of which 44 were American, eight French, one Polish, and the remaining 15 British and Canadian. General Simpson's US 9th Army was to have 12 divisions concentrated for Grenade, as compared with the seven divisions that could be spared, initially, for British 30th Corps in General Crerar's Canadian 1st Army. The remaining nine divisions (including the Polish 1st Armoured) of 21st Army Group were spread out from Moerdijk to Roermond: any additional offensive operations by this group, therefore, depended upon how exhausting Veritable would turn out, for, if it became prolonged, the only reinforcements that could be provided would be at the expense of General Dempsey's British 2nd Army, north of Roermond: in that event replacements for 2nd Army could only be found by means of US 9th Army re-deploying northwards.

The mind boggles at any attempts to compare the strengths of the opposing sides at this stage of the war. The Allied war effort had reached its peak—in the case of the British (whose infantry strength sank in decline) had passed it—but material flowed from the factories in a torrent so that divisions went into battle lacking nothing, with morale in the ascendent and support from artillery, special devices, and air power of a crushing weight. On the other side of the map line, the plethora of German divisional symbols depicting I Parachute and XV Army represented wildly fluctuating values. For instance, the single German division guarding the Reichswald (the 84th) comprised only 10,000 green troops backed by 100 guns and 36 assault guns. Dug into the front line was 276th 'Stomach' Battalion, selected for its task, in preference to an 'Ear' Battalion, by the divisional commander, because the latter would not have heard 'even the opening barrage of an attack'. Further back, however, stood sterner and healthier troops—VII Parachute Division—and in armoured reserve the XLVII Panzer Corps of two half-depleted divisions, 116th Panzer and XV Panzer Grenadier, mustering barely 90 tanks.

Here in defiance stood the pathetic remnants of the once great German army: chronic illness battalions, tattered armoured formations, fanatic paratroops who were never to jump again: all, in varying degrees, ready to die on the soil of the Fatherland for a cause which had lost sense and clarity: all fighting a pitiful battle of annihilation in desperation against an enemy whose sheer weight nothing could gainsay—not even be assuaged by the dream of secret weapons whose manufacture now withered as Allied air power pounded the sources of supply. From this moment every brick shattered and every life lost levied a senseless libation to Hitler's megalomania. But worse still, the Germans had no idea from whence the attack might come, since no signs of large-scale preparations had been detected near Nijmegen, and Field-Marshal von Rundstedt expected the blow to fall across the Maas north of Roermond. This the Allied deception plan had aimed to achieve: now, at least, strategic surprise had been attained.

'Veritable' rolls forward
Canadian 1st Army's blow dropped from the air during the night of February 8 when

The Meuse, the Maas, the Niers, the Rhine—to the infantryman there seemed to be no end to the rivers to cross . . .

A British sergeant, clutching rifle and spade, staggers ashore after crossing the Niers

Imperial War Museum

heavy bombers struck Cleve and Goch with subsidiary attacks on other route centres. Next, over 1,000 guns in conjunction with the 2nd Tactical Air Force swamped the German field defences; then at 1030 hours three British and one Canadian infantry division grouped within General Horrocks's British 30th Corps, rolled forward at the rate of 300 yards every 12 minutes, beginning one of the most complex and hard-fought battles of the whole North-West Europe campaign.

Key to the first phase after the initial breach of the forward German defences was the high ground called 'the Materborn feature'. With this in the hands of British divisions, a Canadian division could swim in Buffaloes and DUKWs from village to village across the deeply flooded Rhine lowlands around the north of Cleve: simultaneously the Reichswald barrier would be outflanked and operations could be projected past Cleve in the direction of Udem. At first all went well. The front edge of the Siegfried Line succumbed in a welter of fire and churned-up mud and next day Scottish 15th Division, rushing ahead, seized the Materborn feature just a few minutes before elements of VII Parachute Division could get there, and pushed patrols into and beyond Cleve. Behind them the most appalling traffic congestion choked the broken roads and sodden tracks, massive specialised armoured devices becoming jammed together with tanks and infantry, and now solidified by General Horrocks when he prematurely launched 43rd Division through Scottish 15th in an attempt to overwhelm the more open country beyond.

From this moment Veritable lost its impetus. Instead of creating fresh forces on the instance of the breakout in the manner of the Great Captains, Horrocks actually managed to starve Scottish 15th of support. So, while Canadian 3rd Division hopped from village to village along the Rhine, shielded from view to the other bank by a continuous smoke screen, and 51st and 53rd Divisions hacked their way through the Reichswald where assault guns, firing on the defensive down the rides from concealed positions, scored heavily over the British armour wallowing and bogged in the mud. Cleve, deeply cratered and blocked by the bombing, held out and gave the Germans time to rebuild their front and to transform the situation.

Rundstedt recognised on February 10 that Veritable threatened the entire structure of the German front and the Ruhr itself. Already, on the 9th, shortly before the Roer dams fell, the water had poured down the Roer, stalemating the US 9th Army. Now, temporarily safe in the south, the Germans flung troops towards Cleve; VI Parachute Division and XLVII Panzer Corps arriving piecemeal between February 9 and 12—the former to consolidate a line with VII Parachute, the latter to act as an armoured reserve and retake the Materborn feature. But Rundstedt's initial strategic mistake proved fatal: already on the 12th, the 43rd Division was through and breaking out of Cleve, making for Goch and Udem via Bedburg, there to become involved in some of the grimmest fighting of the war. On this escarpment, Veritable was decided.

Still the Reichswald held out, still the glutinous soil bogged the tanks and left the infantry to face it out against a fanatical and skilful enemy who used every trick and a new-found strength in artillery to dispute every yard. Day and night the brawl seethed and flamed until at last the Reichswald was freed on the 16th, permitting 51st Division to stream towards Goch and along the bank of the Maas. On the previous day, the Canadian 3rd Division, relieved of its watery task north of Cleve, took over from the exhausted Scottish 15th Division to struggle towards Calcar in repeated and costly attack and counterattack against a foe who never gave up. This was attrition most bloody, to which Canadian 2nd Division returned on February 19 while, on the German side, elements of 346th Division and Panzer Lehr put in an appearance, crashing into the Canadian infantry along the Calcar road just after its supporting tanks had been withdrawn for the night. Here the battle paused and switched to Goch upon which three British divisions converged on the 20th —finally completing its capture on the 21st to mark the end of Veritable.

Another brutal slogging match
Quite apart from little gems in the art of war, such as 43rd Division's advance from Cleve to Goch, the fighting around the Reichswald had seemed to emulate the worst sequences of the First World War; nor could the simile with Montgomery's Normandy strategy be overlooked as, once again, the British shouldered the brunt of the fighting, and, by so doing, lured the German reserves away from the American front. From sectors all over the Western Front, Veritable drew nine German divisions into it by February 21, with the promise of more to come if US 9th Army could not start Operation Grenade at once. General Simpson knew that, by February 24, the dams would have emptied and the way would be clear to cross the Roer. He also knew that Canadian 1st Army had temporarily shot its bolt: fresh divisions to relieve those exhausted in Veritable were being supplied by British 2nd Army—their place, on the line of the Maas, taken by two of Simpson's 12 divisions. The next major push in the north, Operation 'Blockbuster', could not be mounted until February 26, although subsidiary attacks would continue to expand 30th Corps' holding around Goch. Calculating that the Germans might be caught unawares if he attacked 24 hours before the water level had finally fallen, Simpson ordered his army across the Roer on February 23.

Over 1,000 guns from British 2nd and US 1st, as well as US 9th Army, battered the Germans at 0245 hours that morning and, at 0330 hours, four infantry divisions began to cross the river, delayed almost as much by the turbulent waters as the enemy. Yet the Germans fought hard, hanging on tenaciously to each riverside town and being eliminated only after stiff fighting. First priority for the Americans had to be the construction of as many bridges as possible: then would come a build-up of men and heavy equipment within a steadily expanding bridgehead. At some time counterattacks might have to be smothered, even though most of the German armoured reserve had already been sucked into the maelstrom up north. Finally, a series of jabs should open the way for armour to race for the Rhine to seize a bridge or two if it could.

At the end of the first day's action it became plain for all to see that Veritable had smoothed Grenade's path. Some 28 infantry battalions had crossed, seven tank-bearing bridges were all but ready, no major counterattack had developed, US 9th Army's casu-

THE LAST STAND-UP FIGHT

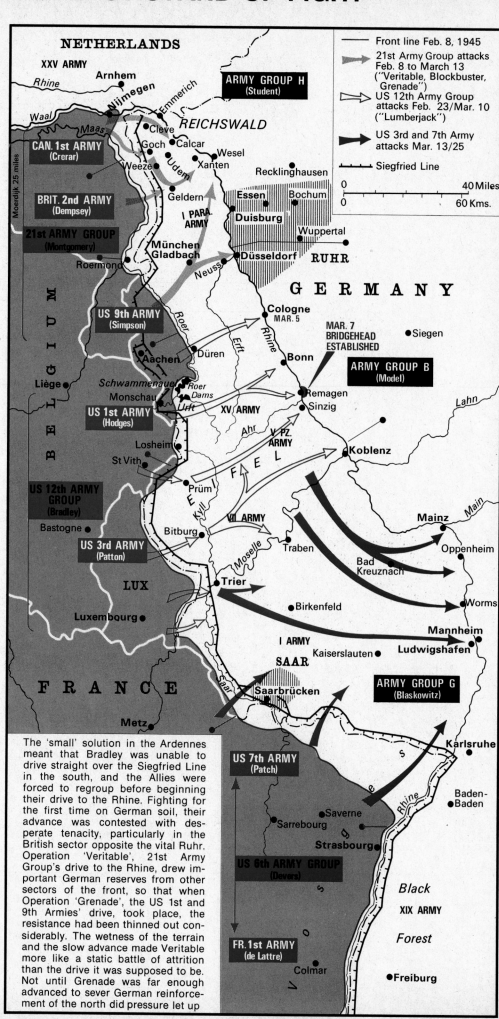

The 'small' solution in the Ardennes meant that Bradley was unable to drive straight over the Siegfried Line in the south, and the Allies were forced to regroup before beginning their drive to the Rhine. Fighting for the first time on German soil, their advance was contested with desperate tenacity, particularly in the British sector opposite the vital Ruhr. Operation 'Veritable', 21st Army Group's drive to the Rhine, drew important German reserves from other sectors of the front, so that when Operation 'Grenade', the US 1st and 9th Armies' drive, took place, the resistance had been thinned out considerably. The wetness of the terrain and the slow advance made Veritable more like a static battle of attrition than the drive it was supposed to be. Not until Grenade was far enough advanced to sever German reinforcement of the north did pressure let up

2256

Using the gatepost as rudimentary cover, the PIAT operator (lying) waits as his comrades dash for cover

A German machine-gun group moves up

Seaforth Highlanders tackle a sniper-ridden house

alties only just topped the thousand mark and only 1,500 of the enemy had been accounted for. From then on the build-up went as smoothly as could be wished, despite repeated raids on the bridges by German aircraft, some of them jet-propelled. Fragmentary German armoured counterattacks cut tentatively into the southern flank but faded away from sheer lack of numbers. Perceptibly, the German defences were cracking and the pace of the American advance increased in response, aimed at München

Gladbach. On the eve of Blockbuster, Grenade's bridgehead spanned a width of 20 miles and 10 in depth, catching in its path enemy units either on their way to fight Canadian 1st Army or from the front immediately opposite US 1st Army.

Ironically, Rundstedt told Hitler on February 25 that he saw no immediate danger of a breakthrough between the Rhine and Maas—his worries turning, instead, with increasing concern towards the American threat along the Moselle; but next day

this opinion blew up in his face. US 9th Army threw all three of its corps into action and began to move 2nd Armoured Division over the Roer—notification of Simpson's confidence that breaking point had been reached, for to commit armour along waterlogged and undermined routes contained a serious element of risk—as Horrocks had discovered in the north. In US 1st Army's sector adjacent to 9th Army, US 3rd Armoured Division showed the way, completing a 10-mile dash from Düren towards Cologne, crushing the remains of XI Panzer Division on the way. And up north Blockbuster fell full blast upon I Parachute Army where it dug in before the Hochwald—the last ditch guarding Rhine bridges at Wesel.

Blockbuster, an attack by Canadian 2nd Corps with two infantry divisions, drove forward at tank pace under the eye of General Simonds—infantry in Kangaroos, led by tanks, with artillery pounding the way ahead in the last hour of darkness. To schedule, but against the usual suicidal opposition, a narrow passage was cleared for Canadian 4th and British 11th Armoured Divisions, allowing the attack to plunge forward through Udem until it came against the sinister loom of the Hochwald. Again the armour ground to a halt, leaving the Canadian infantry to grope forward while 30th Corps began to wheel along the Maas through Weeze, directed on Geldern. By comparison with the Americans, British progress crawled snail-like, as US 2nd Armoured Division entered battle ('. . . a long row of throbbing tanks moving like heavy dark beetles over the green cabbage fields of Germany in a wide swathe'), followed soon after by US 5th and 8th Armoured Divisions bursting the whole front open. Then, at last, Rundstedt turned in despair to Hitler, asking sanction to withdraw and getting it 'with a heavy heart'.

The Rhine is reached

The Germans could hold no longer, try though Hitler might to patch a bridgehead between Wesel and Krefeld. München Gladbach, the largest German town yet to fall, became the property of a single American infantry regiment on March 1 and, a day later, the Canadians broke bloodily through the Hochwald. Some 15 German divisions began to back up against the Rhine, caught in the jaws of the Anglo-American pincer: eight bridges remained to carry their survivors (but equipment was not to be evacuated). There was to be no retreat, said Hitler, who told each bridge commander to delay demolition to the last minute even though he would be shot if the bridge fell intact into enemy hands. In hot pursuit of broken remnants, 9th Army lapped up the miles to the Rhine, reaching Neuss early on the 2nd in the knowledge that one bridge into Düsseldorf at Obercassel still stood.

A *coup de main* had long been planned, sending an armoured column by night, disguised as German and led by German-speaking personnel, to catch the bridge garrison off its guard. Discreetly mixed up with German stragglers, the column drew close to the bridge when a German cyclist recognised his companions for what they were. A quick skirmish, a burst of fire, and then the alarm siren could be heard wailing ahead, the overture to the detonation of the charges. And so it went on, bridge after bridge collapsing to leave a horde of prisoners and mountains of vehicles high and dry on the west bank. Hitler was right when he told Jodl that withdrawal only meant shifting the catastrophe elsewhere—this Simpson could see and turned to Montgomery on March 4 with a plan to bounce across the Rhine there and then, with or without the help of a German bridge.

That it could have been done there is little doubt. What remained of the best of the German army had been trapped or was heavily engaged west of the Rhine, could not be extricated quickly, and might be mopped up at leisure. The defences covering the east

Above: British troops cross the Niers, main obstacle between the Maas and the Rhine

Top right: Stalwart of the British artillery, a 25-pounder supports the drive through Goch

Right: Not all towns were undefended, and costly house-to-house fighting took place in many. In Geilkirchen, last-minute orders before storming a house

Below: Delighted not to have to fight their way through it, smiling British troops occupy Kevelaer

bank were sparse, a central reserve hardly existed and, anyway, the Russian front had first call upon it. Simpson planned at top speed and on March 5 gave his ideas to Montgomery – which is as far as they got. For Montgomery was already well committed to a set-piece crossing of the Rhine with all the trimmings of air support, airborne landings, amphibious craft, and a massed drive north of the Ruhr in the direction of Berlin and the Baltic. To adopt Simpson's plan might catch the administrative build-up at half stretch since major stocks lay behind the Maas river and could not be hauled close to the Rhine until the west flank had been cleared.

So, rather than jeopardise a positive success in three weeks' time, Montgomery withheld permission to extemporise a crossing. In two days the Americans were to do just that at Remagen and get involved in severe and costly fighting – with long-term effects of its own. But by this time it really did not matter how or where the Rhine was crossed: bigger political issues were beginning to arise against which the battle plans and ambitions of individual generals palled. Germany lay wide open to the conquerors as a result of the victory on the west bank of the Rhine – he who moved fastest and furthest once the crossing came would acquire most political power. Thus, until March 10, the 21st Army Group went on with frontal attacks, chopping down the obstinate I Parachute Army crammed into the Wesel pocket.

From March 6, at which moment the Germans decided they must, at last, evacuate by the 10th, a slowly contracting triangle built up in front of Wesel where the German forces came under only sporadic air attack, since bad weather restricted flying and much traffic got across to the east. Hold though they could in the close defensive country between the Hochwald and Xanten, to do so in the more open country to the south, with US 9th Army pounding up, was impossible. British infantry and armour swung south of the Hochwald and pivoted north in step with the Americans curling up by Geldern – the latter beginning to understand from the ferocity of the resistance just what had held back and inflicted such grievous casualties on Canadian 1st Army.

The end came on the 10th when both bridges at Wesel crashed into the river leaving a few rearguards and stragglers to be mopped up on the wrong side in company with a mass of abandoned equipment. True to his military orientation, Field-Marshal Montgomery rated the German decision to fight on the west bank as one of their major blunders, and combined losses of 90,000 Germans on 21st Army Group's front go some way – militarily – to substantiate this claim.

However, putting aside the truism that Germany should have sought peace not later than the Ardennes failure, there can be no doubt that the Ruhr had to be preserved to the bitter end – it would have been a far worse political and economic mistake to have fought from within the area instead of in front of it.

In victory, the price in casualties paid by the 21st Army Group amounted to 22,934 of which 7,300 were American, 5,304 Canadian, and 10,330 British. It marked the last great stand-up fight between the Allies and the Germans: the Germans had been worsted by numbers but not in tenacity and outright desperate courage.

As the US 1st and 3rd Armies wiped out the last of the bulge the Germans had created in US lines with their winter counteroffensive in the Ardennes, the commander of the 12th Army Group, Lieutenant-General Omar N. Bradley, was sharply mindful that the focus of Allied attack soon was to shift from his command. The Supreme Allied Commander, General Dwight D. Eisenhower, had already made clear his intent to return to the strategy he had been pursuing when the Germans had launched their surprise assault.

This was a main effort in the north aimed at the Ruhr industrial region.

Because of the realignment imposed on American troops by the German counteroffensive, this meant a main effort invested in Field-Marshal Bernard L. Montgomery's 21st Army Group. It meant too that Bradley's armies would have to give up divisions to flesh out Lieutenant-General William H. Simpson's US 9th Army. Although Eisenhower had returned the US 1st Army to Bradley following temporary assignment to Montgomery during the Ardennes fighting, he had left the 9th Army with Montgomery to participate in the drive for the Ruhr, in which Bradley's 12th Army Group was scheduled for only a support role.

For several reasons, Bradley and his two army commanders, Courtney Hodges of the 1st Army and George Patton of the 3rd, were anxious to avoid relinquishing divisions to Montgomery. In the first place, they hoped to push on beyond the Ardennes to the Rhine, capitalising on the momentum generated in erasing the bulge and hopefully catching the Germans off balance. They also wanted to by-pass the Roer river dams near Monschau in order to forego another gruelling battle, like those fought the preceding fall, for dams that in German hands might be used to manipulate the waters of the Roer and deny a crossing of the river downstream in the sector of the 9th Army near Aachen.

There was, too, the understandable human reaction of an American command that had incurred a reverse wanting to take a leading part in any new offensive.

Even though Bradley's armies faced inhospitable terrain in the Eifel—the region contiguous to the Ardennes that has the same dense fir forests, limited road network, and mountain-like configuration—much could be said for Bradley's approach. While contemplating a main effort in the north, General Eisenhower was still promoting what had become known as a 'broad front strategy', which in current terms meant an advance generally all along the front as far as the Rhine before sending the main effort across the river to seize the Ruhr. If Bradley could penetrate swiftly through the Eifel against a retreating enemy that already was shifting troops northward in anticipation of renewed attack by Montgomery, he might early gain the Rhine and possibly unhinge the enemy in front of Montgomery.

It was on this thesis that the Supreme Commander afforded Bradley a chance in the Eifel, but it was an approval hedged with stringent qualifications. Nothing short of a quick, decisive penetration of the enemy's frontier fortifications, the Siegfried Line, and swift exploitation was to spare Bradley from shifting divisions northward to the 9th Army and assuming a supporting role.

Since the German VI Panzer Army, which had formed the steel heart of the counter-

BRADLEY'S DRIVE TO THE RHINE

Rhineland, January/March 1945

Charles B. MacDonald

As the Ardennes fighting ended, Bradley's 12th Army Group tried to swing east and jump the Rhine. The attempt failed and Bradley had to wait until the British in the north unhinged the German flank. Then, immediately, the Americans were rewarded with the capture of an intact bridge

US Army

offensive, was moving to the Eastern Front, defence of the Eifel rested with the V Panzer Army and the VII Army, both badly mauled in the Ardennes. Because nobody on the German side expected a major American offensive through the Eifel, the V Panzer Army was pulling out to move north to oppose the US 9th Army, while the VII Army and a neighbour to the north, the XV Army, split between them responsibility for the Eifel.

As Bradley hoped, this posed an ideal situation for exploiting the momentum of the attack erasing the Ardennes bulge. Yet that was reckoning without the deep snow and bitter cold that gripped the front. It was reckoning too without the inroads that the six-week fight to contain and eliminate the bulge had made on Bradley's divisions.

Under the circumstances, there was precious little momentum left.

For five days, from January 28 to February 1, two corps of Hodges' 1st Army and one of Patton's 3rd tried to penetrate the frontier defences north-east of St Vith astride the Losheim Gap, which had served the Germans well in 1914, 1940, and again the preceding December as a débouché in the opposite direction. Yet even when the enemy was nowhere in evidence, as was sometimes the case, progress was slow. Infantrymen had to plough through snow piled in places in waist-high drifts, while tanks, artillery pieces, and trucks coagulated on icy roads in traffic jams that took hours to disentangle. By February 1 the American divisions had done little more than draw up to the first pillboxes of the Siegfried Line.

That looked depressingly little like breakthrough, so that on that day the Damocles sword that had hung over the offensive from the start fell with a clatter. Eisenhower ordered Bradley to halt and begin shifting seven divisions to the 9th Army. Although he afforded a few day's grace for securing the shoulders of the Losheim Gap for subsequent operations, the 1st Army was to move immediately to seize the Roer dams and then prepare to jump the Roer nearby to protect the right flank of the 9th Army in Montgomery's drive to the Rhine. Eisenhower also authorised Patton to nibble at the Eifel as resources permitted to gain a line of departure that might be useful once Montgomery had reached the Rhine.

Blessed from the first with little more than ambition, Bradley's attempt to swing the main effort to the Eifel had ground to a predictable halt. The main effort was to shift now to the north where on February 8 the Canadian 1st Army was to attack southeast between the Maas and the Rhine (Operation Veritable), followed a day later by a north-eastward attack by Simpson's 9th Army across the Roer (Operation Grenade).

Eliminating the Colmar Pocket

A swift penetration of the Eifel having failed, the American forces faced two other assignments in addition to taking the Roer dams before they could turn full attention to a drive to the Rhine. They had to clear the Germans from a triangle embracing some 100 square miles between the Saar and Moselle rivers south of their confluence near Trier, a triangle protected along its base by a spur of the Siegfried Line that the Germans called the 'Orscholz Switch'. They also had to eliminate an expansive bridgehead, measuring 30 by 50 miles, that the Germans still maintained on the west bank of the Rhine south of Strasbourg around the town of Colmar, a bridgehead known to

Allied troops as the 'Colmar Pocket'.

Eliminating the Colmar Pocket was essential to General Eisenhower's plan to build an economical line along the Rhine before jumping the river. It was the responsibility of Lieutenant-General Jacob L. Devers' 6th Army Group, composed of the 1st French and 7th US Armies.

In the final weeks of January an American division and five French divisions of General Jean de Lattre de Tassigny's French 1st Army had begun probing the pocket; then on the 29th a corps with one French and four American divisions loaned from the adjacent 7th Army joined the attack. With the French advancing from the south, the Americans from the north, the Allied forces linked up to split the pocket on February 5; but by this time Field-Marshal Gerd von Rundstedt had at last wrung from Hitler permission to pull the XIX Army back across the Rhine. At a cost to French and Americans of 18,000 casualties and to the Germans probably double that number, the west bank of the Rhine south of Strasbourg was by February 9 at last free of Germans.

Eliminating the little Saar-Moselle triangle involved no such numbers; but in the cruel winter weather of late January and early February, it was a grim enough task for those involved in it. Before getting on with the job, the American 94th Division had first to defeat a spoiling attack launched by the XI Panzer Division during the third week of January. For the next three weeks the Americans staged limited objective attacks to eliminate the pillboxes of the Orscholz Switch, then on the 19th executed an all-out attack. Three days later armoured reinforcements erased the last Germans from the triangle.

In the meantime, the eyes of almost every Allied commander on the Western Front had been focused on another one-division attack, this one designed finally to secure the two dams on the headwaters of the Roer river near Monschau that for months had plagued the American command.

The upstream dam, the Urft, fell quickly into American hands, a fact explained later when engineers discovered that the Germans already had destroyed discharge valves on a viaduct carrying waters of the Urft reservoir to a point downstream from the other dam, the Schwammenauel. Against the downstream dam, an American division began to attack on February 5; but such strength did the defending German division gain from pillboxes of the Siegfried Line, from dense woods, and from roller-coaster terrain that February 9, the target date for the 9th Army's attack across the Roer, arrived with the Germans still in control of the dam.

A long-lasting flood

When at midnight American engineers at last reached the dam, they found that the Germans had blown the discharge valves. The demolitions released no great cascade of water but a steady flow calculated to create a long-lasting flood in the valley of the Roer downstream in front of the 9th Army.

As the 9th Army waited impotently for the waters of the Roer to recede, the Germans were free to turn all their reserves—however meagre—against the Canadian 1st Army's Operation Veritable. It would be the early hours of February 23, almost a fortnight after the original target date, before the 9th Army would dare to chal-

'Quick decisive penetration' was what Bradley wanted. But his forces were worn down by the Battle of the Bulge, and impetus was lost . . .

American troops advance through an already devastated village

lenge the swollen Roer.

The role drawn by General Hodges' 1st Army in assisting Operation Grenade was to send the 7th Corps under Major-General J. Lawton Collins across the Roer close on the 9th Army's southern flank to see the 9th Army safely to the little Erft river, midway between the Roer and the Rhine. Although only a supporting attack, it proved to be the toughest assignment in the opening blow of Operation Grenade.

Collins' two leading divisions launched their assault before Düren, an oft-bombed town located where the Roer tumbles out of a gorge piercing the Eifel highlands to emerge on the Rhine plain. Here the river was a veritable torrent, tossing assault boats around like chips of wood and stopping engineers from putting in infantry and vehicular bridges. Because the foothills of the Eifel afforded vantage points for German observers, mortar and artillery fire on the crossing sites was distressingly accurate. The 7th Corps got across but at a cost of 66 killed, two-thirds as many as were lost in the entire 9th Army. Yet even this figure was low for an assault across such an obstacle as the rampaging Roer and against a position the enemy had had long months to prepare.

As the 9th Army broke out swiftly from its bridgeheads to turn north-east to link with the Canadians along the Rhine, only Collins' 7th Corps remained pointed toward the objective at which the Germans at first believed Operation Grenade to be aimed, the Rhine city of Cologne. Thus the Germans focused their only reserve of two Panzer divisions against Collins' troops; but so depleted were the German divisions that they proved no match for Collins' own armour. By nightfall of February 27, four days after crossing the Roer, the 7th Corps gained a bridgehead over the Erft.

With the 7th Corps predictably about to be assigned a further mission of seeing the 9th Army the rest of the way to the Rhine, General Hodges had already begun to get the rest of his 1st Army across the Roer. Rather than stage other assault crossings, Hodges evolved a plan whereby one division after another would use the bridges of the adjacent division, then shift south to create other bridging sites. In this way the divisions of the 3rd Corps (Major-General John Millikin) were across the river with dry feet by the last day of February and were building up alongside the 7th Corps, while the units of a third corps were getting ready to repeat the process.

All this was part of a new plan devised by General Bradley to carry his 12th Army Group to the Rhine. Called Operation Lumberjack, the plan anticipated the 7th Corps protecting the 9th Army all the way to the Rhine, then turning to take Cologne and heading south along the Rhine. As Collins turned south, other contingents of the 1st Army were to drive beyond the Erft southeast towards the confluence of the little Ahr river with the Rhine at the town of Sinzig, there to converge with a thrust by Patton's 3rd Army through the Eifel to create a pocket of trapped Germans in the northern reaches of the Eifel.

Despite having relinquished units to flesh out the 9th Army, Bradley's army group still was a powerful force. Hodges' 1st Army had 12 divisions (as many as had the 9th Army), while Patton had ten. What was more, Patton all through February had been taking advantage of General Eisenhower's having authorised his nibbling at the Germans in the Eifel to achieve considerable gains. Against what the enemy's XV and VII Armies could muster once the V Panzer Army had pulled out for the north, Patton had seized the two main road centres in the western Eifel—Prüm and Bitburg—and had driven beyond Bitburg to the Kyll river, almost 20 miles inside the German frontier. By constantly inveigling Eisenhower for assistance, Patton also had obtained an armoured division to exploit the victory in the Saar-Moselle triangle and take Trier.

The Germans wait helplessly
By the first of March, the Germans confronting both the 1st and 3rd Armies could do little but await the obviously pending American blow. In the north, the north wing of the XV Army already had been shattered by the advance of Collins' 7th Corps. In the south, Patton's probing attacks had done the same to the main body of the VII Army. A strike by Patton across the Kyll might trap the two corps forming the centre and south wing of the XV Army and finish off the VII Army, thereby dealing a death blow to Field-Marshal Walther Model's Army Group B. In pushing through the Eifel, the US 3rd Army would also be clearing the north bank of the Moselle river, which would imperil the rear of the German I Army, forming the north wing of Army Group G in defence of the Saar industrial region to the south.

To German commanders, it was obvious that the length of time they might hold depended entirely on how soon the Americans struck. As the VII Army's commander, General Hans Felber, saw it, the only hope for his army and Army Group G's I Army was to give Patton free path to the Rhine, withdrawing the VII Army behind the Moselle to protect the I Army's rear. Yet in view of continuing orders from Hitler to stand fast, nobody took Felber's proposal seriously. The only change was to transfer the faltering VII Army from Army Group B to Army Group G, which accomplished nothing more than to shift from one headquarters to another the dolorous task of presiding over the VII Army's impending agony.

Without pause at the Erft, General Collins' 7th Corps on February 28 began the US 1st Army's drive to the Rhine. On March 3, as a combat command of armour gained the river north of Cologne, Collins turned the rest of his corps against the cathedral city. Despite last-ditch defence from anti-aircraft guns turned against American tanks and from a smattering of Volksturm, a levy of ineffective old men and youths Hitler had ordered to rally to a final defence of the Reich, Collins' armour broke into Cologne on March 5 and plunged swiftly to the Rhine past a cathedral still miraculously standing amid acres of bomb-blasted rubble.

In the meantime, General Millikin's 3rd Corps had completed pushing out its bridgehead over the Roer and on March 2 had begun to exploit against crumbling German defences. Despite orders from Bradley through Hodges that the goal of the 3rd Corps was not the Rhine but crossings of the Ahr river to link with the 3rd Army, Millikin and his divisional commanders still saw the fabled Rhine as the objective. Under Millikin's plan, the 3rd Corps was to direct the main effort against the Rhine on either side of Bonn with only one column of an armoured division—the 9th—directed toward the Ahr.

This emphasis on the Rhine around Bonn coincided with expectations of the German army group commander, Field-Marshal Model. He made valiant but generally futile efforts to reinforce defences of the city. His subordinate, General Gustav von Zangen, commanding the XV Army, saw it another way. By driving to the Erft, Zangen might note, the 3rd Corps had entered what the terrain described as the cup of a funnel, whose spout led south-east to the Ahr and thence to the Rhine at Sinzig and the nearby Rhine town of Remagen.

The town of Remagen was important because of the location there of the Ludendorff railroad bridge, which was being covered with a plank flooring to provide a vital supply artery—and escape route—for the XV Army. To block the spout of the funnel leading to Remagen, Zangen begged permission to withdraw the two corps forming his centre and south wing; for even if those corps managed to hold their Siegfried Line positions, they soon would be trapped by the converging 1st and 3rd Army drives.

Yet Model said no. Not a single pillbox of the Siegfried Line, Hitler had decreed, was to be abandoned without a fight.

To Zangen and any other German commander on the scene, probably including Model himself, the absurdity of further attempts to hold west of the Rhine was all too apparent. Yet in view of the stranglehold the word of Hitler still exercised at every level of command, nobody would authorise withdrawal. At division, at corps, at army, at army group, and even at the level of Rundstedt, commanders focused their General Staff-trained minds on issuing defence, assembly, and counterattack orders that looked as pretty as a war game on paper but made no sense in the grim reality of the situation in the Eifel and along the Rhine. In the process, each protested to his next higher commander the idiocy of it all.

Patton unleashes his armour
The long-anticipated hammer blow by Patton's 3rd Army came on March 3 as Major-General Troy Middleton's 8th Corps struck eastward from Prüm and Major-General Manton Eddy's 12th Corps jumped the Kyll east of Bitburg. Because the Germans before Prüm had had several weeks to dig in, the 8th Corps found the going slow. Not so at the Kyll, where the 5th Infantry Division, veteran of many a river crossing, sent patrols across in pre-dawn darkness, then hurriedly threw in foot bridges. The only question remaining was when General Patton might choose to turn loose his veteran 4th Armoured Division.

Patton and his subordinate commanders had only one concern: weather. Days of alternating snow and rain, freeze and thaw had wreaked havoc with the generally poor roads of the Eifel, and continued precipitation could severely cramp a plan for the armour to stick to the roads and leave the wooded ridges to be neutralised by artillery and by fighter-bombers of the 19th Tactical Air Command. Yet in view of an obviously faltering German defence, weather alone was hardly sufficient reason to delay the exploitation.

At daylight on March 5 the armour began to move, cutting first to the north to trap German units still holding along the Kyll, then swinging north-east toward the Rhine. Although rain, snow flurries, and overcast denied air support, the attack quickly picked

Four hours after this photograph was taken, the Ludendorff bridge collapsed under the weight of men and material rushed on to it by US 12th Army Group

2262

up speed, so that reports back to the division headquarters soon began to read like a railroad timetable. By nightfall the armour was 12 miles beyond the Kyll.

This first day did the Germans in. Despite another day of fog and rain on the 6th, again denying support from the air, the tanks raced forward almost at will, clearing the enemy from little more than the roads and shoulders but prompting the Germans to stream from the hills, woods, and villages in great bunches to surrender. At one point a German corps commander saw so many German soldiers clustered about a group of tanks that he assumed it was a German unit. Too late he discovered that the tanks were American. In a matter of minutes he was part of the growing bag of prisoners.

The advance on the 6th carried the 4th Armoured Division another 13 miles to a position half the distance from the Kyll to the Rhine. The next day armour of the 8th Corps also broke loose, but the big news remained in the achievements of the 4th Armoured Division. Despite crumbling roads and another day of rain and fog, the advance became little more than a road march with the tankers signalling German soldiers rearward to be taken prisoner by those who followed. The coming of night saw the armour coiling on the reverse slope of the last high ground short of the Rhine.

In just over two and a half days the 4th Armoured Division had driven 44 miles as the crow flies — much longer by road — taking 5,000 prisoners, capturing or destroying volumes of equipment, and spreading havoc through whatever cohesion still remained in the German defence west of the Rhine and north of the Moselle. Everywhere irregular columns of foot troops interspersed with a confusion of motor and horse-drawn vehicles toiled toward the Rhine, hoping to find a barge, a ferry, or a bridge still standing.

Even more spectacular results

Incredibly, in view of these accomplishments, the drive by the 1st Army's 9th Armoured Division had in the meantime produced even more spectacular results.

As the 1st Army's 3rd Corps approached the Rhine, General Hodges acted to remove any doubt that General Millikin's goal was not the Rhine but crossings over the Ahr to link with the 3rd Army. That prompted the 9th Armoured Division's commander, Major-General John Leonard, to put the bulk of his division driving down the spout of the funnel toward the Ahr, yet it still left one small tank infantry task force heading for the Rhine at Remagen.

The Germans could not so readily resolve their differences over how to defend against the multiple American thrusts. Indeed, as Allied columns all along the line poured toward the Rhine, order and efficiency had little part in German preparations to hold the historic moat guarding their homeland. Nowhere was this more apparent than at Remagen where a small miscellany of troops operated under a variety of commands. A junior army officer commanded all army troops in the vicinity, but an engineer officer was separately in charge of the railroad bridge. A Luftwaffe officer commanded an anti-aircraft detachment, while men of the Volkssturm were responsible to officials of the Nazi Party.

The command situation at Remagen was destined for even further complications. To hold a bridgehead around Bonn and Remagen, Field-Marshal Model set up a separate command responsible directly to Zangen's XV Army. The commander was just becoming familiar with the diverse command complex along the Rhine when Model pulled him out to take the place of the captured corps commander in the VII Army. The general who took his place had little time to check on the situation because he became involved in a dispute with a local commander at Bonn as to just who was in command of the city.

When the XV Army commander, General von Zangen, learned of the shift in command, he entertained new fears lest the Americans capture the bridge at Remagen. He ordered the corps commander in whose sector Remagen fell to send an officer to the town to check personally on the situation.

Before daylight on March 7, the corps adjutant, Major Hans Scheller, headed under blackout conditions over roads jammed with retreating troops for Remagen. It was an hour before noon on the 7th when Scheller reached the railroad bridge, in no time, as events developed, to enable him to get a real grasp of the situation. Sounds of battle already could be heard from the hills to the west.

The American troops heading toward the Rhine had, for their part, no specific plans for taking a bridge intact across the river. Although the possibility intrigued their commanders all the way up to Eisenhower, so remote was the chance that the methodical Germans would neglect to demolish a bridge that nobody entertained any genuine expectations.

That made it all the more astounding when an hour after midday on March 7, Second-Lieutenant Emmet J. Burrows, commanding the leading infantry platoon with a tank/infantry task force of the 9th Armoured Division, emerged from the woods on a bluff overlooking Remagen to see below him German troops streaming in retreat toward a railroad bridge on the southern fringe of the town. Incredibly, the bridge still stood.

Lieutenant Burrows quickly called his company commander, Lieutenant Karl Timmerman, to the scene. As excited by the discovery as was his platoon leader, Timmerman called forward his task force commander, who ordered Timmerman to start moving with his infantry cross-country to seize the bridge. When the commander of Combat Command B, Brigadier-General William M. Hoge, reached the bluff, he confirmed the order and directed a platoon of tanks to plunge downhill to help.

Lieutenant Timmerman, his infantrymen, and the platoon of tanks neared the bridge in mid-afternoon. As they approached, a volcano of rocks, dirt, and noise erupted. Although for a moment Timmerman thought this meant the end of the bridge, it was instead a charge placed on the western approach designed to deny the bridge to tanks.

On the east bank, meanwhile, confusion was rife. The engineer commander whose responsibility it was to demolish the bridge spent 15 minutes on his face, knocked unconscious from the blast of an exploding shell. Even when he came to, he had to await a specific order from Major Scheller before turning the key to set off the prepared demolitions. That order at last received, he turned the key. Nothing happened. He turned ed it again and yet a third time. Still no response.

When the engineer commander called for

a volunteer to do the job by hand, a sergeant responded. Crouching to avoid shells and bullets, he dashed on to the bridge, ignited a stretch of primer cord, then raced back to safety.

Seemingly endless moments passed before the anxious Germans heard at last a booming roar. Timbers flew into the air and the bridge lifted as if to rise from its foundations.

Yet when the noise and smoke cleared, the bridge still stood.

'We've got a bridge'

At the west end of the bridge, Timmerman and his men were as surprised as the Germans when the explosion failed to demolish the bridge. Although Timmerman could see as the dust cleared that big holes had been torn in the planking over the railroad tracks, footpaths on either side of the tracks were intact. His orders were to take the bridge. Calling for his platoon leaders, he signalled attack.

Bobbing and weaving, dashing from one metal girder to another, the men made their way on to the bridge. Machine-gun fire from stone towers at the east end splattered about them, but fire from the tanks on the Remagen side quickly silenced most of the German guns. Close behind the riflemen came engineers, cutting every wire they thought might lead to additional demolitions and shooting apart heavy cables with their carbines.

In a matter of minutes Timmerman and his men gained the far end of the bridge, fanned out to capture cowering German soldiers hiding in a railroad tunnel, then began to climb a precipitous cliff commanding the countryside.

Back on the west bank, American command reaction to the *coup* was swift, despite the orders to concentrate not on the Rhine but on crossing the Ahr. The 9th Armoured Division's commander, General Leonard, supported General Hoge's reaction and rushed reinforcements to the bridge. When the news reached General Hodges at headquarters of the 1st Army, he ordered engineers to hurry to Remagen even before reporting the news to General Bradley. The 12th Army Group commander was in turn equally stirred. 'Shove everything you can across it,' he told Hodges.

General Eisenhower, too, reacted with enthusiasm. While recognising that the terrain on the east bank opposite Remagen afforded little promise for exploitation, he told Bradley to put at least five divisions in the bridgehead immediately. What they would do with the bridgehead could be decided later.

So swift was American reaction to capture of the bridge and so confused and depleted were the German forces falling back across the Rhine that German chances of dislodging the foothold beyond the Rhine were from the start almost nonexistent. Hitler himself reacted with febrile intensity, relieving Field-Marshal von Rundstedt, putting in his place as Commander-in-Chief in the West Field-Marshal Albert Kesselring, brought up from supreme command in Italy, and for the unfortunate local commanders at Remagen, ordering mock trials and swift executions. Yet these acts did little to set the situation right again.

As the first excitement over seizing the bridge passed, General Eisenhower decided to stick with his plan of a main effort across the Rhine north of the Ruhr with Field-Marshal Montgomery's 21st Army Group, while using the Remagen bridgehead as a magnet to draw German forces from other sectors. In keeping with this plan, the 1st Army made no effort to break out of the bridgehead. The men fought merely to defeat German counterattacks and gradually to expand the holding to a depth from which eventually a breakout might be made southeastward to tie in with an anticipated Rhine crossing by the 3rd Army.

Seldom were the counterattacks in strength, for with such desperation did German commanders view the presence of American troops over the Rhine that they threw in units piecemeal as they reached the scene. Although the fighting was fierce enough for the American troops involved, never was the integrity of the bridgehead genuinely threatened.

One more highly dramatic event remained. It happened on March 17 during a period of relative quiet, with no German aircraft about and German artillery silent. About 200 American engineers with heavy equipment were working on the bridge.

First came a sharp report like the crack of a rifle. Then another. The deck of the bridge began to tremble, then to sway as if moved by an earthquake. With a grinding roar of twisting, tearing steel, the Ludendorff railroad bridge slipped, sagged, and with a convulsive twist plunged into the Rhine, carrying 28 US engineers to their deaths.

Bombings dating from as far back as 1940, the weight of the heavy planking to make the bridge serviceable for vehicles, fire of American tanks on the day the bridge was taken, the German demolitions, the drumbeat of hundreds of infantry feet and the heavy tread of vehicles, the pounding of German artillery and near misses by German bombs — all these, plus the weight of the heavy engineer equipment, produced the

US Army

△ US combat engineers catch their first glimpse of the Rhine. Preparations for crossing are in hand

◁ US troops embus for battle. Mud like this followed the bitter cold of early winter

▷ A German infantryman hugs the ground as shells burst. Hastily contrived defences were unable to delay the American advance

▽ Like a range day at home. US infantry fire across the Rhine at retreating Germans

US Army

Bibliothek für Zeitgeschichte

Imperial eagles still erect, but with flagstaff bare, the battle-scarred gate of Fort Blücher falls to American troops as they reach the Rhine

US Army

cumulative effect that wrote an end to the Ludendorff bridge. As to why the German demolitions had failed, the answer plunged into the Rhine with the bridge itself.

The loss of the bridge had no effect on operations in the bridgehead. For several days before the bridge collapsed, it had been closed for repairs, leaving to tactical pontoon bridges the task of handling the flow of traffic to and fro across the Rhine.

For all the speed of the American thrusts to the Rhine, the bag of prisoners was a little disappointing—probably about 35,000. Many another German made his way ahead of or through the thin armoured spearheads across the Rhine or south across the Moselle. Yet those Germans who escaped did so in disarray, unit integrity in most cases gone, and left behind them small mountains of equipment, ammunition, weapons, vehicles.

That meant, as General Felber had warned when anticipating the demise of his VII Army, that the rear of Army Group G's I Army in the Saar would be virtually undefended. This was a situation hardly calculated to escape the practised eye of a George Patton. His 4th Armoured Division had scarcely reached the Rhine before Patton was entreating Bradley and Eisenhower to let him turn swiftly southward across the

Moselle to trap the I Army in the pillboxes of the Siegfried Line in front of the US 7th Army.

No German commander could have been unaware of the threat. Unless reinforcement could be provided for the remnants of the VII Army along the Moselle, warned Generaloberst Paul Hausser, commanding Army Group G, 'envelopment and annihilation of I Army will be imminent'.

Yet the word came back from the top—hold in place.

That set the stage for the kind of driving, slashing attack that Patton lived for. While Lieutenant-General Alexander M. Patch's 7th Army, with a contingent of General de Lattre's French 1st Army close along the Rhine, assaulted the Siegfried Line, pinning the German I Army in place, Patton turned his 3rd Army across the Moselle. Although Patch's 7th Army was involved in shifting divisions and bringing up supplies that would delay attack until March 15, Patton insisted on going ahead on his own.

A driving, slashing attack

On March 12 Patton sent a corps eastward from Trier to attract any available German reserve. Signs of a disintegrating German defence already were apparent in front of

this corps when on the 14th Manton Eddy's 12th Corps jumped the lower Moselle not far from the Rhine. That posed an obvious threat to cut off the entire I Army by a drive southward down the west bank of the Rhine. By the 16th the threat was distressingly and personally real to the German VII Army commander, General Felber, forced by American fighter-bombers into an afternoon of hiding with his Chief-of-Staff in a forest while hostile armoured columns rolled by. On the same day a third corps of the 3rd Army entered the fight, jumping the Moselle between the 12th Corps and Trier against rapidly disintegrating resistance.

Stiffened by the pillboxes of the Siegfried Line, the German I Army still was making a fight of it against the US 7th Army, yet how long the I Army might hold depended less on American pressure against the front of the pillboxes than the rear. While spring weather afforded free rein to American fighter-bombers, the trace of Patton's columns soon looked, in the words of his colleague, Courtney Hodges of the 1st Army, 'like an intestinal tract'.

While Army Group G's General Hausser did what he could to rush in divisions from the near defunct XIX Army, only recently relieved from the Colmar Pocket, he appeal-

The tall chimneys of the factories that had fed Germany's war machine for six years—in sight at last

ed time after time to the new Commander-in-Chief in the West, Field-Marshal Kesselring, for authority to pull back across the Rhine. Still restricted by Hitler's long-standing and oft-repeated injunction against any voluntary withdrawal, Kesselring on March 17 issued an ambiguous order. While directing 'the retention of present positions', he added that 'encirclement and with it the annihilation of the main body of the troops' was to be avoided.

That was, in Hausser's mind, no authority for wholesale withdrawal, but it was enough to justify pulling out the most seriously threatened troops. Division by division he began to peel them back from the western-most positions of the Siegfried Line.

By this time Patton's columns were rampaging far and wide, often overrunning the boundary between the 3rd and 7th Armies before a new one could be negotiated. As American armoured columns appeared without warning, seemingly over every hill and around every curve, and as American air-craft staged a circus in the sky, hardly any semblance of organisation remained in German ranks. It became less withdrawal than *sauve qui peut*.

Still denied authority to withdraw behind the sacred Rhine, German commanders nevertheless continued to build up new lines and to shift units, but mainly on paper. Yet somehow, here and there, they managed to impose some delays, however brief. On March 20 even the Luftwaffe came out of hiding to stage some 300 sorties, though to small avail. That same day word came' at last for what was left of Felber's VII Army to pull back across the Rhine, while remnants of the I Army were reduced to trying to hold little enclaves around the west ends of three remaining bridges over the Rhine, increasingly wary lest they set the scene for another Remagen.

This way the Germans denied a formal linking of the US 3rd and 7th Armies until the 22nd. Approval finally came to withdraw across the Rhine the next day, the 23rd, by which time most Germans that were going to make it already had done so, with or without orders. By nightfall of the 24th only stragglers remained on the west bank.

Just how many Germans escaped from the Saar to fight another day, or how much equipment they managed to take with them, would never be determined. Yet the losses obviously were severe. In prisoners alone the 3rd and 7th Armies eliminated close to 100,000 Germans.

What was more important, the west bank of the Rhine from the Channel to the Swiss frontier now was free of the foe; and while there might be no repetition of Remagen, that was hardly necessary in light of other ways, already demonstrated, of how the Allies might cross the Rhine.

[*For Charles MacDonald's biography, see Vol 5, p. 2016.*]

1945 **January 25:** British 12th Corps completes the capture of the Roermond triangle.
February 1: US 3rd Army reaches the Siegfried Line.
February 8: Canadian 1st Army begins Operation 'Veritable'.
February 9: US 6th Army completes the elimination of the Colmar Pocket.
February 10: US 1st Army captures the Roer dams, but too late to prevent flooding.
February 23: Operation 'Grenade' begins: US 9th Army seizes a bridgehead across the Roer.
March 1: US troops capture München Gladbach.
March 5: US 7th Corps captures Cologne.
March 10: 21st Army Group completes clearance of its part of the west bank of the Rhine.
March 7: Units of 3rd Corps (US 1st Army) capture the Rhine bridge at Remagen.
March 14: US 3rd Army crosses the lower Moselle to cut behind the Siegfried Line.
March 24: 12th Army completes clearance of the west bank of the Rhine.

On this bitter, bleak Dutch day of February 1945, as I sit huddled in my draughty observation tower scanning across the river through my field glasses for signs of German movement, it is the Rhine that is in the news, that involves all the speculative energy of the strategists.

Moerdijk is a little village on the Maas, where the river widens and goes to meet the sea. To be exact, it overlooks the waters known as the Hollandsch Diep (as renowned among wild-fowlers as the Pripet marshes), where the opposite bank is all of 2,000 yards distant.

You will probably not find more than a line or two about Moerdijk in most guide-books, although perhaps the industrious Karl Baedeker has noted that it is near the main road from Breda to Dordrecht and Rotterdam; and with his usual thoroughness it is more than likely that he has something to say about the bridge over the Hollandsch Diep near here, the number of its arches, their span, and with what aptitude they fit their task. Actually there are two bridges, not one, as the railway also crosses the Maas, close to the road. They were memorably captured by German parachutists and gliders in 1940 with the aid of Fifth Columnists. Both of them are fine jobs of engineering, but they were very thoroughly demolished by the Germans when they had to retreat last November.

I imagine that in peacetime Moerdijk was a sleepy, contented, and insignificant village just like many others on the banks of the Maas. The people were simple and honest and kindhearted, and worked hard to wrest their living from the unforgiving land. Possibly there was a small fishing-fleet. There were not many shops in Moerdijk, but enough to supply necessities and simple luxuries. You could easily buy Persil and Van Nelle's coffee and tea, Dobbelman's tobacco to fill your pipe and Silvikrin for your hair. There was no cinema in Moerdijk, and the sanitation was a little primitive, to say no more. But there was a school, and a church, and a convent; at least it appears to have been a convent, but a mere mass of rubble and charred beams and a few religious images lying broken in the dust do not volunteer much information. Anyway, Moerdijk had a life of its own, and a happy, well-ordered little community.

There are no people left in Moerdijk now. They have all gone, taking with them as many of their worldly goods as they could, if they were lucky enough to have any left. There are also no houses left in Moerdijk; intact, I mean. I walked through the village this afternoon to see if I could find one, just one house that was not in ruins. I could not.

I do not know what happened to Moerdijk. It appears to have been bombed and shelled, and then the fires did the rest. Possibly our Typhoons had a go at it. There is a German self-propelled 75-mm gun in the main street (I nearly left out the word 'main', but that would not be entirely true), and a small 20-mm ack-ack gun opposite the convent. Obviously they did not last long. Other than those, and the grave of one of the German ack-ack gunners, a rough affair with four empty shell-cases to mark the corners, the usual scrap of paper in a bottle, and two pieces of packing-case nailed together to make a rough cross, there is nothing left of the German occupation of Moerdijk.

A score or so Germans were captured

THE SPARROW AND THE TYPEWRITER

Holland, February 1945

Not all the Allied troops were caught up in the massive operation to cross the Rhine. For many of them the war had become a cold and tedious business of holding the flanks far from the main action. Here Richard Brett-Smith describes the life and feelings of one such unit marooned in a small Dutch village during the bleak winter of 1944/45

near the bridges; I like to think that their comrades panicked and blew up their escape-route too soon, as I believe indeed happened. The abandoned ones must have been considerably annoyed, especially as they had boasted to the people of Moerdijk about what they were going to do to the Tommies in the future.

There is something not of this world about Moerdijk. To describe it as eerie, or deathly, or horrible, or ghostly—each of these words is apt, yet each falls short. I am reminded of the many villages in Normandy that Moerdijk so resembles. In Holland, thank heaven, Moerdijk is the exception, not the rule. Anyone who has passed through the wrecked and charred villages of Normandy will remember how strangely they were affected—most of all, I think, by that vivid, peculiar, unforgettable smell of death, not merely a figure of speech but a grim reality, acrid, roasted, and bitterly sweet.

The only live things left in Moerdijk besides a few soldiers are the cats—rangy, furtive animals, who will suddenly streak across the street from one ruin to another—and of course the birds, sparrows and pigeons and, on the neighbouring *polders,* mallard, teal, and coot. But even the birds are quiet here; I have been in Moerdijk three days now, and surely spring is coming, but I have heard no bird sing.

You cannot help noticing the absolute shamelessness of war in this place. The havoc it brings is tempered by no reticence or pity, but rather made the more flamboyant by its grotesqueness. In a house

which is otherwise reduced to a heap of rubble and charred wood one wall stands still intact, and inside it there are a fireplace, a radiator, a mirror and a cheap print of the Crucifixion, all hanging on untouched. The plaster figures of Jesus and the Virgin Mary that you will find in every poor Dutch home now rub shoulders with a strange company—smashed pots of home-made jam, empty beer bottles, brass bedsteads, garish pieces of curtain, and in one case a rusty Spandau machine-gun.

Everywhere are dust, broken glass, chipped bricks, ashes, clothes of all kinds, and bedding, sodden with rain and strewn at random about the houses and gardens. Cupboard doors have been wrenched open, old letters and picture-postcards scattered in all directions. Here you see a piano upended in a front garden, riddled with bullet holes, there an old Ford two-seater lurching lopsided on its rims in a blackened garage, its tyres reduced to a heap of grey ashes. No home is too humble to have been exposed to the world in all its shame, no secret too intimate to have been ripped open in savage fury. What the natural devastation of war failed to achieve in Moerdijk, German looters completed in cold hatred before they left.

On the ground floor of the convent, of all places, I see five or six charred typewriters; resting on one of them where he has fallen is a dead sparrow. Somehow that seems symbolic—the work of man, and the work of nature: and neither has escaped. Behind me in the garden of the convent, surrounded by jagged tin cans that once contained bully beef, stew, or powdered milk, and by all sorts of rubbish, stands a grave, grey figure, the statue of St Francis of Assisi, his eyes staring unseeingly, his hand raised in benediction. It is perhaps as well that he cannot see what is around him; especially the sparrow on the typewriter.

From the top of this tallest building in Moerdijk (to attain which is a tricky, but perfectly feasible climb, for there are disconcerting gaps in the staircase and even more disturbing hiatuses in the flanking wall) you can see the whole deserted village in panorama. It is like turning a corner and coming unexpectedly upon a funeral. You feel an embarrassed intruder.

In this observation point my soldiers have somehow found a place to keep them dry and warm, although even the veterans admit that it is more than difficult. Hence we can see, on a fine day, the conspicuous church of Dordrecht (or is it perhaps a cathedral?), once the richest city in the Netherlands, and all the villages, spires, and windmills in between. Today on the far bank of the Hollandsch Diep the red and grey-roofed cottages stand out boldly, and the long black lines of the dykes are clear. I can see German pillboxes, and now and then a few soldiers walking about in the sun; once this afternoon a hand-cart came up to one of the houses, bringing the rations. It is too far for small-arms fire to be of any use, and shelling does not do much good. They go to ground after the first shot.

The other side of the river looks a lot pleasanter and healthier than Moerdijk; in fact rather like a peaceful country scene such as van Ruysdael or Hobbema might have painted. Here there are undertones of the Brueghels if not of Hieronymus Bosch. Today the Germans feel safe across the river. It will not always be so.

LUZON

Philippine Islands, January/June 1945

Stanley L. Falk

THE GREATEST BATTLE

If Iwo Jima was the bloodiest battle of the Pacific war, the campaign on Luzon was the largest. It dwarfed the 1941/42 fight for Luzon, and all Pacific battles that followed. Only on Luzon could men and material fight battles on a scale anywhere near those which took place in the Desert and Europe. More Japanese troops fought on Luzon than on any other Pacific island, and more American troops were committed here than in *any* American campaign except the drive through northern France. In the Pacific, only a full-scale invasion of Japan itself could have eclipsed the size or scope of the battle for Luzon

The Japanese defeat at Leyte in the autumn of 1944 opened the way for American reconquest of the rest of the Philippines. But strong, numerous, and determined Japanese forces still held the main island of Luzon, and their destruction or defeat was essential if the entire archipelago was to be liberated. For a while, American planners had considered by-passing Luzon in favour of a direct invasion of Formosa. By October 1944, however, the American Joint Chiefs-of-Staff had decided to recapture Luzon. The stubborn Japanese defence of Leyte forced a delay in this decision, but by the end of November General MacArthur was able to fix the target date for the assault on Luzon as January 9, 1945.

The American organisation for the invasion of Luzon was similar to that employed against Leyte. Ground operations were again the responsibility of General Walter Krueger's 6th Army: well over 200,000 troops, with tens of thousands more available for reinforcement. The 6th Army's mission was to land at Lingayen Gulf, drive south into the central plain to secure the tactical heart of the island, and then seize Manila. Vice-Admiral Thomas C. Kinkaid's 7th Fleet—more than 850 combat, transport, and support ships—was charged once more, as at Leyte, with putting Krueger ashore and providing initial protection and support. The powerful carrier task forces of Admiral William F. Halsey's 3rd Fleet would offer strategic cover by hitting Formosa and northern Luzon while General George F. Kenney's Far East Air Forces would strike at Luzon from Leyte and Mindoro and then stage forward to Luzon as soon as suitable bases were available.

To meet the American assault, General Tomoyuki Yamashita had more than 250,000 men of the XIV Area Army on Luzon. This was a sizeable force, including a large number of recently-arrived reinforcements. But Yamashita's troops were poorly organised, led, and deployed. Most units were under strength and short of food, ammunition, vehicles, and fuel. There was no longer any Japanese fleet to shield them, and only about 150 combat aircraft were still operational on Luzon. The overall command organization was somewhat better, however, than it had been during the Leyte campaign: Yamashita for the first time controlled all army forces in the Philippines, and his superior, Field-Marshal Count Hisaichi Terauchi, had transferred his Southern Army headquarters to Indo-China and could no longer look at operations over Yamashita's shoulder.

Yet there still remained an important naval headquarters in Manila, along with a large body of naval troops, and these elements were not under Yamashita's command—a situation that was to cause considerable difficulty for both sides during the subsequent battle.

Landing at Lingayen expected

It was clear to Yamashita that, despite his numerical strength, he could not give battle to the Americans on equal terms, and that he could not successfully defend all of Luzon. He expected MacArthur to land at Lingayen Gulf—where the Japanese themselves had made their main assault three years earlier—but he did not deceive himself with the notion that he could thwart this landing. Nor, in the face of superior American air strength, firepower, and manoeuvrability, could he oppose MacArthur in open combat. The best he could hope to do would be to delay the conquest of Luzon as long as possible, to tie down as many American combat formations as he could, and thus slow the inevitable Allied advance on the Japanese home islands.

The XIV Area Army commander therefore made no plans to hold the central plains and Manila. This area, the primary objective of Krueger's forces, would be all but undefended while Yamashita's troops would concentrate on securing three mountain strongholds. The first of these was the vast rugged wilderness of northern Luzon, including the fertile Cagayen Valley, to which Yamashita would withdraw with the bulk of his army. The second largest Japanese force would defend the rough heights east of Manila, site of the dams and reservoirs that controlled the capital city's water supply. The third and smallest force would hold the mountainous area west of the central plains, protecting the Clark Field complex and threatening Krueger's right flank as he moved south. In these redoubts, the Japanese would make their last stand. With determination and fortitude, Yamashita believed, they could hold off the Americans for months or even years.

The combat formations of the US 7th Fleet began leaving Leyte Gulf for Lingayen on January 2, 1945. Commanded by Vice-Admiral Jesse B. Oldendorf—who had crossed the Japanese 'T' at Surigao Strait in October 1944—this force of battleships, escort carriers, minesweepers, and other support vessels had the task of clearing the shore approaches and bombarding Japanese defences before the invasion. In the event, however, their most important role seems to have been to attract the bulk of Japanese *Kamikaze* attacks, absorbing their sting which otherwise would have hit the more vulnerable transports and supply ships.

The first blow struck Oldendorf on the 4th, catching him in the Sulu Sea, west of Panay. A two-engined Japanese bomber slipped through the American combat air patrol, crash-dived into the flight deck of the escort carrier *Ommaney Bay,* and so badly damaged her that she had to be sunk. The next afternoon, off Manila Bay, no less than 16 suicide planes broke through. Nearly a dozen Allied vessels, including HMAS *Arunta* and *Australia,* suffered hits or near misses, some quite serious.

The attacks reached a crescendo on January 6, as the American force entered Lingayen Gulf. From just before noon until dusk, Japanese pilots struck again and again. in vicious, punishing *Kamikaze* assaults. Despite heavy losses to themselves, the suicide planes managed to crash into nearly a score of vessels, some of which had been hit on the 4th as well. Two battleships were badly hurt, a minesweeper was sunk, and cruisers, destroyers, and other ships also took heavy damage and casualties. In three days, the *Kamikazes* had killed and wounded more than 1,000 Americans and Australians, and seriously injured a disconcerting number of ships.

Despite the severity of the Japanese air attacks, they could not prevent the pre-invasion bombardment of the Lingayen beaches. This got under way as scheduled, for the fact of the matter was that the Japanese had few planes left to throw against Oldendorf. For several days now, Halsey's 3rd Fleet carrier pilots had been hitting fields on Formosa and Luzon, cutting off any Japanese aerial reinforcement of the Philippines and destroying most of the Japanese planes still available. In response to a special request from Kinkaid, Halsey made a particularly heavy strike on Luzon on January 7. So effective was this blow that the Japanese decided to move whatever aircraft they had left out of the Philippines. After the 7th, only a few individual Japanese planes ventured forth against the invaders. The *Kamikaze* threat continued for another week, but organised air opposition had ended.

An unopposed US landing

Nor was there any opposition to the 6th Army's landing. The convoys of assault troops entered Lingayen Gulf early on the morning of the 9th. Their approach through the central Philippines had not been unopposed and a number of ships had been hit by *Kamikazes*, yet these sporadic attacks had failed to slow the passage of the force. At 0930 hours, just on schedule, the first assault waves hit the southern Lingayen beaches. The landing took place under cover of a heavy and sustained air and naval gunfire bombardment—which, in fact, was entirely unnecessary. The Japanese, with no intention of opposing the landing, had wisely evacuated the beach area.

Terrain thus proved more of a problem than the Japanese. No sooner had the invaders rushed across the open beaches than they encountered a series of flooded rice fields, fish ponds, marshes, and streams. But the Japanese had made no attempt to defend these obstacles, beyond the obvious tactic of destroying bridges, and Krueger's troops crossed the water barriers easily on amphibious tractors. They received only occasional, scattered artillery fire and encountered very few Japanese soldiers. By the night of January 9, some 68,000 men of the 6th Army and a great quantity of supplies had come ashore, forming a beach-head 17 miles wide and as deep, in some places, as 4 miles. General MacArthur, as he had at Leyte, had also landed on the first day of the operation, splashing triumphantly to the beach through the warm Lingayen surf.

The American reaction to the lack of Japanese opposition was as much one of surprise as of gratification. But as the advance continued against only light resistance in the next few days, this surprise gradually turned into suspicion that the Japanese might be laying a deep and dangerous trap. The 6th Army's deployment was therefore a slow and careful one. As Japanese resistance gradually increased, however, it became clear that the greatest threat to the beach-head lay on the left or north-east flank. Major-General Oscar W. Griswold's 14th Corps was advancing slowly but easily on the right.

But on the left, Major-General Innis P. Swift's 1st Corps was beginning to push up against the northernmost of General Yamashita's three defensive areas. The Japanese here were in a good position to sweep down on Krueger's flank and, if successful, sever what might easily prove to be an overextended and vulnerable 6th Army line of communications. Even if this remained only a threat, the danger to the supply base at Lingayen could not be overlooked, for until the Manila Bay area could be captured, it would be the only American supply facility on Luzon. It was imperative, then, that General Swift drive back and defeat the Japanese on his left front in order to safeguard the way for the 6th Army's drive south to Manila. **2272** ▷

Part of the invasion fleet in position in Lingayen Gulf; an air-sea rescue flying-boat patrol keeps watch

On the last lap, heading in to the Lingayen beaches on the morning of January 9

US Coast Guard

Massive descent on the Filipino heartland

'Looking through the gunsight' as a rocket-firing landing-craft bombards the preliminary target of Mindoro

A helpless victim of US air power. In Manila Bay, a Japanese heavy cruiser is bracketed by exploding bombs

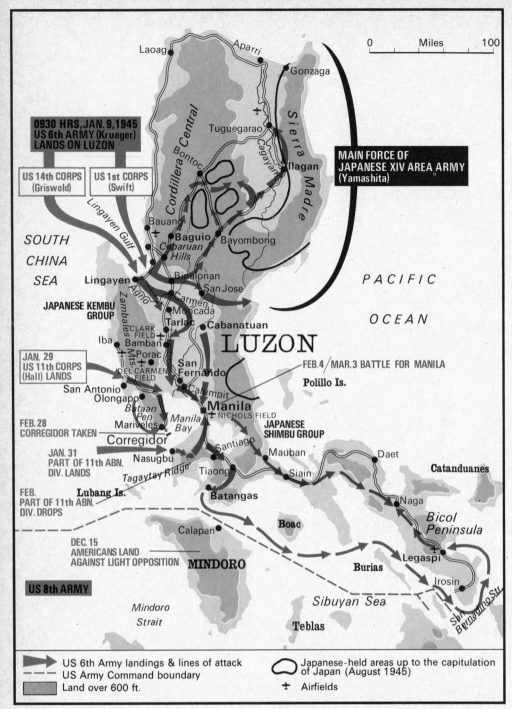

0 Miles 100

0930 HRS, JAN. 9, 1945
US 6th ARMY (Krueger)
LANDS ON LUZON

US 14th CORPS (Griswold)	US 1st CORPS (Swift)

Laoag
Aparri
Gonzaga
Tuguegarao
Bontoc
Cordillera Central
Sierra Madre
Cagayan
Ilagan
Bauang
Baguio
Cabaruan Hills
Bayombong
MAIN FORCE OF JAPANESE XIV AREA ARMY (Yamashita)

SOUTH CHINA SEA

Lingayen Gulf
Lingayen
Binalonan
San Jose
Agno
Zambales
Carmen
Moncada
JAPANESE KEMBU GROUP
CLARK FIELD
Tarlac
Cabanatuan
Iba
Bamban
Porac
DEL CARMEN FIELD
San Fernando

PACIFIC OCEAN

LUZON

JAN. 29 US 11th CORPS (Hall) LANDS

San Antonio
Olongapo
Bataan Pen
Mariveles
FEB. 28 CORREGIDOR TAKEN
Calumpit
Manila
NICHOLS FIELD
Manila Bay
JAPANESE SHIMBU GROUP
FEB. 4/MAR. 3 BATTLE FOR MANILA
Polillo Is.

JAN. 31 PART OF 11th ABN. DIV. LANDS
Nasugbu
Santiago
Mauban
Daet
Corregidor
Tagaytay Ridge
Tiaong
Siain
Catanduanes

FEB. PART OF 11th ABN. DIV. DROPS
Lubang Is.
Batangas
Naga
Boac
Bicol Peninsula
Calapan
Legaspi

DEC. 15 AMERICANS LAND AGAINST LIGHT OPPOSITION
MINDORO
Burias
Irosin

US 8th ARMY

Mindoro Strait
Sibuyan Sea
Teblas

➤ US 6th Army landings & lines of attack	◯ Japanese-held areas up to the capitulation of Japan (August 1945)
– – – US Army Command boundary	✛ Airfields
▬ Land over 600 ft.	

△ In 1942, the Japanese had ended their conquest of Luzon with the US remnants penned helplessly in the Bataan peninsula; in 1945 the tables were turned. Gradually, the Japanese forces under Yamashita were forced back to the hill fastnesses in the north, where many of them were still fighting at the end of the war. ▽ Scene on one of the Lingayen beaches, where the bulk of Krueger's army flooded ashore in the first fortnight of January

As Swift's troops moved inland, they quickly found their way blocked by an arc of well-emplaced Japanese defences along a series of ridges extending east and south from the eastern shores of Lingayen Gulf for some 25 miles to the steep, rugged Cabaruan Hills. The Japanese with their customary skill with the shovel had succeeded in building an intricate network of caves, tunnels, pillboxes, and connecting fortifications, well supported with artillery and automatic weapons, and difficult to knock out except at dangerously close range. Against these formidable positions, the 1st Corps launched a vigorous three-division attack. Progress was slow, hampered by the stubborn fixed defences and repeated small but punishing counterattacks and raids. The drive east and south-east struck and gradually overwhelmed a series of strongpoints at key road junctions and in the Cabaruan Hills. The climax came on January 28 when General Swift's forces decisively repulsed a fierce tank attack after several days of savage fighting at San Manuel.

The struggle in the north was even more difficult, as 1st Corps' troops sought to secure the extreme left shoulder of the 6th Army's beach-head. With the help of additional reinforcements here, Swift gradually forged ahead until by the end of the month he had cleared the Japanese from their most threatening positions and was himself probing the mountain approaches to General Yamashita's headquarters at Baguio. The danger of a large-scale counterattack from the north was now ended. Many months of hard fighting remained in the mountain fastness of northern Luzon, but Krueger's left flank was at last secure.

Meanwhile, Griswold's 14th Corps had been moving south against negligible resistance. Within a week of landing, the corps had crossed the undefended Agno river, cheered on by happy Filipino civilians who lined the roads to shout their welcome. Fearing a trap, however, Griswold hesitated to advance too rapidly, and Krueger, no less cautious, was unwilling to mount a major drive inland until the 1st Corps had secured the 6th Army's left flank. But on January 17, MacArthur ordered the advance continued. Not only was he anxious to reach Manila and rescue Allied prisoners and civilian internees there, but he also realised the necessity of seizing the Clark Field area to provide major bases for General Kenney's air units.

Griswold drove forward. His troops continued to encounter only scattered pockets of resistance, easily eliminated. On the 23rd, however, they ran into strong opposition at the town of Bamban on the corps' right, and it was clear that they had finally caught up with the Japanese in strength. These Japanese were the forward elements of the Kembu Group, the 30,000-man force ordered by General Yamashita to hold Clark Field and the mountains west of the central plains. Griswold's left was well in the air by now because of the delay in the 1st Corps' advance, but reconnaissance to his east had uncovered no enemy concentrations and the 14th Corps commander concluded that the primary Japanese threat lay on his right. So, leaving only small forces to guard his exposed flank, he swung the bulk of his units toward the west for an attack on Clark Field.

The Clark Field air centre was a vast complex of pre-war and Japanese-built bases. It lay on the forward edge of the mountains, dominated by those heights but vulnerable to a determined assault from the east. For three days, Griswold's troops probed the edges of the Kembu Group's defences. The men moved easily at first, over relatively flat terrain, but when they entered the foothills they discovered a vast defensive network of caves and tunnels well protected by artillery and machine-guns. Overcoming these positions was arduous and costly work. Many could not be reached by tanks or artillery, and infantry assault squads had to lay siege to one cave after another with machine-guns, flame-throwers, and demolitions. By the 27th, only limited gains had been won, US casualties were beginning to mount.

After a brief pause, Griswold attacked again on the 28th, this time in greater strength. The Japanese continued to resist stubbornly, throwing heavy fire against their assailants and launching numerous counterattacks against the 14th Corps. Yet soon the attrition began to tell. By the evening of the 31st, more than 2,500 men of the Kembu Group had fallen and Griswold's troops, despite their own considerable casualties, were at last in possession of the Clark Field complex. The Japanese still held the mountains to the west—from which they would have to be driven, or destroyed—but Griswold's main force could now return to its primary mission of pushing on toward Manila.

Even as the 14th Corps seized Clark Field, American forces were making other strong moves on the broad Luzon chessboard. Under cover of darkness on January 30, a small force of American Rangers and Filipino guerrillas penetrated deep within Japanese lines to strike a prisoner-of-war camp near Cabanatuan. They surprised and quickly subdued the Japanese guards, rescued more than 500 Allied prisoners, and successfully fought off their pursuers during the night as they made their way back to friendly territory.

Further north, at the same time, 1st Corps' forces opened a major attack on Japanese positions in the San Jose area. The Japanese defences were, as usual, well prepared. Tanks, in many instances, were dug in to their turrets, forming strong and effective pillboxes, while artillery and anti-tank guns were carefully emplaced and vulnerable only to direct hits by heavy shells. In a week of stiff fighting, however, General Swift's troops overcame or bypassed these obstacles, seized San Jose, and destroyed the II Tank Division, the only Japanese armoured force on Luzon. Elements of the attacking American units continued to push east until they reached the shores of the Philippine Sea, effectively cutting land communications between Yamashita's northern command and the Japanese in the Manila area.

On January 29, meanwhile, Major-General Charles P. Hall's 11th Corps landed unopposed on the west coast of Luzon, just north of Bataan Peninsula, and pushed rapidly inland. Hall's first objective was to seize a nearby airfield and the Olongapo naval base. Then he would drive east to cut off Bataan from northern Luzon and prevent Japanese forces from withdrawing into that peninsula as MacArthur had done in 1942.

Yamashita had no intention whatsoever of allowing any sizeable forces to be trapped on Bataan, but Japanese units already there put up a stiff fight in the rugged, jungle fastness along the top of the peninsula. It took Hall's men two weeks of rough, difficult combat before they succeeded in destroying

Japanese resistance and reaching Manila Bay. This action now completely sealed off those enemy forces still holding out in the mountains north of Bataan and west of Clark Field.

Still another landing took place south of Manila Bay. On January 31, the greater part of the 11th Airborne Division went ashore against negligible resistance at Nasugbu Bay, only 50 miles south-west of Manila. Hoping to tie down Japanese units in southern Luzon and at the same time provide an additional approach route to the capital city, the paratroops made good initial progress. Three days later the rest of the division dropped on Tagaytay Ridge, 20 miles or so inland, but found no Japanese on this highly defensible terrain feature. The whole division then joined up and, with little resistance before it, drove rapidly along the main highway toward Manila. By the evening of February 4, the paratroops were approaching the southern outskirts of the city. Here they were finally halted by strong Japanese defences.

Japanese relic: an off-limits sign

'Go to Manila!'

The main attack on Manila would come from the north. Late on January 30, at the insistent urging of MacArthur, General Krueger directed the 14th Corps to 'advance aggressively southward' on the capital. Spearheading the drive were two veteran divisions, the 1st Cavalry on the left and the 37th Infantry on the right, and for the next few days they would be in a race for the honour of making the first entrance into the city. 'Go to Manila,' MacArthur exhorted them. 'Go around the Nips, bounce off the Nips, but go to Manila!'

The two American divisions pressed ahead, MacArthur continuing to urge them on. Foremost in his mind were the 3,500 Allied civilians held prisoner at Santo Tomas University in the northern part of the city. Fortunately, the advance encountered only scattered resistance and by February 3, after a bitter night battle, forward elements of the 1st Cavalry were poised for a final dash. For this, the division organised a special 'flying column' of tanks and motorised elements. The 'flying column' rolled forward swiftly, reaching the last bridge above Manila just in time to prevent

its defenders from blowing it up. Then it sliced through weak Japanese forces in the city's northern suburbs and, late that afternoon, reached the university grounds.

Inside the stockade, the prisoners could hear the noise of furious battle, the rumble of tanks, and then the welcome sound of an American voice shouting, 'Where the hell's the front gate?' A tank crashed through the entrance and then another: the prisoners were free. In a nearby building, however, a small Japanese force still held nearly 300 women and children hostage. The Japanese commander demanded a safe-conduct guarantee before he would release his captives and, after about an hour of tense negotiating, the Japanese were permitted to leave unmolested. A final group of 1,300 Allied prisoners-of-war and civilian internees was rescued that evening by 37th Division troops who entered Manila shortly after the cavalry 'flying column' and captured Old Bilibid Prison where the captives were held.

The Japanese in Manila totalled some 17,000 men, most of them naval troops, under the command of Rear-Admiral Sanji Iwabuchi. As a naval commander, Iwabuchi was not subject to General Yamashita's control and, despite Yamashita's expressed wish to evacuate Manila, was determined to fight to the end in the city. For this purpose, he divided his forces into several subordinate commands, each charged with holding a portion of the city more or less independently of the others. He planned no specific tactics other than the widespread use of demolitions to destroy installations and create obstacles and the all-out defence of strongpoints. Of these, the most formidable were the many heavily reinforced concrete buildings in the downtown area and the ancient walled inner city of Intramuros.

Almost every major structure in Manila became a minor fort as the Japanese blocked the entrances, put barricades on the stairways and in the corridors, cut firing slits in the walls, and dug connecting tunnels to nearby buildings or bunkers. Streets were barricaded and mined, automatic weapons were deployed in great numbers, and heavy naval guns and other artillery were emplaced in and around the city. For the first time in the Pacific War, American forces were faced with the task of capturing a large, well-defended metropolitan area.

Following a fairly simple plan of assault, the 37th Division attacked south along the Manila waterfront, the 1st Cavalry swung around to make its push from the north-east and east, and the 11th Airborne drove up from the south. The Japanese were heavily outnumbered. But their defences were strong and Iwabuchi had no intention of giving up.

As resistance mounted so did American casualties, and the attackers were forced to the unhappy conclusion that there was no longer any hope of saving Manila's buildings. Reluctantly the word went out to lift the restrictions on artillery fire, and the entire force of 14th Corps artillery was now thrown against Japanese positions. Any strongpoint that blocked the advance was pounded into a shambles. While churches and hospitals were spared, the toll in large structures and civilian lives was high. But the added firepower did the job. By the 12th, the two American divisions had penned most of the Japanese defenders in and around Intramuros and the waterfront area to its south.

The attack of the 11th Airborne Division from below Manila had run into equal difficulties. The primary obstacle before the

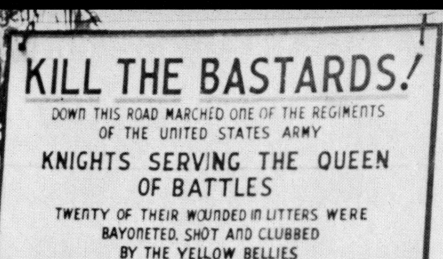

KILL THE BASTARDS!

DOWN THIS ROAD MARCHED ONE OF THE REGIMENTS
OF THE UNITED STATES ARMY

KNIGHTS SERVING THE QUEEN
OF BATTLES

TWENTY OF THEIR WOUNDED IN LITTERS WERE
BAYONETED, SHOT AND CLUBBED
BY THE YELLOW BELLIES

KILL THE BASTARDS!

US military propagandists pulled no punches in whipping up bitter memories of the Bataan 'Death March', notorious aftermath of the fall of Bataan in April 1942. This sign was suspended over one of the main roads on Luzon

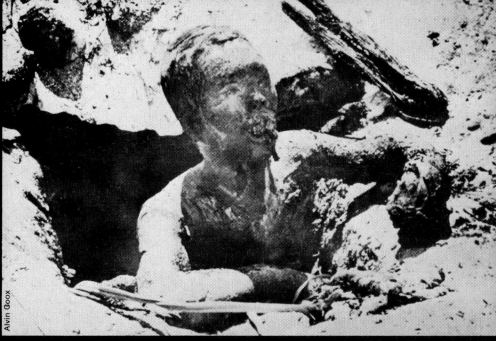

American flame-throwers proved as effective as ever . . .

Japanese resistance was its fanatical, futile self

paratroops was Nichols Field, where Admiral Iwabuchi's sailors had built strong concrete and steel pillboxes and emplacements to house a powerful assortment of automatic weapons and artillery as large as 6-inch naval guns.

Supported by 14th Corps' artillery firing from north of Manila, the paratroops attacked with their tanks but found the going so treacherous that they were forced to call for close air support before they could begin to make any progress. Slowly but surely they pressed forward across the airfield, taking heavy casualties but just about wiping out some 3,000 Japanese naval troops. 'Tell Halsey to stop looking for the Jap Fleet,' signalled one company commander. 'It's dying on Nichols Field.' Late on the 12th, the paratroops linked up with the 1st Cavalrymen, who had fought their way around the capital and reached Manila Bay 2 miles north of Nichols Field. If the Japanese still in Manila had any hope of escaping, it was now gone. But it was more than a week before the attackers were close enough to Intramuros to begin an assault on this last bastion.

The old 16th-century citadel was a formidable fortress even by modern standards. The stone wall around it stood 15 feet high and was as thick as 40 at its base. Its gates were protected by stout redoubts and heavily-fortified concrete buildings. The presence of a large number of civilians within the walls ruled out air bombardment of Intramuros but, after the Japanese had refused requests to evacuate non-combatants, there was no alternative but to unleash a powerful artillery and mortar assault to prepare the way for the infantry. The actual attack went in on the 23rd, and for two bloody days, it continued until the last Japanese was dead. Intramuros, or what was left of it, was finally in American hands.

The struggle for the rest of the city went on for another week. The most difficult nut to crack was a small area south of Intramuros where stood many modern fireproof government buildings. Again the pattern was the same: heavy shelling by artillery, attacks by tanks and infantry, and then the brutal, difficult room-by-room advance against an enemy who refused to surrender. Not until March 3, with the reduction of the last Japanese remnants in the shell of the Finance Building, was all resistance eliminated. The month's struggle for Manila had cost the Americans more than 1,000 killed and 5,500 wounded. Almost no Japanese survived. The city itself was in ruins and as many as 100,000 Filipino civilians may have died, victims of the savage battle and killed by the Japanese in a last frenzy.

Even before the struggle was over, General MacArthur had re-established the Philippine Commonwealth Government in Manila. Addressing a provisional assembly of Filipino officials on February 28, the American commander recalled his earlier pledge to liberate the Philippines. 'My country has kept the faith!' he declared. The Philippine government was once more in power, the Philippine people nearly free. 'Your capital city, cruelly punished though it be, has regained its rightful place – Citadel of Democracy in the East.'

But MacArthur could not enjoy the full fruits of Manila's liberation unless he also cleared the Japanese from the entrance to Manila Bay. For – as the Japanese themselves had discovered in 1942 – whoever held Bataan and Corregidor effectively pre-

vented anyone else from using the harbour and port facilities of the Philippine capital. MacArthur well understood this and, at his insistence, General Krueger had begun operations to open Manila Bay while the fighting in the city was still at its height.

No sooner had the 11th Corps sealed off the top of Bataan than it swung south in an effort to capture the entire peninsula. On February 14, a reinforced regiment began pushing down the east coast, practically unopposed, and the next day a second force of equal size landed at Mariveles, at the southern tip of Bataan, also without meeting resistance. The Japanese did not hold Bataan in force and within a week American troops had overrun the whole peninsula. There had been little hard fighting.

Corregidor did not fall as easily. 'The Rock,' as it was called, was a heavily fortified, tadpole-shaped island defended by some 5,000 Japanese, most of them naval troops. Since the last week in January, General Kenney's planes and Admiral Kinkaid's warships had dropped tons of explosives and napalm on Corregidor, shattering and crumbling its exposed defences but inflicting few casualties on its defenders, who remained snugly underground during the worst of the pounding.

On February 16, in a co-ordinated airborne and amphibious assault, a battalion of American paratroops dropped on the south-west heights of the island – at the head of the tadpole – while a battalion of infantry landed on the southern shore. Shaken by the bombardment and thoroughly surprised by the parachute assault, the Japanese offered little initial resistance. But they quickly recovered, and poured out of caves and tunnels to provide an extremely warm reception for the invaders.

American reinforcements now arrived, sufficient, by the next day, to split the island in half. The Japanese, forced back into their underground network of defences, fought bitterly to hold each position. But the attackers struck with tanks, Bazookas, and flame-throwers and, one by one, gradually cleared or sealed off these retreats. Often, in desperation, the Japanese blew up their own underground defences, killing themselves and frequently taking some of the Americans with them. During the night of February 23, they set off a huge explosion in the tunnel housing their main ammunition stores, shaking the entire island and sending reverberations echoing along the whole of Manila Harbor. By the evening of the 26th almost all of Corregidor was in American hands and two days later the island was declared secure. American casualties totalled almost 1,000, most of them wounded, while only 19 Japanese survived to be taken.

On March 2, only nine days short of three years since he had left the island, General MacArthur returned to the site of his former headquarters. Colonel George M. Jones, the paratroop officer who had led the assault, stepped forward and saluted proudly. 'Sir,' he declared, 'I present you the fortress Corregidor!'

Manila Bay was now safe for Allied shipping, although it took an additional seven weeks to clear the Japanese from the south shore of the bay and from several small fortified islands in the middle of the water. Despite the fact that they lacked the power to interfere with passing vessels, the Japanese in these positions refused to surrender and held out to the death. To prevent useless casualties on the islands, the Americans

were forced to lower demolitions into the Japanese fortifications or to pour burning oil or gasoline in on the defenders. This grim method was the only means of finishing the job.

With Manila Bay and the capital city in American hands, the decisive phase of the Luzon campaign was ended by early March 1945. There still remained some 170,000 Japanese in strong positions in northern Luzon, west of Clark Field, and east and south-east of Manila. Many of these continued to hold out until the war's end six months later, but most would be killed or would die of disease or starvation.

The largest force of Japanese, those in the north under Yamashita's direct control, proved the most difficult to cope with. Although the 1st Corps took Baguio in late April, Japanese defences in the vast rugged wilderness to the north-east held out until the end of the war. 'The terrain features of these areas provided impregnable fortifications,' recalled Yamashita's Chief-of-Staff, Lieutenant-General Akira Muto. He continued:

However, the American forces started attacking . . . and kept it up incessantly. [Their] superior . . . bombardment and shelling gradually obliterated the jungle area. Bulldozers accomplished the impossible. Tanks and artillery appeared in positions where we had thought they would never penetrate. Our front line troops destroyed bulldozers, tanks, and artillery by valiant hand-to-hand fighting. However, the enemy advanced inch by inch, capturing this mountain, taking this hill.

Despite starvation, disease, exhaustion, and increasing casualties, Yamashita's forces managed to tie down more than four American divisions as well as large Filipino guerrilla forces. In so doing, they came closest to accomplishing the mission their commander first set for the XIV Area Army on Luzon: to engage and occupy as many American troops as possible and thus delay as long as it could the inevitable assault on Japan.

The Japanese, of whom only about 60,000 were to survive out of an original force of more than 250,000, were soundly defeated. American casualties were to reach 8,000 killed and 30,000 wounded. An additional 2,000 American and Australian sailors were killed or wounded in *Kamikaze* attacks. But by the end of June 1945 – when control of Luzon passed from the 6th to the 8th Army – everything of tactical, political, or economic value on the island was in American hands.

STANLEY L. FALK was born in New York in 1927. He served in the US Army between 1945-48, including a spell with the occupation forces in Japan, as Intelligence officer, linguist, and historian, and still holds a reserve commission with the rank of lieutenant-colonel. Before joining the faculty of the Industrial College of the Armed Forces (where he is at present Associate Professor of National Security Affairs), he was for almost 14 years an historian with the official historical programmes of the US Army and Joint Chiefs-of-Staff. He has also been a lecturer and consultant in the fields of military history and national security affairs. He holds a PhD diploma in American History from Georgetown University, Washington; his doctoral dissertation was a study of American army ordnance development in the period before the American Civil War. His many publications include *Decision at Leyte*, *Bataan, the March of Death*, and his next book is to be a study of the Malayan-Singapore campaign of 1941/42.

US soldiers examine knocked-out tanks of the Japanese II Armoured Division, largest Japanese tank force on Luzon. *Bottom:* US parachute bombs go down on Clark Field, centre of the Manila airfield complex. Note wrecked Japanese aircraft, another sign of the dramatic reversal of the 1941/42 campaign, which saw the US air strength on Luzon virtually destroyed on the ground

◁◁ General Yama-
shita, C-in-C
Japanese XIV Area
Army on Luzon
◁ General Krueger,
C-in-C US 6th
Army, which had
conquered Leyte
by December 1944

Manila—the first urban battle of the Pacific war

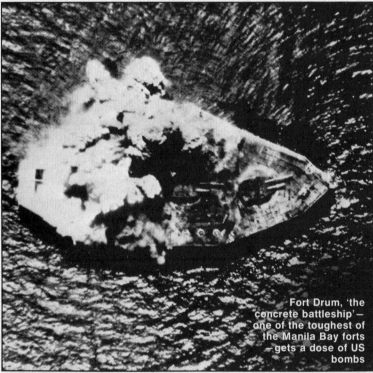

Fort Drum, 'the
concrete battleship'—
one of the toughest of
the Manila Bay forts
— gets a dose of US
bombs

Keystone

US troops in action
near Olongapo, to the
north of the old
Bataan battlefield

US Army

Filipino townsfolk in
the rubble of Manila

Central Press

ACROSS THE

Burma, August 1944/March 1945

A 14th Army troop ferry on the Chindwin river, main start-line for Slim's offensive

Imperial War Museum

After the pursuit of the beaten Japanese from Kohima and Imphal and the crossing of the Chindwin, Slim's forces were now faced with the task of driving south to the great river barrier of the Irrawaddy and then overcoming it. There could be no question of an offensive towards Rangoon in the south until this had been accomplished. With consummate generalship which fooled the Japanese at nearly every stage, Slim embarked on his task. And by the first week of March 1945 northern Burma had been recovered and the spearheads of 14th Army were across the Irrawaddy

By the end of August 1944, the battle of Imphal was over and the Japanese XV Army was in full retreat. The remnants of the Japanese XV and XXXI Divisions, which had attacked Imphal and Kohima respectively, were struggling to cross the Chindwin, while the more redoubtable Japanese XXXIII Division continued to resist strongly in the Kabaw Valley and on the Tiddim road to cover the withdrawal and the supply dumps in the rear.

Although the battle may have been won, the monsoon, as formidable an enemy as the Japanese, was still in full swing. By day and by night the rain descended in torrents to wash away long stretches of road and track or to turn the surface into glutinous mud several inches deep. Jeeps in four-wheel drive, with chains on the wheels and following the ruts of the vehicles ahead, ploughed their way through the morass only to bog again and again; gun teams, with

torsos bare, sweated to manhandle their guns forward, the towing vehicles being quite incapable of moving them; mules, without which many of the operations would have been impossible, plodded and squelched up and down hill with heavy loads of equipment and ammunition, while their leaders slipped and stumbled to keep up.

Despite the appalling conditions of weather and terrain, in which in pre-war days it would have been considered that operations were quite out of the question, the infantry, invariably soaked to the skin by the incessant rain or by their own sweat, forced their way up the hillsides, through dripping trees and undergrowth, to destroy Japanese rearguards or to drive them back. But somehow the acute discomfort and seemingly overwhelming difficulties were overcome, in no small part due to the pilots of the Royal Air Force who, in atrocious flying conditions, dropped supplies and attacked Japanese positions.

IRRAWADDY

Lieutenant-General Sir Geoffrey Evans

Popperfoto

Swimming pack mules cross the Irrawaddy during 36th Division's march to Katha

If conditions were bad for the British and Indian soldiers, they were a great deal worse for the Japanese. Often reduced to a diet of snails, roots, and grass until they could reach the supply dumps further back, with scant medical stores to treat their wounds and none to ward off the many indigenous diseases, they died like flies. When troops of Slim's 14th Army re-entered Tamu in the Kabaw Valley, it could only be described as 'a village of the dead'. Corpses lay everywhere, in makeshift hospitals, in the so-called street, at the feet of placid-looking Buddhas; many were huddled grotesquely in rusting motor cars abandoned during 1942, and in the houses into which they had crawled to die. Patrols pushing on towards the Chindwin river had a similar story to tell: the small huts along the banks were crammed with dead and dying and in one hut alone 80 were found lying in indescribable filth and, of them, only one was alive. So disgusting was the

stench that frequently the men of the patrols had to move around with handkerchiefs soaked in mosquito repellant over their faces: even so they were nauseated.

The Burmans in the valleys and riverine villages, too, had been quick to take advantage of the plight of their recent oppressors; lone Japanese, weakened by disease or hunger, were captured and ghastly tortures inflicted upon them before being put to death. It was war at its most bestial.

'To recapture all Burma . . .'

Following months of discussion between the British and American Chiefs-of-Staff, a decision had ultimately been reached as to the shape of future operations in Burma and, on September 16, 1944, a directive was issued to the Supreme Allied Commander, South-East Asia (SACSEA), Admiral Mountbatten, which involved two opera-

tions, the code-names of which were 'Capital' and 'Dracula'.

Operation Capital envisaged an advance by 14th Army and Stilwell's NCAC to the line Pakkoku/Mandalay/Lashio, which would make safe the land communications to China—in other words the road being built by NCAC to join up with the old Burma Road north of Lashio, and the oil pipeline being laid alongside it.

Operation Dracula referred to the capture of Rangoon by an amphibious cum airborne operation.

The opening sentence of this directive laid down Mountbatten's aim with unmistakable clarity: 'Your object is the recapture of all Burma at the earliest date', and it went on to say that without prejudice to the security of the air and land communications with China, the following operations were approved:

● First, those stages of Capital necessary to the

security of communications with China.
● Second, the vigorous prosecution of Capital and the execution of Dracula before the 1945 monsoon, with a target date of March 15.
● Third, if Dracula had to be postponed until after the monsoon, the exploitation of Capital as far as possible without prejudice to the launching of Dracula in November 1945.

But as far back as June, when 4th Corps was still under siege at Imphal, Mountbatten had given instructions to General Giffard, commander of 11th Army Group responsible for all operations in Assam and Arakan. He was not only to re-establish communications between Diampur and Imphal, but to oust the Japanese from west of the Chindwin between Yuwa in the south to Tamanthi in the north, 130 miles of river line, and to be prepared to exploit across the river between these two places after the monsoon. These instructions having been passed on to General Slim, planning had begun at 14th Army to put them into effect.

Even then, Slim, with Giffard's approval, was thinking in broader terms: of bringing the Japanese to battle and inflicting on them the final *coup de grâce.* What he needed was strong bridgeheads from which he could launch 14th Army against the Japanese before they had time to recover from the effects of defeat at Imphal. As will be seen, it was with the object of destroying the enemy always in mind that he based his plans throughout the reconquest of Burma.

To give effect to the instructions of 11th Army Group, General Slim issued orders on August 6 to General Stopford, in charge of all operations on the central front, to pursue the Japanese relentlessly and without delay on three routes—along the Tiddim road to Kalemyo; through the Kabaw Valley from Tamu to Kalemyo; and along the track from Tamu to Sittaung on the Chindwin (see map). He further ordered him to occupy Sittaung and, if possible, to capture Kalewa where he was to be prepared to make a bridgehead. The Japanese were consequently assailed from a number of different directions at the same time, a feature of the Allied strategy and tactics which was to continue throughout the campaign.

Within a few days of the issue of these orders, the pursuit began with 11th East African Division in the Kabaw Valley and 5th Indian Division on the Tiddim road. In both cases the physical obstacles to be overcome were greater than the enemy opposition. In the Kabaw Valley, notorious for tropical diseases of all kinds, the numerous *chaungs* crossing the muddy cart track were in spate, necessitating the building of bridges before the advance could be resumed, while on the Tiddim road, besides the raging torrent of the Manipur river barring the way and the unspeakable state of the road, closely hemmed in by jungle on either side, the deadly scrub typhus took a heavy toll of the British and Indian soldiers. And all the while General Tanaka's Japanese XXXIII Division continued to fight with great determination on both routes, despite mounting casualties and loss of equipment.

Very largely due to the enormous physical difficulties, it was not until November 13, three months later, that 11th East African Division and 5th Indian Division joined hands at Kalewa, during which time bridgeheads had been established at Mawlaik and Sittaung. On December 2, Kalewa was captured by the East Africans and, within eight days, a Bailey bridge 1,150 feet long—the longest in history—spanned the Chindwin. The opening phase of Capital had been completed and 14th Army was poised to begin the advance on Mandalay.

The Japanese tasks
But meanwhile what of the Japanese? What were the plans of General Kimura, reputed to be one of the most outstanding of all Japanese generals and now in command of Burma Area Army in place of Kawabe, relieved after the Imphal *débâcle?*

In brief, his instructions were to cover the vital strategical areas of southern Burma, including the south-west coast, and at the same time to interrupt, if possible, Allied communications with China. To effect this, he had three armies under his command, comprising ten divisions and two regiments (brigades)—on paper a formidable

force, but in reality far less so, since all formations were under strength though that situation would improve as expected reinforcements arrived.

In his opinion, the Yenangyaung oilfields and the rice-producing country of the Irrawaddy delta were essential to keep his armies in being, and to protect these indispensable areas he would have to hold a general line from Mandalay through Yenangyaung and on to Ramree Island. As for his opponent, he anticipated that General Slim might attempt crossings of the Irrawaddy at a number of points, the main effort being directed somewhere between the Ava bridge west of Mandalay and Myinmu, with subsidiary crossings about Singu, north of Mandalay and between Myingyan and Pakkoku. Nor did he rule out the possibility of airborne operations against Maymyo and Meiktila. With these considerations in mind he disposed his forces in the following manner.
● In the north, XXXIII Army (General Honda), consisting of two divisions and a regiment, was to hold the Lashio/Mandalay line.
● In the centre, XV Army (General Katamura), with XV, XXXI, XXXIII, and 53rd Divisions mustering some 21,500 men, was to be responsible for the defence of the river line from Mandalay to Pakkoku and as far back as Meiktila.
● Further south, XXVIII Army (General Sakurai), with two divisions and one regiment, was to cover the Yenangyaung oilfields, the Arakan coast, and the Irrawaddy delta.

The reserve Kimura kept centrally placed on the main lines of communication so as to be able to send it quickly to the assistance of either XV or XXVIII Armies. For the actual defence of the Irrawaddy line, after fighting delaying actions north of the river, he proposed to bring his formations back behind the river, on December 1, where they were to take up defensive positions, but at the same time be prepared to counter-attack when opportunity offered.

Picking the final plan
For weeks before the Combined Chiefs-of-Staff issued their directive of September 16, a variety of plans had been under study at SEAC and, among them, one envisaging the securing of the Shwebo Plain by 14th Army, while Stilwell's forces and those Chinese formations in Yunnan advanced southwards from the direction of Myitkyina to join up with 14th Army about Maymyo. This plan had appealed to both Generals Giffard and Slim and had resulted in the former giving Slim instructions which had not only included the carrying out of the phase just completed, but also required him to prepare for an overland and airborne advance to liberate that area of Burma between the Chindwin and Irrawaddy as far south as Mandalay.

Although General Slim was well aware of the political importance of the capture of Mandalay, he was, as ever, intent on the destruction of Burma Area Army at the earliest moment, since he knew that with the return of the monsoon and its effects on the maintenance of his formations across the Chindwin, 14th Army would have to be reduced in size after crossing the Irrawaddy. Moreover it was axiomatic that once the Japanese armies had been destroyed the whole of Burma would fall into his hands. It was with this object that the staff set to work to plan the future operations, fraught with a number of well-nigh insoluble problems.

Of primary importance was the decision where to compel the Japanese to give battle—and here General Slim selected the Shwebo Plain, in the dry belt of Burma, which provided conditions not unlike the Western Desert, where full scope could be given to his armour, superior both in numbers and quality to the Japanese tanks, and where the advantages of air superiority could be used to the maximum. Furthermore, it was obvious that if Kimura could be forced to fight in the Irrawaddy loop, he would suffer the grave disadvantage of the Irrawaddy behind him. Across this wide river all his supplies would have to come—in the face of British air attack—and across it a withdrawal would have to be made if his troops were defeated. Clearly speed was vital and the sooner 14th Army could move with all available divisions, armour, and aircraft, the better the prospects of success.

By far the greatest problems were those of the supply and maintenance of 14th Army once across the Chindwin. From railhead at Dimapur to Shwebo was 400 miles, of which 250 were over an earth-surfaced road which would be impassable unless made to withstand all weathers before the monsoon to be expected in May; air supply bases would be 260 miles in the rear, slightly above the maximum economic range for supply aircraft; in addition vehicles, aircraft, airfields, and engineering resources were well short of what would be required. And finally, the lines of communication would run through the disease-ridden Kabaw Valley: casualties among the administrative troops were bound to be high.

Therefore, for administrative reasons alone there was a limit to the strength of 14th Army trans-Chindwin; and, despite every permutation and combination, out of the six divisions and two tank brigades available to General Slim, a maximum four and two-third divisions plus the two tank brigades.

In November 1944, as General Slim had hoped, all Intelligence reports pointed to the probability that Kimura intended to stand north of the Irrawaddy, his northern flank resting on the 120-mile-long Zibyu Taungdan range of hills, a little more than 25 miles east of the Chindwin and coming to an end at Pyingaing, commonly known as 'Pink Gin', on the road from Kalewa to Shwebo. Beyond a labyrinth of jungle-covered foot hills and steep ravines, the main range rose in a sheer escarpment to just over 2,000 feet, and there were only two reasonable tracks through this very difficult country.

In every way it was ideal for defence, and the Japanese could be expected to offer stiff resistance while the Japanese XV Army reorganised its battered divisions. It was on this Intelligence assessment that General Slim made his plan for the offensive by 4th and 33rd Corps, scheduled to start on December 3.

His objective was the Japanese airfields in the area of Yeu and Shwebo, and both corps were directed towards this target. On the left was 4th Corps, under command of Lieutenant-General F. W. Messervy, the very experienced commander of 4th Indian Division, of 1st and 7th Armoured Divisions in North Africa, and of 7th Indian Division in Arakan and Kohima. The 9th Corps comprised 7th Division (Major-General G. C. Evans), 19th Division (Major-General T. W. Rees), 268th Brigade, and 255th Tank Brigade. The 4th Corps' task was to break out of the Sittaung bridgehead and, forcing the Zibyu Taungdan range, capture Pinlebu and Pinbon, and then turn south to capture Shwebo, if necessary in combination with an airborne assault. For this last operation, one division was to be held back west of the Chindwin until required.

On the right, 33rd Corps (Lieutenant-General Stopford), consisting of 2nd British Division (Major-General C. C. G. Nicholson), 20th Division (Major-General D. D. Gracey), and 254th Tank Brigade, having moved out of the Kalewa bridgehead, was to advance on a broad front astride the road from Kalewa towards Yeu and Monywa.

For the protection of the right flank, the Lushai Brigade and a newly arrived East African Brigade, the 28th, were ordered to move down the right bank of the Chindwin in the direction of Gangaw: once 14th Army was under way, 11th East African Division was to be flown out of the battle area.

On December 4, the 19th Division, spearhead of 4th Corps, burst from the Sittaung bridgehead and headed for Pinlebu and Pinbon. It was a completely untried division and moreover was to suffer from the handicap of being without its artillery and motor transport for a considerable time because of the lack of sufficient boats and rafts to ship these across the 600-yard-wide Chindwin. Yet, in accordance with the final sentence of the 14th Army order which, after reference to the facts that the enemy was neither in great strength nor in good shape, read 'it is therefore legitimate for you to take certain risks which in other circumstances would not be justified in order to achieve a rapid advance to the area of Indaw and Wintho'—and, roused by the inspiring leadership of its intrepid commander, it made surprisingly quick progress. Of Rees, who

INDIA
CHINA
Imphal
Myitkyina
Yunnan
Kalewa
Lashio
Mandalay
AREA COVERED BY MAIN MAP
B U R M A
Meiktila
Arakan
Irrawaddy
Ramree
THAILAND
Rangoon

Central Burma: Slim's master plan

When Slim began to chase the Japanese armies into central and southern Burma, he was determined to force a decisive battle to complete the destruction of the Japanese in Burma. At first, he believed that his opposite number General Kimura, commanding the Burma Area Army (an area army being the equivalent of an army group) intended to stand and fight between the Chindwin and the Irrawaddy. But when it became clear that Kimura had pulled back the bulk of his forces across the Irrawaddy, Slim was forced to think again. His new plan proved to be one of the most daring and momentous of the war. Half of 14th Army was to be slipped across the Irrawaddy to seize the key Japanese supply centre of Meiktila, a *coup* which the Japanese could not dare to ignore. Further to the north, other 14th Army units were to close up to the Irrawaddy and seize bridgeheads, giving the impression that 14th Army's sole objective was Mandalay. Such a complex reshuffle of Slim's forces would need complete secrecy, and a series of brilliantly successful deceptive operations was set in motion. The campaign was launched on January 19; by February 1, 14th Army was up to the Irrawaddy along a 200-mile front and the Japanese had no idea where Slim's blow would fall. All was now ready for the decisive trial of strength at Mandalay and Meiktila, in which Slim would make his bid for final victory

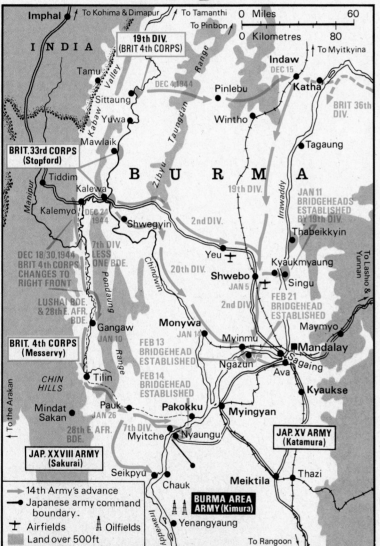

Imphal — To Kohima & Dimapur — To Tamanthi — To Pinbon
0 Miles 60
0 Kilometres 80
I N D I A
19th DIV. (BRIT 4th CORPS)
To Myitkyina
Tamu
Indaw DEC 15
Sittaung DEC 4, 1944
Pinlebu
Katha
Yuwa
Winthö
BRIT 36th DIV.
Mawlaik
Tagaung
BRIT. 33rd CORPS (Stopford)
B U R M A
Tiddim
19th DIV.
Kalewa
DEC 24 1944
Thabeikkyin
Shwegyin
2nd DIV.
DEC 18/30, 1944 BRIT 4th CORPS CHANGES TO RIGHT FRONT
7th DIV. LESS ONE BDE.
Yeu
Kyaukmyaung
To Lashio & Yunnan
20th DIV.
Shwebo
Singu
LUSHAI BDE. & 28th E. AFR. BDE.
JAN 5
2nd DIV.
FEB 21 BRIDGEHEAD ESTABLISHED
Monywa
Gangaw
JAN 14
Maymyo
FEB 13 BRIDGEHEAD ESTABLISHED
Myinmu
BRIT. 4th CORPS (Messervy)
JAN 10
Mandalay
Ngazun
Sagaing
CHIN HILLS
Tilin
FEB 14 BRIDGEHEAD ESTABLISHED
Ava
Kyaukse
Mindat Sakan
Pauk
Pakokku
JAN 26
Myingyan
28th E. AFR. BDE.
7th DIV.
JAP. XV ARMY (Katamura)
Myitche
Nyaungu
JAP. XXVIII ARMY (Sakurai)
Seikpyu
Thazi
Chauk
Meiktila
BURMA AREA ARMY (Kimura)
Yenangyaung
To Rangoon

→ 14th Army's advance
● Japanese army command boundary.
✈ Airfields
⛏ Oilfields
Land over 500ft

ing XV and XXXIII Armies. Besides containing all the supply and ammunition dumps, the airfields and the hospitals, this area was the nodal point of rail and road communications from Rangoon and from it these communications again radiated in all directions. A tight ligament on this administrative artery would paralyse all Japanese forces in north Burma, and Kimura would be forced to take steps to loosen it. In all it was an extremely attractive target — but the problem was how to put a force into Meiktila of sufficient strength to hold out until other formations could make contact.

A bold step to take

Neither airborne forces nor aircraft were available for such an operation, and the bypassing of Mandalay from the east was not feasible as the north-to-south communications were not good enough to take large forces with armour. But there was a bullock-cart track which ran southwards from Kalemyo through Gangaw/Tilin/Pauk, where the jungle ended, and then on to Pakkoku on the Irrawaddy bank, whence suitable roads led east to Meiktila.

It was a bold step to take, yet it was along this route that General Slim decided to send half his army and to surprise the Japanese. But before the move could get under way, much replanning was necessary, regrouping had to be carried out and a great deal of speedy work by the engineers would be required if the fresh project were to be launched in time.

On December 16, Slim warned Headquarters Allied Land Forces South-East Asia that he was changing his plan and he followed this up two days later with an outline of his proposed operations, to which the code-name 'Extended Capital' was allotted. On this day also, he met his two corps commanders at Tamu and issued orders to implement the new plan.

The operation was planned in four phases.

● First, 33rd Corps, taking 19th Division and 268th Brigade under its command, was to occupy the area of Shwebo and Monywa as originally ordered, close up to the Irrawaddy and give every indication that Mandalay was the sole 14th Army objective. At the same time 4th Corps, with 7th Division and 17th Division (at that time refitting in India), 28th East African Brigade and 255th Tank Brigade, was to move south through Gangaw, Tilin, and Pauk and seize a bridgehead in the neighbourhood of Pakkoku, holding 17th Division back until it was wanted.

● Second, while 33rd Corps was investing Mandalay and forcing crossings of the Irrawaddy north and west of it, 4th Corps was to seize Meiktila, thereby compelling Kimura to commit his reserve. The target dates given to 4th Corps were Pakkoku (January 31), and Meiktila (February 28), but some modification was later found to be necessary.

The third and fourth phases dealt with the pursuit by both corps until a port in south Burma was captured, if necessary with the help of an airborne operation. For the air landing of supplies each corps was to construct temporary airfields every 50 miles, a comparatively simple task with mechanical equipment in the dry open country at this time of the year.

Fooling the Japanese

It was vitally important to conceal the change of plan from the Japanese and to this end certain deceptive measures were ordered. A dummy 4th Corps Headquarters was established in the north, through which all signal traffic to 19th Division was passed, together with fictitious and sometimes indiscreet messages, to give the impression that the corps was still operating on this flank; complete wireless silence was to be maintained by all units of the real 4th Corps until the crossing was about to begin; 28th East African Brigade was to lead the advance of 4th Corps, with the object of misleading the Japanese into thinking 11th East African Division was the only force operating in this area.

The most northerly troops of the Japanese XXXIII Division covering the approach to Pakkoku were in touch with the Lushai Brigade at Gangaw, but following an airstrike by a large number of heavy bombers on January 10, their positions

stood just over 5 feet high and was appropriately nicknamed by the Press the 'pocket Napoleon', General Slim wrote later to the effect: 'What he lacked in inches he made up in the miles he advanced and the only criticism I made to him was to point out that the best huntsman did not invariably ride ahead of his hounds!'

In eight days, 19th Division was through the Zibyu Taungdan hills and by December 15 its patrols had made contact with 36th Division (Major-General F. W. Festing), at Indaw, 90 miles east of Sittaung: this division was under the orders of Stilwell and was advancing south along the east bank of the Irrawaddy. At long last, a connected front now existed throughout northern Burma.

But, for some days past, General Slim was becoming suspicious that his forecast of Kimura's intention to stand north of the Irrawaddy had been incorrect, since captured documents and

information from local Burmans indicated that with the exception of rearguards the bulk of the Japanese had crossed the river, and this assumption was strengthened by the comparatively slight opposition to 19th Division's advance. A point had been reached when a decision had to be taken whether to continue with the operation as arranged or to change the plan completely: of the alternatives, General Slim chose the bolder course as giving him a better chance of completing the enemy's destruction. In effect the situation was that instead of destroying the Japanese first and then crossing the river, the army would now have to cross the river and then bring the Japanese to battle south and east of the Irrawaddy. The plan he evolved was to prove the master stroke of strategy in the Burma campaign.

Approximately 70 miles south of Mandalay, as the crow flies, lay Meiktila and Thazi, the main links in the Japanese administrative chain supply-

were obliterated, and 28th East African Brigade occupied the village and took over the front. Close behind was 7th Division, less its third brigade which was over 350 miles to the rear at Kohima and with little transport to move itself forward. It was touch and go, therefore, whether Messervy's date of February 15, as the latest for the crossing, could be fulfilled. Besides the wide gap which existed between the head and tail of 7th Division, 150 miles of execrable track, suitable for demolition at a number of points, lay between Gangaw and Pakkoku—and the Japanese could be expected to put up a vigorous resistance.

In an atmosphere of warm sunny days and coolish nights, the advance began on January 19 with the East Africans in the van: a week later, four days ahead of the timetable, Pauk was captured by a brigade of 7th Division with a turning movement through the mountains. From the high ground east of the village the first exciting glimpse of the mighty Irrawaddy was obtained, the whitish cliffs on the further bank being just visible, through glasses, 40 miles ahead. About the same time, the last brigade of 7th Division, destined to carry out the assault crossing, struggled into Gangaw to begin training on the local river with the few boats and outboard engines which it had been possible to collect.

Meanwhile, the engineers toiled incessantly to improve the track. To make it fit to carry the heavy tanks on their transporters and the gigantic bridging equipment lorries was a colossal task requiring the employment not only of every available field engineer, but of a large number of elephants to build the bridges across the innumerable *chaungs*. The fact that it was completed in time to enable these monster vehicles to pass through almost virgin country, was a fine tribute to the skill, determination and stamina of the Indian Sapper and Miners.

From the outset Messervy's plan had been that after 7th Division had formed the bridgehead, 17th Division, which had been reorganised into two motorised and one air-transportable brigades, together with the tanks, were to make the dash to Meiktila, but, at that stage, it had not been possible to determine the exact crossing site. Pakkoku was the obvious place as it afforded the shortest route to Meiktila, yet it was too obvious and, as more air photographs became available, Nyaungu, 20 miles south, was finally selected. Besides offering the shortest crossing—even so the river was half a mile wide at this point—thereby speeding up the ferrying across of the striking force when the moment arrived, a number of roads radiated from Nyaungu to make the breakout easier. Fortunately, no better place could have been selected, because unknown to 4th Corps, the boundary between the Japanese XV and XXVIII Armies passed through Nyaungu and neither had taken adequate measures to make it secure. Instead, its defence had been left to elements of the Indian National Army who at no time had shown great willingness to fight.

How far 14th Army's and 4th Corps' deception plans were successful is evident from the postwar remarks of General Tanaka. Concerning 4th Corps' advance to the Irrawaddy, he wrote: 'At the end of January, our aircraft reported a long line of vehicles on the road from Tilin to Pauk, but these were not considered as part of a powerful mechanised force nor was it regarded as important by Army HQ. If the information had been repeatedly reported by our aircraft it would have received more attention, but they only reported it once and consequently it did not attract special attention.'

'Fake' river-crossing plans
As for the crossing itself, in order to ensure that as far as it was humanly possible, it would not be opposed in strength, further elaborate plans were evolved to deceive the Japanese that Nyaungu was the chosen place.

Some 45 miles south of Pauk was the village of Seikpyu, opposite the Chauk oilfields, the scene of demolitions in 1942. This was clearly a desirable target and on February 2 the East African Brigade, trailing brushwood behind its vehicles to raise more dust thereby making the column appear stronger than it actually was, hurried towards Seikpyu to give the impression that the main crossing was to be launched opposite Chauk; dummy parachute landings were also made east of Chauk and marked maps dropped in suitable places.

Coincidental with this move, 7th Division exerted strong pressure towards Pakkoku as if it was intended to cross at that point. Ultimately, when both operations were well under way and the Japanese fully occupied at both places, it was planned to side-slip the bulk of 7th Division south to the area of Myitche at the last moment and to force the crossing.

That the Japanese were mystified there was no doubt, for Tanaka's comments on the operations between February 5/14 were: 'As I mentioned before, our defensive line was too wide and we could not know where the Allies would cross the river.'

A good deal of work would be necessary on the near bank opposite Nyaungu before it could be made fit for vehicles to reach the water's edge, and this could not be done in full view of the opposite bank. The beach chosen for the assault crossing was therefore a mile or so upstream, but here the distance from bank to bank was almost 2 miles. Once across, the first objective was the capture of Nyaungu, to enable the engineers to begin work on the main crossing site.

Although the Japanese reacted violently by holding on grimly to the approaches to Pakkoku and hurling heavy counterattacks against the East Africans, the condition of the boating equipment now gave rise to much anxiety. After travelling over shocking roads for hundreds of miles it was in a sorry state—no less than 90 out of 96 smaller type of outboard engines alone required repair. Time was pressing, and to the everlasting credit of the technicians of Indian Electrical and Mechanical Engineers, the necessary overhauls were carried out just before the boats and rafts were needed.

Shortly after midnight on February 13 preparations were complete—the assault brigade was in position, the boating equipment had joined them, the guns were ready to open fire when necessary. So far the Japanese had shown no signs of suspicion. In complete silence, at 0400 hours on the morning of St Valentine's Day, February 14, the widest crossing in the history of the Second World War—possibly in all history—began. The target date had been beaten by one day.

After an initial setback, when only one company of the assault battalion succeeded in getting ashore, a massive onslaught was opened by all the artillery, a regiment of tanks lining the near bank, and by six squadrons of Royal Air Force and United States Army Air Force aircraft. The far bank became an inferno of bursting bombs and shells; a dense pall of smoke, through which only the flashes of high explosive were visible, covered the enemy beaches and the second wave went across without a shot being fired by the Japanese.

The opposition that had been offered came from a battalion sent by Tanaka, who had always been apprehensive of the inter-army boundary, but since it arrived about the same time as the crossing took place it was too late. 'The Allied units in front of Nyaungu attained their object under the protection of overwhelming bombing and shelling. The battalion lost its commander and retreated,' was Tanaka's summing up.

After three days—breakthrough
By nightfall, the assault brigade with six tanks and a few mules and jeeps had established itself on the far bank and by the following evening the bridgehead was 2,500 yards deep. Three days later, after Nyaungu had been taken, 17th Division and the tank brigade began to cross and, on February 21, a week following the first assault, they broke out of the bridgehead. Clouds of dust rose from the sandy roads as the tanks and lorried infantry streamed northwards to Taungtha and the road to Meiktila.

On Christmas Eve, Stopford's 33rd Corps had begun to move out of the Kalewa bridgehead, 20th Division making for Monywa and 2nd Division for Shwebo. The 19th Division, turning south, also headed for Shwebo, at the same time preparing to establish a bridgehead across the Irrawaddy about Thabeikkyin as a prelude to advancing on Mandalay.

◁ Lieutenant-General Sir William Slim, C-in-C 14th Army: victor of Imphal, and soon to prove himself the master general of the war in Burma

▷ His army's movements, like those of the Japanese, were dictated by the monsoon rains; and the usual solution to ground transport difficulties was the muscle power of the troops

At Shwegyin, east of Kalewa, the troops of 2nd Division passed the tanks of 7th Armoured Brigade, which had been abandoned during the 1942 retreat (at that time it had been possible to evacuate only one, and this was now returning to Burma with one of the regiments of 254th Tank Brigade, which was determined to return to Rangoon where it had started its career in Burma). These derelicts appeared remarkably unaffected by three monsoons, and in fact *were* unaffected, since technicians were able to extract sound parts and use them as spares in future operations.

Following delays due to stubborn Japanese resistance and unseasonable rain which temporarily halted all transport, 20th Division was in the outskirts of Monywa on January 14: nine days earlier a combination of 2nd and 19th Divisions had taken Shwebo, and by January 11 the latter was reinforcing its bridgeheads at Thabeikkyin and Kyaukmyaung.

One of the thousands of Japanese who fell between Imphal and the Irrawaddy

Allied air power strikes at the Yenangyaung oil-fields, one of the most valuable strategic targets in Japanese-occupied Burma.
▷ Medical aid for a Japanese soldier, wounded and captured by the British on the road to Mandalay

Now the problems of administration took a hand for 33rd Corps—especially 19th Division, which had outrun its communications; further-more, the weather had delayed the arrival of 254th Tank Brigade on its transporters, and these tanks would be urgently required when the river was reached. A fortnight was necessary to build up supplies before closing up to the Irrawaddy.

From the middle to the end of January elements of Katamura's Japanese XV Army launched fanatical and continuous attacks at 19th Division's bridgeheads, in efforts to drive them back across the river and relieve the threat to Mandalay from this direction. Meanwhile, the only strongly-defended Japanese position remaining north of the Irrawaddy was that covering the approach to Mandalay over the Ava bridge and the com-munications back to Meiktila.

So, by February 1, for a distance of approxi-mately 200 miles, 14th Army was almost up to the Irrawaddy everywhere, and in places across it. Kimura and Katamura were still mystified as to where the main weight of 14th Army was to fall, and these doubts General Slim intensified by the timing and wide dispersion of the various crossings.

Already there had been 19th Division's bridge-head which had attracted all the attention and to the Japanese there was every indication that the capture of Mandalay was the Allied aim, the more so since 19th Division began moving south on February 11.

When darkness fell on February 12, the 20th Division began to cross at Myinmu, 30 miles east of Monywa, and thus became the next focus of Japanese attention. For three weeks, until March 5, the bridgehead was the scene of desperate fighting during which no less than 13 battalions of four different Japanese divisions were identified. Casualties were heavy on both sides but so closely were the Japanese engaged by 20th Division that when 7th Division crossed at Nyaungu on the next night they were in no position to counterattack 14th Army's threat to Meiktila.

Finally, 2nd Division which, owing to the shortage of boats and rafts, was compelled to wait until 20th Division's bridgehead was secure, began to cross on February 21 at Ngazun, a few miles west of Sagaing. Again the Japanese fought tenaciously to the extent that Japanese officers were seen clambering on to the British tanks and attacking the crews with their swords through the open turrets: by March 5, the 2nd Division was over the river and preparing to move east towards Mandalay. Along the whole front of 14th Army, therefore, the scene was set for the operations which were to bring to an end all further organised Japanese resistance in Burma. [General Evans' biography is in Vol 2, p. 669.]

From the spring of 1942, when the Japanese drove the British-Indian forces out of the plains of central Burma, until the autumn of 1944, when Slim's 14th Army returned to destroy them there, the war was fought in the jungle, along a 600-mile arc from the Himalayan foothills to the swamps of the Arakan coast. In this vast area, tens of thousands of square miles of mountain and jungle, even large armies are lost to sight. The man on the ground can see only a few yards round him: even the airman sees nothing but a carpet of trees, like a rumpled green rug under his wings, broken only by occasional clearings and a few huts.

Before 1941, it was assumed that the jungle favours the defence, but this is by no means entirely true. Fighting in the jungle is like fighting in a fog: it smothers long-range weapons, and enables the attacker to come to close quarters with small loss. Heavy bombers and heavy guns are useless if there is no visible target upon which they can be directed, and tanks are reduced to the role of mobile pillboxes, each needing a close escort of infantry to protect it from the enemy who can rise up unseen within a yard of it.

At first, the Japanese infantry, tough, resolute, lightly armed, and trained for these very conditions, had every advantage over an opponent accustomed to rely upon a wide range of supporting weapons. But by 1944, the British and Indian troops had learned the rules of this highly specialised form of warfare, and were quite as tough and skilful at it as their opponents. As the prospects of a full-scale invasion to throw the Japanese right out of Burma grew, it became more necessary than ever to gain exact information of their positions and strength. Normal patrolling could and did maintain contact with the forward positions, but special arrangements had to be devised to find out what was going on further back.

The Allied 'V-Force' had been in it from the beginning. Officers who knew the language and the people lived and moved in the Japanese back areas for weeks and months at a time, building up an Intelligence network among the tribesmen—Chins and Kachins, Arakanese, Lushais, and the faithful Nagas—collecting information and passing it back. (The Japanese imitated this technique with a V-Force of their own, and some adroit individuals managed to belong to both organisations at the same time.)

An influx of special forces

When the war in Europe moved on to the Continent, various small amphibious units were released to the eastern theatre and formed into a Small Operations Group (SOG) under Colonel H. T. Tollemache, R.M.

● There was the Combined Operations Pilotage Patrol (COPP), a mixed army and navy unit, who worked chiefly from canoes, and specialised in the reconnaissance of beaches and the pilotage of amphibious assaults. There was the Swimming Reconnaissance Unit (SRU), who swam where even canoes could not go, and No. 2 Commando Special Boat Section (SBS), who would go anywhere and do anything which could be done in canoes.

● Besides SOG, there was 'D-Force', specially trained and equipped for deception, whose small parties could simulate the attack of a brigade in one place, while the real assault went in elsewhere, and who used ingenious techniques to induce the Japanese to reveal their positions prematurely.

● Force 136 was an offshoot of SOE, but they conducted their mysterious operations without reference to anyone else, and reported their results to their own HQ in Delhi.

● And in Arakan there was a superbly equipped American unit of the OSS, about 40 strong—but it was thought in some quarters that they were more interested in post-war oil concessions than in the current activities of the Japanese.

Between them, these various units carried out hundreds of small operations of all sorts in the Japanese rear areas. On the sea coast and on the great rivers—the Irrawaddy is more than 2 miles wide at its junction with the Chindwin—they reconnoitred landing beaches under the noses of the Japanese, laid buoys and planted markers to guide the assault boats. They searched for lost airmen in the jungle, helped the gunners to establish observation posts behind the enemy, laid booby-traps, and occasionally ambushed a Japanese patrol and brought in a prisoner for questioning. On one occasion, Major D. H. Sidders, with two canoes, intercepted a motor-boat on the Chindwin and captured it, killing a crew of eight. On another, an SBS party under Major H. V. Holden-White, met a Japanese V-Force officer in the jungle, killed him, and carried off all the papers from his headquarters.

Above all, they kept up a constant flow of information about Japanese positions and movements, so that the main army might bring its strength to bear on the elusive Japanese under their screen of trees. Sometimes there were skirmishes, but generally it was desirable to conceal from the Japanese that their movements were being watched, and if the watchers suffered few casualties, this was the measure of their skill and jungle craft.

It is scarcely possible to say that there ever was a 'typical' operation, but the extract from a diary given below illustrates the atmosphere in which much of the work was done.

Having occupied Akyab on January 2, 1945, 15th Corps immediately began to plan another leap to Kyaukpyu, 60 miles further south on the northern tip of Ramree Island. The information available suggested that the Japanese were withdrawing from the islands, that no serious resistance was likely, and that there were only about 50 Japanese at Kyaukpyu. Nevertheless, General Christison ordered No. 2 SBS to reconnoitre the area, and bring back one or more locals for questioning.

Teknaf. 14/1/45: The boats were all loaded last night, and we sailed from Teknaf at 0800, with nine teams in two MLs (one team being two men in a folboat). Passing the black and white lighthouse on Oyster Reef, we were well out in Combermere Bay by dusk, the land only a pale mountainous outline in the fading light. A chain of pale blue blobs on the horizon ahead marked the line of islands which shelter Kyaukpyu on the north. This time, we had chosen the cove under Catherine Bluff as our slipping point, and the MLs lay rocking on the smooth swell with

their engines humming as the boats were slung over the side, meeting the water in a surge of phosphorescence, and we climbed down into them as they bobbed alongside. Torch, binoculars, R/T set, weapons, rations, water-bottles were passed down and stowed away, and last of all the long paddles. One by one the boats pushed off and took up their stations, the crews raising their paddles as soon as they were ready to go.

We got away at midnight, following the narrow channel between Tankharo Island and Sinbaikchaing, slipping along between the steep, wooded heights with a strong tide under us. After a couple of miles, we saw a fire blazing among the trees on the Tankharo side, casting a red glare across the channel. Remembering Harry's report about Jap watchfires and Burmese lookouts, we stopped paddling and let ourselves drift slowly past on the tide. There were several men—Burmese—round the fire, but they did not see us.

At last we emerged into the open water of the harbour, and saw the shadowy hill of Laws Island 4 miles away in front. A tedious spell of paddling brought us to it, and we felt our way in under the black shadow of the land to a sandy cove fringed with bushes. Having made sure that no one was about and posted sentries on the approaches, we got the boats into cover and settled down to doze for an hour before dawn.

Laws Island, Kyaukpyu. 15/1/45: As soon as it was light, we reconnoitred the whole area and arranged a defence plan, though the country people say that the Japs seldom visit the islands. Corporals did sentry, while officers and sergeants maintained a watch on Kyaukpyu with binoculars. Though we had found the town itself ruined and overgrown when we visited it last week, from this distance it seemed intact, with the red-roofed houses rising out of the trees, the monastery on a hillock in the middle, and the low wooded hills behind. There seemed to be some wire on the beach, and what looked like bunkers here and there. Canoes were drawn up in front of Pyinpyumaw, where we bumped into a Japanese post on our last visit, and Burmese in brightly coloured clothes were walking about. The most significant thing was that from dawn to 0800, a constant stream of people could be seen crossing Ngalapwe creek by the ferry from Zaingchaung, all going into Kyaukpyu. This suggested market day—if any—or, more likely, forced labour. In either case, there must be people in Zaingchaung who knew what was going on in Kyaukpyu. I sat down with maps and tables to plan a visit there during the night.

In the afternoon, a sentry reported a local approaching: he was gathering shell-fish, it being low tide. When he got near enough, we gathered him in, pale and shivering with funk, and Sergeant Braganza (Burma Intelligence Corps, interpreter), set to work to calm him down. We gave him biscuits and cigarettes, but it took over an hour to get him coherent. He confirmed that the Japs seldom come to the islands, that there were none in Kyaukpyu itself (which we knew) and none in Zaingchaung, which was good news, if true. There were about 200 in Gonschwein, on the sea-side of Kyaukpyu, where they were digging defences (probably a company: say 150, as we know Jap units are under strength).

BURMA: THE WAR OF STEALTH

Burma, January 1945
Richard Livingstone
Even in Burma, one of the war's 'Forgotten Battlegrounds', British Commando operations were of vital importance in preparing the ground for Slim's offensive against the Japanese. This article describes a typical 'undercover action' before the Anglo-Indian offensive of 1945 — and throws a fascinating sidelight on how the British followed up their success in Arakan

Left: the author (with his Number 2 at the machine-gun) on a river in Burma

We could not move until dark, and I did not want the islanders to know of our presence before that, so we decided to hold the man until then, when I would take four teams across to Zaingchaung, while Stan, with the rest, took him back to his village and saw to it that no one left the island until we came back, after which we must find a new hide for the next day.

We pushed off at 2000. Fires could be seen burning on the far shore, near Careening Point, and I steered for it, intending to catch a fisherman as guide to Zaingchaung, which is about 2 miles inland. The tide was rushing up the estuary, and we had to negotiate some awkward boils and rips on the way over. We made a cautious approach and slipped quietly into a narrow stony beach. The fire was the other side of the point, and we managed to get up to it without being seen. The fishermen sitting round it were jumpy, and one bolted, but returned when he was not pursued. After some negotiation, a young man in a white *longyi* agreed to guide us to Zaingchaung, and six of us started off inland, leaving Corporals Burns and Palmer to guard the boats.

Our guide led the way at breakneck speed along a narrow jungle path, and then across dry paddyfields, where we were constantly stumbling over the *bunds*, invisible in the starlight. After three-quarters of an hour, we came to a group of houses scattered about in fenced gardens: here and there one saw the dying embers of a fire, and sometimes a murmur of soft voices came out of the darkness as we passed. The headman lived in a fine wooden house on piles, with an outside stair leading up to the door. I left one man on guard outside and sent the others to watch the approaches to the village, arranging a system of whistle signals in case of emergency. The guide knocked at the door: there was a stir inside, and a sound of voices, and an old man with white moustaches peered out. A quick exchange of Burmese followed, and then he held back the door, and let us into a bare, spotlessly clean room that was walled, floored, and roofed with brown teak planks. Inside, there was another old man, and a young woman with a baby lying on a mat. The headman waved a hand at her, and she disappeared silently into an inner room, while he lit a lamp like an oil-can. A yellow, smoky flame guttered at the spout, casting flickering shadows over the room. An ancient deck-chair was set for me, and the others sat round on mats.

I began by telling Corporal Ba Than (Burma Intelligence Corps, interpreter) to make a soothing speech to the effect that we were friends who had come to drive the 'Japani' away, and that when this had been done, there would be peace and prosperity once more: that we needed his help in telling us all about the enemy, and that when we came back, we should remember those who had helped us, and also those who had not. Ba Than put this over sentence by sentence, the others nodding their heads gravely. It seemed to go down all right. The old man replied that they were tired of the 'Japani', and would be glad to see the 'Ingaleik' back again.

We then got down to the actual situation at Kyaukpyu, and the old man gave us a lot of information. He said there were about 300 Japanese at Gonschwein (*two* companies?). They had guns, and they had conscripted everyone to dig defences — not at all what 15th Corps were expecting. The Japs seem to have behaved fairly well, but have ruthlessly rounded up everyone, young and old, fit and unfit, for forced labour. They encourage the recalcitrant by pouring boiling water in their ears. There was a lot more useful stuff about enemy movements, motor-boats, supply routes, etc, but not much about their actual positions. After an hour and a half it was time to go. I said that the General wanted to talk to someone who knew what was going on in Kyaukpyu. The headman objected strongly, and said that the Japs would have his head: naturally, if a disgruntled villager reported the transaction, and he had said nothing about it, he would get short shrift. I replied that the General's orders must be obeyed, and that, incidentally, there would be 50 rupees for anyone willing to come, as well as 20 rupees for the headman. Eventually, our guide, whose name was Aung Chan U, agreed to come, if he could hand the money over to his wife before leaving. So I produced my money-belt, and the interview ended with polite obeisances all round.

Returned to the boats at 0030. Stowing Aung Chan U under the deck of Sergeant Penn's boat, so that only his head showed, we paddled back across the river to Laws Island, where we divided. Jimmy and Penn, with Aung Chan U, started on their 10-mile paddle to Catherine Bluff, where they would meet an ML at dawn, and return to Teknaf to report progress to date. The rest of us crept round the steep shore until we saw the flashes of Stan's torch, and he guided us in to a tiny cove behind a ridge of rocks. Here by the water's edge we found Stan with a slight Burmese in white shirt and trousers who could speak English. His name was San Hla Baw, and he had been a clerk in the District Commissioner's office until that morning when the Japs had closed the office and dismissed the staff. They were expecting attack, and San Hla Baw had brought his family over to the island to escape the wrath to come.

Leaving a picket on guard over the boats, we adjourned to his house, a small bamboo *basha* standing among palms and bananas. Here we were introduced to his grandmother, a wrinkled, genial witch who spoke only Arakanese, a young and pretty wife, and five small children sleeping in a row under a blanket. The ceremonial deck-chair was produced and the lamp lit, while the wife blew up the embers of the fire and set about making tea. We handed round biscuits and cigarettes, but the grandmother preferred her cheroot. I got out maps and notebooks, and went into details with San Hla Baw by the light of the flickering lamp. His information confirmed that of Aung Chan U and the headman of Zaingchaung, but in much greater detail. It seems the Japs may have the whole 121st Regiment on Ramree. Its II Battalion is in the Kyaukpyu area, with two companies on the beach at Gonschwein and the rest heavily entrenched on Mount Peter and Black Hill. They have artillery and their HQ is in the cave temple. This, I thought, will cause a stir at 15th Corps.

But when I raised the question of his returning with us, San Hla Baw went off the deep end. He

besought us not to take him, he said the Japs would massacre his family, he pointed to the children — who slept serenely through the uproar — and said they would be left fatherless, while the grandmother sat in the background sucking her cigar and interjecting what I took to be sardonic remarks in Arakanese. Eventually, he calmed down and said that if we would leave him in peace, he would go back to Kyaukpyu the next night — no one will venture on the water in daylight for fear of the RAF — and get some more information. He would come back the night after and meet us again. Obviously, there was a chance of treachery, but I thought we could take care of that. So I agreed, gave him 50 rupees, promised him another 50 when he returned, and briefed him on the additional information required.

Tankharo Island. 16/1/45: Left at 0330 and crossed to Tankharo to find a new hide for the day. Mud and mangrove obstruct much of the shore, but by dawn we were established under cover with sentries posted. Mess-tins were soon simmering over the blue flames of the little cookers, and after breakfast we cleaned the mud off ourselves and our weapons and settled down to catch up on our sleep. In the afternoon a party of deer hunters came along the beach, with dogs, nets, and long spears. They knew little about Kyaukpyu, but confirmed some other items of information. They knew of Jimmy's visit to Thechaung last week, but said that the Japs had not heard of it yet. They showed us a spring where we could fill our waterbottles, and went their way smiling.

Laws Island. 17/1/45: Left at 0130 and went back to Laws Island, where we found a new but uncomfortable hide among some rocks. The islanders knew we had left, and I did not want them to know that we had come back. But in case San Hla Baw gave us away, it was desirable to be on the spot before the Japs could get there, so that it would be they and not we who would be ambushed.

But everything went off quietly. San Hla Baw turned up on time. He had done extremely well, filled in a lot of detail, and in particular had located the exact positions of two out of the three guns. We now had a pretty complete blueprint of the Japanese positions. All that remained was to get it back to Corps HQ.

San Hla Baw still objected to coming with us. For an hour we argued with him, flattered him, offered him rewards. I did not want to carry him off by force if it could be avoided. Grandma told him to pull himself together, and be a man (Braganza's translation) and finally he agreed, on the promise of a chit from me, a chit from the General, 50 rupees, and a new suit of clothes.

Akyab. 18/1/45: The tide would not serve before midnight, so we sat smoking and drinking tea. The stars sparkled among the wind-tossed tree-tops, and the lamplight flickered on faces brown and pale. At last, it was time to go. In single file, we picked our way along the narrow path, and climbed down among the rocks to the little cove where Stan had the boats already ranged along the water's edge. San Hla Baw was tucked into Sergeant Smith's boat, and we started on the four hours' paddle to the rendezvous. The wide spaces of the harbour, the low land of Kyaukpyu in the distance, and the high wooded islands all lay dark and silent as we passed through Tankharo Channel on the ebb tide, and emerged near Catherine Bluff. The ML was hard to see in the shadow of that high crag, but we steered inshore and soon picked her up against the clear horizon. She called up her partner from the alternative rendezvous at Pagoda Rocks, and soon we had got the boats on board, and were heading out past Satellite Island as dawn came up over the mountains.

In the event, the information provided by this reconnaissance enabled 15th Corps to recast its plans for the attack, and when 26th Indian Division landed at Kyaukpyu on January 21, the Japanese defences were smothered by an accurate bombardment from sea and air. The place was occupied at a cost of only 14 casualties. But it took another six weeks to clear the whole of Ramree.

[*For Capt Livingstone's biography, see Vol 3, p. 1119.*]

THE FIGHT FOR IWO JIMA

Pacific Theatre,
February 16/April 7, 1945
Don Yoder

Before the Marines even set foot on
Iwo Jima the island citadel had been
given the heaviest bombardment of the
entire Pacific war. Yet the 36-day battle
for the island was the bloodiest in
Marine Corps history, a campaign that
cost the lives of more than 6,000
Americans and 22,000 Japanese. 'This
fight,' said Marine General Holland
Smith, 'is the toughest we've run across
in 168 years.' *Right:* The Marines hit
the beach and the ordeal begins. In the
background is Mount Suribachi, Iwo
Jima's dominating feature

US Marine Corps

Did Iwo Jima *have* to be taken by force? Could it not, like certain other Japanese-held strongholds in the Pacific, have been bypassed, cut off, and left 'to wither on the vine'? The answer is no, and for four good reasons, most of them dictated by Allied air strategy:

● First, heavy B-29 bomber losses over Japan emphasised the need for fighter escorts, and since the 2,800-mile round trip from US air bases in the Marianas to Japan and back was beyond the range of the fighters, a nearer staging point had to be captured.

● Second, Iwo Jima, with its two completed airbases and its proximity to Tokyo (660 nautical miles or three air hours) would itself make an excellent base for Allied bombers.

● Third, since Iwo Jima was traditional Japanese territory, administered by the Tokyo prefecture, its conquest would mean a severe psychological blow to the homeland, as well as a vital strategic outpost denied to the Japanese.

● Fourth, Iwo Jima was a necessary link in the air defences of the Marianas. So to isolate Iwo Jima would not be enough: it would have to be seized.

Preliminary planning for the invasion of Iwo Jima began as early as September 1943, and 13 months later, after the Marianas had been secured, Admiral Chester Nimitz informed Lieutenant-General Holland M. ('Howling Mad') Smith, one of the leading exponents of amphibious warfare and commander of all the Marines in the Pacific, that he would be in charge of an operation to take Iwo Jima. Handling the invasion itself would be Major-General Harry Schmidt's 5th Amphibious Corps, veterans of the Gilberts, the Marshalls, and the Marianas campaigns. Schmidt would control three divisions:

● The 3rd Marine Division (Maj-Gen G. B. Erskine), a veteran unit that had seen action on Guam, would be held offshore Iwo Jima as a floating reserve.

● The 4th Marine Division (Maj-Gen C. B. Cates) was also a battle-hardened unit, one that had been in on the Saipan and Tinian landings. It would take part in the initial assault along with the 5th Division.

● The 5th Marine Division (Maj-Gen K. E. Rockey), though yet untried in combat as a unit, was composed of 40% seasoned veterans.

Longest bombardment

Once the target had been selected, the Marines began a rigorous training programme for the invasion: practice landings were made on beaches as similar to Iwo's as possible, and a hill shaped much like Mount Suribachi, Iwo Jima's dominating feature (see map), was taken time and time again in mock assault. Meanwhile, as preparations continued, the air force had begun, on December 8, 1944, the longest and heaviest aerial bombardment of the whole Pacific war, a 72-day 'softening-up' by B-24s and B-25s. A few optimists thought that the island had been neutralised. Only the Marines who had to hit the beaches would be able to verify this.

The US navy, too, laid down its bombardments, which began in November 1944 and continued with intervals until February 16, 1945, when it began its pre-assault barrage. For three days US warships pounded the island from the sea in an attempt to pulverise, or at least neutralise, the Japanese guns capable of hitting the

Marine firepower

In the amphibious landings the worst moment of all was at the moment of contact with the shore, when the first wave of the landing force came under the fire of enemy beach defences with no heavy firepower of their own in support. The British met this problem with the DD swimming tank—but in the Pacific war the Americans preferred to improve on the well-tried 'Landing Vehicle, Tracked'—the Buffalo. Two armed versions helped the Iwo Jima landings, one armed with twin cannons for light support and one with a 75-mm howitzer for heavy support. The former was able to fire at ground targets while acting as a troop transport, while the howitzer version played the same role as the DD tank

The course of the battle. The Marines landed on Iwo Jima without much opposition and within five days had conquered the southern part of the island, including Mount Suribachi. But the drive to the north was an agonising battle of attrition against an enemy who had sworn to kill ten Americans for each Japanese before dying. US casualties after the 36-day fight totalled almost 25,000

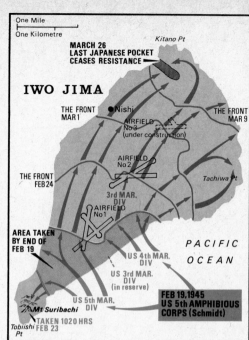

LVT(A) (Howitzer)
Weight: 13·7 tons. *Crew:* four. *Speed:* 20 mph on land, 7½ mph afloat. *Armament:* one 75-mm M-3 howitzer, two ·50-inch Browning machine-guns

LVT(A) (Twin Cannons)
Weight: 12·5 tons. *Crew:* six. *Troop capacity:* 15. *Speed:* 20 mph on land, 7½ mph afloat. *Armament:* two 20-mm cannon, two ·50-inch Browning machine-guns

beaches. Like their counterparts in the air force, the navy too believed they had succeeded. Again, the verdict of the Marines would be the one that counted.

On February 17, two days before the actual invasion was scheduled to begin, LCI gunboats and rocket boats came close inshore to cover the frogmen clearing the beach approaches and checking beach and surf conditions. Suddenly, at 1100 hours, the Japanese, who felt certain that this was the invasion they had so long awaited, opened fire with their heaviest artillery. Some 170 casualties were suffered in this action, but the frogmen did return with a full report of beach and surf conditions. Moreover, by revealing their carefully concealed positions the massive coastal guns had marked themselves for certain destruction. They could have raised havoc on D-Day itself.

The morning of D-Day, February 19, found 450 vessels of the US 5th Fleet gathered offshore the tiny island—the largest collection of ships yet for a Pacific operation. And around and among these vessels swarmed the 482 LVT(A)s, packed with troops, that would carry the eight Marine battalions into action. The bombarding warships closed in to 1,000 yards and began firing. Then the air strikes began and the navy laid down a creeping barrage, the first time it was used in the Pacific. The first wave, 68 LVT(A)s, aligned itself for battle. Every few minutes one of these waves would begin the 4,000-yard dash to the shore and certain violence. If all went according to schedule, the first seven battalions of fighting Marines would be ashore within 45 minutes.

At 0902 hours the first wave of Marines hit the beach, the 5th Division on the left, the 4th on the right, and for the first few minutes reported only light resistance and scattered Japanese fire. Could the defences have been exaggerated? Had the preliminary bombardment really worked after all? It seemed too good to be true. Then, after 20 minutes, the deadly fire of all the Japanese weapons—all the artillery and mortars so carefully sited beforehand—opened up in a vicious barrage. Suddenly, the Marines, by now 200 to 300 yards inland, found themselves pinned down. Then the small-arms fire opened up—from underground pillboxes, from harmless looking sand hummocks, from apparently everywhere. The most costly operation in Marine history had begun in earnest.

Fatal Japanese mistake

The Japanese plan had been clever, but they had made one mistake, a fatal one: they had allowed the Marines to get ashore with all the equipment they would need. By 1030 hours elements of all eight assault battalions were ashore and the bigger LSMs were following up with tanks, bulldozers, and artillery. By the end of the day some 30,000 Marines had been landed and although their casualties had been high, very high, they knew they were there to stay: the entire neck of the island was now secure. By the end of the second day the Marines were at the foot of Suribachi. The next move was obvious.

For three days the Marines fought for control of Suribachi, and at 1020 hours on February 23 a 40-man patrol clawed its way to the summit and raised the American flag. But the fall of Suribachi by no means meant the fall of Iwo. The 4th and 5th

Divisions had now to turn north and face the first line of the main Japanese defence belt, and the savage days that followed were evidence of how carefully it had been prepared. The advance had been stopped cold: a battle of attrition, fought with bayonet, flamethrower, rifle, and grenade, had begun. Each time the Marines managed to penetrate one defence line they would find themselves facing another, seemingly more formidable than the last. Artillery was useless against these positions, and the terrain handicapped the tanks. To escape the Marine artillery barrages the Japanese would hug the US front lines as close as possible. So convincing was their camouflage that time after time they would deliberately allow the Marines to overrun their positions, holding their fire until the last possible moment not to give themselves away. By D+10 it had become clear that US strength was being bled off just as relentlessly as Japanese: casualties, and sheer exhaustion, had reduced many combat units to only 50% efficiency.

Not until D+18 (March 9) was a final breakthrough to the north-east shore of the island made by patrols of 3rd Division. But elsewhere on the island the 4th Division was forced to deal with a Japanese counterblow which, if not a formal Banzai charge, was definitely suicidal in nature: 650 Japanese were found dead in one area alone, and reports from other sectors brought the total to nearly 800. In no way had the

One month of the bloodiest fighting in US Marine history

Marine advance been blocked. From now on it was 'simply' a case of mopping up.

It was during this phase that the Marines discovered what the Japanese had been doing since they first occupied the island. Complex mazes of interwoven caves; networks of underground bunkers; ridges, gorges, ledges: the island was one vast lattice of defensive positions. In one area, 1,000 yards wide by 200 deep, 800 separate fortifications, pillboxes, and blockhouses were counted. Entire hills had been hollowed out and rebuilt to house hundreds of defenders, all of whom had sworn to kill ten Marines before dying. It was like nothing the Marines had ever encountered before.

An Intelligence officer of 4th Division described the action like this:

The enemy remains below ground in his maze of tunnels throughout our preliminary artillery fire. When the fire ceases he pushes OPs out of the entrances not demolished by our fire. Then, choosing a suitable exit, he moves as many men and weapons to the surface as he can, often as close as 75 yards from our front. As our troops advance toward this point he delivers all the fire at his disposal, rifle, machine-gun, and mortar. When he has inflicted sufficient casualties to pin down our advance he then withdraws through his underground tunnels most of his forces, possibly leaving a few machine-gunners and mortars. Meanwhile we have delivered a concentration of rockets, mortars, and artillery. Our tanks then push in, supported by infantry. When the hot spot is over-run we find a handful of dead Japs and few if any enemy weapons. While this is happening, the enemy has repeated the process and another sector of our advance is engaged in a vicious fire fight. And so the cycle continues.

It was not until D+25 that the Marines dared declare organised resistance on Iwo to have ceased, but even so, the actual mopping up lasted until D+34. On the night of March 25/26 the Marines witnessed the last convulsions of the desperate Japanese forces: a 300-man Banzai attack on a bivouac area. It had no effect.

Bloodiest prize in the Pacific

Iwo was the bloodiest prize in the Pacific, but its value had not been exaggerated. On March 4, twelve days before the island was declared secure, the first B-29 landed there. On April 7, 108 P-51 Mustangs left from Iwo for the first time to escort a daylight B-29 attack on Tokyo, and within three months of the island's fall more than 850 B-29s had made emergency landings there; without Iwo most of them would have been lost.

Yet the price of Iwo had been extraordinarily high, and whether the dead were Japanese or Americans they had died with the utmost violence. Of the 23,000 men defending Iwo only 1,083 were ever taken prisoner. As for the Americans, some 6,821 soldiers and sailors lost their lives in the struggle for the 8 square miles of Iwo: 24 Medals of Honor were won: 12,600 pints of blood were transfused: 2,650 men were classified 'casualties of combat fatigue'. It had been a fight with a fury unprecedented in the Pacific, and must have left America's military leaders with one haunting thought at least: if to conquer tiny Iwo it took a 72-day air bombardment, a three-day naval hammering, and 36 days of the best the Marines could offer, how long would it take to overwhelm Japan herself? And at what cost?

Far left: **A wounded Marine is rushed to an aid station. But in the early days of the battle there were no safe areas, even for the wounded**

D+1: Marines move up during the fight for an airfield— the *raison d'être* of the whole Marine invasion

D+4: Suribachi falls. This is one of several famous photos celebrating its capture

D+5: The drive to the north begins. In most areas the US tanks were handicapped by the terrain, and artillery was often quite useless against the carefully prepared defence positions

IWO JIMA

THE JAPANESE VIEW

Pacific Theatre,
June 1944/April 1945
Major Yoshitaka Horie

'If by chance the prisoners of war should have returned to their homeland afterwards, they would have been treated as cowards by their countrymen.' These prisoners were taken early in the battle. But of the 23,000 men defending Iwo Jima only 1,000 were ever captured

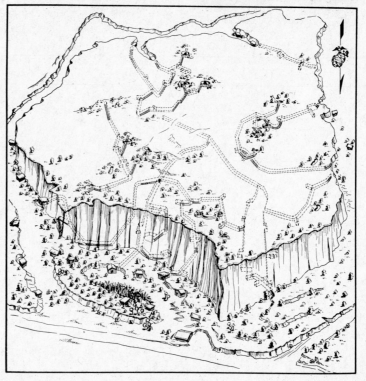

'In order to connect each defensive position in the Motoyama district, we planned to dig almost 18 miles of underground tunnels.' This sketch of a typical fortified position (made by a US Seabee unit) shows how well the Japanese prepared their defence system

When the battle for Iwo Jima ended, the Americans had certainly had one of their most shattering experiences in the entire Pacific war. But what of the Japanese side of the story? Iwo Jima became an epic of Japanese history, a glorious battle in defence of an outlying part of the homeland, which found its expression in the 'Song of Iwo Jima', composed for the occasion and broadcast to the embattled Japanese at the height of their ordeal. Our account is written by a key Japanese staff officer during the battle

I welcome this opportunity to write about the Iwo Jima campaign. Already 23 years have passed since the campaign, but I am unable to forget it for even a moment. I devoted my body and soul to the defence plan and supply of Iwo Jima under my respected General Kuribayashi. I am also unable to write this without tears in my heart for the many officers and men of Japan and America who sacrificed their lives there.

In 1891 Iwo Jima, along with Chichi Jima and Haha Jima, became the territory of Japan, but because the island had no special product it had been written off in geography books as 'an island of sulphur springs, with no water, no sparrows, no swallows'. It was only after Truk Island was raided by an American task force in February 1944, and our Combined Fleet retired from there, that we (except for several officers) began to give much thought to this island in connection with our strategy.

In 1943, our navy constructed the first airfield (near Mt Suribachi) on Iwo Jima and made it an intermediate aircraft base from Japan to the Marianas, as well as an aircraft base from which to protect our convoys. In February 1944, we had only 1,500 naval air force men and 20 aircraft on the island. From February to March, Japanese Im-

perial Headquarters increased the strength on Iwo Jima to 3,000 army and 2,000 navy personnel. In those days the army was under the command of the Chichi Jima Fortress; the navy was under the command of Yokosuka Air Force.

From January to June, 1944, Japanese Imperial Headquarters had sent about six divisions to the general Pacific area, especially to strengthen Saipan, Guam, and Palau and to re-establish our Combined Fleet. At about the same time, Japanese Imperial Headquarters came to recognise the value of Iwo Jima and began to study what influence this isolated island would have on the mainland of Japan if the Marianas fell into enemy hands. From March to June, the army and navy in the Bonin Islands were under the single control of the Chichi Jima Fortress commander, who was himself under the command of the XXXI Army on Saipan.

On June 15, US forces landed on Saipan and four days later our Combined Fleet was defeated by the US 5th Fleet 270 sea miles north of Yap Island. Japanese Imperial Headquarters gave up their plan of retaking Saipan and decided to reinforce Iwo Jima with part of this strength.

On June 15, about 100 of our naval aircraft

were destroyed by the first American air raids on Iwo Jima. In those days we did not have any strong defensive fortifications on this island and it was as hazardous as being on a pile of eggs. If American forces had invaded Iwo Jima at that time, it could have been occupied in one or two days.

On June 30, Japanese Imperial Headquarters activated the 109th Division and appointed Lieutenant-General Kuribayashi as its commander, putting him under the direct command of Imperial Headquarters. On the same day I, who had been involved in the plan to retake Saipan as a staff officer of the XXXI Army, became one of General Kuribayashi's staff officers. At the end of June, the navy created the III Aircraft Fleet at Kisarazu and brought the air forces of Iwo Jima under the command of this fleet as the XXVII Air Wing.

We planned to send the following army strength (about 14,000 men in all) to Iwo Jima from Japan through Chichi Jima after July: the 145th Infantry Regiment; the III Battalion of the XVII Mixed Regiment; the XXVI Tank Regiment; four independent anti-tank gun battalions; two independent machine-gun battalions; two 25-mm machine-gun companies; two medium howitzer battalions; one mortar company;

Into the death-warrens

For the attacking Americans, Iwo Jima presented a nightmare succession of lethal Japanese defences, designed to give the maximum protection and the greatest possible number of surprise bolt-holes, summed up by these two illustrations. *Left:* A US patrol has located a Japanese sniper and moves in to 'take him out' with flamethrowers. *Below:* When the Americans attack, the Japanese take to a warren of connecting burrows, which lead either to fire positions in the American rear, or to the next defence network further up the hill. Waiting for any American attempt to enter the tunnels are bamboo-sliver pitfalls, and blind corners round which the Japanese can lurk

Chris Harrison

one rocket-gun company; one assault company; one radar unit, and other units.

The following men were responsible for Iwo Jima's defence.

Lieutenant-General Kuribayashi, a cavalry officer, who had graduated from Military Academy and War College, had stayed in the USA for three years and in Canada for two. He was also a poet and had written two songs, one about loving horses and another about loving his nation. On Iwo Jima, one night, I talked with him at length and he told me: 'When I was in America I saw many factories. I pay my respects to the greatness of American mass production. I think that "Victory or Defeat" in this war will be decided by production power. Don't you think so?'

Major-General Ohsuga was an artillery officer who had graduated from Military Academy and War College. In March 1944 he had been appointed as the Chichi Jima Fortress commander; on June 30 he was appointed commander of the II Mixed Brigade when the 109th Division was formed. In December he was hospitalised in a field hospital on Iwo Jima, suffering from paratyphus.

Major-General Senda (commander of the II Mixed Brigade after Major-General Ohsuga) graduated from Military Academy. He came from the commandant of the Sendai Reserve Military Academy and was well acquainted with infantry battle tactics.

Colonel Takaishi (Chief-of-Staff) graduated from Military Academy and had attended the War College. An infantry officer, he was appointed Chief-of-Staff in December 1944, succeeding Colonel Hori. He was well acquainted with infantry battle tactics, very energetic, and a poet.

Lieutenant-Colonel Nishi (commander of the XXVI Tank Regiment) was a baron, a cavalry officer, and a champion of Olympic horse games.

Other staff officers included (from old to young by age) Lieutenant-Colonel Nakane, operations staff; Lieutenant-Colonel Mishikawa, supply staff; Major Yoshida, fortifications staff; Major Yamanouchi, intelligence staff; and Major Horie, head of the Chichi Jima detached headquarters. Rear-Admiral Ichimaru (commander of the XXVII Air Wing) had graduated from the Naval Academy and was a famous naval pilot.

Because Iwo Jima was very near to the mainland of Japan and could accommodate many aircraft, we often discussed the value of the island in Tokyo and on Iwo Jima.

First, at Iwo Jima, some officers said: 'We will not be left as an isolated force. We can keep on fighting, expecting the assistance of the air forces and fleets from the mainland of Japan. So the plan should be an offensive defence.'

In Tokyo, some officers said: 'We must make a plan of how to use this Iwo Jima. We need not be anxious about its fall.'

'We must sink this island'

At that time, I was one of the officers who observed the overall military situation most pessimistically and insisted upon stating my opinion. Briefly, I had this to say:

'Now we have no fleet and no air forces. If American forces assault this island it will fall into their hands in one month. Therefore, it is absolutely necessary not to let the enemy use this island. The best plan is to sink this island in the sea or cut the island in half. At least we must endeavour to sink the first airfield. In the future, if by any chance we have an opportunity to take an offensive step again in the Pacific area, we will not use Iwo Jima.'

At the General Staff Office and Naval Staff Office, there were some officers who had the same ideas. One staff officer in particular asked me to calculate the explosive needed to sink Iwo Jima. Lieutenant-General Kuribayashi also agreed with me, but in September 1944 he inspected the whole island with me and investigated how to dispose of it. We found that the disposal of this island was quite impossible. We would have to make it stronger by fortification.

However, we both agreed that even if we placed any strength on the first airfield it would immediately be defeated by a severe air and naval bombardment and so it would be better to place our strength elsewhere. Later, one staff officer of the III Air Fleet came to Iwo Jima and insisted on distributing many 25-mm machine-guns and materials from the navy so that numerous pillboxes could be built around the first airfield.

He declared that his instructions came from the Naval General Staff, and argued that 360 pillboxes would prevent the enemy from invading. I opposed him very seriously at first, saying that he had no knowledge of the real power of the hostile navy. General Kuribayashi joined me against his ideas, but later he came to concur with him, asking him to let the army use half of the weapons and materials—particularly cement—for its own purposes. In October the general ordered the pillboxes made, using several battalions every day, and after three months they had built 135. When the American forces landed on Iwo Jima all 360 had been completed, but barely. In fact, this airfield was captured by the Americans in only two days. If we had directed this great strength, many materials, and the three months of labour which were used on the airfield, into the defence of Motoyama district and Mt Suribachi, we could have made these areas much stronger.

We received information that many American vessels were gathering at Ulithi, Guam, and Saipan from the end of January 1945, and we thought at Tokyo and Iwo Jima that the Americans would land on Iwo Jima or Okinawa. In my opinion, the possibility of the landing of American forces at Iwo Jima was 40% and at Okinawa 60%. We thought that if American forces landed on Iwo Jima they would occupy the first airfield, make an offensive base there, and use many tanks. Therefore, we endeavoured especially to strengthen the defence of Mt Suribachi, the front of Minamiburaku, Tankuiwa, and Osakayama, while emphasising training for anti-tank battle.

Many officers insisted that since Iwo Jima was the first front line of the homeland it would be better to let the II Brigade commander be island commander, and that the divisional commander should stay at Chichi Jima, where it was convenient to control the supply and communications of all the Bonin Islands. But Vice Chief-of-Staff General Ushiroku and General Kuribayashi said: 'Iwo Jima is the most important island and the enemy will surely come to get it, so we should place the division headquarters there.' Then General Kuribayashi decided to place the detached headquarters at Chichi Jima in order to supply and communicate with each island.

The army was of the opinion that they should be disposed for defence all over the island and that naval troops should be disposed under the control of each sector army commander. But Rear-Admiral Ichimaru was very anxious to defend one district itself and insisted that it would be better to make plans for mutual understanding, strengthening our union, and displaying fighting power. So the main power of the navy was put into

General Kuribayashi: cavalry officer, poet, and determined commander of the Japanese forces on Iwo

Keystone

2294

the defence of the Minamiburaku district, while the army was charged with defending all the rest of the island.

Each position a graveyard

In June 1944, the plan was to strengthen the Motoyama and Mt Suribachi districts and especially to hold a big reserve (including the XXVI Tank Regiment); if the enemy landed on the first airfield, we would make offensive operations towards the coast and annihilate him. In January 1945, the plan was changed to having each man think of his defence position as his graveyard, to fight until the last, and to inflict as much damage as possible on the enemy.

I insisted that we should use most of the anti-aircraft guns as artillery and retain only a few of them as anti-aircraft guns: they were good for protecting disclosed targets, especially ships, but worthless for covering the land defences.

But the staff officers of Iwo Jima tended to feel that because the natural features of Iwo Jima were weaker than those of Chichi Jima, if we had no anti-aircraft guns, our defensive positions would be completely destroyed by the enemy's air raids.

Eventually most of the 300 anti-aircraft guns were used as artillery. When the Americans landed on Iwo Jima, they silenced these anti-aircraft guns in one or two days. There was evidence that anti-aircraft guns were not valuable. But the 75-mm anti-aircraft guns, prepared and used as anti-tank guns, were very valuable indeed.

In order to connect each defensive position in the Motoyama district, we planned to make almost 18 miles of underground tunnel. We began this work in December 1944, but by the time the Americans landed we had only finished 3 miles.

General Kuribayashi insisted on emphasising training in bodily attacks against enemy tanks, infiltration attacks, and sniping. He had special badges made for the men in charge of bodily attack against enemy tanks, and on the men in charge of infiltration attack.

By February 1, 1945, the island was defended by 21,000 men (15,500 army and 5,500 navy). Our weapons included the following:
- 120 big guns (more than 75-mm) with 100,000 rounds of ammunition.
- 300 anti-aircraft guns (more than 25-mm) with 500 rounds for each.
- 20,000 small guns (including all machine-guns) with 22 million rounds.
- 130 howitzers (8- and 12-cm) with 90 rounds for each.
- 20 mortars (20-cm) with 40 rounds for each.
- 70 rocket-guns (20-cm) with 50 rounds for each.
- 40 anti-tank guns (47-mm) with 600 rounds for each.
- 20 anti-tank guns (37-mm) with 500 rounds for each.
- 27 tanks.

The army and navy used two systems to supply Iwo Jima: Tokyo/Iwo Jima, by destroyer, high-speed transport, and SB (something like the American LST but smaller); and Tokyo/Chichi Jima/Iwo Jima, by ship and high-speed transport and then by sailing boat, fishing boat, or SB.

After August 1944, the power of the American air forces and submarines was very obvious, and our supply vessels suffered much damage on the run from Tokyo to

Last stage of the battle: the fight from cave to cave against a suicidal enemy

'Each man will make it his duty to kill ten of the enemy before dying'

Iwo Jima's 8 square miles of bunkers, caves, and pillboxes made it one of the most strongly fortified areas in the world

Futami Harbour of Chichi Jima, and especially from Chichi Jima to Iwo Jima. We lost on the sea more than 1,500 men and 50,000 tons of materials.

When materials were sent to Chichi Jima from the mainland of Japan (usually by fishing or sailing boat) we unloaded them on Omura during darkness and in between the enemy's air raids. The supplies were then dispersed to the interior of the island. This was very hard work and many times we used 2,000 men and 50 trucks for a whole day without sleeping or resting. The lack of a harbour, rough waves, and severe air raids greatly hindered the unloading work at Iwo Jima. We could not leave landing craft on the sea there, so when we finished unloading we had to pull them up on the land.

In November 1944, we had only a 30-day supply of grain and a 15-day supply of supplementary food, a very dangerous situation. But afterwards we were able to increase the food a little by brave and self-sacrificing transportation. By February 1, 1945, army and navy had on hand on Iwo Jima about a 70-day supply of grain and a 60-day supply of supplementary food.

Until June 1944, American aircraft did not come to the Chichi Jima area, so we thought only of protecting our convoys from submarines. Our transports were protected primarily by our destroyers or coastal defence ships with a little assistance from aircraft at Tateyama, Hachijyo Jima, Chichi Jima, and Iwo Jima. After June, American aircraft started attacking our transports in this area and we were obliged to use night transportation and night work, and, to protect our ships, we were forced to send one army aircraft squadron to Iwo Jima. It was then that I experienced, bitterly, how miserable our transportation by sea was when the air was in the control of the enemy.

Officers and men were suffering from lack of water. They gathered rain water in empty barrels and used it. As they were unable to take baths because of the water shortage, they were obliged to go to Kitano Hama to take hot sulphur-spring baths. I also went to that hot spring once. There were no fresh vegetables, and many of us suffered from malnutrition and paratyphus. And in those days, I think, 20% of all the troops were patients.

'We could not take countermeasures'

On February 19, 1945, American forces landed on the beaches near the first airfield under cover of keen bombardments by aircraft and warships. Although their landing direction, strength, and fighting methods were as we had predicted, we could not take any countermeasures. The 135 pillboxes we had built at the first airfield were overrun and occupied only two days after the landing. We laid down a strong barrage with the artillery we had at Motoyama and Mt Suribachi, but the guns were immediately destroyed by the enemy's counterfiring. At that time we had many opportunities to make offensive attacks against the enemy, but we knew very well that if we did we would suffer much damage from bombardments by the American aircraft and vessels. Our officers and men therefore waited for the enemy to come closer to their own positions.

We were very discouraged when we heard of the fall of Mt Suribachi after only five days' fighting. On Chichi Jima I received a telegram from the district commander of

Mt Suribachi, Colonel Atsuji, who informed General Kuribayashi that the 'enemy's bombardments from air and sea and their assaults with explosions are very fierce and if we try to stay and defend our present position it will just lead us to self-destruction. We would rather go out from our positions and choose death by a Banzai charge'. I was filled with emotion. I knew about the fall of the first airfield, but I never thought of losing Mt Suribachi in only five days. General Kuribayashi was very angry when he received this telegram.

When the American M-4 (Sherman) tanks appeared in front of Osakayama, General Kuribayashi was anxious to know how to to dispose of them. Even our 47-mm anti-tank gun could not destroy them, and he at last came to the conclusion that bodily attacks with explosives were the only way.

General Kuribayashi informed Tokyo by wireless that he was not afraid of the fighting power of only three US Marine divisions if there were no bombardment from aircraft and warships. This was the only reason we were in such a miserable situation, he said.

General Kuribayashi was usually at his command post in the cave. As soon as his staff officers composed telegrams (sometimes he composed them himself), using information that came into their hands from time to time from all troops, he inspected, revised, and ordered them dispatched. As he was a very skilful writer, his telegrams made all Japanese weep in those days.

At first we received information that our infiltration attacks were inflicting great damage on the enemy. But early in March the information sent to Tokyo by wire was: 'The security of the American forces has become very strict and it is difficult to pass through their guarded line. Don't overestimate the value of infiltration attacks.'

At this point, I would like to pay my respects to the brave aviators who supplied weapons to Iwo Jima by aircraft. They made arrangements with the Iwo Jima commander and left Hamamatsu airfield on the mainland and supplied some hand grenades and flamethrowers. It is indeed difficult to express what was in the hearts of the fighting youth of Iwo Jima, as they stood facing death, when they saw those brave fliers.

Kuribayashi's last messages
According to the telegrams of General Kuribayashi, we have knowledge of the following desperate fights:

March 7: All troops of Tamanayama district fighting desperately, facing enemy at only 87-yard distance. Seven small units sent for infiltration attack from Tamanayama on sixth night. Not back yet. Results unknown.

March 8, 1000 hours: Enemy attacking northern district. Bombardments with mortars and warships very severe. Several enemy troops advancing toward Naval HQ (near Kitaburaku) and Hyoriuboku. All surviving fighting positions have sustained heavy losses, but fighting spirit running high. Inflicting great damage on enemy.

March 8, 1800 hours: Troops at Tamanayama and northern districts still holding positions. Continue to inflict damage on enemy. Fighting spirit, believing in country's victory, looks god-like.

March 8, 2000 hours: Am very sorry I have let the enemy occupy one part of Japanese territory, but am taking comfort in inflicting great damage on enemy.

March 10, 1930 hours: Enemy attacks against northern districts continuing day and night. Our troops still fighting bravely and holding positions. Divisional radio station besieged by many enemy troops. Had to destroy radio-telegraph today at 1130 hours. 200 or 300 American infantrymen, with several tanks, attacked Tenzan all day. Enemy bombardments—one battleship, 11 destroyers, and aircraft—very severe. Bombing and machine-gun firing against divisional HQ from 30 fighters and bombers so fierce I cannot express nor write of it here. Before American forces landed there were many trees around my HQ. Now not even a grasp of grass remaining. Surface of the earth changed completely. We can see numerous bombardment holes.

March 10, 2000 hours: At Tamanayama the II Mixed Brigade HQ in danger. Might have gone out for a Banzai charge at midnight on the 8th. No contact with them after that time.

March 11, 1050 hours: Surviving strength of northern districts (army and navy) is 1,500 men. On the 9th we inflicted enemy losses of 798 men and one tank.

March 11, 1400 hours: On the 8th, M-4 tank stopped on rugged ground of northern district. One man tried to go out from canopy. Superior Private Gondo sniped at him, threw hand grenade into tank, and burnt it. No contact with commander of Tamanayama district since yesterday. This morning enemy began to concentrate firepower from warships, mortars, and heavy artillery, and bombing on northern district.

March 13, 0800 hours: Captured documents say enemy is 3rd, 4th, and 5th Marine Divisions. 5th Division now in Tenzan area. On the 12th, inflicted following losses on enemy in northern district alone: one aircraft shot down, 200 men killed.

March 14, 1500 hours: Attack on northern district this morning. Much more severe than before. Around noon one part of enemy with about 10 tanks broke through our left front line and approached to 220 yards of divisional HQ.

March 15, 0800 hours: To Chichi Jima Signal Corps Commander from Iwo Jima Signal Corps Commander. Situation very dangerous. Do your best to contact us. Present strength of northern district about 900 men.

March 17, 0200 hours: From General Kuribayashi to all surviving officers and men. Battle situation come to last moment. I want surviving officers and men to go out and attack enemy until the last. You have devoted yourself to the Emperor. Do not think of yourselves. I am always at the head of you all.

March 17, 0500 hours: 145th Infantry Regiment fought bravely near Hyoriuboku, holding regimental flag in centre. Last telegram sent to me on 15th read: 'Completely burnt our brilliant regimental flag. Goodbye. . . .'

March 21, 1200 hours: At midnight on 17th went out of cave and gathered all surviving men of 145th Infantry Regiment, Tamanayama, northern, eastern, and western districts, westward of Kitaburaku. Are continuing to fight. Have 400 men under my control. Enemy besieged us and on 18th and 19th approached us by shelling and flamethrowers from tanks. Are trying to approach entrance to cave with explosives.

March 21, 1300 hours: Enemy front line 200 or 300 yards away. Attacking us with tanks. Advised us to surrender by loudspeaker. Only laughed at this childish trick.

Did not set ourselves against them.

March 22, 0910 hours: Divisional commander, officers, and men continuing to fight.

General Kuribayashi commanded his battle by candlelight without having a single rest or any sleep day after day. Radio broadcasts, newspapers, and magazines of Japan encouraged him continually. Old and young men, boys and girls of his native place, all prayed to God for his victory. On March 14, the Song of Iwo Jima, composed by the fighting men of Iwo Jima before the American forces landed, was broadcast from Tokyo to General Kuribayashi and his officers and men, and he sent his thankful message to all Japanese.

On March 15, he informed Tokyo by wire: 'Am determined to go out and make Banzai charges against enemy at midnight on 17th. Now I say goodbye to all senior and friend officers forever.' He added three farewell songs in this telegram.

From the morning of the 17th, the day he was promoted to full general, we were unable to communicate with him. We thought the 17th was his last day. We were all greatly surprised when we received his telegram on the morning of the 21st. We know from this telegram that he and his men (army and navy, altogether about 400 men) went out at midnight on the 17th and shut themselves in a cave about 150 yards north-west of his old cave. He sent the following last telegram to us: 'Have not eaten nor drunk for five days. But fighting spirit is running high. We are going to fight bravely to last moment.' I tried at Chichi Jima to send him the telegram of his promotion to general on March 17.

On the evening of the 23rd one radio operator informed me that he had heard this message from Iwo Jima: 'To all officers and men of Chichi Jima. Good-bye.' I tried to communicate with Iwo Jima three days after that. I did not get any answer. Iwo Jima had fallen.

In conclusion, I would like to explain why Japanese soldiers do not surrender. To the Japanese way of thinking, if a Japanese soldier stands on a battlefield he ought to devote his body and soul to the only outcome: victory or honourable death. From ancient times this has been the Japanese soldiers' custom, tradition, and common sense, and if by chance the prisoners of war should have returned to their homeland afterwards, they would have been treated as cowards by all Japanese. After the Second World War, however, the feeling of the Japanese about this matter seems to have changed completely.

MAJOR YOSHITAKA HORIE was born in Japan in 1914 and graduated from the Imperial Military Academy in 1936. He fought and was wounded in Northern China, and in 1942 graduated from the Imperial War College with the rank of captain. He then served as a staff officer in the Army Shipment Headquarters, as a liaison officer between army and navy, as a staff officer with XXXI Army, and finally as a staff officer for General Kuribayashi, last commander of Iwo Jima. By that time he had been promoted major. Mr Horie has written several books (*Fighting Spirit: Iwo Jima, Fighting Spirit: Pelipiu*, and *Death for Honour: Saipan*) and has translated several others from English into Japanese, including the Memoirs of Harry S. Truman. He is currently working with the US Air Force in Japan, while teaching English as a part-time university instructor in Tokyo.

TO THE GATES OF BERLIN

East Prussia, October 1944/February 1945 At the end of 1944
came an ominous pause on the Eastern Front, while the Russians,
who had gained their foothold in East Prussia, built up their
forces to complete the occupation of the 'cradle of German
militarism'. The Germans tried desperately to improvise defences.
But when the attack came it was of such massive strength and
ferocity that their front was soon torn wide open—and Russian
forces swept to within striking distance of Berlin. *By Earl Ziemke*

Father and son, already proud possessors
of Iron Crosses, wait in the cold during
the pause before the Russian onslaught

Ullstein

East Prussia was a symbol to both the Russians and the Germans, to the former of rampant German militarism, to the latter of a centuries-old conviction of military and cultural superiority over the Slavs. In the summer of 1944, as German Army Group Centre retreated across Belorussia, it manoeuvred desperately to halt the Russians forward of the East Prussian border. The Russians, just as desperately, tried to get a handhold on the 'cradle of German militarism'. On August 17 one Soviet platoon crossed the border north-west of Vilkaviškis but was wiped out before the day's end.

Two months later, on October 16, three Soviet armies drove across the border between Schirwindt and the Romintener Heide. In three days they had taken Goldap, the first German city in the east to fall, and were threatening Gumbinnen, on the direct route to Königsberg (see map on p. 2303). Shaken, Hitler cancelled plans he had been making to restore contact between Army Group Centre and Army Group North, then cut off in Courland. Instead, he ordered Colonel General Hans Reinhardt, commanding Army Group Centre, to take III Panzer Army on his north flank back behind the Niemen river and use its armour to drive the Russians out of East Prussia. Reinhardt held Gumbinnen and retook Goldap, but he had to leave the Russians in possession of a 15- by 50-mile strip of East Prussian territory when the battle ended in the first week of November. By then an ominous quiet was falling on the whole Eastern Front north of the Carpathians as both sides worked to get set for the next clash.

Army Group Centre needed time. In the summer, when Reinhardt moved his headquarters in to East Prussia, he had discovered with dismay that Gauleiter Erich Koch, who was also Defence Commissar for East Prussia, had done nothing about building fortifications and had not even made provisions for evacuating civilians from the threatened border areas. Subsequently, Koch, with Hitler's approval, continued to resist taking any precautions that he regarded as defeatist. On the border and around Königsberg, particularly in the so-called Heilsberg triangle which had been built in the 1920's by the Reichswehr, the army group had some concrete emplacements, but most of the moveable equipment had been taken out of them long ago and put into the Atlantic Wall.

In November and December, awaiting the battle, Reinhardt's three armies, using military and civilian labour, dug a network of trenches that reached back to the coast. The front, although it followed some theoretically good natural lines of defence, was weak in critical places. On the left, the III Panzer Army line followed the Niemen river from the coast to a point 55 miles upstream and then bent south at almost a right angle to tie in with IV Army east of Gumbinnen. The IV Army line ran east of Gumbinnen, east of Goldap (where it angled south-westward to Augustow 15 miles beyond the border), and then followed several small watercourses to the Narew river to tie in with II Army at Nowogrod. The II Army held a front on the Narew from Nowogrod to the Army Group Centre/Army Group A boundary at the junction of the Narew and Vistula rivers 10 miles north of Warsaw. The river lines were already badly weakened. The Russian attack toward Gumbinnen in October had created the entering wedge for a thrust toward Königsberg behind the III Panzer Army line on the Niemen. In the II Army sector on the lower Narew, the Russians had taken bridgeheads at Rozan and Serock before the end of the summer offensive.

Under military circumstances like those the Germans were facing at the end of 1944, a pause can be as debilitating as continuous battle. At the beginning of December, Army Group Centre had 33 infantry divisions and 12 Panzer or Panzer Grenadier divisions. Of the latter, Reinhardt held nine in reserve. With that strong an armoured reserve and with the front-line divisions each holding, roughly, 10 miles of the 360-mile army group front, he was about as well off as a German commander could expect to be at that stage of the war. But Hitler was planning offensives in the West and the Russians were still on the move in Hungary. By the end of the month, five of the Panzer divisions had been transferred, while on

January 4 Reinhardt reported that the Russians had five armies on the Narew and an equally strong array of 50 to 60 divisions south of the Niemen in the Goldap-Schillfelde area. Since he was on notice to give up another Panzer division (ordered a few days later), he concluded, with obvious irony, that OKH (Army High Command) considered East Prussia less important than other areas and was willing to risk a large loss of territory there. He received no answer.

Good cause to expect the worst

As the Germans watched and waited, the Intelligence picture darkened. At first, in November, the Eastern Intelligence Branch of OKH thought that the next Soviet moves would be against East Prussia and, south of the Carpathians, toward Vienna, to form a wide pincers that would also reach into Czechoslovakia and Upper Silesia. In December the estimate changed: the main effort, Intelligence predicted, would be against Army Group A on the Vistula and would go straight west. A simultaneous thrust against Army Group Centre could be expected but possibly with a more limited objective than the full conquest of East Prussia since Army Group North was still holding out in Courland and so tying down Soviet strength on the northern flank. By early January it appeared that the Russians would undertake the 'big solution' against Army Group Centre, the thrust to the lower Vistula to cut off East Prussia, and also thrust deep against Army Group A, possibly to Berlin.

From what they could see, the German Intelligence officers had good cause to expect the worst. Their strength comparisons showed that opposite 160 German units of roughly division or brigade size on the whole Eastern Front the Russians had 414 units in the front, 261 in front reserves, and 219 in reserves in depth. Even if one allows for a Soviet unit size 30% smaller than the German and for the fact that they were usually 40% under authorised strengths (with no similar understrength allowance for the German units), the Soviet superiority worked out at over 2·3 : 1.

During the first week of the new year, the German Army Chief-of-Staff, Colonel-General Heinz Guderian, visited the army group headquarters on the Eastern Front. At Army Groups Centre and A he heard the same story: the Russians were so strong at the critical points, the bridgeheads on the Narew and the Vistula, that the front could not hold. Reinhardt proposed that he be allowed to take his front back from the Narew to the East Prussian border and thus at least escape the initial blow that the Russians had by then had three months to prepare.

On January 9, Guderian reported to Hitler in the Alderhorst, the Führer Headquarters near Bad Nauheim from which Hitler had directed the 1940 campaign against France and where he was now trying to salvage what he could from the Ardennes offensive. According to Guderian, Hitler refused to believe the Intelligence estimates of Soviet strength and told him whoever concocted them ought to be put in an asylum. He rejected Reinhardt's proposal and a similar one from the Army Group A command. The stenographer, whom Hitler insisted on having present at every conference with a general, recorded in the fragment of his notes that has survived a series of rambling remarks by Hitler on the folly of ever having given ground in the Soviet Union in the first place. Those who were 'beginning to whine', he said, ought to look at the example of what the Russians had gone through in the early years of the war.

Whether Hitler wanted to believe it or not, the respite on the Eastern Front was over. German Intelligence believed the Soviet armies were ready to move on December 15 and thereafter were waiting for a change in the weather. They could have been right. The early winter that year was cold, which favoured overland armoured movement, but persistent cloudiness, snow, and fog hampered air operations and artillery observation. The Soviet accounts say the winter offensive had originally not been scheduled to start until January 20, but had been moved ahead eight days after Winston Churchill asked Stalin what he could do to take some of the pressure off the British and Americans in the West.

Stavka had prepared two offensives, related but separated geographically by the course of the Vistula west of Warsaw. The stronger of the two was to be against Army Group A between Warsaw and the Carpathians. It was aimed toward the Oder and Berlin. The other was to run north of the Vistula bend into East Prussia. The operation in East Prussia was conceived as a sweeping double envelopment. The 2nd Belorussian Front, with Marshal Rokossovsky in command, was to break out of the Serock and Rozan bridgeheads on the lower Narew, strike north-west to the Baltic coast, cut off East Prussia, and clear the line of the lower Vistula. On Rokossovsky's right, 3rd Belorussian Front, under General Chernyakovsky, was to attack due west south of the Pregel river toward Königsberg, split III Panzer Army off from the Army Group Centre main force, and envelop IV Army among and west of the Masurian Lakes.

Strategically, Stavka intended nothing less than to end the war—in about a 45-day operation, according to its estimates. To make certain that the attack in the main direction, toward Berlin, would be sufficiently strong, the East Prussian operation had been cut down somewhat, particularly in rations and artillery ammunition. Because of that and because Army Group Centre appeared relatively stronger than Army Group A, the Soviet Command intended, 'in the least favourable situation', to settle for the immobilization of the German forces in East Prussia.

Attack south of Warsaw

On January 12, the day the offensive began south of Warsaw, the Russians opposite Army Group Centre attacked IV Army north and south of the Romintener Heide in an attempt to mislead the Germans and tie down their reserves. The next day, opening the attack in earnest, 3rd Belorussian Front hit III Panzer Army at Stallupönen and Pillkallen, and on the 14th, 2nd Belorussian Front attacked II Army out of the Serock and Rozan bridgeheads. Both German armies held up well the first two days, falling back to the main battle line and patching up the holes. Fog prevented the Russians from bringing their air power and armour into full play.

Unfortunately for Reinhardt, this momentary success looked almost like a defensive victory by comparison with what was happening south of Warsaw. In two days the Army Group A front had crumbled completely, and on the 14th, trying to find a bright spot, Guderian reported to Hitler that apparently Reinhardt could prevent tactical breakthroughs on the Narew and the Pregel. Hitler seized the opportunity and ordered the Panzer Corps 'Grossdeutschland', which with its two Panzer divisions formed the heart of Reinhardt's reserves, transferred to Army Group A.

On January 15, II Army was pushed back to the first switch position. In the north the weather was clearing, and during the day heavy air and tank attacks forced III Panzer Army to start drawing back the front south of Pillkallen to prevent its breaking apart.

The next day the weather also cleared in the II Army sector, and a Soviet tank spearhead broke through past Nowe Miasto; 2nd Belorussian Front's main force—five armies, one of them a tank army, plus a tanks corps, a mechanised corps, and a cavalry corps—was beginning to move out of the Rozan bridgehead in full force. From the vicinity of Nowe Miasto it aimed north toward the mouth of the Vistula. The two armies and a tank corps on the left, pushing out of the Serock area to provide cover in the direction of Bielsk and Bromberg, would have no trouble: the Army Group A flank had broken away south of the Vistula. In the north, 3rd Belorussian Front, having failed to break through on a broad front, began shifting its weight northward to the Pillkallen area. For Army Group Centre the obvious next move was to start pulling back the still untouched IV Army so as to get divisions to close the breakthrough against II Army and prevent, if it could, the envelopment of its right flank. Reinhardt proposed this on the 16th.

By the 17th, II Army was clearly strained to the limit. After Guderian told him that afternoon that Hitler refused to let IV Army withdraw, Reinhardt called Hitler and was treated to a lengthy

Russian tanks occupy Heiligenbeil in East Prussia. The Soviet predominance in armour told heavily in their favour, and the hasty German defences were no match for them

lecture on the futility of withdrawals—they released as much enemy as German strength. The most Hitler would agree to was taking two divisions from IV Army by thinning its front.

The next day II Army's front snapped, opening a gap on both sides of Mlawa. Reinhardt put in a Panzer corps HQ and all the reinforcements he could scrape together, seven divisions, but knew they were not likely to be enough. In twenty-four hours the leading Soviet tanks stood south of Gilgenburg; 5th Guards Tank Army was ready for the dash to the coast. In the meantime, III Panzer Army's front had broken open north of the Pregel river.

The 20th was a relatively quiet day. Rokossovsky and Chernyakovsky were getting ready to shift into high gear, but Hitler again refused to let IV Army move. He promised a Panzer division from Army Group North and 20 naval replacement battalions from Denmark.

The Russian offensive picked up speed on January 21. Against II Army, 2nd Belorussian Front went as far as Deutsch Eylau and turned a force north toward Allenstein, while 3rd Belorussian Front took Gumbinnen, removing that obstacle on the route to Königsberg along the Pregel. Obviously, the thrust to the coast to cut off the army group was developing, and II Army reported that it might delay but could not prevent it. More alarming, the attacks south of the Pregel and toward Allenstein presaged an attempt to force the whole army group away from the coast and into an encirclement in the interior of East Prussia. The IV Army was already lying in the bottom of a lopsided sack, 130 miles from the coast.

After Reinhardt reported that all the lower commands were pressing for relief and that a complete loss of confidence in the higher leadership was impending, Hitler finally agreed to let IV Army withdraw to the eastern edge of the Masurian Lakes. This was something, but far from enough. Reinhardt noted in his diary that in the long run the army group would have to take everything back to the Heilsberg triangle, the fortifications built when all the 100,000-man Reichswehr had expected to be able to defend was Königsberg and a foothold in East Prussia. For a decade or more no one had imagined that that relic of German weakness would ever again figure in a military plan.

Surprise attack on Elbing
By nightfall on January 23, the 2nd Belorussian Front had cut all the roads and railroads crossing the Vistula except the coastal road through Elbing. After dark that day, the 5th Guards Tank Army's lead tank detachment approached the city. Finding that it had not been alerted—the streetcars were running and on one street German soldiers from a local armoured school were marching in formation—the Russian crews turned on the headlights of their tanks and rolled through the main streets firing as they went. By daylight, when the next wave of Soviet tanks arrived, the Germans in Elbing had recovered enough to fight them off and force them to detour east around the city. In the meantime, however, the Russian lead detachment reached the coast. With that the Army Group Centre main force, IV Army and III Panzer Army, was isolated in East Prussia. The II Army held Elbing but along the rest of its line was being forced to fall back to the west across the lower Vistula.

Reinhardt reported that he would put all the troops he could muster into counterattacks from east and west to restore the contact. Hitler, anticipating withdrawals elsewhere to get the troops, countered with an order forbidding Reinhardt to take IV Army any farther west than Lötzen and Ortelsburg. As reinforcements, he offered instead two divisions from Memel, which he had insisted until then on holding as 'a springboard to Army Group North'. The divisions would have to be brought south by small boats or over the Kurische Nehrung, the narrow, 60-mile-long tongue of sand hills spanning the Bay of Courland.

On Reinhardt's north flank, III Panzer Army had managed for nine days to preserve a front of sorts by retreating gradually toward Königsberg; but on January 24 the Russians broke through

south of the Pregel and threatened to cut off Königsberg on the south. The army group command was trapped between reality and Hitler's illusions. Reinhardt knew he could not hold Königsberg and the Samland Peninsula, let the IV Army front continue to bulge eastward toward the Masurian Lakes, and still counterattack to the west. But he could not bring himself to confront Hitler with those issues, and he went so far as to transfer to III Panzer Army two divisions IV Army had taken out for the counterattack. When IV Army evacuated the outer defences of Lötzen without permission during the day of the 24th, Reinhardt said nothing; he knew the army would have to go back farther, much farther: but he also accepted Hitler's demand for a full-scale investigation in silence.

Hossbach decides to break out
On the morning of the 24th the Commanding General, IV Army, General Friedrich Hossbach, acting independently, called in his three corps commanders. He told them that the army's land communications with Germany were cut and no relief could be expected. Therefore, he had decided to break out to the west. The breakout and retreat would begin on the night of the 26th, or the next day. He intended to put the whole army into it and give up East Prussia. The civilians would have to stay behind. This sounded horrible, he said, but it could not be changed; the paramount objective had to be to get the army back to Germany proper with its combat potential intact. He did not mention III Panzer Army. Probably he assumed that it would have to make its own choice whether to go or stay when the time came. On the necessity for an attack to the west he and Reinhardt agreed in general terms, and the withdrawal east of Lötzen had showed that Reinhardt was not determined to hold in the east. Hossbach apparently concluded that it was not worthwhile to tell him more.

On the 25th Chernyakovsky's troops got to within 12 miles of Königsberg in the south-east. They seemed again to be intent on pinching off the neck of the sack in which IV Army was caught. The IV Army's east front was 90 miles from the coast; on the coast IV and III Panzer Armies' fronts, back to back, were less than 40 miles apart. That night Reinhardt, who had been wounded in an air raid during the day, tried to persuade Guderian that the time had come to reduce the bulge. Guderian insisted that the front stay where it was; he refused to hear of any withdrawals. During the day Army Group Centre had been renamed Army Group North. (In a flurry of name changes that had no discernible purpose unless it were to confuse future scholars of the war, Army Group North became Army Group Courland and Army Group A became Army Group Centre.) At the same time, II Army was transferred to the newly-created Army Group Vistula, which, under the command of the Reichsführer-SS Heinrich Himmler, had been given the mission of defending Pomerania, West Prussia, and Danzig on a line from the Oder to the Vistula.

The 5th Guards Tank Army had a solid hold on the Baltic coast north-east of Elbing by January 26. On its right, IV Army deployed divisions for the breakout. The movement weakened the army's south-east and north-east fronts; Lötzen was lost; and the Russians, crossing the frozen lakes, punched numerous holes in the front. Before noon that day, Reinhardt reported that he was about to order IV Army to withdraw 30 miles to the line Wartenburg/Bischofsburg/Schippenbeil/Friedland. Talking to Hitler, Reinhardt added that he intended further to break out to the west and take the front into the Heilsburg triangle. Hitler replied that he would give a decision later and hung up.

Realising that he was being presented with a *fait accompli*, even though he apparently did not guess the full extent at least of Hossbach's intentions, Hitler fell into a rage. He told Guderian that what Reinhardt projected was diametrically opposed to his, Hitler's, basic plan and was treason. He demanded that Reinhardt and Hossbach be relieved immediately. To the army group he sent an order forbidding any withdrawal beyond the line Wartenburg/Nikolaiken—which would only have cut a narrow slice off the south-eastern tip

of the IV Army bulge. Thereafter communications with the Army High Command suddenly ceased; no one with any authority would talk to the army group. Finally, at 1915 hours, Reinhardt decided on his own responsibility to let IV Army withdraw to the line he had originally proposed. He tried to sweeten the dose by reporting that he would try to get a solid front 'at the latest' in the line Wartenburg/Bischofsburg/Schippenbeil/Friedland. Two hours later a telegram came through relieving him and his chief-of-staff.

Before noon the next day, Colonel-General Lothar Rendulic arrived from Army Group Courland to take command. He had orders from Hitler to hold Königsburg and what was left of East Prussia. The counterattack to the west had begun during the night, although by then it was wasted effort. Only the breakout and retreat that Hossbach had planned could have succeeded, and with Rendulic in command and Hitler alerted that was impossible.

Three days later, General Friedrich Müller, who had made a reputation as an improviser during the retreat from Greece, replaced Hossbach. Müller was a specialist in carrying out orders. In his efficiency reports he was described as *krisenfest* ('reliable in crises'), which at this stage of the war denoted an ability to lead his troops through successive disasters without any apparent qualms.

The withdrawal Reinhardt had ordered before he was dismissed took some of the pressure off IV Army's east front, but in the north General Bagramyan's 1st Baltic Front had added its weight to the advance on Königsberg and had pushed III Panzer Army away from Königsberg and on to the Samland Peninsula. South of Königsberg, IV Army still held open a narrow corridor into the city. The greatest danger for the moment was that the Russians on Samland might go the remaining 15 miles or so to Pillau on the Frische Nehrung and cut the army group's sea supply line. (From Pillau trucks could cross the frozen bay to Heiligenbeil.)

On February 1, the IV Army made a last attempt to break through to Elbing. It ran into a counterattack and was stopped dead.

35 miles from Berlin
During the succeeding days the flood of civilian refugees out of East Prussia reached its peak. Some were taken out by boat, most walked or made their way by horse and wagon to Danzig across the Frische Nehrung and the Vistula delta. Many died on the way from cold and exhaustion. Many others were killed in Russian air and artillery attacks. By mid-February 1,300,000 of the 2,300,000 population of East Prussia had left. Of those who stayed about half were *Volkssturm* ('Home Guard') men and others who had been absorbed into the Wehrmacht.

Rendulic, in the last few months left in the war, was working to assure himself of a niche in history as one of the most ruthless of the German generals in the treatment of his own troops. The one characteristic all his former superiors had remarked on was his absolute nervelessness. For him, keeping the army group in East Prussia raised no question other than how it could best be accomplished. In one order he made the battalion and regimental commanders responsible for 'every foot of ground' voluntarily given up and appended the example of a captain he had ordered shot the day before for taking his battalion back a mile after it had been broken through. In another, he ordered 'flying courts-martial' created to scour the rear area. Every soldier, not wounded, picked up outside his unit area was to be tried and shot on the spot.

In the first week of February all Germany was stunned by the wave of destruction that had rolled in from the east. Three weeks earlier, the front had still been deep in Poland and except for the strip in East Prussia, nowhere on German soil. Now, the Russians were on the Oder, 35 miles from Berlin. Upper Silesia was lost. In East Prussia a German army group was being cut to pieces, and if the Russians maintained their rate of advance, there seemed to be no reason why they could not be on the Rhine in another three weeks.

[Earl Ziemke's biography is in Vol 5, p. 2156.]

In March 1945 the Red Army reached Danzig. A Soviet tank covers a street with its machine-gun as German opposition is cleared up. In street fighting tanks were used mainly in a house-breaking role

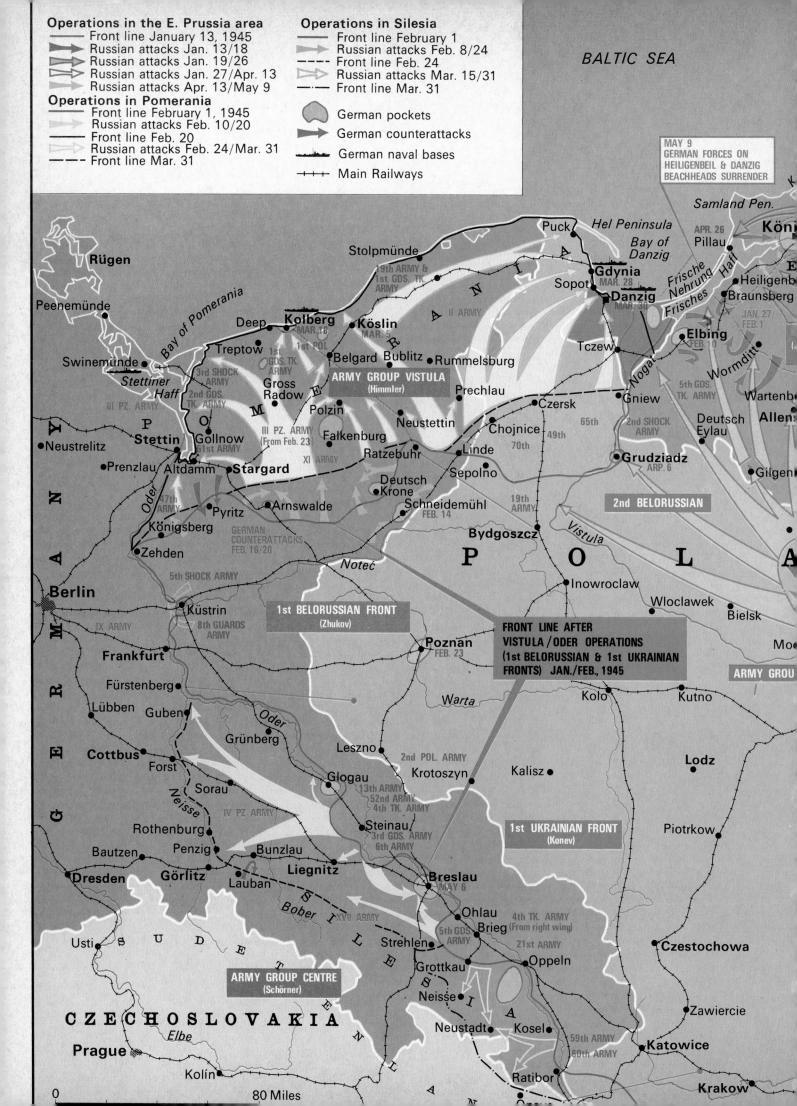

Operations in the E. Prussia area
— Front line January 13, 1945
→ Russian attacks Jan. 13/18
⇒ Russian attacks Jan. 19/26
⇨ Russian attacks Jan. 27/Apr. 13
⇨ Russian attacks Apr. 13/May 9

Operations in Pomerania
— Front line February 1, 1945
⇨ Russian attacks Feb. 10/20
— Front line Feb. 20
⇨ Russian attacks Feb. 24/Mar. 31
-·-· Front line Mar. 31

Operations in Silesia
— Front line February 1
⇨ Russian attacks Feb. 8/24
--- Front line Feb. 24
⇨ Russian attacks Mar. 15/31
-·-· Front line Mar. 31

⬢ German pockets
➤ German counterattacks
⚓ German naval bases
+++ Main Railways

BALTIC SEA

MAY 9
GERMAN FORCES ON
HEILIGENBEIL & DANZIG
BEACHHEADS SURRENDER

Samland Pen.
Köni...
APR. 26
Pillau

Rügen

Hel Peninsula
Bay of Danzig
Puck
Stolpmünde
19th ARMY &
1st GDS. TK.
ARMY
II ARMY
Gdynia
Sopot
MAR. 28
Danzig
MAR. 30
Heiligenb...
Frische Nehrung
Frisches Haff
Braunsberg

Peenemünde
Bay of Pomerania
Deep
MAR. 18
Kolberg
Köslin
MAR. 5
1st POL
ARMY
Belgard Bublitz
Rummelsburg
Prechlau
Czersk
Tczew
Nogat
Gniew
Elbing
FEB. 10
Wormditt
Wartenb...
Allen

Swinemünde
Stettiner Haff
Treptow
1st
GDS. TK.
ARMY
3rd SHOCK
ARMY
2nd GDS.
TK. ARMY
III PZ. ARMY
Gross Radow
Polzin
ARMY GROUP VISTULA
(Himmler)
Neustettin
Chojnice
49th
Linde
70th
65th
2nd SHOCK
ARMY
5th GDS.
TK. ARMY
Deutsch Eylau

Stettin
61st ARMY
Gollnow
III PZ. ARMY
(From Feb. 23)
Falkenburg
XI ARMY
Ratzebuhr
Sepolno
19th
ARMY
Grudziadz
ARP. 6
Gilgen...

Neustrelitz
Prenzlau
Altdamm
Stargard
Deutsch Krone
Schneidemühl
FEB. 14
2nd BELORUSSIAN

Königsberg
47th
ARMY
Pyritz
Arnswalde
GERMAN COUNTERATTACKS
FEB. 16/20
Noteć
Vistula
Bydgoszcz
Inowroclaw
Wloclawek
Bielsk

Zehden
5th SHOCK ARMY
P   O   L
A
Mo...

Berlin
Küstrin
1st BELORUSSIAN FRONT
(Zhukov)
IX ARMY
8th GUARDS
ARMY
Poznań
FEB. 23
**FRONT LINE AFTER
VISTULA / ODER OPERATIONS
(1st BELORUSSIAN & 1st UKRAINIAN
FRONTS) JAN./FEB., 1945**
Kolo
Kutno
ARMY GROU

Frankfurt
Fürstenberg
Warta
Oder
Krotoszyn
Kalisz
Lodz

Lübben
Guben
Grünberg
Leszno
2nd POL. ARMY

Cottbus
Forst
Neisse
Oder
Sorau
Glogau
13th ARMY
52nd ARMY
4th TK. ARMY
Steinau
3rd GDS. ARMY
6th ARMY
1st UKRAINIAN FRONT
(Konev)
Piotrkow

Rothenburg
Penzig
Bunzlau
IV PZ ARMY
Liegnitz
Breslau
MAY 6
4th TK. ARMY
(From right wing)
21st ARMY

Bautzen
Dresden
Görlitz
Lauban
Bober
XVII ARMY
Ohlau
Brieg
5th GDS
ARMY
Czestochowa

Usti
Neisse
Strehlen
Grottkau
Oppeln
Zawiercie

ARMY GROUP CENTRE
(Schörner)
Neisse
Neustadt
Kosel
59th ARMY
60th ARMY
Katowice

C Z E C H O S L O V A K I A
Elbe
Ratibor

Prague
Kolin
Krakow

0 _____ 80 Miles

Annexed by Germany from Lithuania 1939

LITHUANIA

1st BALTIC FRONT
(Bagramyan)

43rd
ARMY

Niemen

Tilsit

39th ARMY

III PZ.
ARMY

Pillkallen

Schirwindt

Kraupishken

28th
ARMY

Vilkaviškis

Pregel

nsterburg

Stallupönen

Gumbinnen

**3rd BELORUSSIAN
FRONT**
(Chernyakhovsky)

2nd
GDS.
ARMY

riedland

SSIA

Schippenbeil

Goldap

UP CENTRE
NORTH JAN 25)
hardt)

Suwalki

Masurian

IV ARMY

chofsburg

Lakes

Augustow

kolaiken

31st ARMY

urg

50th ARMY

Nowogrod

Bialystok

49th
ARMY

N   D

Rozan

3rd & 48th
ARMIES

2nd BELORUSSIAN FRONT
(Rokossovsky)

2nd SHOCK
ARMY

6th GDS.
TK. ARMY

65th ARMY

70th ARMY

Serock

Warsaw

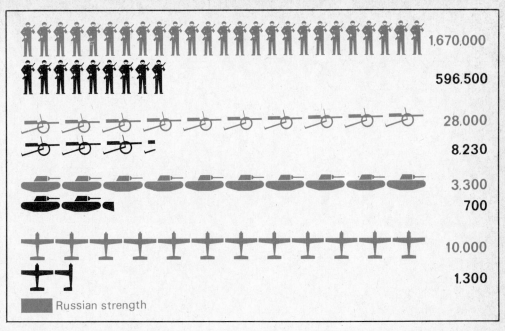

1,670,000

596,500

28,000

8,230

3,300

700

10,000

1,300

Russian strength

Drive to the Gates of Berlin

East Prussia, the birthplace of Prussian militarism, and Silesia, the young Prussia's first territorial acquisition, were both wrested from the Reich by the Red Army in four months. Often seen as the triumph of a superior ideology, a superior political system, and superior generals, the Red Army's successful offensive is more readily explainable in terms of superior numbers, weapons, and supplies. The 2nd and 3rd Belorussian Fronts in East Prussia had a massive superiority in men and machines (see chart above), and the German forces, abandoned in East Prussia after the Russian advances south of Warsaw in January, were in no condition to resist them. All the same, no further Russian advance could take place until the remaining German forces in East Prussia had been removed from their flanks. The map shows the two offensives, one in East Prussia and one in Silesia, necessary to secure the Red Army's flanks before they could launch their final, massive attack on Berlin

Russia's SU-37: Light tanks or self-propelled guns were used extensively for close infantry support; their small size and low silhouette made them less vulnerable than their heavier brethren. What they lacked in punch and firepower, they made up in speed and manoeuvrability. *Length:* 15 feet 9 inches. *Weight:* 10·5 tons. *Range:* 166 miles. *Top speed:* 32 mph. *Armament:* One 37-mm gun. *Armour:* 35-mm in front

John Batchelor

DRIVE TO THE ODER

Above: Bowed down by the barrel, ammunition, and baseplate, a Russian mortar crew dashes to a new position down a Danzig street

Eastern Prussia and Silesia, February/April 1945 To the horrified Germans, there now seemed little to stop the Russians from sweeping over the whole of their country. But the Russians were having their own problems—not only had they again outrun their supply lines, but their flanks were now threatened by sizeable German forces which had to be cleared before the final assault on Berlin could begin. *Victor Zhelanov* presents the Russian view

The success of the winter offensive of January 1945 had swept units of the Red Army deep into German territory, to form a massive bulge running south from Frisches Haff bay to Graudenz, west through Ratzebuhr to Zehden, and then south-west along the Oder to Ratibor (see map on page 2302). Although this bulge, which was held by 1st Belorussian Front under Marshal Rokossovsky and 1st Ukrainian Front under Marshal Konev, was only 40 to 45 miles from Berlin, there were several factors which made an immediate offensive to seize the city impossible.

The Soviet forces were tired after their offensive, units were seriously understrength in both men and equipment, and reinforcements were not arriving in adequate numbers. The rear elements of the Fronts and armies were a long way behind the forward troops, and the speed of the offensive had outstripped the rate at which railways and roads could be prepared. The Germans had fortified the line of the Oder—particularly the towns of Küstrin, Glogau, Breslau, and Ratibor—and it would take time to reduce these in preparation for a major advance.

Although the German Army Group North had been cut off in the Königsberg/Samland area, it was still tying down considerable Russian forces, and in Eastern Pomerania, Army Group Vistula lay, with its back to the Baltic, overhanging the right flank of the Russian forces. After the disasters in January, Hitler had put this army group—which consisted of II and XI Armies, supported by Luftflotte VI—under the command of the Reichsführer SS, Heinrich Himmler, and ordered him to defend both Danzig and Berlin and establish a front along the Vistula and Oder rivers which would protect Pomerania and West Prussia.

When the Russian forces had first reached the Oder, the German High Command had also worked out a counteroffensive which involved holding the river line with III Panzer and IX Armies while making two major strikes out of Pomerania and East Silesia—where Army Group Centre under General Schörner was situated—to crush the Russian forces on the Oder. This, in the words of General Guderian, would 'strengthen the defence of Berlin, and gain the time which was needed to negotiate an armistice with the Western Powers'. It would also have enabled the Germans to hold on to Eastern Pomerania with its important naval bases in the Bays of Danzig and Pomerania through which their forces in Courland and East Prussia were supplied, and to retain the Upper Silesia industrial area.

But the means were lacking: the only substantial force in Army Group Vistula was II Army, and this was not only tied down in defending the Danzig area, but had been ordered by Hitler to clear Elbing and 'resume' the advance towards Army Group North; while the units in Silesia were seriously understrength. So OKW planned a single attack, to be carried out by units of XI Army from the Stargard area in Eastern Pomerania towards Pyritz. This was designed to smash units of the 1st Belorussian Front, and was to begin on February 15 with, as Guderian said, 'lightning speed, before the Russians brought large forces up to the front and guessed our intentions'.

Thus, the German forces in Eastern Pomerania were a threat which could not be ignored by Stavka, and 2nd Belorussian Front was ordered to move west, liquidating Army Group Vistula and closing the lightly-held gap between its left flank and the right flank of 1st Belorussian Front. The order to attack on February 10 did not reach 2nd Belorussian Front, which was still weakened by its exertions, until February 8: it was to strike west of the Vistula and have seized a line running from the mouth of the Vistula to Neustettin via Rummelsburg. Then, when 19th Army had arrived from reserve, the Front was to advance towards Stettin, capturing the Danzig/Gdynia area, and clearing the Baltic coast as far as the Bay of Pomerania.

In spite of the ambitious scope of this offensive, the forces of 1st Belorussian Front were not to be used, and they were ordered by Marshal Zhukov to concentrate on consolidating their bridgeheads across the Oder, take steps to wipe out the German fortifications at Küstrin and Frankfurt-on-Oder, prepare for the next offensive towards Berlin, and guard against possible attacks from the north.

A serious reverse

The 2nd Belorussian Front launched its offensive on February 10 in the Grudziadz/Sepolno sector, heading north-west. But units of the German II Army made good use of their strong defence lines and put up a dogged resistance so that the Soviet forces could advance only slowly. By February 20 they had gained only about 25 to 40 miles and were forced to halt on a line running from Gniew to Linde. Meanwhile, the encircled German garrison at Elbing was wiped out, but Grudziadz remained untaken.

There were several basic reasons for the slowness of the advance: the operation had been planned too hastily, and was now shown to be too much for only one Front; German resistance had been underestimated; and Soviet forces were still below strength, with their supply units too far back and their air support coming from a considerable way off.

Nevertheless, the offensive had caused great concern to the Germans, and General Weiss, the commander of II Army, warned Himmler that in the long run he could either defend the Danzig area or keep contact on his right, but not both, and that Grudziadz must be evacuated. Himmler's reply was to order Weiss to remember the glorious traditions of Prussian militarism, and hold all these objectives.

Meanwhile, the units of 1st Belorussian Front had been active on their right flank, annihilating the German garrisons in Deutsch Krone and Arnswalde, and advancing between 12 and 30 miles to the north by the end of February. The German force in Schneidemühl, which had been surrounded during January, was wiped out on February 14, and the siege of Poznan ended on February 23. The Polish 2nd Army, which was just completing formation, took part in this latter battle.

On February 16, the Germans made a strong counterattack in the Stargard/Pyritz area, and XI Army was not driven back until the 20th, but its defeat did not mean an end to the threat which the German forces in Eastern Pomerania posed to the right flank of the Soviet forces.

There was also considerable action in East Prussia, where 3rd Belorussian Front under Marshal Chernyakovsky forced IV Army out of the Heilberg area, while 1st Baltic Front under Marshal Bagramyan thrust the remnants of III Panzer Army, now named Army Detachment Samland, back to the tip of the Samland Peninsula by February 13. Königsberg was surrounded and, a week later, IV Army was confined to a 35-mile by 15-mile beach-head around Heiligenbeil. It was during this battle that Marshal Chernyakovsky was killed and Marshal Vasilevsky took command of 3rd Belorussian Front.

Stavka now ordered 1st Baltic Front to disregard Königsberg temporarily and concentrate on clearing the Samland Peninsula, while Vasilevsky was to concentrate on the Heiligenbeil area. But a sudden attack by Army Detachment Samland succeeded in breaking through to Königsberg, and so Stavka decided to halt all further operations, merge 1st Baltic and 3rd Belorussian Fronts under Marshal Vasilevsky, and prepare for a final operation to clear East Prussia.

The German attack on the right wing of 1st Belorussian Front had emphasised the need for a new and larger offensive to complete the elimination of the entire German force in Eastern Pomerania. Only if this were done, could the situation on the central strategic axis be prevented from becoming too complicated, and the projected Berlin offensive launched without risk. The Front commanders were well aware of this, and by February 15 they had submitted to Stavka their plans for further operations in the area.

Marshal Rokossovsky proposed to reduce the area of 2nd Belorussian Front's operations, change the direction of the main blow, and limit the task set to his troops. Instead of making another frontal assault on the whole German line in Eastern Pomerania, he intended to strike north to the coast in the Köslin area, thus cutting off and destroying the German II Army. Marshal Zhukov asked for permission for 1st Belorussian to use large forces in similar thrusts towards the Baltic coast.

Stavka accepted these proposals, and ordered 2nd Belorussian Front to use 19th Army and 3rd Guards Tank Corps to strike the main blow on the left flank of the Front, while 1st Belorussian Front used its right wing in a thrust towards Falkenburg, and other forces in an attack towards Gollnow. The 3rd Belorussian Front was to prevent enemy withdrawal from the Frische Nehrung peninsula, while the Baltic Fleet used aircraft, MTBs, and submarines to attack German sea communications in the southern Baltic. The new concept of the operation was to cut Army Group Vistula into sections, and then to destroy it piecemeal.

Opposite 2nd Belorussian Front, the Germans had been able to reinforce their II Army with units taken from reserve so that it now had 18 infantry, two Panzer, and one motorised divisions, with 230,000 men, 800 tanks, 4,000 guns and mortars, and 20 armoured trains. The 2nd Belorussian Front had received virtually no reinforcement while the operation was being prepared, and Marshal Rokossovsky and his staff had to rely on redisposition of their forces to establish a superiority of almost 3 to 1 in infantry, 2 to 1 in tanks and assault guns, 4·5 to 1 in mortars, and 3 to 1 in artillery on the 10½-mile sector chosen for the main assault.

Facing 1st Belorussian Front, the German III Panzer Army had absorbed the forces of XI Army, and now consisted of 11 infantry, one Panzer, and two motorised divisions plus one brigade and various other units—a total of 200,000 men, 700 tanks and assault guns, 2,500 field-guns and mortars, and about 100 coastal artillery and fixed AA guns which had been adapted to fire at land targets.

Marshal Zhukov assigned four combined arms armies (3rd Shock, 47th, 61st, and Polish 1st), two tank armies (1st and 2nd Guards), and two cavalry corps (2nd and 7th Guards) to the task of beating III Panzer Army; a force of about one cavalry and 18 infantry divisions, one mechanised and four tank corps, three 'breakthrough' artillery divisions, and other units including about 70% of his artillery—this had a considerable superiority over the Germans in the assault sector.

The offensive began on February 24 when the assault group on the left flank of 2nd Belorussian Front broke through the main belt of German defences, and by the end of the third day had driven a wedge 30 miles deep and 37 miles wide into the German positions. The 3rd Guards Cavalry Corps was fed into the breach, and joined in the battle for Neustettin. Desperate German attempts to hold this advance were unsuccessful, and on February 28 the Soviet forces widened the breach to 44 miles and captured the towns of Prechlau and Neustettin. On the right and centre of the front there was no advance.

The Germans again cut off

On March 5, the assault group took Köslin and reached the Baltic on a sector about 12½ miles wide. The German II Army was isolated from the remaining forces of Army Group Vistula and could only keep contact by air or by sea through Danzig or Gdynia. The main force of 19th Army now swung east and began to work along the coast towards Gdynia, while part of the force in the Köslin area turned west to prevent any counterattack from the rear. Throughout, the success of the assault group had been greatly helped by the strong support given by the 4th Air Army, which flew more than 8,500 sorties between February 24 and March 5.

The offensive by 1st Belorussian Front on March 1 was heralded by a 50-minute bombardment. It broke through the German defences on a broad front, and both tank armies were fed into the breach—1st Guards racing to the north in an attempt to fight through to the sea as soon as possible.

On the 3rd, the Polish 1st Army on the right wing of 1st Belorussian Front took advantage of the success of 2nd Belorussian Front to bypass Polzin and make a lightning attack on Kolberg. The 1st Guards had reached the Gross **2308** ▷

Scraping the barrel

Sceptical Germans inspect the latest symptom of the Führer's infallibility—the order conscripting old and young alike. *Below:* 17 and 18 years old respectively, these two boys had only 12 weeks' training before being thrown into action

Peering myopically at an unfamiliar weapon, an elderly Volkssturmer struggles to revise his memories of war as a machinegun and bayonetting match. On his left a youthful colleague clutches his *Panzerfaust*, Germany's version of the Bazooka

Armed only with small arms and *Panzerfausts* these cycle troops were nonetheless expected to stem the tide of Allied armour *Below:* Two last-ditch defenders of the Fatherland appear not unduly downcast by their capture in March 1945

Among the prisoners taken when Antwerp was occupied was this ten-year-old. By this stage in the war even regular units were made up of very young recruits. Hitler was obviously determined to fight to the very last boy

Radow area, but the 2nd Guards, which had swung to the left, was making little headway—with its accompanying 61st Army it had been met by a strong German counterattack in the Stargard area. Meanwhile, 47th Army was on the east bank of the Oder, fighting hard to break the first line of German defences but having little success.

By March 5, the right wing consolidated its hold on the coast along a 10-mile sector between Kolberg and Deep, and had set about mopping up isolated enemy units: south-west of Polzin, the Poles and 3rd Shock Army had encircled X SS Corps and Corps Group 'Tettau', while east of Kolberg units of both Soviet Fronts had surrounded more than 20,000 Germans and several battalions were pinned in the forests north of Belgored. On the same day, 61st Army beat back another German counterattack and seized Stargard. Here they liberated a large group of Western prisoners-of-war and many Soviet citizens who had been driven into slavery by the Nazis.

As they reached the coast, the main forces of 1st Belorussian Front turned west and continued their offensive along the coast towards Stettiner Haff lagoon. On March 5 Stavka had felt able to detach 1st Guards Tank Army and send it to be used on the left flank of 2nd Belorussian flank during the operation to capture the Danzig/Gdynia area.

The 1st Belorussian Front quickly completed its task: the German force surrounded near Polzin was wiped out by March 7, and the remnant of III Panzer Army withdrew over the Oder. On March 18, Kolberg was taken by units of the Polish 1st Army, and when, on March 20, Altdamm was stormed, the last German foothold on the east bank of the northern Oder had been eliminated. The 1st Belorussian Front was now able to go over to the defensive.

But 2nd Belorussian Front was still on the offensive, and it was only after slow and bitter fighting that it succeeded in driving the Germans back behind the fortifications of the Danzig/Gdynia area. After the fall of Köslin, Hitler had sent General Rendulic to command Army Group Courland, and transferred II Army to Army Group North, giving Weiss command of the army group with orders to hold the Gdynia/Danzig area, the Hel Peninsula, Pillau, and the Frische Nehrung—and the surrounded Germans fought desperately.

On March 22, Soviet troops breached the German lines west of Sopot, captured the town, and reached the coast, thus splitting the German force whose remnants were now concentrated in the port areas of Danzig and Gdynia and the Hel Peninsula. Gdynia naval base was stormed on March 28, and about 9,000 prisoners and much equipment were taken. Two days later the last of the Danzig defenders were mopped up, and the city itself was occupied. Over 10,000 prisoners were taken and 45 submarines captured in the harbour.

Now all that remained of Army Group North was the force on the Hel Peninsula and some troops who had retreated to the Vistula delta with the II Army HQ, where they were joined by the rem-

nants of IV Army. This had been pressed back in its Heiligenbeil bridgehead by the assaults of 3rd Belorussian Front, and, at last, on March 29, Hitler allowed it to cross the Frische Nehrung.

So 3rd Belorussian Front was able to turn on Königsberg. On April 6, Vasilevsky threw four armies into the attack, and three days later, its commander, General Lasch, surrendered the city—to be condemned *in absentia* to death by hanging. On April 15, the German Front on the Samland Peninsula was broken, and civilians and troops streamed back across the Frische Nehrung to the positions in the Vistula delta until the Russians captured Pillau. There the Germans remained blockaded until May 9, when General von Saucken, who was now in command, surrendered.

The Soviet successes in Eastern Pomerania had not only caused the Germans great losses—91,460 men being taken prisoner, and considerably more killed—but the threat to the Soviet right flank had been removed. The German navy had lost one of its three main U-boat training areas, and this brought considerable relief to both Russian and Western navies—in his memoirs, Churchill acknowledged that '. . . the capture of Danzig and the consequent annihilation of one of the three main U-boat bases is an event bringing great relief to the Admiralty. The renewal of U-boat warfare on the scale which they had predicted is plainly now impossible'.

In his rage at these disasters, Hitler removed Himmler from command of Army Group Vistula and replaced him by General Heinrici. The Führer did not even have the satisfaction of seeing the remnants of Army Group North in the Vistula delta pinning down any large Russian forces, for Marshal Rokossovsky was able to leave only nine divisions to keep an eye on it, and march the rest of his forces to new positions on the Oder.

Here, on the left wing of 1st Belorussian Front, there had been heavy fighting as Soviet troops sought to reduce the Küstrin and Frankfurt strongholds. The 5th Shock and 8th Guards Armies had had to overcome stubborn opposition by the German IX Army, and it was not until the end of March that they were able to surround Küstrin and extend their bridgehead round it so as to form an important springboard for a future offensive. The Germans made a number of counterattacks to try and throw the Soviet troops back over the river and relieve Küstrin, but all these attempts failed—and this was one of the main reasons for the dismissal of Guderian from his post of Chief-of-Staff of OKH.

Important fighting in the south
All the time that the East Pomeranian operations had been under way, there had been much activity in Silesia: two operations had been undertaken by 1st Ukrainian Front under Marshal Konev—one in Lower Silesia in February, and one in Upper Silesia during March—both intended to disrupt the German plan to stop further Soviet penetration into Germany by setting up an impregnable defence line along the southern Oder.

Marshal Konev decided to begin in Lower Silesia by using his right wing to break through the German defences between Grünberg and Breslau, and advancing to the Neisse. This would bring his forces level with the left wing of 1st Belorussian Front, and enlarge the wedge driven into Germany by the Soviet forces. Afterwards, he would transfer his weight to the left wing so as to throw the Germans back to the south-west—away from the Oder—and to advance to the Czechoslovakian frontier.

All his proposals were accepted by Stavka, and in less than a week Konev gathered an assault force of the 3rd Guards and 4th Tank Armies, the 25th and 7th Guards Mechanised Corps, most of his artillery, and 2nd Air Army. The Soviet force enjoyed a very favourable superiority over IV Panzer Army, which had 18 infantry, four Panzer, and two motorised divisions, a number of other formations, and the Corps Group 'Breslau'.

The operation began on February 8, when, after a short artillery barrage, six Soviet armies (3rd Guards Tank, 4th Tank, 3rd Guards, 6th, 13th, and 52nd) burst out of their Oder bridgehead and headed for Cottbus and Penzig. After

three days of fighting the attack force had made a 90-mile-wide gap in the strongly-defended German line, advanced about 37 miles, cut the Berlin-Silesia railway, and surrounded the fortress of Glogau with its garrison of about 18,000.

On February 14, the 5th Guards Army joined the offensive by breaking out of its bridgehead in the Olau/Brieg area, and heading north-west against the German XVII Army. The next day, with 6th Army, it had surrounded Breslau, thus cutting off 40,000 German troops. By February 24, units of 1st Ukrainian Front had swept forward 60 to 75 miles, forced the Bober river off the march, and seized 60 miles of the eastern bank of the Neisse north of Penzig. Here German resistance stiffened, but the Soviet forces had achieved their objectives: seizing Lower Silesia, coming up to the same line as 1st Belorussian Front, and reaching positions in the Liegnitz/Breslau/Brieg area from which German forces in Upper Silesia—deployed south of Oppeln—could be outflanked. During the offensive, more than 91,300 Soviet citizens and 22,500 foreigners had been liberated from Nazi imprisonment.

At the end of February, the Germans threw a series of counterattacks against the Russian positions to try and recapture the lost defences on the Oder; the strongest of these attacks was on March 3 when IV Panzer Army struck out of the Lauban area towards Glogau, but the Soviet troops were well entrenched and able to beat off all attacks.

Marshal Konev was now able to transfer 4th Tank Army and 7th Guards Mechanised Group south into the zones of 21st, 59th, and 60th Armies to join the 9th Guards and 31st Tank Corps which were already there preparing for the Upper Silesian operation. This was to consist of two blows, north and south of Oppeln, which would outflank the main German force and meet in the Neustadt area so as to encircle it. The northern force, consisting of 4th Tank and 21st Armies, with parts of 5th Guards Army and 4th Independent Guards Tank Corps, was to attack from the Glottkau area, while the southern—59th and 60th Armies, 31st Tank, and 7th Guards Mechanised Corps—would strike from the vicinity of Kosel.

The assault began on March 15, and the attacking forces were soon well through the German lines and beginning the encirclement. By the fourth day, the Germans near Oppeln, five divisions and a number of other units, had been wiped out. During the fighting, Colonel-General Lelyushenko's 4th Tank Army was particularly skilful and effective, and on March 17 it was awarded the title of 'Guards'. By March 20, the 1st Ukrainian Front's forces had widened the breach to 70 miles and advanced some 30 miles.

The troops of the Front had now captured the important industrial towns of Neisse, Neustadt, and Ratibor, and by March 31 were approaching the foothills of the Sudeten mountains and crossing into Czechoslovakia in some areas. On their left flank was 38th Army of 4th Ukrainian Front, which had advanced some 22 miles and was also on the Czechoslovakian border.

These successes had meant that the entire Oder river line was now clear of Germans on the main axis of attack, and large German forces had been annihilated. The Red Army had eliminated all threats of a flank attack and had taken up positions from which the decisive blow against the Third Reich could be made.

The battle for Berlin was about to begin.

VICTOR IVANOVITCH ZHELANOV was born in 1908. He completed courses at the Artillery and General Staff Academies, and gained an M.Sc. in history. For the past 22 years he has been teaching history, and is now a senior academic worker and consultant to the section dealing with the Great Patriotic War at the Institute of Marxism-Leninism under the Central Committee of the Communist Party of the Soviet Union. He has published over 100 books and articles on military history, and was one of the authors of the works *The USSR in the Struggle for Austria's Independence* (Moscow, 1965) and *The Second World War* (Moscow, 1966).

General Konstantin Rokossovsky, commander of the 2nd Belorussian Front, scored notable successes in East Prussia, driving forward at 15 miles a day

Novosti Press Agency

Russian infantry advance through a Pomeranian town. The wool hats, great-coats, and slung weapons typify Russian infantry, who by this time were almost completely motorised

ACROSS THE RHINE

Western Germany, March/April 1945

For both Allies and Germans, the Rhine was not only a vital military objective—the last defence of the Ruhr and the last ditch before breaking out into the north German plain—it was also an important psychological barrier: the Rhine has always symbolised German national strength and figures largely in Wagnerian legend. Thus both sides were prepared to fight bitterly for it. The main assault was to be made in the north against the Ruhr by the British and Canadians, but it was the Americans, with a brilliantly improvised crossing, who were first across. *By Martin Blumenson*

In eastern Switzerland, near the Italian border, two glacier-fed mountain streams flow eastward for several miles to their juncture and there become the Rhine river. Still more torrent than river, the Rhine goes north along the edge of Austria and Lichtenstein to Lake Constance. West beyond the lake, the river plunges 70 feet at Schaffhausen, then winds between Switzerland and Germany to Basel, where it turns sharply to the north. Now 225 yards wide and getting larger as it goes, eventually reaching a width of half a mile, the river separates Germany's Black Forest on the right and France's Vosges Mountains on the left. The water is deep enough for boats, but the current too swift for river traffic, which moves instead through the Rhône-Rhine Canal to Strasbourg. The river continues past Speyer to Mannheim, where it receives the waters of the Neckar, past Worms to Mainz, where it takes the waters of the Main river, then bends sharply west to Bingen. There, quite suddenly, as it swings generally north again, the Rhine enters a gorge that constricts its passage.

Here is the fabled domain of history, romance, and legend—of Attila the Hun, brave Roland and Siegfried, and the Lorelei maiden 'of wondrous form and fair', who sat on a huge rock near the town of St Goar and lured boatmen to destruction. Here are the peaks crowned with ruined castles, strongholds of robber barons who exacted toll from passing boats. Here is the Rhine of 'gemütlichkeit' and tourists, spectacular scenery, a river of barges and tugs, overarching bridges, quaint villages, and toy-like trains on both banks.

The gorge ends at Koblenz, and there the Mosel joins the Rhine. Continuing, the Rhine passes Remagen and Bonn, moves to Cologne, then Düsseldorf, Duisburg, Dinslaken, and Wesel. As it turns left and west to enter Holland near Emmerich, the Rhine is lost in a delta, but one channel wends past Arnhem to Rotterdam, and beyond to the North Sea.

About 850 miles long and draining an area of about 75,000 square miles, the Rhine is connected with the Danube by the Ludwigs Canal, to the Rhône and thereby to the Mediterranean by two man-made waterways, and on the north by a canal to Amsterdam. Significant in terms of trade and commerce, the river has been important in European history since Julius Caesar spanned it with a timber bridge. Except for a short time when Roman legions pushed eastward from Mannheim and Mainz to the Main river, the Rhine served for 400 years as the boundary between the Romans and the barbarians. The west bank cities of Basel, Strasbourg, Mainz, Koblenz, Bonn, and Cologne are Roman in origin. The east bank is thoroughly German.

During the Middle Ages, Germans ruled both sides of the Rhine from Basel to the Netherlands. The river valley became a prize of contention during the Thirty Years' War, and in 1648 France gained a foothold on the west bank. Louis XIV made additional gains, and Napoleon established the French frontier along the old Roman boundary. France lost the left bank, Alsace, after the war with Prussia, until the Treaty of Versailles restored it. But the Germans occupied it again, along with the rest of the country, during most of the Second World War.

Germany's national river, the Rhine is an important symbol of German history and national strength. In Wagner's operas, the Nibelungen ring was made of gold guarded by maidens deep in the clear waters of the Rhine. This treasure, somehow, granted to its possessors a power over the whole world. So too the Rhine guarded Germany and conferred the same mystique. So long as its waters protected the country from invasion, the Germans could keep alive hope that all was well. Despite adversity and defeat, devastation and suffering, the power of the nation remained intact. But if the river were crossed and the fortress-sanctuary penetrated, all would be lost.

The vital triangle

Even before the invasion of Normandy in June 1944, the Allies had been very much aware of the Rhine river, the most significant water obstacle to military forces in western Europe. Having been assigned the mission of liberating the occupied countries in the west and of striking to the heart of Germany, Eisenhower's Allied planners had looked all the way to Berlin as the ultimate objective, then, for reasons of practicality, fixed on the nearer target of the Ruhr, one of the great steel and munitions producing areas in the world and the heart of industrial Germany.

Resembling a triangle, the Ruhr presses one side against the Rhine river from Cologne for 50 miles downstream to Duisburg. From Cologne generally eastward for about 50 miles along the Lippe river and from Duisburg eastward about the same distance along the Ruhr river, the two other sides converge at Dortmund. The principle cities within this industrial heartland are Essen, Düsseldorf, and Wuppertal.

Allied pre-invasion planning projected two major thrusts into Germany. One was to pass north of the Ardennes and aim at the Ruhr. The other was to go south of the Ardennes and eliminate the lesser Saar industrial area. The forces making both thrusts were then to cross the Rhine, which bars the western approach to the Ruhr, then encircle the region, thereby cutting its products from the German war machine. Meanwhile, the advances would continue into Germany, the main drive moving across the north German plain, a secondary operation tentatively heading from Frankfurt north-eastward to Kassel.

The tremendous breakout of Allied forces in Normandy, starting at the end of July and exploited during August, carried the Allied armies across France into Belgium and Holland, to the Siegfried Line which protected the German border, and brought the Rhine within immediate reach. In the first days of September, as the Allied leaders began to look all the way to the river, to think of bridgeheads on the east bank, and to consider even where to go beyond, Montgomery suggested carrying the momentum of the pursuit to Berlin. Judging this idea unrealistic, Eisenhower instead permitted him to launch his daring airborne-ground operation, Market Garden, in a vain attempt, as it turned out, to get the 21st Army Group across the lower Rhine at Arnhem in the Netherlands. By then, Bradley had oriented the armies of his 12th Army Group to the objectives of Cologne, Bonn, Koblenz, Mannheim, and Mainz.

Before these thrilling events could come to pass, the Allied pursuit came to an end, the German armies stiffened at the West Wall, the difficult and desperate battles of the Siegfried Line and of Holland had to be fought, and the Ardennes counteroffensive had to be stopped. Not until the turn of the year, with the Bulge almost flattened, could the Allies start thinking again of crossing the Rhine, the last major barrier before the heart of the enemy homeland.

Both flanks of the Allied front touched the Rhine in January 1945, but these forces would be the last to cross. In the north on the extreme left, General Crerar's Canadian 1st Army held the lower reaches of the river in the Netherlands and even a slender bridgehead at Nijmegen, the latter the result of Operation Market Garden. But extensive flooded areas made it difficult, if not impossible, to cross the river in strength. And a substantial crossing, besides being a risky endeavour, would not take the Allies toward their main objectives in Germany.

In the south too, from Switzerland to a point north of Strasbourg, Jacob B. Devers' 6th Army Group had Jean de Lattre de Tassigny's French 1st Army at the water's edge.

Britain's 'Tetrarch': This tank, developed for an air-portable role for use with the Hamilcar glider, was also used for conventional fighting in an infantry close support role. Its generous ground clearance made it vulnerable to mines, hence the thickening of the floor armour. It could be fitted with flotation screens, and was ideally suited for landing operations and river crossings. *Length:* 14 feet. *Top speed:* 40 mph on road; 28 mph cross country. *Armament:* One 40-mm gun; one 7·92-mm Besa. *Armour:* 10-mm front, 14-mm floor

▽ A bridge collapses in smoke and dirt as in the nick of time the Germans frustrate Allied attempts to capture it intact

John Batchelor

Scots disembark on the 'hot' side of
the Rhine. The crossing in craft of this
size was hazardous even without enemy
opposition, particularly as the Germans
were able to increase the river's flow
by controlling several dams

But a crossing in that area led only to lesser Allied objectives. Besides, De Lattre and Patch's US 7th Army would be so occupied turning back the German New Year's offensive in Alsace and eliminating the Colmar Pocket that they would be unable to give attention to the Rhine until late in March.

The first crossings, then, would take place somewhere between Emmerich near the Dutch border and Strasbourg, in the zone of the 21st Army Group on the left or the 12th Army Group in the centre (see map). Between these army groups would soon develop a marked rivalry.

Germans exhausted but dangerous

When the Allied Combined Chiefs-of-Staff (CCS) met at Malta for four days in January and February 1945, they estimated the Germans to be exhausted but still dangerous despite the pressures exerted from the west and by the Russians who were crossing the Oder and menacing Vienna. Further German resistance appeared futile, yet would certainly continue. How then should the CCS direct Eisenhower to end the war? This question revived briefly the controversy over broad front versus narrow front strategy that had been argued somewhat noisily in September.

Eisenhower had prepared for the CCS at Malta a tentative plan to seize two bridgeheads across the formidable Rhine. Following the pre-invasion outlines, he contemplated a crossing north of the Ruhr between Emmerich and Wesel, another upstream and south of the Ruhr between Mainz and Karlsruhe. A heavy attack in the north offered the quickest means of eliminating the industrial capacity of the Ruhr and of reaching the north German plain, excellent territory for mobile operations. But suitable sites for crossing between Emmerich and Wesel existed only along 20 miles of the river. This was space enough to employ initially over three divisions, and they would be vulnerable to quick German concentration. Upstream, between Mainz and Karlsruhe, there were enough sites to accommodate at least five assault divisions, and there would be less danger of effective opposition.

The British Chiefs-of-Staff asked whether it was wise for Eisenhower thus to disperse his forces. Feeling that he lacked sufficient strength to make two major operations across the Rhine, they suggested a single, overwhelming assault crossing. This, they believed, should be executed in the north. Nearer the important base of Antwerp and thus more easily supplied, it would provide a more direct menace to the Ruhr and get troops more quickly on the north German plain. They also raised a subsidiary question: would Eisenhower wait to make his crossings until all the armies had closed to the western bank of the Rhine?

Eisenhower assured the Combined Chiefs that he would seize Rhine crossings in the north as soon as such action became feasible and without waiting for everyone to close to the river; that he would make his main effort in the north; and that he would advance in the north with maximum strength.

This, the CCS agreed, would be satisfactory.

In the north, since the setback at Arnhem in September, Montgomery had been meticulously preparing to have Dempsey's British 2nd Army cross the Rhine. As early as October, engineer and ordnance specialists met periodically to discuss the problems and

to devise solutions for the gigantic task of crossing. By November an outline plan had been drawn for general planning, and engineer units were designated to undergo special training and to experiment with amphibious equipment and river crossing techniques.

After the Ardennes counterblow, intensive planning was resumed. Eisenhower called river crossing specialists from all the army groups to his headquarters for a three-day conference, where the experts pooled their knowledge. Since the army groups in the south were to cross soon after the major effort in the north, logisticians raised the issue of whether there were adequate supplies of amphibious assault and bridging equipment for all. A theatre-wide survey, including stocks in Britain, disclosed the possibility of shortages, so Eisenhower then asked that additional shipments be rushed from the United States. When SHAEF estimated that each division securing a bridgehead on the east bank would require 540 tons of supplies per day, Montgomery acted at once to forestall a supply bottleneck behind the front by ordering eight more bridges constructed over the Maas river in the rear to supplement the existing spans.

Since the Rhine was wide and treacherous, particularly in its northern reaches, and since the level of the water and the speed of the current might be manipulated by the Germans who controlled several dams on the river's eastern tributaries, the projected crossing operations resembled a beach assault after an amphibious voyage over tidal waters. British and US naval contingents therefore provided vessels large enough to transport tanks and other heavy equipment across the river almost simultaneously with the assaulting infantrymen.

Apotheosis of the 'Seamule'

Naval Force 'U' under Captain P. H. G. James, RN, brought overland from Antwerp to Nijmegen a flotilla of LCVPs and a flotilla of LCMs, together with crews and maintenance facilities, to ferry troops and vehicles across the Rhine. Some of these craft were 50 feet long, and transporting them over the roads of Belgium and Holland was no mean feat; 24 of each type of boat were attached to the 2nd Army, 12 of each went to the Canadian 1st Army. Eventually, similar naval elements were attached to the American armies. In addition, 'Seamules', 38-foot harbour tugs powered by two engines, were disassembled into four sections for overland shipment to the armies, together with a harbour craft company to instruct engineers on how to operate them.

Late in January it was obvious that at least a preliminary assignment of zones was necessary in the north. Montgomery controlled three armies, Crerar's Canadian, Dempsey's British, and Simpson's US 9th, all of which had accumulated river assault and bridging equipment in expectation of getting across the Rhine. On January 21, though the Rhineland and Palatinate regions west of the Rhine had still to be cleared, Montgomery issued his first order. He directed Dempsey to be ready to cross the Rhine at three places:

● Near Rees, 25 miles upstream from Arnhem
● Near Xanten, 7 miles upstream and close to Wesel
● Near Rheinberg, 10 miles farther upstream at the north-west corner of the Ruhr.

Simpson's 9th Army was to contribute a

corps of two infantry divisions to be attached to the 2nd Army for use in exploiting a bridgehead already gained.

'Flabbergasted', as the army historian recorded it, that the 9th Army was to make no assault crossing, the Americans were unable to believe that Montgomery intended the river crossing material they had laboriously collected to go to waste. Nor did it make sense to keep the 12 divisions of the 9th Army out of action at the Rhine. Finally, since the 9th Army would have to pass through the British bridgehead to get started on a drive east of the river, the logistical and traffic regulating problems would be immense.

New plan for the crossing

Staff officers of British 2nd and US 9th Armies, who enjoyed a close relationship based on mutual friendship and respect, submitted a revised plan calling for fuller American and Canadian participation. They proposed that the British sector be narrowed, that the Xanten area be split between the American and British armies, that the 9th Army make a two-corps assault between Xanten and Rheinberg, and that the assault across the river be extended to the northwest to make room for crossings by the Canadians on the British left.

Montgomery then modified his plan and issued new instructions on February 4. He assigned the Rheinberg area to the 9th Army for a one-corps assault in order to obviate logistical and traffic difficulties. He expressed his intention to transfer Wesel to the Americans once a bridgehead there was secure. He rejected an assault crossing by the Canadian army downstream from Rees because flood plains, poor approaches, and dominating ground on the east bank made river crossings there too risky. But he decided to attach a Canadian brigade to the British army and to commit additional Canadian forces in the Rees bridgehead, these troops to drive downstream on the right bank to clear a crossing site for the Canadian army near Emmerich. In mid-February, Montgomery told Crerar he could mount a raid at Emmerich as a diversion; and if there was only light opposition and if equipment was available without prejudicing the main crossings, Crerar could launch a full-scale assault. The Rhine crossings, Montgomery specified, would take place on March 31, but early in March he advanced the target date by one week to March 24.

In a letter to his senior subordinate commanders on February 20, Eisenhower reiterated his plan to have Montgomery's 21st Army Group launch a massive thrust across the Rhine even as Bradley's 12th Army Group and Devers' 6th Army Group were clearing the west bank for later crossings. Once all the armies were safely across, the two main avenues of advance were to be the area north of the Ruhr and the Frankfurt-Kassel corridor.

Bradley's planners, looking toward the Frankfurt-Kassel corridor, found two sites where the Rhine valley is relatively broad and the river appropriate for crossings. One was between Koblenz and Andernach, the other downstream between Bonn and Cologne. Troops across the river would find access fairly easy to the Ruhr-Frankfurt autobahn, then to the Lahn river valley leading to the Kassel corridor. Toward the end of February and the beginning of March, there was a flurry of hope that US **2316** ▷

Imperial War Museum

◁ Rubber floats for a pontoon bridge are carried down to the Rhine. Building bridges in the swift current posed many problems for the engineers
▽ Slow but sure. A raft is used to ferry across armour, one at a time

Imperial War Museum

US Army

△ A 'Duck' takes to the water. This legendary amphibian was the main US infantry carrier used for the Rhine crossing. Hundreds of these in constant use hastened the buildup on the east bank
▽ Another amphibian. A 'Buffalo' wallows across under a load of British infantry

Rijksinstituut voor Oorlogsdocumentatie

◁ In two assault craft lashed together, French troops cross the Rhine. In the French sector the crossing was less wide, but more hazardous
▽ From the steep east bank the Germans hotly opposed the crossings. Dis-embarking under fire was a dangerous moment

Imperial War Museum

US Army

▷ A Sherman rolls east to link up with airborne forces, whose abandoned gliders can be seen in the background
Below right: A Commando machine-gun section fire their Vickers at German positions. Its handlers believed this gun to be the most accurate of its kind

△ A US mortar crew duck to avoid the blast, as they bombard enemy positions holding up their advance on the east bank of the Rhine
▷ British troops pass the results of their handiwork as they push deeper into Germany

Above right: Allied troops were constantly shocked by the extreme youth of their enemies
▷ Enough POWs to fill a bomb crater. POWs were beginning to come in in growing numbers and formed one of the major Allied administrative problems

units might capture a Rhine river bridge intact—which would avoid the necessity of an assault crossing. But after several attempts came painfully close to success, general opinion solidified on the point that the Germans would methodically destroy all the bridges over the river. Amphibious assaults of the broad stream, difficult for planners and executors, would be necessary.

And then suddenly, on March 7, came a surprising occurrence in the zone of Bradley's 12th Army Group. Men of Hodges' US 1st Army captured a bridge intact at Remagen, between Bonn and Koblenz.

The electrifying event was more dramatic than significant. Though Eisenhower immediately permitted a build-up of the bridgehead, the terrain on the east bank was difficult and gave no ready access to the important objectives. Because an expansion of the bridgehead would eat up troops to be used in the major efforts to be made elsewhere along the river, the Remagen bridgehead had little effect on the preparations to cross the Rhine. On March 13, Eisenhower indicated that the Remagen bridgehead was to be used to draw enemy units from the Ruhr, to attract German troops that would otherwise face and oppose the scheduled crossings in the zones of the 21st and 6th Army Groups.

And now the Americans in Bradley's 12th Army Group began to show pique. They resented Eisenhower's continued emphasis on the importance of the crossings in the north. They regarded Montgomery's elaborate preparations for his 21st Army Group crossings as overcautious, needless, wasteful, and time-consuming. And they determined to jump the Rhine as an extension and exploitation of their west-bank operations in the Saar-Palatinate. If the crossing at Remagen could be dismissed as a lucky fluke, Patton's US 3rd Army would show how easily the Americans could cross the Rhine without even pausing.

A quick, spectacular crossing would prompt newspaper headlines that would draw the spotlight from Hodges. In addition, Patton had a hankering to beat Montgomery across the river. But an even more serious motive was the feeling that Bradley and Hodges shared with Patton: concern that Eisenhower might halt the 1st and 3rd Armies in order to give Montgomery additional American divisions.

The three American commanders met on March 19, after Bradley had conferred earlier that day with Eisenhower. Bradley authorised Hodges to put more strength into his Remagen bridgehead, and he approved agreements made by Hodges and Patton with respect to co-ordinating their advances beyond the Rhine. The 3rd Army would cross near Mainz and make a subsequent drive to meet the 1st Army in the Lahn river valley. Both armies, massing considerable force side by side, would then open the Frankfurt-Kassel corridor in such strength that Bradley's 12th Army Group rather than Montgomery's 21st Army Group 'could', as Patton said, 'carry the ball'.

The magnitude of bringing assault boats, bridging, and other engineer equipment from depôts in the rear argued against an immediate crossing. But Patton ordered convoys to start at once from Lorraine with the necessary material. He rationalised his action by saying that he wanted speed in order to give the Germans no time to recover from the Saar-Palatinate campaign and to prepare defences along the Rhine.

Since Montgomery had scheduled his crossings for the night of March 23, Patton decided to cross after darkness on March 22. This was 72 hours away.

'A bankrupt estate'

The fierce battles west of the Rhine had virtually settled the outcome of the Rhine crossings. The German units were depleted, their reserves exhausted. Albert Kesselring, who in March replaced Gerd von Rundstedt as Commander-in-Chief West, 'inherited', in the words of a British Intelligence report, 'a bankrupt estate'.

But Kesselring took energetic steps to defend the Rhine, and he used the two-week period between the end of the Rhineland and Palatinate fighting and the beginning of the main crossing attempts to good advantage. The German troops built a narrow belt of rifle and machine-gun pits along the river, concentrating their defensive works on the most probable crossing sites. They had managed to preserve a large number of artillery and anti-aircraft artillery pieces that could fire effectively, and these they placed in excellent positions. They would make a real attempt to hold back the Allies, while at the same time trying to contain the Remagen bridgehead.

Yet their efforts to defend the water barrier were doomed to failure from the outset. According to a German general officer, the Germans had only 'a shadow of an army' on the east bank. Morale varied 'from suspicion to callous resignation', while officers often 'lacked confidence and wondered just what were the demands of duty'. The ground forces, in general, 'could only pretend to resist'.

The most logical place for a crossing in the 3rd Army zone was downstream from and north of Mainz, below the confluence of the Main and Rhine rivers. This would avoid the necessity of making a second assault crossing at the Main. But Patton figured that the Germans would be expecting the obvious, and he decided to opt for surprise. He told Manton Eddy, commander of the 12th Corps, to make a feint near Mainz while actually crossing 10 miles upstream at Oppenheim. Later, Patton would write that he thought it had been a 'great mistake' on his part to have crossed above Mainz rather than below the city.

As 12th Corps closed to the Rhine, the 5th Division was about to go into corps reserve. Eddy summoned the division commander, Leroy Irwin, to his headquarters on March 21 and directed him to be ready to cross the Rhine that night at Oppenheim while another division feinted and demonstrated behind a smoke screen at Mainz. Though the 5th Division was thoroughly experienced in river assault crossings, having made 22 in past campaigns in France, Belgium, and Germany, Irwin protested the short time available for preparations.

As it turned out, Irwin would have another 24 hours to get ready. Eddy told him on the morning of March 22 that Patton insisted he cross that night. Irwin was reluctant—he said it would be impossible to make a 'well-planned and ordered crossing'. But he admitted he would probably be able 'to get some sort of bridgehead'. That, of course, was all that Patton wanted.

The assault regiment of the 5th Division planned to send one battalion across at Nierstein, another at Oppenheim, starting at 2200 hours on March 23. An artillery group of 13 battalions was on hand to lay

down supporting fire, but there would be no preparatory concentrations in the interest of attaining surprise. The Rhine at this point was from 800 to 1,200 feet wide, and the assault battalions would cross on about 500 craft. The first waves were to paddle in assault boats; reinforcements would go in motor-propelled craft, DUKWs, and a dozen LCVPs, the latter manned by US naval personnel.

Despite the necessity for haste, 7,500 engineers made elaborate preparations to support the infantry and to bridge the Rhine. Early assault waves would take bulldozers and air compressors to the far bank to enable work to begin at once on cutting ramps for the DUKWs and on readying bridge and ferry sites. Using searchlights mounted on tanks to give illumination, engineers were to start building a bridge soon after the first infantrymen reached the far shore.

Once the regiment was established on the east bank, Irwin would send over the two other regiments. Eddy then planned to commit an armoured division through the bridgehead to exploit to the north-east to the Main river at Hanau. An additional armoured division and two infantry divisions were available to drive north to junction with the US 1st Army in the Lahn valley.

There were few Germans opposite the 5th Division. Occasional shells fell in the streets of Nierstein and Oppenheim, but American artillery observers could find no lucrative targets on the German side of the river. Responsible for more than 50 miles of the river from Mainz to Mannheim, the German VII Army had only one regular corps headquarters, a local military district headquarters (Wehrkreis XII) upgraded to a provisional corps headquarters, and no divisions as such. In the entire VII Army sector, four divisions that were little more than remnants grouped around surviving staffs, rear-echelon detachments, students and instructors of nearby training schools, convalescent companies, and a hodgepodge of miscellaneous units comprised the troop list. Furthermore, contact and communication had been lost with the adjacent I Army in the south.

As a bright moon shone during much of the night of March 22, the leading American elements at Nierstein pushed into the Rhine half an hour behind schedule. There was no protest from the opposite bank, and the first arrivals quickly captured seven German soldiers who volunteered to return an assault boat to the west bank. At Oppenheim, assault boats were midstream when machine-guns opened fire on them. A fierce skirmish lasted half an hour before the Germans, probably in platoon strength, surrendered. All told, the American assault regiment took 20 casualties and was entirely across the river by midnight and ready to drive to the first line of villages while the second regiment began to cross. Perhaps 50 rounds of German artillery fire fell on Oppenheim during the night. Shortly after dawn, 12 German aircraft strafed and bombed the crossing sites, the first of several raids, usually of one or two aircraft, that occurred during March 23, but they caused little damage. By the end of the day, the 5th Division was wholly over, a second infantry division was crossing, tanks and tank destroyers were being ferried over on LCVPs, and a treadway bridge was open to traffic. Eddy ordered an armoured division to move into the bridgehead early on March 24 and

The small map shows the strategic situation in March 1945: the Allies at the Rhine, the Russians on the Oder. The large map shows the Allied crossings of the Rhine. Operation 'Plunder', the crossing by Montgomery's 21st Army Group, was, in contrast to the American crossings, exhaustively planned, and heavily supported by airstrikes, smoke, and artillery. The harsh opposition encountered by 'Veritable', Montgomery's earlier operation, was mainly responsible for this caution, but the US 12th Army Group had no such inhibitions: the American crossing was quick, improvised, and extremely successful

head for Hanau. A German counterattack, launched around midnight by officer candidate students from a school in Wiesbaden, had no effect on the situation.

Meanwhile, Bradley had announced to representatives of press and radio that American forces could cross the Rhine practically anywhere without preliminary air bombardment. As a matter of fact, he said, the 3rd Army had crossed without even an artillery preparation.

Patton had readied two more assault crossings downstream from Oppenheim. Concerned that Eddy's 12th Corps might have trouble crossing the Rhine and later the Main, he ordered Middleton's 8th Corps to jump the river in the 8th Corps zone. One division was to cross near Boppard, a few miles upstream from Koblenz, another near St Goar, 8 miles farther south, then head for Giessen in the Lahn valley to make contact with 1st Army forces breaking out of their Remagen bridgehead.

Boppard and St Goar are in the Rhine gorge, an unlikely area for assault crossings. The river flows through a deep canyon with cliff-like sides rising 300 to 400 feet in height. Between river and cliff is room usually for only a highway and railroad, and the towns and villages are at the mouths of small cross valleys, where narrow, twisting roads provide the only way out for vehicles. The Rhine was swift and treacherous, and its banks were revetted in many places with stone, anti-erosion walls 15 feet high.

Defenders of the Rhine
Höhne's 84th Corps defended the Rhine gorge with a division of about 400 infantrymen and ten howitzers, an anti-aircraft artillery brigade, a collection of *Volkssturm* units, several police companies, and miscellaneous elements. These troops had been on the east bank for almost a week and were prepared to oppose crossing attempts.

Four battalions of the 87th Division started to cross just before midnight, March 24. Near Rhens, one assault battalion received such heavy fire from German machine-guns, mortars, anti-aircraft guns, and artillery pieces that it took almost an hour to get some men across. A few hundred yards downstream, another battalion crossed undetected but drew heavy fire upon landing. On the following day, March 25, these crossing sites would be abandoned in favour of those established upstream at Boppard, where two battalions had crossed easily, then moved forward to take the town of Oberlahnstein at the confluence of the Lahn and Rhine rivers.

Upstream at St Goar and Oberwesel, the 89th Division crossed during the night of March 25. Discovered by German defenders, the assault troops, despite enemy flares, erratic smoke screens, and effective anti-aircraft-gun fire, forced their way across, and resistance opposite St Goar and Oberwesel soon ceased. Not long thereafter, the American flag flew from the Lorelei rock.

By March 26, Allied fighter pilots were reporting German motorised columns moving east bumper to bumper, retreating soldiers clogging the roads. But the big news in the 8th Corps zone came from reports that the 1st Army on the left had sent an armoured column streaking out of the Remagen bridgehead down the Ruhr-Frankfurt autobahn to Limburg and pointing across the 8th Corps front towards Wiesbaden. Also, the Oppenheim bridgehead in the south had exploded into pursuit action. **2321** ▷

2317

Top Generals of the Western Front
Major K. J. Macksey

General Dwight D. Eisenhower

In 1941, Eisenhower was totally unknown outside the narrow circle of the peacetime American army: thereafter, at war, his translation from an unassuming staff officer to Supreme Commander at SHAEF ranks among the most rapid promotions achieved by a senior officer since the days of Napoleon. Eisenhower spent most of his career on the staff, developing skills at organisation and in the weaving of command decisions into a common operational design. In the field of command he had little personal experience —none of it in action. This apprenticeship served him well when it came to building working relationships among Allies whose strong-willed leaders each had to be persuaded into co-operation one with the other. To Eisenhower must be accorded the creation of the military teams that finished the war in North Africa, opened the Second Front in Normandy, and then prosecuted the final victory —all with a cordiality that bore happy comparison with the stormy alliances of the First World War. As the war progressed, Eisenhower's impact upon strategy became increasingly positive—his selection of the Broad Front Policy, his re-organisation of responsibilities to counter the Ardennes offensive, and his concentration of the main effort in the North German Plain the symbols of his expanding authority.

Lieutenant-General George Patton

Most renowned among all American field commanders of the Second World War, Patton was a cavalryman who saw active service in US tanks in the First World War. Between the wars he did much to save US armour from mismanagement, and in Tunisia, by discreet yet bold handling, restored self respect to American forces after their defeat at Kasserine. When commanding in Sicily he marred his success by a personal indiscretion involving a shell-shocked soldier in hospital, but Eisenhower knew that this man, with his innate sense of mobility, possessed the ability to beat the German Panzer leaders at their own game. Patton's handling of US 3rd Army from the breakout in Normandy, through the pursuit to Metz, the fighting on the frontiers, the counterblow in the Ardennes, and the final race across the Rhine to Czechoslovakia, are garnished with tales of skill, magnificent élan, superb character, and a glorious evasiveness. For Patton found it hard to recognise a master, and his success embodied many a deflection of orders —some of which caused his superiors unwanted concern. An educated soldier, Patton merely copied the habits of most great masters of mobility with the dash and disregard of the conventional that are the essence of decision—right or wrong.

Lieutenant-General Omar Bradley

As much a protégé of Eisenhower as Dempsey was of Montgomery, Bradley, a quiet sincere man, came to light on the tail of Patton's bright comet. Taking over US 2nd Corps in North Africa from Patton, Bradley demonstrated his vigour by the grasp and leadership that he rapidly imposed upon his divisions and the way he stormed Bizerta. He exhibited the qualifications needed for high command, planned shrewdly, executed those plans with determination and, as commander of US 1st Army before, during, and after D-Day until he took over US 12th Army Group, he pressed every advantage. However, only rarely was his command forced into precipitate difficulties: unlimited resources were at his disposal—he was neither in a position to lose the war nor the peace until the German Ardennes offensive caught him as far off balance as it caught every other senior Allied leader. This was Bradley's most testing hour, when the difficulties of re-knitting a torn front had to be reconciled with the pressures exerted by the conflicting demands of those surrounding him with a plethora of advice. Thereafter his exploitation of every opportunity in the final invasion of Germany showed him as the sound soldier he undoubtedly was.

Lieutenant-General Courtney Hodges

Fate and the machinations of military seniorities ordained that Hodges should play second fiddle in the American hierarchical orchestra. When Eisenhower gave Bradley command of US 1st Army as an essential stepping stone before becoming commander of US 12th Army Group, Hodges had to wait upon events as Bradley's deputy. And after Bradley had handed 1st Army to Hodges, the change coincided with, and was overshadowed by, Patton's meteoric dash to Paris and beyond. Because Patton was actually senior to Bradley, and Hodges junior to them both, Bradley found it easier to deal with Hodges, though Hodges's position became more difficult once his army had taken position on the boundary of 12th and 21st Army Groups—to be shuttled under command of first one, then the other. An infantryman, Hodges was temperamentally better adjusted to the close fighting of Normandy and the Siegfried Line as opposed to slashing exploitations and, as the rock upon which the German Ardennes offensive broke, he kept a cool head, filling the gaps and assembling new reserves for offensive action. In any other company or theatre of war, Hodges might have hit the headlines: as it is he is among the least celebrated of those American leaders who played a significant part in winning the war.

General de Lattre de Tassigny

De Lattre de Tassigny, one of a select band of untarnished French divisional commanders involved in the French collapse in 1940, won his successes as the prize of personal leadership in the forefront of the battle at a time when the accepted system of command imposed control from headquarters in rear. Thereafter the stormy career of this dashing leader implicated him in subversive activities against the German Occupation and Vichy authorities that forced him to make a dramatic escape to England. His dynamic training of French forces in North Africa prior to 'Dragoon' implanted a true sense of recovery in the minds of his soldiers and a yearning for deeds of valour that would help expunge the shame of 1940. Thus the impetus behind the French 1st Army's exploitation from Marseilles to Strasbourg owed as much to de Lattre's zeal, exuberance, and professional single-mindedness as to French patriotism, for no amount of the latter could compensate for lack of up-to-date techniques in modern war. Like Patton and the other great exponents of mobility, de Lattre was tough and a hard task-master who could not suffer fools. And, after the war, when he took charge in Indo-China, he demonstrated that inventiveness and improvisation are at the heart of true military virtue.

Lieutenant-General Guy Simonds

Of all the Allied corps commanders, Simonds was among the most versatile and best equipped to deal with the wide variety of operations posed to his Canadian 2nd Corps. He had commanded, in action, both an infantry division in Sicily and an armoured division in Italy, was young, ruthless, and aggressively intolerant. Yet his educated approach to battle made use of every possible modern aid to help reduce casualties and still achieve striking penetrations of the enemy line. The highly original armoured thrust towards Falaise on August 8, 1944 (Operation 'Totalise') employing armoured infantry carriers by night, sprang from Simonds' mind; the surge of his corps through the Pas de Calais to the Scheldt illustrate his driving energy; and his meticulous reduction of the German defences along the waterway guarding Antwerp's approaches, and later near Nijmegen, emphasises his grasp of detail. It must not be forgotten that Simonds twice commanded the whole of Canadian 1st Army in General Crerar's absence—throughout the Scheldt campaign, and again (this time from 2nd Corps HQ) during the last phase of the advance into Northern Germany. No Canadian field commander had greater experience or acquired more respect from friend or foe.

Eisenhower

Patton

Bradley

Hodges

de Lattre

Simonds

Field-Marshal Sir Bernard Montgomery

By appointing Montgomery to command the combined Allied forces for the Normandy landing, Eisenhower made full use of the mind and personality of one of the most professional military commanders ever produced by the British army. In 1944 Montgomery's whole attention was riveted on the military problems, to the exclusion of waspish provocations, national prejudices, and anything else not immediately associated with the battlefield. His application of the principles of war were hardly intuitive: each plan and each move, evolved from the studies of a lifetime, related to deep and careful thought and expounded with such clarity that they could sometimes appear rigid and ponderous. To Montgomery's eternal credit he never squandered soldiers' lives and, despite his authoritarianism, sought advice on technical subjects when he recognised these as being outside his knowledge. The crushing Allied victory in Normandy was his, the ultimate overrunning of Western Europe (including his inspired, but abortive, attempt to lay the airborne carpet to Arnhem) its inevitable outcome. If, thereafter, he fell foul of his American colleagues it can only be stated that at the time of the Ardennes offensive, a firm hand was needed and Montgomery supplied it—with or without finesse. But—he never lost a battle.

Lieutenant-General Miles Dempsey

It is a tantalising thought that all four corps in Dempsey's British 2nd Army were commanded by men who had commanded a corps before he had. O'Connor had been taken prisoner in Africa and not released until 1943, Ritchie had suffered a set-back when commanding 8th Army at Gazala, and both Crocker and Horrocks had been wounded. Dempsey's quiet, unassuming manner in many ways likened him to Eisenhower, his task of controlling strong corps commanders no less easy than Eisenhower's with powerful army commanders. Dempsey was lucky—an essential prerequisite in a successful commander. He had been brought to prominence by Montgomery after following the latter's star since being one of the Field-Marshal's students at Staff College—but because he stepped up after the others had faltered in no way diminishes his reputation, for he possessed the inner calmness that an army commander must have but a corps commander can do without. His British 2nd Army fought and won the toughest of the Normandy battles, exploited to Antwerp at a faster rate than any other, and never once gave ground. The credit is Dempsey's, a man who dwelt in the background, but one who had the confidence of his subordinates.

Field-Marshal Gerd von Rundstedt

From first to last Rundstedt owned the confidence of the Wehrmacht and never seriously became involved with the factions dividing Germany. In so doing, this phlegmatic officer seems to have detached himself from the turmoil engulfing Germany in 1944/45 even though he occupied one of the top military posts— C-in-C West. A symbol of Germany military propriety, Rundstedt was sacked and restored to active service by Hitler on no less than three occasions—a record! For two years he tried to strengthen the Atlantic Wall and, above all, create a Central Mobile Reserve which alone, in his opinion, would defeat an Allied landing. The story of his frustration in building that reserve and of its dispersal at the hands of Rommel, who understood the Allied aerial threat better than his chief, is the story of the bankruptcy of German military power, just as Rundstedt's failure to assuage Hitler reflects the subjugation of the Wehrmacht to Hitler's will. Yet Rundstedt's continuance in office as a sop to Hitler's faded regard for the Wehrmacht indicates the loyalty of a soldier who put duty before self even when he knew perfectly well that his cause was undermined and also lost.

Field-Marshal Erwin Rommel

Rommel's appointment to command the German Army Group B in January 1944 succeeded his disillusionment with Hitler's direction of the war as well as his faith in the viability of mobile armoured warfare in the face of overwhelming Allied air superiority. In consequence, his attempts to radically realign strategy and reshuffle resources to counter the coming invasion merely led to bad compromises between the mobile school on the one hand and the adherents of linear coastal defence on the other. Events proved Rommel right as it became well nigh impossible, due to the disruption of landward communications, to gather a powerful counterattack force in sufficient time to throw the Allies out of Normandy: hence, without much confidence, he fought a battle of containment, his hopes turning, meanwhile, to the possibility that Hitler's elimination might solve the problem of the Führer's constricting dominance. Nobody can tell what might have been the outcome had not an RAF aircraft wounded Rommel three days before the Bomb Plot, but the turn of events merely condemned Rommel to an enforced suicide disguised as death from wounds—a subterfuge that amply indicated Hitler's appreciation of Rommel's prestige and hold over the imaginations of both friend and foe.

Montgomery

Dempsey

Horrocks

Rundstedt

Rommel

Model

Lieutenant-General Brian Horrocks

One of Montgomery's corps commanders from Alam Halfa to Tunis (at about which time he was seriously wounded) and then from Normandy to the Baltic, Horrocks epitomises the driving energy and endless horizons essential in a man who has to lead armoured motorised forces upon raids of deep exploitation. Although an infantryman by origin, Horrocks possessed the panache of a cavalryman of old, and in his handling of the left hook at Mareth, the record-breaking lunge from the Seine to Antwerp, and the pursuit across the Rhine, practised the sort of personal intervention that best wins mobile battles. In the closer-fought battles of Operation 'Veritable' he must have champed at the difficulty of exploding through the Reichswald when neither the sodden ground nor the desperate enemy permitted sweeping advances. Horrocks figures among the generals who combined drive, ability, and charm with success and good luck. As a battalion commander at the outbreak of war, it was his good fortune to avoid the stigma of early British set-backs and enter the arena as a senior commander on the crest of success with his wagon hitched firmly to the ascendant Montgomery star.

Field-Marshal Walter Model

Model represented the new middle class of Wehrmacht officer which had gradually joined the old aristocracy and reached the highest appointments. As a dashing leader of armoured formations, Model built a reputation in France and Russia for a ruthless, driving energy that categorised him as an arch apostle of the offensive—and also made him a hard task-master. It is possible that his immense personal influence with Hitler did much to persuade the Führer to allow the Panzers' 'death ride' at Kursk in 1943, but thereafter Model had, perforce, to demonstrate his flair as an improviser and master of defensive tactics in adversity. Beyond doubt, Hitler's confidence gave Model a freer hand than most of his contemporaries; partly as a result he managed to restore just sufficient order, after Kluge's lost Normandy battle, to stabilise the front along Germany's frontier and to destroy the British bridgehead at Arnhem. Thereafter his limited spoiling attacks, which kept the front alive and led up to the last all-out German throw in the Ardennes, marked him as a commander whose competence was of the first order. Cornered in the end within the Ruhr Pocket, he committed suicide after nearly three weeks' unavailing resistance.

Even with the Allies across the Rhine and invading the Fatherland, there were still pockets of strong, desperate resistance. Here a Sherman fights its way east

Having passed through the Oppenheim bridgehead on March 24, the 4th Armoured Division was half way around Darmstadt by midnight and at Hanau and Aschaffenburg the next day. Tank crews seized damaged but passable bridges at both towns and crossed the Main.

Clearly now, the 1st and 3rd Armies of the 12th Army Group had broken the Rhine defences. Exploitation and pursuit became the order of the day. But the main prize of the Rhine crossing lay in the north, where the Ruhr remained the only major source of industrial power left to the Germans after their loss of Silesia to the Russians and the Saar to the Americans.

An assault of massive complexity

Montgomery's Rhine crossings would rival the invasion of Normandy in the number of troops involved, the supplies accumulated, the transportation used, the special equipment devised, the supporting firepower assembled, the deception plans implemented. With more than 1,250,000 men under him, Montgomery would execute what was probably the largest assault river crossing operation of all time.

The British 2nd Army alone had collected 60,000 tons of ammunition, 30,000 tons of engineer stores, and 28,000 tons of other supplies above normal daily requirements; the US 9th Army had stockpiled 138,000 tons for the crossings. More than 37,000 British and 22,000 American engineers would participate. More than 5,500 artillery pieces, anti-tank and anti-aircraft guns, and rocket projectors could be called upon for supporting fires. Elaborate schemes of camouflage, complex dummy installations, and thoroughly co-ordinated patrols and artillery fires provided deception, while a dense chemical smoke screen maintained for ten days along a 20-mile front sought to give the preparing troops concealment. Civilians were evacuated from their homes for several miles west of the Rhine. Railheads were pushed forward. New roads were built. And giant trucks brought landing craft and the assorted paraphernalia of amphibious warfare close to the water. So detailed were the preparations that 9th Army engineers went so far as to borrow chemical heating pads from hospital units for the purpose of wrapping outboard motors of assault craft to insure instantaneous starting in the damp and chilly mornings of early spring.

Between 900 and 1,500 feet wide at this point, the Rhine flows at a speed of just under 5 miles per hour and is about 9 feet deep. The land on both sides is low and flat, with numerous creeks, canals, and drainage ditches, many towns, hamlets, settlements, and scattered buildings. The Lippe river, emptying into the Rhine just below Wesel, would serve as boundary between American and British armies.

The focus of the 21st Army Group crossings had to be on Wesel because of its roadnet. While the Canadian 1st Army held the line of the Rhine and Meuse from Emmerich to the sea, ensured the security of the Nijmegen bridgehead, and safeguarded the port of Antwerp, the British 2nd Army was to cross between Rees and Wesel with Horrocks' 30th Corps on the left and Ritchie's 12th Corps on the right. The 9th Brigade of the Canadian 3rd Division was attached to the British 51st (Highland) Division for the Rees crossing and in concert with a brigade of the Highland Division would make the initial assault. While the 51st Division established

a lodgement deep enough for bridges to be built, the Canadians were to thrust westward toward Emmerich on the right bank to help the Canadian 3rd Division make a crossing there. The 2nd Corps on the right would send the 1st Commando Brigade to assault Wesel immediately after a heavy bombing by the Royal Air Force.

The US 9th Army would cross on its 16th Corps front in the Rheinberg area with the 30th and 79th Divisions. Assuming success in these operations launched during the hours of darkness, Montgomery would have the support on the following morning of two airborne divisions, the British 6th and the US 17th, both operating under command of Matthew B. Ridgeway's 18th Airborne Corps. Paratroops and gliders, in an operation codenamed 'Varsity', were to come to earth east of the Rhine, a mile or two from the river, to disrupt the Wesel defences, eliminate German artillery, block enemy movements directed against the crossings, and assist in expanding the bridgehead. With the Rhine defences overcome, with Rhine crossing sites available downstream from Rees, the Canadian 1st Army was to drive north to trap German forces remaining in the Netherlands, the British 2nd Army was to start a deep strike north-east across the German plain, and the US 9th Army was to move to the south-east to seal off the Ruhr.

As a general preliminary to the assault, the Allied air forces had carried out since February a heavy bombing programme called 'Interdiction of North-west Germany'. Attempting to cut the Ruhr from the rest of Germany by attacking railroad bridges, canal traffic, communication centres, and industrial plants, British and American bombers smashed and flattened the area.

Montgomery estimated the total German strength opposite his 22-mile assault zone at 85,000 men. These belonged to the I Parachute Army, which was under Army Group H and controlled three corps. There were very few tanks and assault guns on the east bank, but the Germans had a reasonable amount of artillery and anti-aircraft units. Their hasty field fortifications along the river and the railroad paralleling the stream were fairly solid.

The final and last round

At 1530 hours on March 23, Montgomery gave the order to go. At the same time he issued a message to his armies: on February 7, he said, I told you we were going into the ring for the final and last round. This was now going on. 'The enemy,' he continued, 'possibly thinks he is safe behind this great river obstacle. We all agree that it is a great obstacle; but we will show the enemy that he is far from safe behind it.' Once across the Rhine, Montgomery promised, 'we will crack about in the plains of Northern Germany, chasing the enemy from pillar to post.'

At 1800 hours on March 23, harassing artillery fire began to build up in intensity and volume. By 2100 hours, when the first assault units were to enter the water, the expenditure of ammunition had been enormous. In less than two hours, two batteries of the 4th Light Anti-aircraft Regiment fired almost 14,000 rounds. In return came only sporadic firing characterised as 'practically negligible' and as little more than 'light harassing fire'.

As assault troops moved forward from marshalling areas in the rear and joined the Buffalos, storm boats, DUKWs, and ferries that would take them across the river,

a 'Bank Group' organisation controlled and regulated movements in strict accord with preset priorities. On the far side, another Bank Group would function to direct boatloads of troops and tankers to forward assembly areas.

In the left of the 2nd Army zone, the first wave of the Highland Division was across the river in six minutes. Not until troops reached Speldrop, a mile and a half inland, did opposition develop. The arrival of tanks reinforced the British, but the Germans remained obdurate and prevented movement downstream along the east bank.

On the 2nd Army right, at about 2200 hours, the Commandos paddled across the water to a place about 2 miles west of Wesel, moved quietly toward the town, waited less than a mile outside while 201 RAF planes bombed the city for 15 minutes with 1,100 tons of high explosive, and then moved in. The city was a mass of rubble, but defenders were active. It was well into the following day before the Commandos could pronounce Wesel secure and not until dawn of March 25 would all resistance collapse.

Meanwhile, at 0100 hours on March 24, a mammoth artillery preparation opened near Xanten, and an hour later men of the 15th (Scottish) Division crossed the river northwest of the town and secured their initial objectives against spotty opposition.

The 9th Army, sending two divisions across the river on an 8-mile front, had plenty of artillery, an abundance of engineer assistance, and a plethora of smoke-making machinery. In opposition were two corps of the I Parachute Army, Straube's 86th, holding Wesel and the river line from the Lippe river to Dinslaken, and Abraham's 58th, defending to below Duisberg. A three-quarter moon was dim in the Rheinberg area, and the wind was blowing smoke toward the Germans when artillery pieces fired 65,000 shells in an hour-long preparation, 1,500 bombers attacked a dozen German airfields within range of the crossing sites, and infantrymen and engineers took their places in storm and double assault boats.

The 30th Division committed all three regiments, and each sent a battalion across, one near Büderich, another near Wallach, and the third near Rheinberg. Each battalion had 54 storm boats—each craft was powered by a 55-horsepower motor and was capable of carrying seven infantrymen and an engineer crew of two; and 30 double assault boats—each driven by a 22-horsepower motor and able to transport 14 men and a crew of three. Machine-guns firing tracer bullets guided the first wave, which met hardly any opposition. Men leaped from their craft, ran toward the dike and, virtually before they knew it, had captured a bridgehead. 'There was no real fight to it,' a company commander later said. 'The artillery had done the job for us.'

At 0300 hours, near Rheinberg, the 79th Division dispatched two regiments across the water. The men had some difficulties with smoke that caused some short-lived confusion but hardly any trouble with defenders. They too quickly established a solid bridgehead.

In the words of the official US army historian, these American divisions had 'crossed perhaps the most imposing water obstacle in Western Europe at a cost of 31 casualties'.

Shortly before 1000 hours on March 24, a total of 889 fighters escorted 1,696 transport planes carrying paratroops and towing 2,348

gliders that together totalled 21,680 airborne infantrymen to the Varsity drop zone north-east of Wesel. While 240 four-engine Liberators followed closely with 582 tons of supplies to be dropped to the airborne divisions, another 2,153 aircraft maintained cover or ranged Germany in quest of German aircraft. Altogether, 2,596 heavy bombers and 821 medium bombers attacked airfields, marshalling areas, and other targets.

Desperate moments

The 6th Airborne Division had been brought from airfields in England, the 17th from 12 airfields around Paris. They had made rendezvous over Belgium before flying to the drop zone, while the administrative tails of both divisions were driving overland from France and Belgium.

It was the glider force of the British Air Landing Brigade which caught the first impact of German reaction, and some were caught by flak even before release. Those which escaped this fate, spiralled swiftly and silently down on to the German positions, under immediate and concentrated machine-gun fire, and the survivors were in close action the moment they fought their way clear of their often wrecked gliders. For a short time their position was desperate indeed, but then the paratroops dropped nearby and helped to draw off some of the pressure, and owing to a fortunate error in navigation, some of the American paratroops had been dropped on the landing zone beforehand. These helped to put out of action some 88-mm batteries which could have wrecked the whole scheme.

Once the initial difficulties were overcome, however, things went smoothly and in a matter of hours the airborne troops seized their objectives for the first day of operations. Eliminating artillery and service elements of the German 84th Division, they had firmly linked up with the main force by

nightfall, thus avoiding the fate which had befallen so many of their comrades at Arnhem. Nevertheless it had been a close-run thing, and many men who took part in both operations have said that the Rhine crossing, while it lasted, had been the fiercer battle.

'They fought like madmen'

At the end of March 24, there was concern only on the extreme left, at Speldrop, where British and Canadian troops fought a fierce battle with the forces of Eugen Meindl's II Parachute Corps. Some parties of the Black Watch were cut off and surrounded in Speldrop, and it took two days of hard combat by the Highland Light Infantry of Canada and other formations to take the town and secure the flank. 'The enemy', Canadian troops reported, 'fought like madmen'. The Canadians pressed their advance toward Emmerich in what was termed 'vicious fighting' and finally took the town on April 1.

Three days earlier, on March 28, Montgomery had informed his army commanders: 'We have won the Battle of the Rhine.' Now, he told them, he intended to exploit, to drive hard to the Elbe 'so as to gain quick possession of the plains of northern Germany'.

But there had been no quick breakout. Despite a host of bridges across the Rhine, despite a quick thrust of 17 miles beyond the river—by American paratroops riding tanks of the British 6th Guards Armoured Brigade, it would take a little time to get under way what would turn out to be the final operations of the war. From the Dutch-German border near Emmerich all the way south to Worms, Allied armies had crossed the last

A vain attempt to defy the swelling tide of Allied armour sweeping into Germany. The hasty German slogan reflects the bitter attitudes of last-ditch, die-hard Nazis

US Army

great barrier to the heartland of Germany and were about to start the last deep thrusts across the country.

The crossing at Worms had been made by Patch's US 7th Army. Patch would have preferred making his crossing about 20 miles farther south near Speyer because the terrain gave him better access to the east. But when Eisenhower offered an airborne division to help the army across the river, Patch agreed to go at Worms where the hills and forests of the Odenwald would give the paratroops better protection. An unexpectedly rapid intrusion into the Saar-Palatinate by the 3rd Army then narrowed the 7th Army front, placing Worms at the extreme left of the zone and taking away some of its attractiveness as a crossing site. Word that the airborne troops could not arrive until the end of March was even more disappointing. Finally, when the 3rd Army crossing at Oppenheim clearly indicated that an airborne operation would be unnecessary, Patch told Haislip to take his 15th Corps across at Worms in the main effort.

Haislip mounted a two-division assault that started at 0230 hours on March 26, against remnants of 22 German divisions that lacked substantial strength. The 45th Division met only a weak battle group, which delivered a fierce but brief flurry of opposition before collapsing. The 3rd Division stirred up vigilant German pickets who called such heavy mortar and artillery fire on the crossing sites that the men trying to get to the water's edge to embark for their crossing were seriously hampered. With surprise gone, American artillery pieces opened fire, expending in 38 minutes more than 10,000 rounds and, according to one report, 'painting the skyline a lurid red'. The result of the concentration was a considerable decrease of German fire against the first wave of infantry, which roared across the 1,000 feet of water in storm boats in exactly 30 seconds. By nightfall, 7th Army elements had made contact with the 3rd Army on the left, and leading troops were across the Darmstadt-Mannheim autobahn, 8 miles beyond the Rhine.

Though there were several solid bridgeheads across the Rhine on the evening of March 26, Patton decided to send Walker's 20th Corps across in another assault between the 8th and 12th Corps at Mainz. Why another assault crossing? Patton disdained the thought that the Germans could seriously interfere. He wanted to get on with permanent rail and highway bridges across the Rhine, and he desired the excellent road and rail net of Mainz as well as its central location in his army zone. He figured too that an assault crossing was the quickest way to clear the east bank of Germans.

On the night of March 27, therefore, the 80th Division dispatched a regiment across the river at Mainz while another regiment, having crossed to the east bank by means of a 12th Corps bridge, moved to jump the Main 3 miles above its confluence with the Rhine. Both were to work together to clear the angle formed by the Main and Rhine rivers. The Germans put up a noisy but ineffective opposition; assault boats departing the slips and docks of the Mainz waterfront had no difficulty getting men ashore; and by the end of the day, Wiesbaden was cleared at a human cost of only five wounded.

At that point Patton told his three corps commanders to head for Giessen and link up with the 1st Army. 'I told each Corps Commander,' he later said, 'that I expected

him to get there first so as to produce a proper feeling of rivalry.'

Now, every Allied army had troops on the east bank of the Rhine except the French 1st Army on the extreme right and southern flank of the Allied front. A sensitive Charles de Gaulle, president of the Provisional Government of France, was keenly aware of this fact. On March 29, he sent a telegram to De Lattre, the army commander: 'My dear General, you must cross the Rhine, even if the Americans do not agree and even if you have to cross it in rowboats. It is a matter of the greatest national interest.'

What De Gaulle was referring to was that the Allied governments had yet to designate a portion of Germany for postwar occupation by France. Concerned that the American and British governments might be unwilling to recognise French claims in the postwar period, fearing that the Allies were hoping to freeze out the French, he determined to seize a sector beyond the Rhine that his troops could then hold as a de facto occupation zone.

De Lattre had anticipated his political chief. Because his army's frontage along the Rhine was covered from the east bank by fortifications of the West Wall protecting the city of Karlsruhe, a crossing in the French zone was out of the question. De Lattre consequently went to visit Devers on March 27. Noting that Patch's US 7th Army had crossed at Worms on the extreme northern edge of its zone, De Lattre guessed that the Americans might relinquish part of their frontage in order to free units to press the attack in the north. He was right. Devers expanded De Lattre's frontage along the Rhine as far north as Speyer, more than half the distance from Karlsruhe to Mannheim and well beyond the West Wall fortifications. Devers also authorised De Lattre to cross the Rhine, to seize Karlsruhe, and to drive deep to the south-east to take Stuttgart. But Devers specified no target date.

Suspicious that American columns might drive south from Worms and overrun the French crossing sites, De Lattre instructed de Monsabert, his 2nd Corps commander, to start crossing the Rhine before daylight on March 31. De Gaulle's telegram only prompted De Lattre to tell Monsabert that he no longer had the choice of whether the corps might be ready to cross on that date; now the honour of the nation itself was at stake.

When Devers quite innocently asked De Lattre on March 30 when the French might be ready to start crossing, De Lattre assured him that French troops would be across before daylight on the following day. Devers approved.

At 0330 hours on March 31, the 3rd Algerian Division at Speyer found only a single rubber assault boat on the west bank of the Rhine. The troops used it, shuttling silently across the water ten men at a time. Eventually, soldiers found four more boats and increased the rate of build up. Shortly before daybreak, Germans on the east bank became aware of the crossing and began to shell the site. It was too late. An entire infantry company was already well established on the far shore and receiving reinforcements.

Several miles upstream at Germersheim, the 2nd Moroccan Division staged a more conventional crossing, with an artillery preparation and assault boats carrying troops according to pre-arranged waves. Un-

fortunately, there was some confusion at the hastily chosen embarkation points, and the initial wave got into the water only after daylight. By then, the effect of the artillery shelling was gone, and German small arms and mortar fire destroyed 17 of 20 storm boats. The 30 men surviving the crossing managed to hang on to a toehold on the east bank while French artillery ringed them with fire. Subsequent waves, taking heavy losses, built up the bridgehead, and by nightfall the fact that the bulk of two battalions was across assured the solidity of the bridgehead.

On April 1, the neighbouring 6th Corps of the US 7th Army gave permission for French vehicles to cross an American bridge at Mannheim. Quickly taking advantage of the offer, French reconnaissance units were 18 miles beyond the Rhine by the end of the day.

On the following day, De Lattre made a third Rhine crossing at Leimersheim, between Germersheim and Karlsruhe, in order to speed the capture of Karlsruhe. Several days later, there was a fourth crossing at Strasbourg. By then, the campaign had entered a new phase of operations.

The fact that the French had crossed last could not extinguish the great pride they had in their achievement. Like the armies of Turenne and Napoleon and for the first time since then, they too had forced crossings of the Rhine river.

'The German is whipped'

The Allied armies had crossed the Rhine with comparative ease and extremely light losses. And for that the Allies owed much to Adolf Hitler. Had the Germans withdrawn from the west bank during the winter to make a decisive stand on the east bank, had they conserved their resources instead of expending them in the Ardennes, they would have exacted a deadly toll of the attacking armies.

But that possibility had passed. With the Rhine behind them, all the Allied armies manning the long front from the North Sea to Switzerland were embarked on the last offensive.

'My dear General,' Churchill had said to Eisenhower at the Rhine, 'the German is whipped. We've got him. He is all through.'

The statement was true. But there would be one more month of combat, one more month of exertion, heroism, travail, and suffering, before the Allies won the war in Europe.

[Martin Blumenson's biography is in Vol 3, p. 1204.]

Crossing the Rhine

1945 **March 22/23:** The 5th Division of US 3rd Army crosses the Rhine near Nierstein and Oppenheim to establish bridgeheads.
March 23/24: The British 51st (Highland) Division and the Canadian 3rd Division cross near Rees and Emmerich, while the US 9th Division crosses near Rheinberg.
March 24/25: The US 87th Division crosses at Boppard and the 89th at St Goar. The US 4th Armoured Division reaches Darmstadt. The British 6th and the US 17th Airborne Divisions land east of the Rhine and link up with advancing British forces.
March 26: The 3rd Division of US 7th Army crosses near Worms and links up with the 3rd Army.
March 27: The 80th Division of the 3rd Army crosses near Mainz and captures Wiesbaden.
March 31: The 3rd Algerian Division of the French 1st Army begins to cross the Rhine near Germersheim.
April 1: Canadian troops capture Emmerich.

Imperial War Museum

8th Army Gurkhas cross the swollen Ronco river during the drive to Ravenna

ITALY: THE AUTUMN BATTLES

Victory in Italy, September/November 1944
Douglas Orgill

After breaking through the Gothic Line, the Allied armies pushed steadily northwards— but it soon became clear that the foul conditions of the Italian autumn were favouring the German defence. Alexander ordered a 'two-handed punch' offensive, but 8th Army became bogged down on the right flank, unable to keep up the pressure on Kesselring. As a result, Kesselring was able to reinforce the German units slowly falling back before 5th Army—and was thus able to carry out Hitler's strict order not to withdraw north of the Po. The Allies were forced to call off their advance for another winter, to build up their resources for a decisive assault in the spring

By the middle of September 1944, General Sir Harold Alexander, commanding the Allied armies in Italy, faced a tactical dilemma. For the past three weeks, the British 8th Army had been attacking the German X Army along the Adriatic coast inland from Pesaro. But in spite of a brilliant initial success in breaking through the actual defensive works of the German Gothic Line, 8th Army was now deeply entangled in and delayed by the formidable defensive positions which lay on the successive ridges south-west of Rimini, crossgrained to the British line of advance.

ander's mind. The weather of the Italian autumn was steadily worsening, and the rain, which made the inadequate roads into quagmires and slowed all movement, was coming more and more often. Alexander was well aware that time was not on his side. He visited the 8th Army front on September 8, and decided to wait no longer for 8th Army's success, but to unleash 5th Army north of Florence.

'As soon as 5th Army had forced the enemy back to the Gothic Line,' he reported later, 'they would launch a full-scale attempt to break through, and by that time I hoped

Rimini on 8th Army's front, successively through Forli, Faenza, Imola, and Bologna (see map). If Clark could cross the mountains and cut Route 9, the German forces on the Adriatic would be put into great peril.

Two major passes through the mountains north of Florence lay in front of 5th Army. One—the better of the two—was the Futa Pass, 20 miles from Florence on Route 65 to Bologna. The Todt engineers who built the Gothic Line had anticipated that this was where the major Allied effort would be made. The Futa defences were involved and formidable, with wire, dug-in tank turrets,

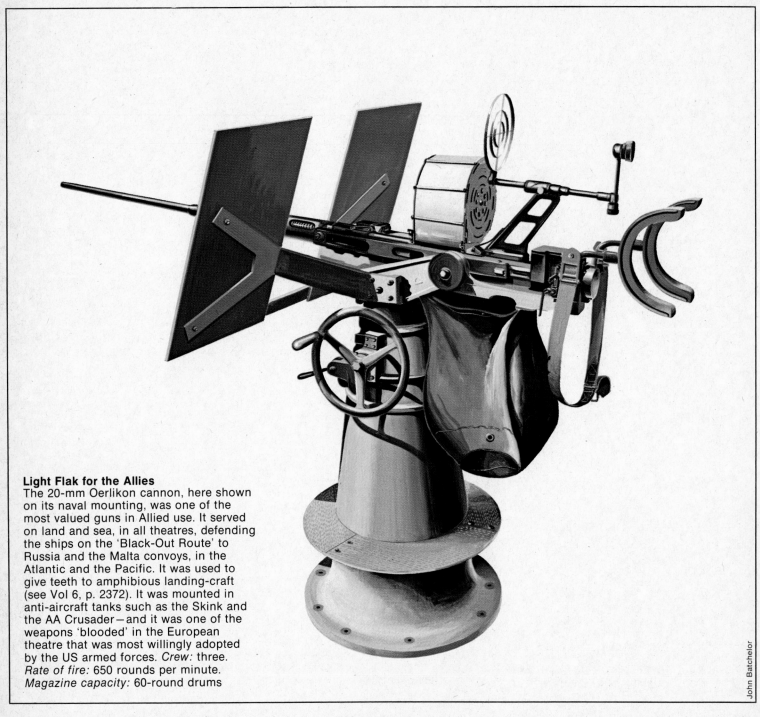

Light Flak for the Allies
The 20-mm Oerlikon cannon, here shown on its naval mounting, was one of the most valued guns in Allied use. It served on land and sea, in all theatres, defending the ships on the 'Black-Out Route' to Russia and the Malta convoys, in the Atlantic and the Pacific. It was used to give teeth to amphibious landing-craft (see Vol 6, p. 2372). It was mounted in anti-aircraft tanks such as the Skink and the AA Crusader—and it was one of the weapons 'blooded' in the European theatre that was most willingly adopted by the US armed forces. *Crew:* three. *Rate of fire:* 650 rounds per minute. *Magazine capacity:* 60-round drums

John Batchelor

Alexander's original plan for the autumn campaign had embodied what he called 'a two-handed punch'—an attack first by Lieutenant-General Sir Oliver Leese's 8th Army along the Adriatic, followed by an attack by General Mark Clark's United States 5th Army on the central front in the Apennines. It had been intended that Clark would not attack until Leese had broken into the plains beyond Rimini, but the delays now suffered by Leese changed Alex-

8th Army would be just about ready for their attack on the Rimini positions and that we should be able to prevent Kesselring from shifting reserves from one army front to another by keeping up a series of heavy blows by our two armies in turn. . . .'

The belt of the Apennines which now faced 5th Army was up to 50 miles deep, and contained peaks of 5,000 feet. Behind the mountains, the long straight highway of Route 9 ran diagonally north-west from

and a 3-mile anti-tank ditch. Some 7 miles to the east was the Il Giogo Pass, on the road which ran from Florence to Firenzuola, and thence to Imola on Route 9. This pass was also well defended by a chain of mountain posts, but the German obsession with the Futa Pass had tended to discount Il Giogo as the ground for an Allied attack.

At first Clark had indeed, as the Todt planners anticipated, intended to attack at Futa, but the quick German withdrawal north of Florence changed his mind. He chose Il Giogo. The choice was excellent, for the boundary between the German X and XIV Armies ran through this sector, giving the Germans the additional confusion of a command shared between two army HQs.

In many ways, Clark's position with regard to the forces under his command was similar to Leese's with 8th Army. Like Leese, he was strong in armour which he could not properly deploy, and weak in infantry, which he desperately needed. He had three army corps at his disposal: two were American – 2nd Corps, with the US

as against the strongest artillery or mortar fire'. . .

Clark attacked on September 10, using the 2nd Corps astride Route 65 to attack Il Giogo, with the British 13th Corps in the more difficult country on the right, and the US 4th Corps along the line to the left, keeping up pressure on the flank. On the next day, both the 2nd and 13th Corps had crossed the Sieve river, and the American infantry were preparing to attack the 3,000-foot peaks of Altuzzo and Monticelli which guarded the entrance to the Il Giogo Pass.

Lieutenant-General Geoffrey Keyes, com-

had to crawl the last mile on their hands and knees. They were too late. The 338th, profiting by the bloody lesson of the past two days, moved swiftly, and by dawn on the 17th the peak was in American hands. Out of 400 men in the rifle companies of the assaulting battalion, 252 had been killed or wounded in the five days of fighting.

Hope flared again for the Allied command. The 5th Army moved forward through the elaborate but now outflanked defence works of the Futa Pass, capturing Firenzuola on September 21, and threatening the vital diagonal road of Route 9. Clark swung his

Vigilance. A holed-up German heavy MG

Oblivion. German POWs, September 1944 vintage

34th, 85th, 88th, and 91st Infantry Divisions; 4th Corps, with the US 1st Armoured Division, the South African 6th Armoured Division, and a regimental combat team of the US 92nd Negro Infantry Division. The third corps was British – Lieutenant-General Sidney Kirkman's 13th Corps, consisting of the British 1st Infantry Division, the British 6th Armoured Division, the 8th Indian Infantry Division, and the Canadian 1st Armoured Brigade.

The German XIV Army, commanded by General Joachim Lemelsen, had two corps in the line: XIV Panzer and I Parachute. Between them, at the end of the first week in September, they disposed of five divisions. West to east, from the Mediterranean, they were XVI SS Panzer Grenadier, 65th Infantry, 362nd Infantry, 334th Infantry, and IV Parachute.

Again: 'last man, last bullet'
Also opposite Clark, to the east of the Futa Pass, was the right-hand division of Vietinghoff's X Army – 715th Infantry. Lemelsen's XIV Army did not have the veteran experience of Vietinghoff's X. It had been badly cut about during the retreat north of Rome, and some of its reserves – those for IV Parachute, for instance – were inexperienced boys who had never fired live ammunition. No allowance, however, was made by the German command for this. On September 8, an order was issued to the division's XII Parachute Regiment, guarding the Il Giogo Pass, that 'the position is to be held to the last man and the last bullet, even if the enemy breaks through on all sides, as well

manding 2nd Corps, used the 85th Infantry Division for his attack. The division's 338th Regiment assaulted Altuzzo in a ragged bloody battle between midnight on September 12 and darkness on the 14th, and received a swift demonstration of just how determined the Germans were to hold the position. They suffered heavy casualties from Spandau and rifle positions in the Altuzzo rocks and scrub, and at dawn on the 15th the mountain crest was still firmly in the hands of XII Parachute Regiment. On the right another American regiment, the 363rd – from the US 91st Infantry Division – had fought its way to within 100 yards of the crest of Monticelli, but was pinned fast by heavy fire.

Farther right still, however, the British 1st Infantry Division, attacking the German 715th Infantry Division on the high ground of the German army boundary, scored an important success. Its 66th Infantry Brigade took Monte Prefetto, one of the forward Gothic Line positions – an opportunity which Clark was quick to exploit by pushing the US 337th Infantry Regiment through the British positions and capturing Monte Pratone, farther still into the German line.

At Altuzzo, moreover, the battered but indomitable US 338th Infantry had returned to the assault, and this time they found revenge. The Germans, too, had suffered heavy losses in the past 48 hours, and they were hastily bringing the Parachute Corps reserve, the Grenadier Lehr Brigade, on to the mountain. So heavy were the attentions of the American artillery and fighter-bombers that some of the German infantry

excellent reserve division, the US 88th, down the Santerno road towards Imola, in an attempt to cut Route 9 and trap the German X Army. But with 8th Army slowing down in a sea of mud, Kesselring was able to plan his withdrawals at leisure, shortening his own line while that of his opponents lengthened. He packed the Santerno valley with the troops of four divisions, and although the 88th captured the key position of Monte Battaglia after a spirited action, the division could get no further.

The 8th Army, for its part, could no longer keep up the pressure which would stop Kesselring reinforcing the front opposite Clark. The weather was appalling, and the British armour was finding that the country north of Rimini was strewn with flooded ditches and canals, instead of being the promised land of which they had dreamed.

Germans in near-despair
Rimini, it will be remembered, fell on September 21, captured by the Canadians and the Greek Mountain Brigade, supported by British armour. But on the previous day, yet another demonstration of how difficult it was for armour to attack fixed defences had been given by the Queen's Bays, one of the armoured regiments of 2nd Armoured Brigade. Obeying orders gallantly but hopelessly, it had assaulted high ground southwest of Rimini, to be promptly cut to pieces, with heavy casualties, by the fire of comparatively few German 88-mm guns. The Allied superiority in armour could no longer be held to be even potentially a decisive factor in the battle.

Yet, briefly, the fall of Rimini had given hope to the Allies and near-despair to the Germans. 'I have the terrible feeling that the whole thing is beginning to slide,' Kesselring had told his staff after he had reluctantly given permission to abandon the town and pull the German X Army back behind the Marecchia river. And 8th Army was jubilant. 'Although the price had been heavy,' Alexander reported later, 'no one in 8th Army doubted that a real victory had been gained, for it was confidently expected that, after breaking in to the flat country of the Romagana, we should be able to exploit rapidly to the Po'. . .

This expectation was dashed almost immediately. The New Zealand Division, Alexander's *corps de chasse*, crossed the Marecchia on the 22nd, and carved fiercely into the battered German 162nd Turkoman Division, recruited from ex-enemy sources on the Russian front. Then the New Zealanders hit the main body of the German defence, which consisted of the veterans of the German I Parachute Division. These defenders stood firm. On September 24, the division's evening report stated proudly: 'During the past 36 hours the division has beaten off 27 attacks in battalion strength. It is still holding a continuous line.'

Heavier and heavier fell the rain. The Marecchia, ankle deep on September 21, was a wild brown torrent 12 feet deep a week later, and the problem of bridging its crumbling banks was becoming an engineering nightmare. From September 29 to October 2, it rained continuously, and every ford over the Marecchia was impassable. The Germans pulled back beyond the next river obstacle, the Uso, but stood firm on the line of the Fiumicino, a little to the north. Resolutely, 8th Army dragged itself up through the mud to the south bank of the river, but it was soon clear that a major assault might be needed to cross it.

The hopes and the impetus of the campaign, in fact, had swung in a way which had not been foreseen to Clark's 5th Army in the centre. Prospects for 8th Army now looked poor; but in spite of the frustration of the US 88th Division in its abortive dash for Imola, the chances for 5th Army still seemed reasonably good. Keyes and the US 2nd Corps were now back on the main axis of advance—Route 65 to Bologna—while Clark brought in the British 1st Guards Brigade to hold the captured positions round Monte Battaglia.

Keyes pushed on steadily down Route 65 in appalling weather, and by October 2 had reached Monghidoro, less than 20 miles from Bologna. The following day Clark drove into the little town, and from a rooftop point looked out over the Po valley to the faint white line of the Alps beyond. 'It seemed to me then,' he said later, 'that our goal was very close.'

Yet no one was more aware of on how slender a margin both 8th and 5th Armies were working in regard to men on the ground. Two days after he had gazed longingly at the distant Alps, Clark signalled the Allied headquarters at Caserta:
Infantry replacement situation is so critical that current operation may be endangered.

Alexander confers with British officers

Supply of infantry replacements and infantry overstrength in divisions only sufficient to maintain divisions at authorised strength through 9th or 10th of October. Losses in my four infantry divisions during the past five days have averaged 550 per day over and above returns to units. Heavy fighting continues, with enemy apparently rushing all available forces to halt our advance on Bologna. All divisions have been in heavy fighting twenty-three to twenty-six days under adverse weather conditions. Continuous supply of infantry replacements is essential.

On both sides of the hill, there was now a clear realisation that the biggest threat to the German position south of the Po came from Clark's 5th Army. Alexander at last had one fresh division to throw into the fight. This was the British 78th Division, newly arrived from the Middle East, and originally destined to join Leese and 8th Army. Now, however, he decided to use it to help Clark. He signalled Wilson at Allied Force Headquarters: 'It is a slow and costly process, and my fears are now that we may not be just strong enough to carry it through. I am reinforcing 5th Army by giving them 78th Division for 13th Corps. It is my last remaining fully fresh division'. . .

While Alexander watched Clark's progress with muted hope, Kesselring observed it anxiously.

'From the middle of October,' he reported, 'the situation south of Bologna gave matter for grave concern. If one or another sector of the Po plain between Bologna and the Adriatic were lost, it might be of secondary importance, but if the front south of Bologna could not be held, then all our positions in the Po plain east of Bologna were automatically gone—in which case they must be evacuated in good time so as at least to save the troops and material.'

Kesselring had already been worried enough by the Allied pressure to ask Hitler to allow him to put into effect Operation *Herbstnebel* ('Autumn Fog')—a contingency plan for a German withdrawal beyond the

Allied left flank: 'chow time' with US 91st Division on the heights of the Apennines

Po. The request was abruptly refused by Hitler early in October, and the OKW informed Kesselring that 'the Führer . . . has decided to defend the Apennine front and to hold upper Italy, not only until late autumn, but indefinitely'. . .

In the short term, Hitler was right, although his decision left his armies in a dangerous position to face any renewed Allied offensive when the weather improved in the spring. Kesselring was over-estimating Allied capabilities in the streaming, sodden mountains. The Americans pushed on through the mud, assaulting the towering escarpment of Livergano, and reaching Monte Grande, only 4½ miles from Route 9, by October 20. Three days later the British 78th Division stormed the nearby peak of Monte Spaduro, and success seemed tantalisingly near. But it was not to be. Between the Americans and Route 9, the broken, difficult country was packed with first-class German troops, and Clark was knocking helplessly on a door he no longer had the strength to open. Since September 10, the four American divisions of 2nd Corps alone had lost 15,716 men in killed and wounded.

Clark's offensive, unsupported by adequate infantry replacements, could not take such losses. Almost within sight of Bologna, the 5th Army's drive slowed and stopped. On October 28, Keyes issued written orders to all his divisions to go on to the defensive.

'After all the effort that had been expended,' Clark said later, 'after all the casualties we had suffered, it seemed almost impossible to give up the idea of completing the breakthrough that autumn . . . at the end of October, a definite date was set for renewal of both the 5th and 8th Army attacks towards Bologna, but we never kept that date'. . .

A hard winter now faced the Allies, in the mountains they had hoped would be far behind them by Christmas 1944. Paradoxically enough, however, the second half of October and the weeks up to Christmas were marked by smaller-scale successful operations by 8th Army, though, as Kesselring had correctly appreciated, these were of secondary tactical importance.

Leese had left 8th Army at the beginning of October, to take command of the Allied land forces in South-East Asia. He was succeeded by General Sir Richard McCreery, who was perhaps more conscious of the hill-fighting qualities of his Indian divisions than Leese had been.

Confronted with the impasse at the flooded Fiumicino, McCreery now swung his 10th Indian Division through the foothills to the west, seized two crossings high up the river, turning the German line and forcing Baade's 90th Panzer Grenadiers to pull back hastily along Route 9. The Indians, accompanied by the British 46th Division, reached Cesena a week later, and the town was entered in force on October 20.

Respite for the winter

Resolutely, through weather that was mostly appalling, 8th Army fought its way forward through the Romagna, though it was basically doing no more than clear the board for its anticipated offensive in the spring. The large town of Forli, on Route 9, fell on November 9. New, limited plans were made for the capture of Bologna and Ravenna, and the latter town was captured early in December. Bologna, however, had to wait until the spring offensive. The shortage of troops on the ground was accentuated by the dispatch of divisions to deal with the crisis in Greece, and the *coup de grâce* to the renewed drive on Bologna was given when the Germans made a limited, local, but alarming attack through the positions of the US 92nd Negro Division in the valley of the Serchio river north of Lucca, on the west flank of the Allied line. This attack was rapidly contained by a swift move of the 8th Indian Division, but it caused the postponement of a projected advance towards Bologna by 5th Army. In deep snow, and under hostile skies, both Germans and Allies settled down for the remaining winter months, roughly along the line of the Senio, stretching across Route 9 south of Imola, to rest and retrain for the advance that both sides knew would surely come in the spring. [*Douglas Orgill's biography is in Vol 5, p. 2091.*]

In the field: a German ammunition detail

In the bag: German POWs in Ravenna

Allied right flank: Greek troops of 8th Army in the fight for Rimini in September

ITALY: THE TOP GENERALS

MAJOR-GENERAL FRANCIS TUKER

LIEUTENANT-GENERAL W. ANDERS

GENERAL SIR HENRY MAITLAND WILSON

Tuker took command of the celebrated 4th Indian Division at the height of Operation 'Crusader' in 1941, and commanded it until mid-way through the Italian campaign. As an officer of Goorkhas, Tuker saw active service in the First World War, on the Indian Frontier between the wars, in Abyssinia, in the desert, and then in the mountains of Tunisia. By inclination he was a mountain fighter and thus more at home in the Italian theatre of operations than almost any other Allied divisional commander. A keen student of war, Tuker may well have thought more deeply about his profession than any other of his contemporaries, and was quite fearless in expressing highly original views even when he knew them to be contrary to common opinion. Such was his influence, that he frequently succeeded in changing the plans of higher authority by means of high-powered persuasion. Tuker represented the finest example of the truly professional pre-war Indian Army, well read, well versed in his trade, and searing in his writings and utterances. The performance of 4th Indian Division at Cassino under his leadership set an example to every other formation at the front and epitomised the excellence of the Indian Army that made up so much of Alexander's commands.

Anders was one of a number of distinguished Polish officers who fell into Russian hands in 1939, but he survived and was released with many compatriots to take a further part in the war alongside the British. As commander of Polish 2nd Corps, Anders led his fellow exiles with the dash and determination that matched the desperation of men whose cause is in doubt and whose future has no clear horizon. At Cassino the Polish infantry suffered casualties it could ill afford—and thereafter Anders had to scrape the barrel in order to maintain a force of operational strength. Quite often his reinforcements came from the Poles who had been driven into the ranks of the German army and then been recaptured. After the death of General Sikorski, Anders became a focal point of Polish hopes, and thus his actions at war became tinged by political motives, since the achievements of Polish arms might strengthen or weaken their claims in the peacemaking. To his countrymen, Anders imparted a vital inspiration: to his Allies he was a dignified colleague whose military ability drew the deepest respect. But, as with all the exiled Poles, his situation exuded a sense of tragedy.

Of all the Allied commanders, Wilson had the longest experience of the Mediterranean theatre. He had arrived in Egypt in 1939 and thereafter played a part in Wavell's early desert campaign, led the British into and out of Greece, handled the offensive and armistice negotiations in Syria, became C-in-C Persia and Iraq to meet the threatened German invasion via the Caucasus, and thence moved to the post of C-in-C Middle East. Thus he presided over peripheral affairs, and weathered the storms that buffeted less fortunate colleagues into oblivion. Like General Alexander, he enjoyed the confidence of Churchill along with the happy knack of anticipating the Prime Minister's wishes. Wilson's support of the abortive invasion of the Aegean Islands in 1943 (when commanding the Middle East) and of the Anzio venture (after becoming Supreme Commander, Mediterranean), along with his opposition to Operation 'Anvil', all reflect his sympathy with Churchill's views. Wilson never achieved the same impact on events as did many of his contemporaries, but he was an imposing figure carrying a prestige which prompted Churchill to send him as Head of the British Military Mission in Washington in December 1944—thus depriving Wilson of the laurels of the final victory in Italy.

In Italy, the southern front of the European battleground, both Allies and Germans were forced to contend with formidable terrain, crippling weather conditions, and the switching of resources to other, more important war fronts. Who were the generals who managed best to deal with these handicaps? *By Major K. J. Macksey*

GENERAL MARK CLARK

GENERAL ALPHONSE JUIN

FIELD-MARSHAL ALBERT KESSELRING

From the moment the campaign in North Africa came to an end, Kesselring guided Axis attempts to forestall Italian peace moves and at the same time beat off successive Allied assaults. However, once the Germans found themselves fighting in a land hostile to their cause, Kesselring was repeatedly denied the vital information which alone could offset his loss of the initiative. From the beginning to the end of his tenure of command, except for one short period, Kesselring fought on the defensive, tested by a series of surprise situations. In consequence, he had to employ a succession of brilliant improvisations in terrain which almost invariably favoured the defensive. Only once, at Salerno, did it look as if he might deliver a decisive counterstroke: normally his entire effort was spent on holding a line and then extricating defeated elements after they had been overwhelmed. Kesselring's nerves were strong—as he demonstrated at the time of the Anzio landing—but his more equable temperament did not combine well with Rommel's, while later, in General Vietinghoff, the commander of X German Army, he discovered a partner with whom he could co-operate at ease.

Although Clark, as Eisenhower's deputy, had played a prominent part in the planning of Operation 'Torch' and had become famous for his daring visit to Africa to negotiate with the French generals prior to the landings, it was not until he took command of US 5th Army and commanded it at Salerno that he enjoyed operational command. Clark was the sort of man whose competence and charm built confidence in both subordinates and superiors—attributes that were essential in the Italian campaign when a commander might find himself co-ordinating elements from a variety of nationalities, in the most trying operational conditions, hampered by the lowest priority for manpower and equipment. From the beginning, Clark was fired with determination to capture Rome and then to conquer Italy. He was not afraid to take risks, but, unhappily, his style was perpetually cramped by terrain which enforced a direct approach and emasculated mobility. At Anzio, caution, for once, overrode his natural aggression and was felt throughout his chain of command. The drain of his resources to other theatres constantly taxed Clark's powers of improvisation, but in the last campaign, after he had succeeded Alexander as commander in Italy, he demonstrated the versatility inherent in so sound a soldier.

Juin became a prisoner of war in 1940 and remained one until the Germans made him C-in-C French Forces in North Africa in the belief that he would have the prestige and inclination to help maintain political stability there. In fact, Juin's inclinations were more Gaullist than Vichyite and although he exhibited greater distrust of the British than the Americans at the time of the 'Torch' landings, he nevertheless fell in step with the Allies. But, reflecting a soldier's natural reticence at becoming involved in political affairs, he 'sat on the fence' and did not recommend himself as a candidate for supreme French leadership. Thereafter his activities found their principal, initial expression in the task of revitalising the French army in preparation for subsequent operations. In Italy he commanded the French Expeditionary Force with gusto and skill, seeming to understand the nature of mountain warfare best of all the senior Allied leaders. His infiltrations of the German defences close to Cassino are classic examples of warfare where the ability to move at maximum speed over trackless terrain can out-manoeuvre fully mechanised armies. Thus, Juin did more than help restore French military prestige—he retaught timeless lessons to the Allied armies.

VICTORY IN ITALY

Italy, April/May 1945

Commandos in a Fantail—Britain's surprise weapon

In January 1945, the Italian front was at a standstill. The 8th Army, after a series of hard-fought river crossings, stood on the banks of the Senio, in the flat dismal plain of the Romagna. The country was sodden with rain; armoured operations were impossible. The 5th Army had reached within 9 miles of Bologna, after some tough fighting, mostly by the Americans, in the mountains north of Florence. There was a shortage of artillery ammunition over all the European theatre; with three months of winter still to come, no further major offensive operations were possible. The Germans had withdrawn slowly and skilfully in the mountains, shortening their communications towards the vital lateral artery of Route 9, the 'Via Emilia': the possession of this valuable road enabled them to switch reserves from one valley to the other in the mountains, and to fill the holes created by any local Allied successes.

Up until Christmas 1944, the Allies had been hoping for a breakthrough, somehow, somewhere. But in the New Year, the front was thinned out, the masses of idle tanks, queued-up, with their crews bivouacking permanently on the road, were withdrawn, and their crews returned on foot to replace the exhausted infantry in the line, or to carry out the interminable chores of mountain warfare—digging supply roads, manhandling casualties over miles of mountain track, or leading the nightly mule trains for the supply of the troops in the front line.

The Americans had done some of their very best fighting in the mountains; the British troops, however, seemed spent, and General Mark Clark, now commanding the 15th Army Group, was inclined to discount their value in further offensive operations.

The Combined Chiefs-of-Staff, who had hamstrung the Allied forces after Cassino by the removal of French and American troops for the invasion of southern France, now proposed to bleed 15th Army Group once more by removing five more divisions (including the splendid Canadian Corps) and two fighter groups, for north-west Europe. They issued a directive to General Alexander—since November 1944 he had been Commander-in-Chief of Allied forces in Italy—telling him to contain the German forces, to prevent their withdrawal, and to take advantage of any weakness.

But that fine general was to show his greatness yet once more. 'I considered'—he wrote in his despatches—'I might yet be able to do something more drastic.'

Alexander's new plan was first to reorganise and regroup his two armies; then, when the weather improved, to strike a final decisive blow to destroy the German armies in Italy.

If the Germans withdrew from Italy, they must swing north-eastwards towards Austria, where, it was rumoured, the Führer had ordered the preparation of an *Alpenfestung*—a mountain fortress—in which the remnants of the Third Reich would fight and die like the Gods in Valhalla. To make this withdrawal the Germans had first the Po river, then the Adige, the Brenta, and the Piave, as delaying positions. Of these the Adige was the most heavily fortified, since it was backed by the Euganean Hills, in which the so-called Venetian Line had been prepared.

The hinge of the pivot, from the German point of view, lay at the Adriatic end of their line, where the inland lake of Comacchio blocks all progress northwards along the eastern coast (see map on p. 2335). At this point, the endless succession of parallel rivers (whose names will be found written on the hearts of many 8th Army veterans) suddenly changes in character. There are more rivers to come after the Senio—the Santerno, Sillaro, and Idice—but all are gathered into one—the Reno, which rises in the mountains west of Bologna, runs north for 30 miles to Cento, then swings south-east until it meets the Senio near the southern shore of Lake Comacchio. Thus between the Reno and the Po there is a strip of comparatively good going, free from major water obstacles. Access to this 'Promised Land' was through a narrow gap between Lake Comacchio and an extensive tract of floods south of the Reno; through this gap ran Route 16, the main Ravenna-Ferrara road. The key was the bridge at Bastia where the road crossed the Reno, and the small town of Argenta, which commanded the exit to the gap.

Alexander's plan was a simple one in conception. The 8th Army would attack westwards, through the Argenta Gap; 5th Army would attack northwards, west of Bologna; the German armies would be caught in a trap between the two.

Though simple in conception, the plan was filled with many difficulties, the greatest of which was that of achieving surprise. Airborne operations to capture Bastia were not considered practicable, owing to the strength of the AA defence; the Germans were as aware of the importance of the Argenta Gap as the Allies. Surprise was therefore to be obtained by:

● Simulating preparations for landing north of the Po, from the Adriatic.

● Persuading the enemy that the main attack would be *south* of the Reno towards Bologna, by attacking in the area of Lugo.

● Making use of many new weapons now available in the theatre. These included 400 Fantails (landing vehicles, tracked)—lightly armoured amphibious carriers.

Concentration was to be obtained by staggering the attacks of 8th and 5th Armies. The 8th Army was to attack first to draw off the German reserves; 5th Army to deliver its blow three days later, so that full air support could be given to both attacks, by the Strategic Air Force. D-Day was to be April 9.

In April 1945 the long stalemate on the Italian front was broken for the last time, as the Allied 5th and 8th Armies launched themselves against the German forces. The battle for the Po valley was on – and only 17 days were to pass between the first Allied attack and the German surrender in northern Italy. It was a complex and skilfully-planned assault, one which included an attack by amphibian vehicles to clear the Argenta Gap, and this account of the action includes a description of the planning written by the 8th Army's last commander in the Italian campaign

Colonel R. L. V. ffrench-Blake

Men of the 2/6th Queens advance through typical waterlogged country

THE 8th ARMY'S BATTLE PLAN
(by its commander, the late General Sir Richard McCreery)

Towards the end of November 1944, when General Alexander had become Commander-in-Chief of the Allied Forces in Italy, General Mark Clark was promoted to command the 15th Army Group, which consisted of General Lucien Truscott's American 5th Army, and the British 8th Army.

The autumn rains, as in 1943, had been tremendous. On one air journey up the Adriatic coast, I saw every Bailey Bridge carried away by raging flood waters. However, at the turn of the year a sudden change took place, and we had a week of bright sun and hard frost, enabling the Canadian 5th Armoured Division to do a most successful sweep from the west to clear the Germans from a large pocket on the right bank of the Senio, north-west of Ravenna. At last the firm going was good for tanks.

This Canadian attack led to the biggest German counterattack for a long time. Three infantry battalions advanced recklessly across open ground, but were driven back with very heavy losses by the tanks of the 9th Armoured Brigade supporting the 1st King's Royal Rifle Corps.

On January 4 the 7th Armoured Brigade with a battalion of the Queen's in Kangaroo personnel carriers cleared another German pocket east of the Senio, capturing nearly 500 prisoners at a cost of only 17 casualties. The 8th Army was now up to the right bank of the Senio everywhere, and suitably placed for the winter pause.

A grave artillery ammunition shortage

had been developing, and now the utmost economy was necessary if sufficient reserves were to be built up for one more great offensive. After the most insistent and urgent pleas to both London and Washington, Allied Force Headquarters calculated that by early April the 15th Army Group would have sufficient artillery ammunition for 12 days' intensive operations. Meanwhile many batteries were restricted to five rounds per gun per day.

Another vital factor was the withdrawal from the 8th Army of the Canadian Corps, to join their comrades in north-west Europe. To make up for this grievous loss, AFHQ was training three Italian *gruppi*, each the equivalent of two infantry brigades, with British equipment. The Polish 2nd Corps was steadily increasing its strength by the enlistment of Poles from prisoner of war camps, men who had been conscripted to fight with the German army.

During these winter months General Clark had one big fear: that he might be an army group commander without the resources to fight a great battle! Winston Churchill disclosed after the war that this was also his own fear, and that of the Combined Chiefs-of-Staff.

After the regrouping for the winter pause, intensive training started in rear areas for the coming battle. The armoured troops were equipped with new tanks. Morale in the 8th Army rose rapidly. The 8th Army was an army of veterans, with two long autumn campaigns and one summer campaign in Italy behind them: therefore they were well trained. A training centre was formed on Lake Trasimeno under Brigadier R. B. B.

Cooke, 9th Armoured Brigade. Our chief task was to train the infantry with the various 'Funnies' – amphibious 'Fantails' and flame-throwing 'Crocodile' tanks, and also the 'Kangaroos', Sherman tanks without turrets to carry assault infantry. All these were available in Italy in very limited numbers for the first time.

This training was a race against time. The Fantails, for example, had to have skilful drivers. These were drawn from tank drivers of the 9th Armoured Brigade, and volunteers from the Royal Army Service Corps, at the suggestion of my enthusiastic Deputy Director of Supplies and Transport, Brigadier S. T. Divers.

The Fantail, developed originally to cross the swamps of Florida, was a large tracked vehicle with thin armour holding up to two sections of men. It was hoped these vehicles would be useful in turning the German left flank by wading the shallow parts of Lake Comacchio.

Along the Senio the 8th Army was now confronted by almost a First World War trench warfare situation. The Germans were dug deeply into the left flood-bank, with weapon pits firing in enfilade (see diagram on page 2338), and with deep dug-outs, and in many places our infantry were holding the right flood-bank. In these sectors it was hoped the flame-throwing Churchill tanks would greatly assist the assault, even if their effect was chiefly on morale.

Training, and morale, were much helped by the weather. After the Christmas snow, followed by frost, the rainfall remained exceptionally low until the final battle. In March and April the Po and its tributaries are often bank-high with melting snow from the Alps and the Apennines, accompanied by heavy thunderstorms. This year, by early April, the rivers running north into the Po were narrow streams at the bottom of high flood-banks, much easing the task of the Royal Engineers with their Bailey Bridges. The high banks were quickly bulldozed down, under comparatively good cover. The conditions were a complete contrast to the autumn of 1944.

It was hoped to exploit one other weapon new to Italy—the amphibious tank—and, later, I had the satisfaction of seeing, from the air, tanks moving across both the Po and the Adige at the same moment.

The good news from Germany at this time, especially the capture of an intact bridge over the Rhine at Remagen, also helped morale.

Strain on the junior commanders

Neither the books produced by the top commanders, nor the official histories have brought out sufficiently clearly the great problems facing the regimental officers of a unit which has been in battle for a long time. Desertion in the infantry in Italy was one of these problems—that is to say, not desertion to the enemy, but to the rear areas, particularly to the thickly populated areas round Naples. A platoon commander in the winter of 1943/44 or the autumn of 1944 never knew exactly how many of his men would parade for yet one more attack across a river, or for a spell in a front line sangar in the mountains in the snow and slush, where they might expect to be heavily mortared for the hundredth time.

The junior leader had a great strain thrown on him, yet no one is more resilient than the British soldier, and many who had failed their duty on one occasion returned to fight hard in this final battle. For instance one young enterprising battalion commander selected 20 men from a detention barracks, and placed them all in one platoon under good NCOs and an outstanding platoon commander. They all fought hard.

It was not surprising that in Italy, and also in Normandy, divisions which had fought for years did not go as far, or as fast, as those which had been well trained at home, with a good leavening of battle-experienced officers and NCOs posted from the active theatres. Therefore the great trial faced by the 8th Army in this last battle was certainly one of its greatest tests.

Another anxiety for some of the married soldiers in the 8th Army was the length of separation from their wives. Although men from units like the New Zealand Division did get home after two years or more overseas, there were exceptions in the case of key officers. One such was Steve Weir, Chief Commander Royal Artillery to General Freyberg, and then acting divisional commander. He finished the war commanding a British division, the 46th. His wife and son joined him in Austria, where he saw his boy, then over four years old, for the first time!

In spite of the winter pause the Allies had fulfilled their task of holding German divisions in Italy. The bombing of the German lines of communication into Italy, like the Brenner Pass, and Hitler's refusal ever to give up ground, both helped, and in early April the Germans still had 23 German and four Italian divisions in Italy. Moreover some of these (such as I and IV Parachute Divisions and XXVI Panzer Division) were some of the best left in the German army,

with a high morale, and up to strength: the two parachute divisions were each 15,000 strong.

The Allies had 17 divisions and four Italian *gruppi*, six armoured brigades, and four infantry brigades. This gave little superiority on paper, but we had overwhelming superiority in the air. Our ration strength was much larger than the Germans', although this was to a great extent due to our much longer supply 'tail'.

As always, the plan for the attack was largely governed by the terrain. The Germans had flooded large areas of ground each side of the Reno, west of Lake Comacchio, but the low rainfall since Christmas was gradually causing these floods to recede. However they were still a formidable problem, and the main road Ravenna-Ferrara formed the only firm ground defile, especially at the village of Argenta.

Several times I went up in an Auster to look at 'the other side of the hill' to try and solve the problem of the Argenta Gap. It was here, we hoped, that the 400 Fantails would help turn the Germans' eastern flank.
● 5th Corps was to attack over the Senio on a wide front with the right of the corps directed on the Argenta Gap. The left would be assaulting the river on the right of Polish 2nd Corps, to be in a position to swing either north or west depending on how the battle progressed.
● Polish 2nd Corps was to attack over the Senio north of the Via Emilia (Route 9) directed on Bologna. Progress made by the New Zealanders and the Poles in the Po plain would directly help the American attack on Bologna if we could make good progress.
● As the 8th Army's advance gained momentum in the plains, 10th Corps and 13th Corps, holding positions in the mountains, would gradually be squeezed out, but I intended to use the troops of 13th Corps at a later stage to keep up the momentum of the attack. The task of Polish 2nd Corps would also be finished after Bologna had fallen.
● 6th Armoured Division was retained as Army Reserve until it was decided on which axis to launch it.

The 8th Army had the close air support of the Desert Air Force, the finest, most experienced tactical air force in the world. Our leading infantry could count on the fighter-bombers destroying farm buildings, or neutralising located German defences in river banks only a few hundred yards ahead of them. On the other hand the support from the bombers of the Strategic Air Force was not so accurate, in spite of all the 'aids' arranged. I had hoped for a dress rehearsal on a small scale, but General Joe Cannon, US Air Force, thought this unnecessary. Unfortunately on D-Day one Polish infantry brigade which was formed up ready to attack, and therefore thick on the ground, received 160 casualties from one group of 22 aircraft who released their bombs several thousand yards short.

The heavy bombers used small 25-pound bombs: a carpet of these in great numbers was laid in the Germans' forward area, but they were so well dug in in the river banks and so thin on the ground elsewhere, that it is thought the 'heavies' caused few casualties.

Before D-Day one very successful preliminary operation was carried out. The 'spit' of land between Lake Comacchio and the Adriatic, right up to Porto Garibaldi, was cleared at small cost, and with 800

prisoners taken from the Turkoman Division. We could now operate along the shores of Lake Comacchio, provided the Fantails could tackle the difficult going.

Now my chief task during the early days of April was to put the army plan across with conviction myself, and even the oldest hands were converted. That veteran warrior General Bernard Freyberg was ready and eager for one more great battle, and I felt that he was determined that his New Zealanders should be in at the kill.

In early March one big uncertainty required tactful handling. General Anders, when he learned details of the agreements reached at Yalta between Roosevelt, Churchill, and Stalin, was shattered. When I visited him he said: 'How can I ask my soldiers to go on fighting? I must withdraw them from the line.' I replied that there were no troops to replace them, and that a 10-mile gap would be opened up! Anders remained silent for a whole minute, then said: 'You can count on the Polish 2nd Corps for this coming battle. We must defeat Hitler first.'

It was, however, a great tragedy that in the closing stages of the war, as at the outset, Great Britain had been able to do nothing to help Poland, and Anders knew that she was being handed over to a Communist régime, to be a Russian satellite.

All was now ready, but April 8 was very windy, with many airfields out of action. However, Mark Clark telephoned that the weather report for the next day was good. At 1920 hours, April 9, the 'balloon would go up'.

THE 5th ARMY'S BATTLE PLAN

There was no easy solution to 5th Army's problems. The Germans were still firmly in occupation of the mountains 10 miles south of Bologna. A diversionary attack would be made at the extreme west of the line, near the Mediterranean coast, at D-4. This sector was held by the US 92nd Infantry Division, and two combat teams, one of Japanese-Americans and one of disbanded AA gunners. In the centre, south of Bologna, 4th Corps (General Grittenberger) on the left of the Reno, would attack in the direction of Bazzano, 10 miles west of Bologna, while 2nd Corps (General Keyes) on the right would attack directly towards Bologna, and be prepared to advance on either side of the city. The intention was to cut the Via Emilia west of Bologna, and to launch the two armoured divisions, US 1st and South African 6th, on an axis west of the Reno, directed on the Po crossing at Ostiglia and north of Bondeno. Bologna was to be by-passed, not more than one division being detached for its capture.

THE GERMAN SITUATION

What was the situation of the German armies?

Kesselring, who had been appointed Commander-in-Chief West, had handed over Army Group C in Italy to General Vietinghoff. Hitler's orders were (as usual) to hold out to the last in the present positions. General Herr and his X Army Staff had calculated exactly the D-Day which 8th Army would use, and had planned a withdrawal from the Senio to the Santerno, 24 hours before the attack was due. This manoeuvre not only would have kept his own troops out of the preliminary bombardment, but would have caused the British

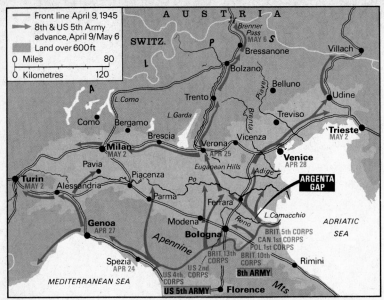

A U S T R I A

SWITZ.

Brenner Pass MAY 6 S

Bressanone

Villach

Bolzano

Belluno

Trento

Udine

L.Como

Treviso

Como

Bergamo

Brescia

Vicenza

Verona

Milan MAY 2

Venice APR 28

Trieste MAY 2

Pavia

Piacenza

Euganean Hills

Adige

ARGENTA GAP

Turin MAY 2

Alessandria

Po

Parma

Ferrara

Genoa APR 27

Modena

L.Comacchio

ADRIATIC SEA

Bologna

Apennine

BRIT. 5th CORPS
CAN. 1st CORPS
POL. 1st CORPS

Spezia APR 24

MEDITERRANEAN SEA

BRIT. 13th CORPS

Reno

Rimini

US 4th CORPS

US 2nd CORPS

BRIT. 10th CORPS

8th ARMY

US 5th ARMY Florence

Mts

DRIVE TO THE ALPS

Left: The last offensive of the Italian campaign. Once through the Argenta Gap and across the Po, the British and US columns, expecting a last-ditch stand in the mountains, would fan out towards the German forces stationed in the Alps

Below: Partisans and Americans talk with captured German officers near Milan

all rail routes leading south from Austria. Now the attack was switched to the Po crossings. No bridges remained, but the Germans kept the flow of supplies going with ferries, heavily camouflaged among the reeds and undergrowth which lined the tall flood-banks on either side of the river. A very large proportion of the German field artillery and transport was horse-drawn, while infantry companies carried their baggage on hand-carts and barrows.

On the shores of Lake Comacchio, one particular German officer had a passion for stewed eel. The local fishermen were allowed to take their boats out from time to time, to keep his mess supplied with his favourite dish. While the fishermen kept the Germans supplied with eels, they kept the British supplied with information, invaluable to the success of the amphibious 'right hook' on which the capture of the Argenta Gap depended.

8th ARMY: THE FIRST CLASH

General McCreery's success in raising the morale of the 8th Army for this last attack was a remarkable achievement. In the middle of March, divisional Intelligence officers had widely disseminated an appreciation on the possibility of the Germans withdrawing to the Austrian mountain 're-doubt', in which they might hold out indefinitely. Thus the idea of the need for a decisive blow in Italy was already planted in everyone's mind, though much of the impact of it was dulled by the emphasis on demobilisation, and post-war rehabilitation, which was being fed to the troops through the channels of Army Education, and which, to a commanding officer trying to raise the fighting spirit of his unit, seemed almost as insidious as enemy propaganda.

McCreery was not well known to all the troops but commanded great respect among his officers: he was a modest man with a positively diffident manner, and it is impossible to imagine him wearing a flamboyant hat, distributing cigarettes, or haranguing open-air assemblies. As a boost to morale, and in keeping with his character as a cavalryman and an amateur rider, he permitted a race-meeting to be held at Cesena, scarcely 30 miles from the Germans, at which, so the story goes, the 8th Army Quartermaster staff brought off a notable *coup* by rapidly transporting from the south a little known but remarkable horse of unlikely appearance. It started at long odds, was never headed, and enabled the Chaplain-General, the Director of Medical Services, and other members of the administrative staff 'in the know', to supplement their pay at the expense of the official 'tote'.

Four days before the battle, McCreery assembled all officers down to lieutenant-colonel in the cinema at Cesena. In his quiet, almost apologetic, voice, he said that the theatre had been stripped of troops for France; that the army was like an old steeplechaser, full of running, but rather careful; that it was his intention to destroy the Germans south of the Po, rather than to allow them to withdraw to further defence lines to the north. The plan was then outlined.

The author went to the same cinema that evening, and saw Laurence Olivier in *Henry V*—a suitable entertainment for the occasion, though the scene where the king

US Army

attack to fall on empty air; and before a fresh attack could have been mounted, all the supporting artillery would have to be moved forward to reach the new positions. Vietinghoff approved the plan, but inevitably it was vetoed by the OKW. Yet, in spite of this crippling handicap, German morale remained good.

The threat of landings from the Adriatic had proved very successful: Vietinghoff moved half his mobile reserve, XXIX Panzer Grenadier Division, north of *both* Po and Adige to the Treviso area, while the diversionary attack by the Americans at the extreme western end of the line drew

off part of 90th Panzer Grenadier Regiment, the only army reserve south of the Po. The Luftwaffe had failed to find or identify the Fantail concentration on the shores of the lake.

Thus, although the Germans were fully aware of the dangers confronting them, they had been forced to conform to every move made by General Alexander, and had been prevented by their own high command from taking the most commonsense step in the face of an impending attack. In addition to all this, their supply problem was acute. The Allied air forces had for months been working on a programme of interdiction of

A GI of US 88th Division in the attack on Vicenza

British troops pick their way through the ruins of Argenta

goes round the camp at night and talks to the young soldier was rather too poignant. The boy says: 'We see yonder the beginning of the day, but I think we shall never see the end.' McCreery's message got through to his troops. The author passed it on to his own regiment, behind closed doors in a school; the thrill of excitement which ran through the audience remains one of his greatest memories of soldiering.

The armoured divisions had difficulties to face: first, doubtful going, for which special spoon-shaped extensions, called 'Platypus Grousers', were fitted to the tracks; second, dead flat ground covered by orchards, below the level of which the German anti-tank gunners could shoot, while the tank commanders and the tank gunners were blinded by the branches; and third, the perennial difficulty of moving up under cover of darkness, and deploying through a narrow gap. This time there must be no failure, as at the Gothic Line the year before.

But it was the infantry who really had the tough task. Outflanking movements and infiltrations were impossible against the relentlessly straight lines of the flood-banks and levées in which the Germans were entrenched, often in dug-outs hollowed out in the thickness of the earth wall. Indeed so deep and secure were these tunnels that when the two sides faced each other across the width of a canal, a technique had been evolved for eliminating the enemy by firing a 17-pounder anti-tank gun clean through the near flood bank and into the far one! The gun was laid by accurate survey, as a result of which an aiming point was marked on the face of the near bank (see diagram).

Whatever happened, the Argenta Gap was likely to prove hard to take; and considering that every man knew that if he survived this battle he had probably survived the war, the courage and determination of the infantry of all nationalities was astounding.

On April 1, Commandos and men of 24th Guards Brigade seized the spit to the north of 56th Division, and followed up on April 5 by taking the islands in the lake. On April 6 the 56th Division crossed the Reno, and took a wedge of ground up to the shores of the lake, thus securing the launching site for the

amphibious flanking movement, and at the same time diverting the enemy's attention to the seaward flank. The only disappointment was the performance of the Fantails, which could not function in the lake: the water was too shallow for flotation, and the mud too soft for tracks. The plan for the amphibious 'hook' had to be rapidly revised.

All was now poised for the battle.

Into the assault

The preliminary air bombardment consisted of 175,000 fragmentation bombs, dropped by 825 heavy bombers on gun areas and reserve assembly areas opposite the assaulting divisions. This type of bomb was chosen in order to avoid churning up the ground. Some 1,000 medium and fighter bombers attacked individual targets, gun and mortar sites, HQs, and vehicles moving behind the lines.

The artillery programme consisted of five 'false alarm' bombardments by 1,500 guns, each lasting 42 minutes, with ten-minute intervals, during which the river bank of the Senio was attacked by aircraft. At 1920 hours, H-Hour, the fighter bombers made a final dummy run along the river, as a signal for the infantry to advance. During the bombardment the leading troops withdrew 400 yards.

General McCreery, airborne in an Auster spotter plane, saw the attack begin: 'In the evening dusk,' he says, 'the spectacle was most impressive, the usual huge artillery and fighter bomber support being supplemented on this occasion by the flame-throwing tanks.'

On the first night – April 9 – the 8th Indian Division and 2nd New Zealand Division attacked towards Lugo across the Senio, with the task of seizing a bridgehead across the Santerno. During the day of April 10, the air bombardment was repeated on the Santerno positions. The 78th Division waited to pass through them, once the Santerno bridgehead was established.

The men of 8th Indian Division, Argylls, Frontier Force Rifles, Mahrattas, and Punjabis, stormed across the river behind a curtain of flame and flung themselves upon the Germans. Close behind, the Sappers built ramps and bridges, while the Mahratta Anti-

Tank Regiment slung its guns across the gulf by cable-slings, in the manner of the famous naval field-gun race in the Royal Tournament.

By dawn on the 10th, the supporting tanks of 21st Army Tank Brigade were crossing the Senio on three bridges, one a two-tier structure of 'Ark' tanks (see diagram). By evening the Punjabis were up to the east bank of the Santerno, while the Jaipurs and West Kents widened the gap for the reserve infantry brigade to pass through; next morning, April 11, after another concentration of bombers and guns upon the Santerno positions, the Gurkhas, Frontier Force Regiment, and Royal Fusiliers crossed behind another barrage of flame. The Santerno bridgehead was won, and the 78th Division came up from reserve to begin the attack on Bastia. On the left, the New Zealanders were equally successful.

The close air support was most effective. A 'cab-rank' of fighter bombers was kept in the air over the battlefield. Observers travelling in tanks with the leading troops called down the aircraft, directing them on to detailed targets by an ingenious use of a card-index of vertical air photos, from which it was possible to identify a single house. The Germans said that even lone vehicles were spotted and attacked by hordes of aircraft. They were now receiving the treatment which they had dealt out to the Allies in Tunisia.

On the right flank, Brigadier Ronald Cooke, commander of the 9th Armoured Brigade, was preparing for the amphibious operation to negotiate the wide, shallow obstacle of Lake Comacchio.

Brigadier Cooke recalls:

So far as 9th Armoured Brigade was concerned, 'Impact Plain' and 'Impact Royal' formed a single operation which started at 1300 hours on April 10 and finished on the evening of April 13 – a period of over 72 hours. Crews and staff put in a tremendous effort and in combination with the infantry of 56th Division brought off a far-reaching success. The long period spent in training was fully repaid, and all ranks now focussed their attention on repair and maintenance, in preparation for the next operation.

As anticipated, 'Impact Royal' had been

more difficult than the first operation, but the quick collapse of the German defences on the Reno which followed, and the speed with which the Argenta Gap was forced was due almost entirely to these two landings behind the German lines. Neither of these two successes would have been possible without the dash with which the Fantail crews pressed home the assault, or the determination with which the infantry overcame the German resistance.

BREAKTHROUGH AND TRIUMPH

By the evening of April 13, while 169th Brigade of 56th Division was carrying out the amphibious operations, 167th Brigade had succeeded in crossing the Reno and was working towards Bastia, in order to turn the north end of the Santerno defences.

South of the Reno the 78th Division, using the Kangaroo armoured carriers, had broken out of the Santerno bridgehead and was also converging on Bastia; the New Zealanders had broken out of their bridgehead, and had reached Massa Lombarda, while the Polish 2nd Corps was attacking Imola. The 5th Army's attack, which should have begun on the 12th, had not yet started, because of bad flying weather which prevented aerial bombardment.

The ruins of Bastia bridge were captured from the south by 78th Division on April 14. The Kangaroo force consisted of a battalion of infantry, carried in the Kangaroos of 4th Hussars; an armoured regiment – the 9th Lancers; and a troop of SP artillery, armoured engineers, and other supporting weapons.

The whole force, commanded by Brigadier John Combe, was on tracks, and was of the greatest value in thrusting against a shaken German defence, since it was able to motor safely up to points of resistance, and disgorge its infantry close to the objective. Many lives would have been saved had these vehicles been available earlier than the closing months of the war. The 78th Division's advance on the bridge was at first confined between the Santerno on the right and an impassable canal on the left. Nearing Bastia, the Santerno swings away to the east, giving more room for manoeuvre. On the morning of the 14th, the London Irish reached the Reno at Bastia, crossed dryshod over the remains of the bridge, and were engaged heavily by Germans defending Bastia on the further side.

Contact was made with the co-belligerent Italian Cremona group on the right, and with 56th Division on the north bank of the Reno. The reserve brigade of 78th Division was switched westward over a bridge built by 56th Division, and 48 hours later, by April 16, both divisions were approaching the main defences of the gap at Argenta itself. Bastia had been evacuated after the initial resistance by the enemy. (The Royal Fusiliers' progress in the outskirts of the town had been impeded by a thick layer of treacle from the burst vats of a sugar factory!) Once the Reno had been crossed, the Germans withdrew to the main position at Argenta. In front of the town the ground was flooded; only the dusty surface of Highway 16 showed above the water; all the canal banks were dug out and fortified, and the whole area was heavily mined.

The main strength of the position was based on the Fossa Marina, a 12-foot canal running north-east from Argenta into Lake Comacchio. Guided by Italian parti-

A massive bag of German POWs

sans, who knew of routes through the minefields, 11th Brigade closed up to the positions till enemy resistance became too strong for further advance. A full-scale attack was made by both 78th and 56th Divisions on April 16; on 78th Division's front the East Surreys and Lancashire Fusiliers won a bridgehead over the Fossa Marina, leaving the waters of the canal 'streaked and laced with blood, and ugly with corpses' in the words of the division's historian, Cyril Ray. On the right, in 56th Division's sector, the London Irish and London Scottish, and 24th Guards Brigade fought to turn the flank of the German position. On the morning of April 17, General Arbuthnot, commanding 78th Division, threw in the weight of the Irish Brigade to make a gap for the Kangaroos and the tanks of 2nd Armoured Brigade. By the afternoon the armoured force was beginning to fan out in the wider country beyond the gap. The worst was now over, and the battle was becoming fluid at last.

The Polish 2nd Corps had a vital task in their thrust parallel to the main road to Bologna, for their success would help to unlock the German defences facing the 5th Army. General Clark, in his *Calculated Risk,* stated: 'In all our plans for the offensive, the Polish corps figured prominently – I had high confidence in their fighting spirit, and they were moved into a vital spot along the north side of the road to Bologna.'

Old rivals from Cassino
At this spot the Poles were confronted with their old enemies, the German I Parachute Division with whom they had clashed on Monastery Hill at Cassino. The Polish attack, conducted with wonderful *élan* (in spite of the shattering news about Yalta which had so depressed them before the battle) was entirely successful. The I Parachute Division was completely disintegrated, the divisional flag eventually falling as a trophy to General Anders.

The attack by 5th Army, originally planned for April 12, was postponed for two days because of the bad weather. It was therefore not until 0945 hours on the morning of the 14th that the offensive was opened on 4th Corps' front. The assault was

preceded by a bombardment by 500 aircraft of the Tactical Air Force, the heavy bomber effort being reserved for the second day.

Reading from the right of the line were the US 34th and US 91st Infantry Divisions astride Route 65, the main road from Florence to Bologna. Next to them US 88th Infantry Division, and then the two armoured divisions, South African 6th, and US 1st, one each side of the Reno, in the valley of which ran Route 64.

On the left lay US 10th Mountain Division and Brazilian 1st Division. The country was still mountainous along the whole front, and rapid progress was not expected. The first attack, on April 14, was made by the three left-hand divisions of 4th Corps, with fair success, 1st Armoured capturing Vergato, 10th Mountain taking the 3,000-foot Rocca di Roffeno, and the Brazilians clearing Montese.

On the second day, April 15, the air force delivered 1,500 tons of bombs on the corps' front, and another 800 on communication targets elsewhere – a record for the campaign. Following this huge bombardment, Polish 2nd Corps attacked by night, starting at 2230 hours. By midnight South African 6th Armoured Division had captured an important strongpoint, Monte Sole. The US 88th and 91st Divisions on their right had as their main objective three strong mountain features: Monte Rumici, Monte Adone, and Monte dei Frati, which covered the approaches to the village of Pianoro; these peaks, about 2,000 feet high, were the last obstacle barring entry into the plains. Once they fell, the Allies would have the advantage of observation for their artillery over the German areas.

After stubborn fighting for 48 hours, the Germans were forced off the heights into the lowest foothills of the mountains, and their defeat became inevitable. General Truscott, the American army commander, released his reserve division in the Reno valley to thrust at Marzabotto; in its wake South African 6th Armoured Division crossed the Reno to the west bank, while US 10th Mountain Division drove on to reach the Via Emilia on the morning of April 20. At almost the same time, 85th Division reached the Via Emilia east of Bologna. The moment was ripe for a breakthrough.

The armour goes through
On April 18, when Argenta was finally cleared, General McCreery released the British 6th Armoured Division from Army Reserve. He had always considered the possibility of launching his mobile reserve on the line Lugo/Massa Lombarda/Budrio, should the Argenta Gap attacks fail. The armour had made careful study of both routes, using detailed aerial photographs, to detect any possible weak spots in the network of canals and watercourses which lay across their path in even the best of tank going. The Argenta Gap route would pay the biggest dividend, since most of the German troops would be enclosed within the encircling sweep of the Reno, over which only one bridge remained – at Poggio Renatico on the main Bologna-Ferrara road.

Once Argenta had fallen, General McCreery decided upon the northern alternative, and put 6th Armoured Division under command of General Keightley's 5th Corps. The mobile reserve could not be flung impetuously into battle, however, since the way through Argenta was constricted, blocked by rubble, and jammed with the supply traffic

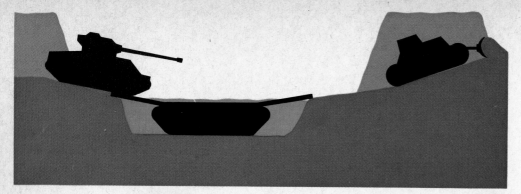

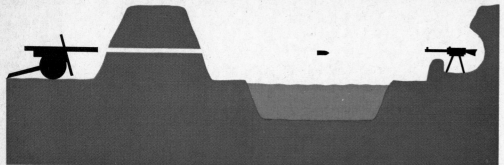

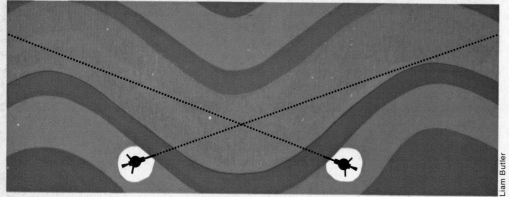

Liam Butler

COPING WITH ITALY'S WATER-BARRIERS

The Allies were sometimes able to cross the narrower water-courses by submerging an Ark bridging tank (see Vol 5, p. 2094) in a position where its twin bridges could reach to either bank. Armour and bulldozers could then be passed across it to widen the breach in the far bank and secure the bridgehead.

The Germans were expert at emplacing machine-guns in the raised banks of the Italian water-courses. The Allies developed an ingenious technique to winkle these out: using 17-pounder guns to shoot straight through the friendly bank, across the water, and into the bank on the far side, where the German positions had already been pinpointed by reconnaissance patrols

A plan view of two typically-sited German machine-gun positions, showing how their mutually-supporting enfilade fire could sweep the far bank and the centre of the water-course, and could also cover small sectors of their own bank

of 56th and 78th Divisions. A nightmare traffic problem faced the corps staff – who solved it, but not without imposing a great strain upon the armoured division, which had to move night after night in the small hours, spending the day in further reconnaissances forward, and in the countless last-minute preparations for battle.

But by April 19 at about 1730 hours the leading two regiments of 26th Armoured Brigade had passed through the leading infantry at Consandolo, and had made contact with the Germans on the Po Morto di Primaro, a canal running obliquely across the front from the Reno to Ferrara. On the morning of the 20th, the 16/5th Lancers on the left gained a bridgehead close up to the Reno flood-bank, through which at midday the last remaining armoured regiment of the reserve – the 17/21st Lancers – was passed. Now only one more water obstacle, the Fossa Cembalina, remained on which the Germans could stand.

The armoured regiments advanced continuously across thickly wooded country, shooting up everything in sight, and searching every possible bit of cover with fire. Roads were avoided, because of the danger of mines. By dark, the leading troops were still a mile short of the Fossa Cembalina, and under fire from German anti-tank guns; they settled into night harbours, locked all the prisoners in the local jail, and prepared to advance at first light. Night patrols reported the Germans digging in on the line of the Fossa.

It was on this day, the 20th, that Vietinghoff – knowing that he was already too late – ordered a general withdrawal to the line

of the Po. The Allied armour was thrusting at him both from Argenta and Bologna: his position was clearly untenable. Three days earlier, reporting this possibility to the OKW, he had received a severe reprimand for being defeatist, and was told to defend 'every inch of the area entrusted to your command'. In the face of such impossible requirements from above, he did what most sensible soldiers will do when expected to carry out an impossible order – he stressed his determination to obey his orders to the last – and continued with his own plan for withdrawal, wrapping it up in the thin disguise of 'abandoning static defence for mobile strategy'.

The initial progress of 6th Armoured Division had been a disappointment to General McCreery. Not only was 8th Army's 'old racehorse' being a bit careful, but it was also considerably out of practice in the art of blitzkrieg. Impatience began to filter down the command net; the leading regiment was ordered to resume the advance in the dark, and to close on the Fossa Cembalina. It arrived at first light to find the bridge blown and the Germans strongly in possession of the further bank at the village of Segni. However, good aerial photo interpretation by the divisional Intelligence staff had revealed the presence of a weak point in the water defences close to the Reno; after a brisk battle, the 17/21st Lancers got through and suddenly found themselves bowling along merrily at full speed in open country.

In a few minutes they had covered 5 miles unopposed and had arrived at the walls of Poggio Renatico, while the other two armoured regiments fanned out to the north

behind them. In 5th Corps HQ, the radio interceptors heard the commander of the German detention centre come up on the radio and say 'there are tanks here at Poggio Renatico' before he was told to shut up by another voice. The last exit from the Reno trap was now shut – the battle was virtually over. The Germans, withdrawing in confusion, started to destroy petrol and ammunition dumps, and to abandon their now useless vehicles, many of which had run out of petrol.

On April 22 the two armoured divisions, South African 6th and British 6th, met beyond the bend of the Reno, near Finale(!) in Emilia; the Poles and the 34th Division had taken Bologna on the 21st; 10th Mountain Division reached the Po on the 22nd, and 8th Indian Division in 8th Army reached it, near Ferrara, on the 23rd.

The final triumph

The Germans left nearly all their guns, tanks, and transport south of the Po; most of their men, including the generals, had to swim across. The pursuit was pressed relentlessly; the magnificent US 10th Mountain Division, which had already covered 55 miles in two days, crossed the Po, seized Verona on April 25, and headed north up Lake Garda. The British 6th Armoured Division sent motor battalions and armoured cars across the Po on April 24, while New Zealand 2nd and British 56th Divisions also got across on the same day. The New Zealanders and 56th Division crossed the Adige neck and neck, while 6th Armoured raced for the Austrian frontier.

The Italian Committee of National Libera-

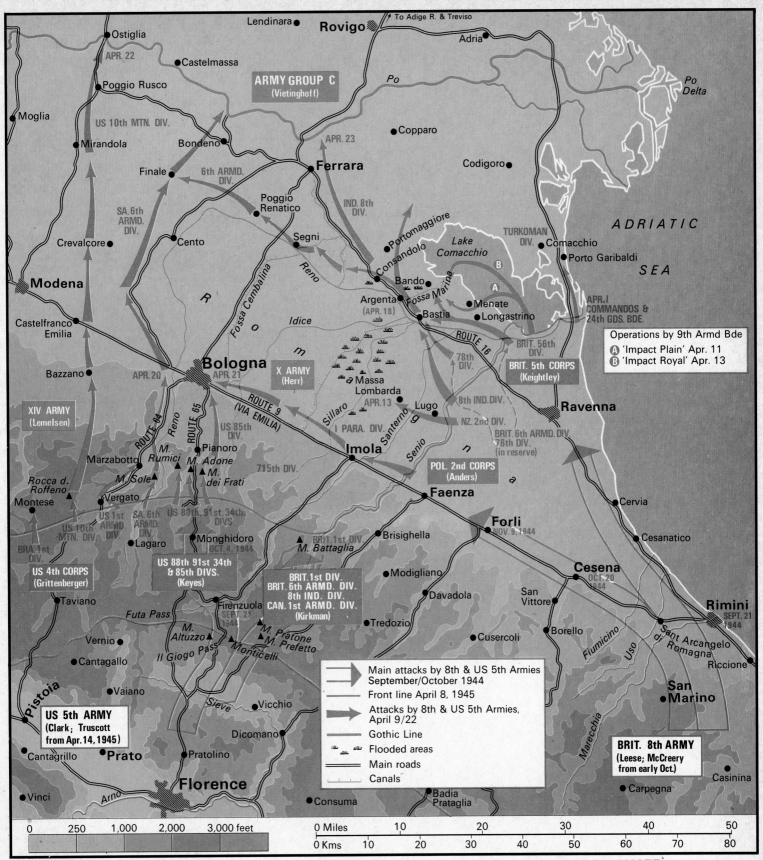

Lendinara • **Rovigo** ↑ To Adige R. & Treviso
Ostiglia • • Castelmassa • Adria
APR. 22 • Po
Poggio Rusco **ARMY GROUP C**
(Vietinghoff) Po
Moglia • Delta
US 10th MTN. DIV. • Copparo
Mirandola • Bondeno APR. 23
Finale • 6th ARMD. **Ferrara** • Codigoro
DIV.
SA. 6th Poggio
ARMD. Renatico IND. 8th
DIV. Segni DIV. Portomaggiore
Crevalcore • Cento • Consandolo TURKOMAN Comacchio
DIV. A D R I A T I C
Reno Bando B Porto Garibaldi
Modena Lake
Comacchio S E A
Castelfranco Argenta Fossa Marina
Emilia (APR. 18) Menate APR. 1
Bastia Longastrino COMMANDOS &
Bazzano APR. 20 **Bologna** X ARMY Idice ROUTE 16 BRIT. 56th 24th GDS. BDE.
APR. 21 (Herr) DIV. 78th Operations by 9th Armd Bde
XIV ARMY ROUTE 9 DIV. BRIT. 5th CORPS A 'Impact Plain' Apr. 11
(Lemelsen) (VIA EMILIA) Massa (Keightley) B 'Impact Royal' Apr. 13
ROUTE 64 Lombarda 8th IND. DIV. **Ravenna**
US 85th APR. 13 Lugo
Reno ROUTE 65 DIV. Sillaro NZ. 2nd DIV.
M. Pianoro Santerno BRIT. 6th ARMD. DIV.
Marzabotto Rumici 715th DIV. I PARA. DIV. Senio 78th DIV.
M. Adone **Imola** (in reserve)
M. Sole M. POL. 2nd CORPS
Rocca d. dei Frati (Anders) Cervia
Roffeno Vergato **Faenza**
Montese US 1st US 88th, 91st, 34th Brisighella **Forli**
US 10th ARMD. DIVS BRIT. 1st DIV. NOV. 9, 1944 Cesenatico
MTN. DIV. DIV. SA. 6th OCT. 4, 1944 M. Battaglia Modigliano
BRA. 1st ARMD. DIV. Lagaro Monghidoro **Cesena**
DIV. US 88th 91st 34th Davadola OCT. 20
US 4th CORPS & 85th DIVS. San 1944
(Grittenberger) (Keyes) Vittore **Rimini**
Taviano Firenzuola BRIT. 1st DIV. Tredozio Borello SEPT. 21
Futa Pass SEPT. 21 BRIT. 6th ARMD. DIV. 1944
M. 1944 8th IND. DIV. Cusercoli Sant Arcangelo
Vernio Altuzzo CAN. 1st ARMD. DIV. di Romagna
M. Pratone (Kirkman) Riccione
Cantagallo Monticelli M. Prefetto San
Il Giogo Pass Marino
Sieve Vicchio **San**
Pistoia **Marino**
Vaiano Main attacks by 8th & US 5th Armies
US 5th ARMY September/October 1944
(Clark; Truscott Dicomano Front line April 8, 1945
from Apr. 14, 1945) **Prato** Attacks by 8th & US 5th Armies, BRIT. 8th ARMY
Cantagrillo Pratolino April 9/22 (Leese; McCreery
Gothic Line from early Oct.)
Florence Flooded areas Casinina
Vinci Arno Consuma Badia Main roads Carpegna
Prataglia Canals

0 250 1,000 2,000 3,000 feet   0 Miles   10   20   30   40   50
0 Kms 10 20 30 40 50 60 70 80

---

tion ordered a general insurrection in
northern Italy. German columns were
attacked everywhere; in Milan and Venice
partisans took control. German formations began to surrender independently. At
1400 hours on April 29, only 17 days after
the start of the offensive, two German
officers, representing General Vietinghoff
and General Wolff (supreme SS commander)
signed an instrument of unconditional surrender—the first German capitulation of
the war. The surrender came into effect on
May 2. Nearly 1,000,000 men in Italy and
Austria laid down their arms.

Twenty-six nationalities had fought in

Italy—in this last great battle, the forces in
the Allied line included Americans, British,
Brazilians, Japanese-Americans, Italians,
New Zealanders, Poles, Indians, Gurkhas,
and a Jewish brigade. They fought a great
battle, against a brave enemy, who strove
well to the very end. The battle was grandly
conceived, and excellently planned; the
staff work was near perfection; the nations
fought as a team, without jealousy or desire
to catch the limelight. For those on the
winning side who survived, it was a lovely
way to end a war.
[Colonel R. L. V. ffrench-Blake's biography
is in Vol 3, p. 1195.]

AUTUMN STALEMATE: SPRING BREAKTHROUGH

The Allies had breached Kesselring's defences in the Gothic Line battles, only to
be halted south of Bologna. The autumn
battles failed to dislodge the Germans—
and for the second time 5th and 8th Armies
spent a winter of recuperation and build-up.
In April 1945 the final assault began,
tackling the formidable Argenta Gap with
an amphibious operation across Lake
Comacchio. Within a fortnight, the Gap
had been cleared and the Germans were
falling back towards the line of the Po river

Elizabeth Wiskemann

SURRENDER IN ITALY

When Mussolini returned to Italy in September 1943 to set up his Neo-Fascist Social Republic, an air of unreality surrounded this new protégé of Germany, the Führer's one-time mentor. Mussolini tried to go back over 20 years to the stirring times of his rise to power by abusing the House of Savoy and by nationalizing industry in such a way as to give the workers nominal control of management. But from the beginning his new Republic seemed to most Italians slightly ridiculous—they called it the *Repubblichetta* of Salò, and its supporters *repubblichini,* also in the diminutive. His plans for social reform they rejected as mere propaganda although Mussolini himself was serious about them, as serious as he was capable of being in his later years. One of the many ironies of the situation was that the northern part of Italy over which Mussolini was trying to establish his rule was the more advanced and industrial part where anti-Fascism was strong—and not only the anti-Fascism of the Communists. In the south, which was occupied by the Allies, conditions were fearfully backward and political attitudes less clear-cut, less positive.

Thus from the beginning serious clandestine resistance to Mussolini's Republic was organised, sabotage making the running of the new régime very sticky. Increasingly the best young people went up into the mountains to form bands of partisans against the Fascists and the Germans; the peasants generally helped the partisans when they could do so. Even within Mussolini's government there was much bickering, for his authority was not what it used to be. Extreme Fascists like Preziosi and Farinacci thought him too liberal (towards the Jews, for example) and too cool towards the Germans; others were shocked that he allowed his son-in-law, Ciano, to be executed in January 1944, apparently as the result of German pressure. The fact that in October the Germans obliged Mussolini to withdraw from the Romagna to Lake Garda, where they could watch him better, meant that he became remote from the Italian public; until December 1944 he never once appeared before it to make a speech.

Mussolini had appointed Marshal Graziani as his Minister of Defence, but this too seemed unreal. On the one hand the Germans enrolled many men Graziani would have liked to recruit into the new Republican Army, sending them to work in factories in Germany: on the other, those he did manage to recruit were whisked away

Graziani, Mussolini's last Defence Minister, in the 'little republic' of Salò

Vietinghoff, German C-in-C: cautious and non-committal in the surrender talks

to Germany to be trained there. The families of all these people, as Mussolini constantly complained to the Germans, were kept uneasy as to what might have happened to them. Mussolini himself felt that the Germans were not prepared to trust him with an army at all.

Mussolini's little Republic was in fact occupied by the Germans in all their Nazi manifestations. It was the presence of General Leyers with his *Rüstungs und Kriegsindustrie* (RUK) organization which blocked any real nationalization of Italian industry, since Leyers was convinced that the Italian factories in Turin and Milan and the shipyards of Genoa would then produce less. These were in 1943-45 some of the most important factories controlled by the Germans. Sauckel's and Todt's organizations impressed Italians to work in the factories in Germany or for the Germans in North Italy.

The German army, at first under Rommel as Commander-in-Chief, but then from November 1943 under Kesselring, had its headquarters at Belluno. The German Ambassador, Rudolf Rahn, represented Ribbentrop and the Foreign Office, and there was a whole network of SS officials with some thousands of SS troops of differing nationalities, *Volksdeutsche,* Czechs, Slovaks, and Ukrainians. Kaltenbrunner, who had succeeded Heydrich as the head of the *Reichssicherheitshauptamt* (RSHA) under Himmler was represented by Wilhelm Harster and his personnel, and Himmler was represented by two more people: Karl Wolff and Eugen Dollmann who, exceptionally, got on with one another. Dollmann was very much the minor figure, but after remarkable triumphs as an interpreter (since he had lived in Italy for many years), Dollmann had been attached just before the war to the German Embassy in Rome nominally as a cultural attaché but actually representing Himmler; he came north with Rahn when Rahn moved to Fasano on Lake Garda. Since the outbreak of war he had worn SS uniform.

Karl Wolff, born in Darmstadt in 1900, had been with the Freikorps between December 1918 and May 1920 and then in the Reichswehr; although little is known about his life in the 1920s, with the conquest of power by the Nazis his rise was meteoric. He joined the Nazi Party and the SS in 1931, becoming ADC to Franz Ritter von Epp, Hitler's man in Bavaria. In July 1933, six months after Hitler came to power, Wolff

Italy and Switzerland, September 1943/April 1945

Ever since the Germans rescued Mussolini and set up his puppet state in northern Italy, there had been a wide-spread resistance to the Italo-German Fascist regime. And as the spring of 1945 drew near, so too did the threat of a renewed Allied offensive and a bloody, drawn-out campaign in Hitler's 'Alpine Fortress'. But behind the preparations for the Axis defence of northern Italy, men were working frantically to negotiate a surrender before irremediable damage was done to northern Italy—and the key man on the German side, a high-ranking SS officer, risked the Gestapo and the concentration camps to arrange the surrender terms

was appointed personal adjutant to Himmler, who was now well on the way to becoming the police chief of all Germany. From being promoted to the SS equivalent of major in November 1933 Wolff reached the SS rank of lieutenant-general *(Gruppenführer)* in January 1937. Wolff was clever and had great charm—it is said that Himmler found in him everything that he himself lacked—and on the outbreak of war Himmler made him his personal liaison officer at Hitler's field headquarters. In 1941 and 1942 he was on the Eastern Front and in 1967 was still in prison for his share in the liquidation of 300,000 Jews in Poland then.

The SS in Italy

In July 1943 Wolff set up an advanced staff in Munich to prepare an operational SS and Police Command in Italy in the event of the possible defection of Badoglio. Then in September, while retaining his position as chief of Himmler's personal staff he was appointed senior commander of the SS and Police in Italy with the title of *Höchster SS und Polizeiführer,* a supremacy shared only with Prützmann in the Ukraine. (Otherwise such officials were only entitled as 'higher', not 'highest'.)

Really, in the last instance, he was the most powerful German in Italy until the war ended; the only person whom he could not coerce was the Commander-in-Chief, Field-Marshal Kesselring, who was responsible not to Himmler but only to Hitler. Wolff's authority extended over the 'rear-occupational zone' of the Tirol south of the Brenner, the Alto Adige which Hitler had always sworn to regard as part of Italy but which he had detached from Italy in September 1943: this had been Mussolini's final humiliation. For general administrative purposes the South Tirol was attached to the Tirolese *Gau* governed by Gauleiter Franz Hofer.

One of Wolff's special responsibilities was the suppression of the partisans. The Italian Resistance soon showed itself to be more serious than anyone had foreseen; and thus Wolff's task of beating it grew fairly steadily, in spite of the fact that the Germans were gradually retreating and the territory of the Republic of Salò was in consequence diminishing. Early in June 1944 the Allies took Rome, and the Germans fell back, after losing Florence in August, to the Gothic Line, stretching from La Spezia to Rimini. Already in the middle of June a meeting of Neo-Fascist generals at Bergamo referred

Kaltenbrunner, SS chief whose vigilance threatened the course of negotiations

Dulles, the man behind the secret talks with the SS leaders in Italy

to 'a greater depression of a spiritual character' after the fall of Rome, and 'a big increase in the number of partisans' in the north. An order from Kesselring at about the same time referred to the deterioration of the partisan situation (from the German point of view), particularly in central Italy, and called for the utmost severity. 'Wherever there is evidence,' Kesselring proclaimed, 'of considerable numbers of partisan groups a proportion of the male population of the area will be arrested, and in the event of an act of violence being committed these men will be shot.' The SS was likely to be less restrained in carrying out such orders than the army.

At the end of July 1944, partly because of Hitler's and Himmler's greater suspicion of the Military High Command after Stauffenberg's attempt on Hitler's life, Wolff was appointed military plenipotentiary in Italy, replacing General Toussaint: he kept all his SS commands.

In November 1944, however, after the Allies had taken Bologna, the switching of reserves to meet the Allied landings in southern France brought the campaign to a halt. From now on German manpower on the ground in Italy was greater than that of the Allies, though the latter remained stronger in the air. On November 13 General Alexander issued a proclamation to the Italian partisans which as good as told them to disperse for the winter: this was a great discouragement, implying as it did that they must not expect supplies could continue to be dropped to them before the spring.

These circumstances made a number of Germans commanding in Italy believe that the moment had come to negotiate with the Allies. Hitler's claim that he was about to launch decisive wonder-weapons had worn thin, but the Germans knew well enough that the Russians were not on the best of terms with the Western Allies; this had been frequently advertised, most obviously perhaps over the Polish Rising against the Germans in the previous August. Officially Hitler, the chief of all the German chiefs, declared that the Germans must fight until the enemy alliance broke up, a fate to which all alliances were foredoomed, he said. And officially the Germans were to scorch the earth wherever they retreated. In Italy this was likely to mean the destruction of some of the most beautiful objects in the world—indeed it had in August 1944 brought the destruction of the exquisite Santa Trinità bridge in Florence. In Italy also it might mean the destruction of the Fiat works outside Turin and of many of the most modern industrial plants left in Europe – the last surviving ones.

Possible German peace feelers
Of the Germans in authority in Italy in January 1945, Ambassador Rahn was far from being an extreme Nazi, nor did he lack sympathy for the arts. He was prodded from time to time by the liberal and art-loving German Consul formerly in Florence, Gerhard Wolf, who had gone north in August 1944. But with the irascible Ribbentrop as his chief it was difficult for Rahn to take any initiative. Nor was Field-Marshal Kesselring the man to attempt any negotiation with the Allies.

On the other hand, the two SS leaders, Wolff and Dollmann, were both temperamentally inclined, and in a more favourable position, to do so. Himmler, their chief, was already thinking in these terms and hoping to gain some kind of timely success by negotiation. The SS, being a relatively new jungle of organisations, was more flexible than the Army or Foreign Office. Moreover, Wolff, and particularly Dollmann, took some interest in the arts and genuinely wished to avoid more destruction; they seem even occasionally to have attracted a few more civilised people to join them as juniors. Their idea was, of course, to save Europe, and Italy in particular, from Communism by in some way joining with the Western Allies against Russia; they did not take seriously the Casablanca formula of unconditional surrender. So much for the point of view of Wolff and Dollmann.

On the part of the Allies there was a great desire to shorten the war combined with the determination that this time the Germans should acknowledge their defeat. The Americans, at that time possibly more than the British, wished on no account even to appear to trifle with the Russians. The head of the American Office of Strategic Services (OSS) in Switzerland since November 1942 was Allen Dulles, a nephew of Robert Lansing. He had served in Switzerland in his youth during the First World War and was a personal friend of President Roosevelt. His position in Berne was unique, as he was also political adviser to the American Minister there. Thus he combined in one person more experience than any other Allied official in Switzerland and more powers. British Intelligence and Special Operations worked separately: Allen Dulles combined all such functions in his person. Thus he had already established contacts with the Italian partisans whose leader in Lombardy, Ferruccio Parri, had illegally crossed the Swiss frontier in order to visit him.

Dulles was constantly approached, as most Allied representatives in Switzerland were, by individuals claiming some kind of eminence and offering to act as intermediaries between the belligerent parties. It was difficult and could indeed be dangerous to deal with them, but it constituted a risk which must sometimes be taken. The Swiss government took its neutrality very seriously, a fact which demanded caution on the part of the British and Americans in Switzerland. On the other hand the representatives of the Allies enjoyed the advantage of the sympathy of the majority of the Swiss, especially those speaking German and Italian dialects.

In January 1945 the Swiss themselves

had every reason to wish that the war, especially in Italy, should end soon and without destruction. Considerable Swiss capital was invested in north Italian industry, and throughout the war the land-bound Swiss had depended on foodstuffs imported via the Italian port of Genoa. And in this last winter (as it turned out to be) of the Second World War the Swiss had a new anxiety. Increasingly rumours crossed the frontiers from Italy and Germany that the Nazis were planning to withdraw into a mountainous redoubt in the Bavarian and Austrian Alps adjacent to Swiss territory to defend themselves there to the last man; this could dislocate that part of Europe for a long time and make it impossible for the Swiss to demobilise.

Such considerations were certainly in the mind of Major Max Waibel, a Swiss Intelligence officer on good professional terms with Dulles. On February 21, 1945, Waibel was rung up by a schoolmaster friend of his, a German-Swiss called Husmann. An Italian acquaintance of Husmann's called Parrilli, after weeks of unwilling delay, had been able to visit Husmann at his home near Lucerne. Parrilli was some kind of businessman from Milan who had been alarmed by Mussolini's threatening speech there on December 16, and who was on friendly terms

SS leaders
who suffered
from conscience . . .

with a German SS official called Guido Zimmer. Zimmer was one of the SS surprises – a devout Catholic and attached to the arts. Zimmer and Parrilli both shivered at the thought of Hitler's 'earth-scorching', and Zimmer had given Parrilli to understand that people senior to himself in the SS had the same feelings: it seems that he actually mentioned Dollmann and Wolff.

Waibel immediately went to Husmann's and met Parrilli; he had the intuition to sense that Parrilli was worth bothering about. On his own responsibility, without consulting higher Swiss authorities, Waibel told Dulles about him and it was arranged that Dulles' chief assistant, Gaevernitz, should meet Parrilli late on the evening of February 25. Gaevernitz was not greatly impressed by Parrilli, but it was conveyed to the Italian that he should try to produce Dollmann, and Parrilli returned to Italy on February 27 to see what he could do. The Swiss soon felt considerable respect for Parrilli: he faced great personal danger on his journeys between Italy and Switzerland, for Allied planes attacked his car and the Italian partisans marked him down as a Nazi agent.

The Swiss seem to have judged well. Parrilli was back in Switzerland (Waibel had given him a password to facilitate his entry) on March 2, with the news that Dollmann with Zimmer would be at the Swiss frontier at Chiasso early the next morning. Dulles agreed to send another of his subordinates, Paul Blum, to meet Dollmann in

Lugano at 3 o'clock on the afternoon of March 3. This left Dollmann to the Swiss for a good eight hours.

Hints of Allied goodwill
The opportunity was used by Husmann, who loved political argument, and who, like many of his kind, was 100% pro-Ally, to break down Dollmann's defences. The Germans, Husmann said, were utterly defeated and had no possibility but surrender. (Rahn had already warned Dollmann of this.) There was no hope of trying to divide the Allies, who would never treat with an emissary of Hitler or Himmler. Apparently Dollmann raised the question of the latter when Blum had arrived, to which the American replied: 'Not a Chinaman's chance.' Otherwise the conversation was in French. Parrilli had brought up the matter of the Allies' attitude toward any German who helped to shorten the war.

Blum's answer was: 'The material and moral destruction in Europe caused by this war is so gigantic that the Allies will need the help of every available man of good will in the work of reconstruction. Everyone who helps to shorten the war gives us proof of his good will.'

Before he left Blum also passed to Dollmann the names of two Italian partisans who had been captured by the Germans – Dulles would take their liberation as proof of goodwill. The names were those of Usmiani and no less a person than Ferruccio Parri himself, who under the pseudonym of Maurizio was a prominent chief of the north Italian partisans (he had been arrested by the Germans in Milan on December 31). Blum had done all this and left after 20 minutes.

Dollmann had come to Switzerland so quickly because Wolff had reacted to Parrilli's first message immediately by holding a meeting of SS chiefs in Italy at 1800 hours on February 28. Harster was present at this and reported on it to Kaltenbrunner, who was no friend of Wolff. If Kaltenbrunner knew, he was likely to inform his chief, Himmler. After the meeting at Lugano on March 3 Parrilli reported to Wolff in person and Wolff proposed to meet the Americans in Zürich on March 8; he also agreed to free Usmiani and even Parri.

Dulles had not at first decided whether he was prepared to meet Wolff, a figure bound to arouse deep suspicion on the Allied side. After persuading Allied headquarters at Caserta that no German general could openly surrender because his preparations for doing so might cause him to disappear into a concentration camp, Dulles obtained agreement from Caserta to possible meetings with Germans in Switzerland. Suddenly he was informed by Waibel via Gaevernitz on March 8 that Wolff was in the train to Zürich, accompanied by Dollmann and two other Germans: he had also brought Parri and Usmiani to Chiasso. The indefatigable Husmann, too, was in the train with Wolff, coaxing him out of his Nazi assumptions. As it happened an avalanche near the St Gotthard Pass had obliged Husmann and Wolff to change trains. Wolff only just succeeded in remaining unnoticed by the other passengers.

The Swiss consider that Husmann's talks to the Germans greatly facilitated the task of the Americans. Indubitably Waibel's arrangements for the journeys were invaluable as it was vital that these should go smoothly in order that they remain secret.

Hitler must not know of them and Allen Dulles must not be compromised.

Karl Wolff's opinions seem to have been bewilderingly confused. As an indoctrinated Nazi he accepted Hitler's gospel, and regarded Slavs and Jews as sub-human. When he first met Husmann he still believed that the Allies wished to destroy the German nation. With such primitive notions he tried to combine aesthetic values such as he felt the *Herrenvolk* should hold. If the war was hopelessly lost he wished to save German lives and property by stopping it. When he had seen Hitler in the middle of February 1945 he had presumed on his personal charm to suggest that a way out must be looked for; the Führer had for once been fairly non-committal which gave Wolff a margin of risk he might take.

When Wolff returned to Italy he explained Hitler's programme of destruction to his subordinates, adding that none of it was to be implemented without his personal consent. It should be added that the Italian partisans were preparing to counter German measures of destruction, but a professional soldier, General Raffaele Cadorna, who led them in northern Italy, afterwards expressed doubt as to whether they would have been successful.

Now when he was to meet Dulles, Wolff did not try to make a personal bargain with the American, but he offered personal references to the Pope, whom he had secretly visited in May 1944, to Rudolf Hess, and to two relatives of the Italian royal house. He also made it known that he had hidden a number of the pictures from the Uffizi and other Italian galleries to save them from bombing, but also from being removed from Italy. This was true. But what curious confusion was here in Wolff's mind. Why should he suppose that the Americans would be impressed by a link with Hitler's deputy, Hess, who had so dramatically flown to Scotland in May 1941 and for whom the only valid excuse with the Allies was that he was fairly mad? And those relatives of the King of Italy, whom the Nazis—and Hitler in particular—accused of foul treason to Germany, seemed an odd choice of reference for the top SS man in Italy. Wolff, incidentally, had taken measures to protect the King of Italy's famous coin collection.

As for the Catholic Church, its representatives were naturally approached by both sides in the war and used their influence to try to reconcile the opposing parties. Once the Allies were in Rome the Pope was cut off from the Germans except for Weizsäcker and his staff at the German Embassy to the Vatican. The Archbishop of Milan, Cardinal Schuster, now became a key figure: after a time he even enjoyed the confidence of some of the Italian partisans. But after June 1944 Schuster could only communicate with Rome through the Nuncios in neutral countries: this added fresh importance to Switzerland and made it more than ever the obvious theatre for peace negotiations or talks about how to persuade the Germans in Italy to surrender. Rahn and Wolff had often talked to Schuster.

Dramatic talks in Zürich

It was on the evening of Thursday, March 8, that Dulles first met Wolff at his, Dulles', flat in Zürich. Although he had by now had a 'go-ahead' signal from Caserta, Dulles was, understandably, still hesitant about Wolff and he tried to visit Parri and Usmiani first to make certain that the right people

had been released—they had, however, been sent separately from Chiasso with an Italian-speaking Swiss Intelligence officer and had not yet arrived. When Dulles saw them later in the Hirslanden nursing-home in Zürich there was a characteristic scene with Parri. He had thought, when removed blindfolded from his prison in Verona, that he was to be shot by the Germans, and he wept as he thanked Dulles for his rescue, but then almost immediately he wished to be assured that no dishonourable deal had been made involving him and that he could quickly return to Italy to lead the Lombard *Resistenza* to victory. Of all Europe's partisans Parri was one of the most splendid characters.

Thanks largely, it would seem, to Husmann's lectures Wolff had now grasped that his talk with the Americans could only be concerned with the unconditional surrender of the Germans in Italy to all three major Allies. Wolff insisted that neither Hitler nor Himmler knew of his journey to Switzerland, though it has been seen that Harster had informed Kaltenbrunner, who was certain to hand on this piece of news to Himmler.

Wolff now assured Dulles that if he, Dulles, really represented Caserta, Wolff would now try to enlist Kesselring as well as Rahn in favour of the surrender of the Germans in Italy. Italy was a quite separate theatre of

. . . welcomed by the Allies as a shortcut to peace

war from any other in which the Germans were fighting: in a sense they were cut off there by the mountains at their back although these were also a defence. Wolff assured Dulles of the vital point that he controlled the formerly Italian province of Alto Adige or South Tirol with the Brenner Pass, so that his surrender would virtually destroy the plans for German resistance in the 'Alpine Redoubt' by cutting it off. Wolff also offered to free a number of Jews and Allied prisoners held in northern Italy.

When Wolff came away he expressed surprise to the Swiss over Allen Dulles' courtesy to him. Only later did he ask a favour for himself. This was the release of a favourite SS adjutant of Hitler's who had been taken prisoner by the Allies. Wolff felt he could justify his visit to Switzerland if he could offer this man to Hitler as a birthday present—the Führer's birthday was on April 20. Dulles tried to find the man but he had been sent to a POW Camp in Canada.

Dulles now suggested to Caserta to send some responsible officers to Switzerland in case Wolff kept his word, and immediately on Friday, March 9, Field-Marshal Alexander replied that he would be sending two senior staff officers: these turned out to be the American General Lemnitzer, Alexander's Deputy Chief-of-Staff, and the British General Airey, Alexander's Chief Intelligence Officer.

On March 11 Parrilli was back from Italy alone with bad news. On the very day of Wolff's meeting with Dulles, Kesselring had

been summoned to Hitler's headquarters in order to be made into the Commander-in-Chief on the Western Front; he did not return to Italy. Into the bargain Kaltenbrunner was pressing Wolff to meet him in Innsbruck, where Wolff knew that Kaltenbrunner might arrest him. Parrilli, with tremendous devotion, travelled from Fasano to Lucerne, and back, and back again, reporting that Wolff was still determined to act on his own, and bringing offers from him to facilitate Allied landings in north Italy. Later Wolff changed and said he could only act if he could persuade Kesselring's successor, Vietinghoff, to act with him: he thought he could. This was the news which Dulles brought to Lemnitzer and Airey when he met them on March 14 at Annemasse.

At this point the Russians claimed that they should be represented at the negotiations, a tricky suggestion since it would be more difficult to disguise a Russian, and Switzerland had no diplomatic relations with the USSR. This suggestion was not followed up for the moment.

On March 19, 1945, Dulles and the two Allied generals in disguise travelled to Ascona on Lake Maggiore; the generals were installed in a house on the hill while a house on the lake was prepared for Wolff and his suite. (Both these houses belonged to an anti-Nazi Stinnes, who was brother-in-law to Dulles' chief assistant, Gaevernitz, and were not conspicuous.) From the Swiss, the Allied, or the German point of view it was essential that Wolff's contact with Dulles should be absolutely secret, and Ascona was something of a fashionable resort, even in wartime, with Easter approaching.

Wolff was uncertain as to where Vietinghoff would stand and suggested that he should visit Kesselring on the Western Front, if there was time, in order perhaps to bring about a complete German surrender all along the line. But he had very great difficulties in reaching Kesselring. After finding him, Wolff was summoned to Berlin by Himmler and had to parry questions from Himmler and Kaltenbrunner, who seemed to know about his journey to Zürich but not the visit to Ascona. Both Himmler and Kaltenbrunner were obviously jealous of Wolff and afraid that he might beat them at trying to intrigue with the Western Allies against Russia. Not till March 28 was Parrilli able to bring a message to Switzerland to say that Wolff would be back in Italy on the following day, ten days after the Ascona meeting. On Good Friday, March 30, Zimmer brought a message to say that Wolff would come to Switzerland, probably with Vietinghoff and Rahn, on Easter Monday, April 2. It looked as if all the obstacles were overcome.

By this time, after much pleading from Parri to be allowed to return to Italy with his colleague, General Cadorna, who had been visiting Dulles, Parri had been flown to Caserta on March 27. Soon after he was able to get back to northern Italy in time for the partisans' uprising.

Blackmail from Himmler

Himmler and the Russians had yet to be reckoned with, however. On Easter Sunday, April 1, 1945, Himmler telephoned to Wolff and obligingly told him that he, Himmler, had had Wolff's wife and children removed from Italian territory and placed under Himmler's authority in Austria. At the same time Himmler ordered Wolff to stay in Italy; if he failed to do so his family might be murdered. For the moment Wolff could not well move. For the moment he could do little but send messages via Parrilli to Switzerland, promising to prevent destruction, to protect political prisoners, and to avoid action against the Italian partisans, promises which on the whole he kept. On several occasions he pointed out that he could not be responsible for what happened in the Italian ports as this was the affair of Admiral Dönitz.

On April 4, with this news which they did not fail to appreciate, Lemnitzer and Airey flew back to Caserta as there seemed nothing more for them to do in Switzerland for the moment, and the Allied spring offensive was due to begin; it seemed a painful irony that it should have to do so. The Allied armies knew nothing of surrender talks though bright young officers in the British 8th Army wondered why on earth the Germans went

again on March 22 (according to Churchill –Dulles says March 23) Molotov showed signs of great irritation, attacking the Americans as having behaved in an 'unexpected and incomprehensible' manner.

On April 3 Stalin sent an offensive communication to Roosevelt, claiming, among other things, that he had information to the effect that the Germans had agreed 'to open the front to the Anglo-American troops and let them move to the east while the British and Americans promised in exchange to ease the armistice terms for the Germans'. When he replied on April 5 Roosevelt confessed to 'bitter resentment . . . for such vile misrepresentations of my actions or those of my trusted subordinates'. On April 7 Stalin backed down both to Roosevelt and Churchill, in the words of the latter sending 'as near as they [the Russians] can get to an apology'. On the morning of April 12, the

duress. This he was able to do throughout. On April 15 he set out to be confronted by Himmler and Kaltenbrunner on April 17 in Berlin with what amounted to an accusation of treason – both of them would have liked to have succeeded as well in approaching the Allies. Wolff bluffed his way through, it seems, by saying that he had driven a wedge between the Anglo-Americans and the Russians, and that he had delayed the Allied spring offensive in Italy. He then decided that he would be wise to speak to Hitler too and reached the Führer's bunker in the early hours of April 18. According to Wolff (and otherwise only Kaltenbrunner was present) – he told about the same story to both the Americans and the Swiss separately afterwards – Hitler reproved him but then accepted Wolff's story that he had made contact with the Allies independently so that Hitler could disown him if he chose. Wolff

The representative of Karl Wolff, supreme head of the SS in Italy, signs the document of unconditional surrender in Caserta

Lieutenant-General Morgan signs for the Allies – the final act in the story of a tenuous, dangerous road to peace

on fighting. At Caserta, besides Lemnitzer and Airey, no one knew a thing about Wolff except for Field-Marshal Alexander, his Chief-of-Staff and Chief Signal Officer, and Harold Macmillan's political office.

On April 8 Parrilli brought an offer of not quite unconditional surrender from Vietinghoff as well as from Wolff. Dulles wired this to Caserta which replied on April 10 that it agreed to one visit of German emissaries fully authorised to surrender. At this stage it was arranged with the help of the Swiss that an Allied radio operator should be installed in Milan since Parrilli was worn out with travelling backwards and forwards in considerable danger, and his journeys wasted precious time. The operator was a truly heroic young Czech, called Václav Hradecky, who had escaped from Dachau. The Swiss organised his journey, concealing his equipment under a raincoat they lent him; they handed him over at the Italian frontier to Zimmer, who established him in SS quarters in Milan: this was on April 13.

Meanwhile the Russians had made themselves very disagreeable. It was thought that they disliked the idea of a German capitulation in Italy as likely to give Trieste to the Anglo-American armies rather than to Tito, and also because it might rob the Italian Communists of the fruits of their big share in the Italian resistance. Moscow had been informed of Dulles' feelers as early as March 12, and on March 13 invited to send its representatives to Caserta. On March 16 and

day of his death, Roosevelt accepted Stalin's 'explanation' and referred to the negotiations in Switzerland as having 'faded into the past without having accomplished any useful purpose'. A visit to Paris gave Dulles fuller information about these developments but he was nonplussed to receive instructions from Washington dated April 20 completely to drop Operation 'Sunrise' as he had christened his dealings with Wolff. Truman later blamed Churchill for this decision but Churchill says nothing to support Truman's assertion, on the face of it improbable and perhaps due to some misunderstanding. Truman had only been in office one week. Dulles hastened to find an excuse to bring Hradecky back from Milan to Switzerland so that he should not be cut off alone among the SS.

Meanwhile the strangest things were happening to Wolff, who, incidentally, had perplexed Dulles by conveying to him through Zimmer a letter of condolence about Roosevelt's death. After three telephone calls from Himmler in the night summoning him to Berlin, Wolff decided it would be best to go after all – he had refused at first telling Himmler by special letter to come to north Italy whence he, Wolff, had established contact with the Allies.

Having decided to go to Berlin, Wolff made an arrangement with Rahn and his own subordinates to intersperse any messages he sent them with the code '2 × 2 = 4' to show that he was not writing or speaking under

had gambled on his own personal charm which worked now as it had often worked before. But Hitler gave him orders to Vietinghoff to hold out at any cost.

For Hitler had decided, he told Wolff, to establish three large strongholds in Germany, one in Berlin, one to the north and one in the south, the 'Alpine redoubt'. All German troops were to retire to whichever they could reach. The Russian and American armies would meet somewhere in the open areas between the strongholds. Then the Russians would provoke the Americans by pushing beyond the line agreed at Yalta. And in the final war which this would bring Hitler would participate on one side or the other. 'He claimed that he could hold out in Berlin against East and West for at least six weeks, possibly even eight weeks, and for this reason he told Wolff that he must hold out in Italy that long. In the meantime Hitler expected the conflict would come about between the Western Allies and Russia, and then Hitler would decide which side he would join.'

Wolff was back in Italy on April 19 but too exhausted to see anyone before April 21, when he received Zimmer and Parrilli and drank a bottle of champagne with them to celebrate his survival. He seemed now, however, almost paralysed, afraid to risk anything further. Now Rahn, not for the first time, came to the rescue and called a meeting at Recoaro of Vietinghoff, his Chief-of-Staff Röttiger, the German Air Chief in

Italy, Ritter von Pohl (long in favour of surrender), the Tirolese Gauleiter Hofer, and Wolff on April 22. This time they all agreed on surrender regardless of instructions from Berlin, and it was decided that Wolff, with a staff colonel called Schweinitz representing Vietinghoff and an adjutant called Wenner, should leave for Switzerland on April 23 to sign the surrender. Before leaving Wolff moved his HQ to Bolzano as Vietinghoff did: Rahn moved to Merano. From now on the German army offered only token resistance to the Allied armies.

Waibel and Husmann rushed to Chiasso to meet the German party, and Waibel invited the Germans to Dorenbach near Lucerne as his guests, having explained that Dulles was temporarily labouring under adverse instructions as well as suffering from a severe attack of gout. It was now April 24. Waibel, having previously shown

The SS in Italy: link between the beaten German armies and the Allied High Command

it to Dulles, handed Wolff a telegram from Himmler dated April 23 saying: 'It is more essential than ever that the Italian front holds and remains intact. No negotiations of any kind should be undertaken.' Wolff smiled when he received it, saying that orders from Berlin no longer affected him. This strengthened the position of Dulles and Alexander, who were pressing the Combined Chiefs-of-Staff to allow the German emissaries to Caserta.

On April 25 Wolff felt bound to return to Italy. The partisans were just moving into the towns and any kind of accident might occur. He left his adjutant, Wenner, empowered to sign capitulation on his behalf. He decided also, apparently in conversation with Husmann on his journey back to Italy, that if necessary he would organise a unilateral surrender in Italy. Schweinitz and Wenner stayed on at Waibel's. Late on April 26 Wolff was rescued from the partisans near Cernobbio by a team organised by Waibel.

Meanwhile Wolff had conveyed orders to the SS chief in Milan, Rauff, not to resist the partisans and indeed to surrender to them if there was no alternative. He had also been visited by Marshal Graziani, who empowered him to negotiate the surrender of all the neo-Fascist armed forces, not much to speak of by now. On April 25 Mussolini—in conference in Milan with Cardinal Schuster, who hoped to make peace between the Duce and the partisans—had been informed by Graziani of Wolff's activities. Mussolini

seemed surprised and expressed indignation. He then got up and left shortly afterwards for Lake Como, near which he was shot by a Communist partisan officer on April 28.

Signing the surrender terms
Meanwhile on April 27 Dulles was ordered to resume the negotiations for the German surrender in Italy. Or rather instructions came that the German emissaries were to be flown to Caserta to sign. On the morning of Mussolini's death Schweinitz and Wenner were flown to Caserta accompanied by Gaevernitz and Waibel. The whole business was still top secret, so that it was better for Dulles to stay in Berne and perhaps more discreet and certainly more urgent for Wolff to attend to his job in north Italy. At Caserta Wenner representing Wolff made no difficulties, but Schweinitz, on behalf of the Wehrmacht, hesitated to surrender unconditionally. However at 2 pm on April 29 both men signed the document which provided for the unconditional surrender of the German troops in Italy at 12 noon Greenwich time (2 pm in Italy) on Wednesday May 2. A Russian Major-General, A. P. Kislenko, was present in addition to the British and American officers. By April 29 young Hradecký had been conveyed to Wolff's headquarters in Bolzano, the palace of the Duke of Pistoia.

The implementation of the surrender created other problems and further crises. The first difficulty for Schweinitz and Wenner on their return journey to Bolzano was that the Swiss had closed the frontier at Buchs, and Dulles was obliged to intervene at top level in order to get them past it. Then it emerged that Hofer had betrayed the whole Wolff programme to Kaltenbrunner, who intended to arrest all the participants. Wolff warned Schweinitz and Wenner to keep south of Innsbruck, where Kaltenbrunner intended to catch them, and so they succeeded in reaching Bolzano.

Kaltenbrunner and Hofer hoped to negotiate a special Austrian surrender. In the meantime Kesselring had been appointed Commander-in-Chief of the whole German army including the troops in Italy; he, too, vetoed Wolff's surrender and prepared to take action against his subordinates who had supported it. The arrival of two fresh generals sent by Kesselring upset Vietinghoff, who had been in two minds most of the time; his vacillation could invalidate the

surrender since Schweinitz had represented him. It seemed really as if Kesselring had taken leave of his senses and would combine with the unrepenting Kaltenbrunner and Hofer against peace. Although Hitler killed himself on April 30, thus releasing Kesselring from his military oath to him, Kesselring did not give way to Wolff's entreaties until very early on May 2, not many hours before the surrender was to come into force.

As Dulles concludes his book: 'On May 2nd, however, listeners monitoring the German radio had picked up broadcasts to German troops sent in the clear from Bolzano, ordering them to cease firing. At two o'clock local time in the afternoon of May 2, the German soldiers began to lay down their arms. The war in Italy was over.'

The war in Europe was within six days of its end and it is generally considered that the surrender in Italy had shortened it by

Imperial War Museum

April 1945: German troops, surrounded by a sullen crowd of Italian civilians, start their journey to the POW cage, after their surrender in Milan

several weeks. Indeed Operation Sunrise had established a line of communication between the Allied and the German High Commands, and the Czech wireless operator at SS headquarters in Bolzano 'served after the surrender in Italy as the link between the defeated Nazi armies in Germany and the Allied High Command'. On the afternoon of May 3 Kesselring used this route to offer surrender in the West and his message was sent on to Eisenhower. The answer, dated May 4, was addressed to Hradecký for Wolff to transmit to Kesselring; it supplied full instructions for the German surrender in the west. The surrender of all the German forces took place at Reims on May 7, hostilities to cease at midnight of May 8. According to Eisenhower the surrender of the German armies in Italy had placed the German units north of them in an impossible military situation.

One of the happiest consequences, in more personal terms, of the German surrender in Italy was that Röttiger and Wolff were able to save from possible liquidation by SS concentration camp guards a company of more or less distinguished political prisoners of Hitler. These people had been herded together at Niederdorf in South Tirol, but were then transported by the Allied authorities to Capri before being sent to their homes. They included Léon Blum, Kurt von Schuschnigg, Niemöller, and Schacht.
[*Elizabeth Wiskemann's biography is in Vol 5, p. 1932.*]

Highlights of the Italian campaign

1. Prelude: British troops during the conquest of Sicily, August 1943

2. The 8th Army moves into Calabria, the 'toe' of Italy, September 1943

4. Allies enter Naples, first major city taken, October 1943

3. US troops land—straight into the Battle of Salerno, September 1943

6. The 8th Army moves up to the Sangro river, October 1943

5. A 5th Army Sherman crosses the Volturno, first major river barrier in the Allies' path, October 1943

7. First round at Cassino: Allied bombs pound the Monastery, Jan/Feb 1944

8. Anzio, the 'cat's claw' shortcut to Rome that failed, January 1944

9. Second round at Cassino: Allies create more ruins that help the Germans, March 1944

10. Pyrrhic victory at Cassino, May 1944

12. Abandoned German position after the Gothic Line battles, September/October 1944

13. The final triumph: Germans captured in the battle for the Senio river, April 1945

11. Kudos for the US Army: General Clark in Rome, June 1944

As German resistance in Italy collapsed, so did Mussolini's government in the north, the *Repubblica Sociale Italiana.* On April 16, 1945, its ministers met for the last time, and three days later its President left for Milan accompanied by a German escort.

Mussolini established his office in Milan in the Prefecture, where for five days he received a stream of visitors, rejecting all suggestions that he should fly out of the country, speaking of a last stand in the mountains of the Valtellina, and of *'l'immortalità della patria e del Fascismo'.*

On April 25, during a discussion about the terms of surrender for the Republic's troops with members of the Committee of National Liberation at the Archbishop of Milan's palace, Mussolini was told of the Germans' surrender in Italy. Angrily protesting against their betrayal of Italy, he left the palace, agreeing to answer the Liberation Committee's demand for the unconditional surrender of his Republican forces within the hour.

Immediately on his return to his office he pointed to a map on his table, and announced: 'We leave Milan immediately. Destination Como!' It was not the most direct route to the Valtellina, but there were reports that the Americans were advancing fast along the Bergamo road, and that the partisans had cut the road to Lecco. Once in the Valtellina, so he had told the Archbishop, he and 3,000 loyal Blackshirts would continue the war in the mountains.

'Duce, do not have any illusions,' the Archbishop had replied, 'I know the Blackshirts who are going to follow you are rather three hundred than three thousand.'

'Perhaps a few more,' Mussolini conceded with a smile. 'Not many, though. I have few illusions.'

And certainly when he left Milan sitting next to his old friend, Nicola Bombacci, in the back of an open Alfa-Romeo, there were few others prepared to share his chosen fate. In front of him rode Luigi Gatti, his secretary, sitting on the bonnet of the leading car with a machine-gun between his knees. Following him were about 30 other cars and lorries, in one of which was his mistress, Claretta Petacci, who had recently written to a friend, using one of her lover's favourite expressions: 'I am following my destiny. What will happen to me I don't know; but I cannot question my fate.'

Close behind her were two lorries of SS soldiers, commanded by Lieutenant Fritz Birzer, the Duce's unwanted yet determinedly conscientious escort; and the Duce's elder son, Vittorio, who had vainly tried to persuade his father to escape to Spain.

Alessandro Pavolini, a political fanatic and Secretary of the Republican Fascist Party, had agreed to meet Mussolini at Como with a large force of loyal Fascists; but when Mussolini arrived in Como at about ten o'clock that night there was no sign of them.

Mussolini, wearing the uniform of the Fascist Militia, hurried up the steps of the Prefecture where the telephone rang stridently every few minutes and a frightened voice would give an account of some new disaster. The Germans were still in headlong retreat; partisans were blocking the Melegnano and Treviglio roads; all the Milan suburbs were in the hands of armed workers.

Mussolini listened silently while his companions, close to panic, gave him contradictory advice. The Inspector of the Fascist Party in Lombardy advised a withdrawal to Cadenabbia; Buffarini-Guidi, a former Minister of the Interior in the Republican Government, urged him to join him in an attempt to cross the frontier into Switzerland; General Mische of the Republican Army said that the Duce must go to Sondrio.

'I shall go to the mountains,' the Duce said.

He did not want to leave, though, until a lorry-load of documents reached him from Milan, documents which a Socialist journalist—who had helped him fill two large bags with them—believed would support his defence in any trial he might have to face after the war. In addition to the documents, the lorry was carrying part of what was later to be known as the 'Dongo Treasure'—gold bars, *objets d'art,* and money belonging to the Republican Government—amounting, it was afterwards suggested, to several thousand

THE DEATH OF MUSSOLINI

Christopher Hibbert
Victory in Italy, April 1945

After his 'liberation' by German commandos, Mussolini had lived a captive life as the head of the puppet Italian Fascist state, entirely dependent on the German military hold on northern Italy. And when Clark's breakthrough shattered the German front in the spring of 1945, Mussolini was left to the mercy of Italian republicans and partisans, now engaged on a witch-hunt against all Fascist leaders and officials. For Mussolini, in his last days, life no longer seemed to have any meaning—and at last the founder of Fascism, hunted down by his own countrymen, met a violent and ignominious death

million lire. But the lorry was intercepted by partisans on its way north from Milan; and Mussolini seemed more distressed by this calamity than by any other. He showed a complete indifference to the loss of the treasure; but the documents he mentioned repeatedly during the two days he had left to live.

With the documents lost, and with Pavolini's Blackshirts nowhere in sight, Mussolini gave orders for the convoy to move on to Menaggio which was reached, in a dreary drizzle of rain, at about half-past five in the morning. Mussolini remained at Menaggio for several hours, resting in the villa of a local Fascist; but there still being

no sign of Pavolini he gave orders for the small but conspicuous convoy to move off the lakeside road, up into the mountains, to the village of Grandola. And here at last Pavolini joined him. How many men had he brought with him? Mussolini asked him eagerly. Pavolini hesitated.

'Well, tell me. How many?'

'Twelve.'

With all hope now lost, Mussolini allowed the commander of his German escort, Lieutenant Fritz Birzer, to arrange for him and his few remaining followers to join a German convoy retreating north along the lakeside road towards Innsbruck, Austria.

Mussolini *gloriosus,* at the height of his career: 'honours due to a hero'

As the convoy drove away Claretta ran after her lover and frantically tried to jump into one of the lorries; and Birzer had to use all his strength to drag her off the tail-board. So Mussolini went on into Dongo alone.

At Dongo the lorries were searched; and a figure, who appeared to be either drunk, or asleep, crouching down beside two tins of petrol in one of them, soon aroused the partisans' curiosity.

'Aren't you an Italian?' asked Urbano Lazzaro, deputy political commissar of the 52nd Garibaldi Brigade. There was a pause, and then Mussolini looked up and said emphatically, 'Yes, I am an Italian.'

'Excellency!' Lazzaro exclaimed, so taken aback by the Duce's suddenly directed gaze that the deferential title escaped from him unthinkingly. 'You *are* here!'

Mussolini's face was 'ashen', Lazzaro noticed. 'It was also expressionless. The stubble on his chin was dark and thick, accentuating the pallor of his cheeks. . . . One read by his eyes that he was extremely tired but not afraid. Spiritual death. He no longer had anything to do among men.'

While the partisans waited for instructions from the Committee of National Liberation, Mussolini was taken up the mountainside out of reach of possible rescuers, to the frontier guards' barracks at Germasino—and then—accompanied by Claretta Petacci who had been allowed to join him —to a small farmhouse near Bonzanigo.

Here, at about four o'clock in the afternoon of April 28, a tall man in a brown mackintosh burst into the bedroom where Mussolini and Claretta Petacci had spent the previous night. He was Walter Audisio, a Communist member of the Volunteer Freedom Corps, authorised to kill Mussolini by various members of the Committee of Liberation who realised what an embarrassment the Duce would be if left alive to testify at a War Crimes trial.

As Audisio came into the bedroom, he called out: 'Hurry up! I have come to rescue you!'

Audisio hustled Mussolini and Claretta out of the house and down the steep lane to the road where his car was waiting. He pushed them both into the back of the car, jumped on to one of the mudguards while two other partisans stepped on to the running-board.

The driver could see his two passengers in the mirror. 'They were close together,' he remembers, 'with their heads almost touching. Mussolini was pale and the Signora tranquil . . . we stopped at the gate of the Villa Belmonte.'

Audisio got off. He walked down to a sharp curve in the road, looked round the corner, and then returned to the car. Ordering Mussolini and Claretta to move over to the villa wall, he 'pronounced a few words very quickly'. The driver thought they referred to an order Audisio had received, but 'everything happened so quickly' he was not sure.

Mussolini remained motionless and impassive, but Claretta lost control of herself and threw her arms around him, jumping up and down and shouting 'No! No! You mustn't do it!'

'Get out of the way if you don't want to die too,' Audisio admits to have shouted at her. Then he shot them both.

Their bodies were put into the back of the car and driven to Azzano, where a removal van was waiting with the corpses of 15 Fascists, including Pavolini, Luigi Gatti, and Claretta's brother, Marcello, who had been captured at the Rocca di Musso and shot that day at Dongo.

Mussolini and Claretta were thrown on top of them. The next day their mutilated bodies were displayed upside down in Piazzale Loreto, Milan, hanging by their ankles from the girders of the roof of a half-built garage. A bystander recalls that a sudden lull cut across the barrage of jeers and insults which assailed the bodies:

'It was as if we had all in those few seconds shared the realisation that the Duce was really dead at last, that he had been slaughtered without trial, and that there had been a time when we would have given his dead body, not insults and degradation, but the honours due to a hero and prayers worthy of a saint.'

[Mr Hibbert's biography is in Vol 1, p. 164]

For a few miles the convoy moved north without being challenged. At first Mussolini drove himself in the Alfa Romeo, but, warned that there were bands of armed partisans in all the surrounding villages, he climbed into an armoured car.

Suddenly, at seven o'clock in the morning, about 6 miles north of Menaggio, three shots rang out; and a moment later the convoy was halted by an enormous tree trunk and several boulders which had been dragged across the road. To the right was the lake, to the left an immense and thickly wooded wall of rock which was known by the name, aptly ironic, of the Rocca di Musso.

More shots were fired as the convoy came to a halt, and then a partisan officer came forward under the protection of a white flag to say that in order to save unnecessary bloodshed he would allow the German soldiers through the road block, but that his men would let no Italian Fascists through. Fritz Birzer urged Mussolini to put on a German overcoat and helmet and to hide in one of the lorries. At first he refused, saying that he could not accept protection which was not available to the others, that he could not leave Claretta Petacci behind. But at length he was persuaded, and when Birzer drove up with the lorry, he put on a German uniform and climbed in silently.

Piazzale Loreto, Milan; April 29, 1945 — a vicious aspect of Italian 'patriotism'

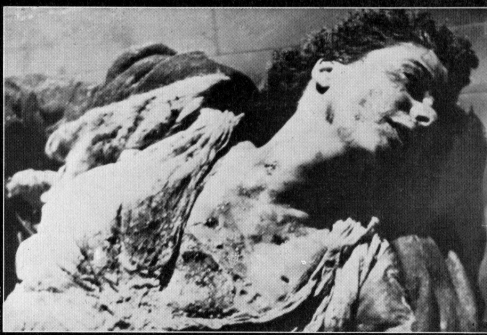

Claretta Petacci... The Duce's mistress

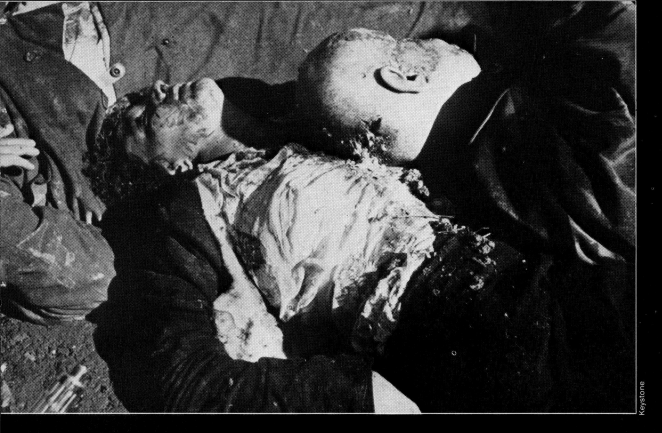

Keystone

Mussolini and his mistress, after mutilation

Tony Bonavita

Audisio, Mussolini's murderer

PopperfoRo

Last respects. In the case is the tattered clothing last worn by the Duce

'The immortality of Fascism'